Ada Programming with Applications

Eugen N. Vasilescu
Hofstra University

Allyn and Bacon, Inc.
Boston London Sydney Toronto

® ADA is a registered trademark of the U.S. Government, Ada Joint Program Office

Copyright © 1987 by Allyn and Bacon, Inc.,
7 Wells Avenue, Newton, Massachusetts 02159.

Library of Congress Cataloging-in-Publication Data

Vasilescu, Eugen N., 1946–
  Ada programming with applications.

  Includes index.
  1. Ada (Computer program language)   I. Title.
QA76.73.A16V37   1986   005.13'3   86–1172
ISBN 0–205–08744–2

Printed in the United States of America.
10 9 8 7 6 5 4 3 2 1   91 90 89 88 87 86

To my wife, Simona, and my children,
Nicole-Valerie and Alexandru

CONTENTS

PREFACE

Ada is a computer programming language designed for the United States Department of Defense in order to cope with the growing software development crisis. Ada was designed as a language whose features are suited for embedded computer systems: parallel processing, real-time control, exception handling, and unique I/O control. However, its features are appealing for a much wider audience. The applications programmer or the systems analyst will find the concept of package an essential design tool. This concept allows abstraction of data structures, separates the specification (roughly, the interface) from the body (the actual implementation), and allows encapsulation of objects and related operations. Ada tasking facilities are also important for a designer of data base systems and for applications where the handling of parallel processes plays a role.

Ada may very well become the language of the eighties, and this potential was recognized quite early by the scientific community. As a result, a number of Ada books were written primarily for computer scientists, providing a migration path from languages like FORTRAN, PL/I, and Pascal.

This book, however, is more concerned with commercial or business uses of Ada and is more in line with a computer information systems approach. An often-stated goal of computer information systems curricula is to prepare the graduate to function adequately in an entry-level position as a systems analyst, applications programmer, or information systems specialist. The book is consistent with this goal. It can be used by undergraduate or graduate students or by any specialist in computer information systems. It can be used for a one- or two-term course and assumes that the reader has had at least an introductory course in computers and some elementary knowledge of a programming language like BASIC, COBOL, Pascal, FORTRAN, or PL/I.

The book is self-contained, and among its objectives are the following:

- To develop an understanding of a strongly typed language and its advantages for efficient and reliable implementation of packages.
- To obtain practical experience and knowledge in designing packages for business use.
- To gain a general understanding of advanced concepts like data encapsulation, concurrency, and modularity.

Readers are not overwhelmed with material. The syntax of Ada is introduced in measured doses, and the presentation of complete Ada programs is emphasized.

At the end of the first chapter readers should know enough about types and statements to be able to write simple programs. Chapters 2 and 3 introduce additional types, such as real types, array types, record types, and access types, and statements like the "for" loop. Concepts like membership operators, records with variants, and more Ada statements (such as the "case" statement) are introduced in Chapter 4. Chapters 5 and 6 cover subprograms and details about type conversions, pragmas, scope, and visibility. Thus the first six chapters of the book deal with concepts one may find (and relate to) in other languages.

The second part of the book (the last five chapters) deals with concepts that make Ada suited for embedded computer systems and systems design, namely, packages, unique I/O control, separate compilation, parallel processing, and exception handling.

Ada is a complex language, and this book is not intended to be a reference manual. It leaves out some features that are not critical for the principal audience. For example, one can learn about the use of generic facilities without getting into the details of writing generic subprograms and packages. While generic facilities are important and valuable in a production environment, they are not as important in a book geared to Ada users with an information systems background. The book also omits implementation-dependent features. The implementation-dependent features are necessary for a systems programmer but are not as critical for persons concerned with implementing business applications. (They are necessary, though, for people who are interested in using external files produced by other languages or in using libraries of programs written in another language.)

This book is based on notes prepared for an Ada course offered to undergraduate students majoring in business computer informations systems at Hofstra University. The programs of this book have been compiled and are reasonably free of syntactic and semantic errors. Earlier versions were run on a JANUS/ADA compiler; the latest versions were compiled on the validated Ada compilers of Data General/ROLM, and Digital Equipment Corporation's VAX–11. An updated diskette, containing the programs of this book together with sample compilations and executions, is available, and inquiries may be addressed directly to the author.

ACKNOWLEDGMENTS

I wish to thank the many people who made valuable contributions during the preparation of this book. In particular, I thank M. Berkowitz for his careful, penetrating, and well-balanced critique of the manuscript. I thank C. Denbaum for the many excellent and detailed comments that improved both the style and the content of the manuscript. I thank the reviewers J. Blaisdell and J. Motil for their many valuable comments. I wish to thank my editor, John Sulzycki, for his support and professional guidance. And above all, I thank my wife, Simona, for her patience and understanding during the preparation of this book.

INTRODUCTION

1.1   INTRODUCING THE ADA LANGUAGE

CHARACTER SET

A program written in Ada uses uppercase letters, the digits, and the following special characters:

```
"  #  '  (  )  *  +  ,  _  .  /  :  ;  <  =  >  _  !
```

as well as the space character. These characters constitute the **basic character set** in Ada, and any Ada program can be written by relying solely on them.

Some Ada implementations use an **expanded character set.** In addition to the basic character set, the expanded character set can use the lowercase letters and the following special characters:

```
!  $  %  ?  @  [  \  ]  ^  `  {  }  ~
```

By adding 52 (the number of letters), 10 (the number of digits), and 23 (the combined total of special characters), one obtains a total of 95. These 95 characters make up the 95-character ASCII graphics set.

This book uses the expanded character set. Appendix C has a complete listing of the 128-character ASCII set, which includes the 95-character graphics set.

FEATURES OF A SIMPLE ADA PROGRAM

The reader with some elementary knowledge of another programming language should be able to follow the program MAX3, given next, with little effort. MAX3 reads three integers and prints the largest integer supplied.

MAX3 Program

```
-- This is a comment. Comments in Ada start with two dashes

-- and continue until the end of the line. These three first

-- lines are all comment lines.

with TEXT_IO; use TEXT_IO;    -- The package TEXT_IO is made

-- available for the program MAX3. Now one can use subprograms

-- included in TEXT_IO like  NEW_LINE, GET, PUT.

-- See Section 1.5 for details on packages and subprograms

procedure MAX3 is              -- the procedure name is MAX3

-- and is introduced here.

    package INT_IO is new INTEGER_IO(INTEGER);

    use INT_IO;

    -- The above two lines make possible the use of subprograms

    -- GET and PUT for integers. INTEGER_IO is part of TEXT_IO.

    -- See Section 1.5 for more details.

    I, J, K, L : INTEGER;

    -- The four variables I, J, K, and L are declared as integer

    -- type variables.

begin                            -- Now the declarations are over

                                 -- and statements will follow.

    GET(I); GET(J); GET(K);

    -- Make use of the GET subprogram of the INT_IO package.

    -- The three statements above are used to read three integers
```

```
-- that   will   placed   in   locations   assoicated   with   the
-- variables I, J, and K.
if I > J
    then
        L := I;                  -- The largest among I and J
else                             -- is placed in the location
        L := J;                  -- associated with L.
end if ;
if L < K
    then                         -- The integer placed in L is
        L := K;                  -- replaced by the integer in K
end if ;                         -- only if L < K.  The largest
                                 -- integer is now in L.

    NEW_LINE;                    -- Make use of the subprogram
                                 -- NEW_LINE of TEXT_IO.
                                 -- It works for output files
                                 -- only and it jumps to the
                                 -- line below.
PUT( " The largest is : " );
-- Print or display the message    The largest is :
PUT ( L );
-- And next to it, print the integer found in the location
-- associated to L.
NEW_LINE;
end MAX3;
    -- The procedure ends here.
```

MAX3 is a complete Ada main program. It is made up of the procedure MAX3 and some additional contextual information needed for compilation and execution. The contextual information for this main program is provided by the line

```
with TEXT_IO; use TEXT_IO;
```

which makes available the text input/output facilities for it. These facilities are needed for reading (from a terminal or other device) and writing (on a terminal, printer, or so on) characters of the expanded character set, in the form humans are used to seeing them.

The procedure itself starts with the line

```
procedure MAX3 is
```

which gives the name of the procedure and signals the start of the body of the procedure. The procedure ends with the line

```
end MAX3;
```

Every line of an Ada program is made up of a sequence of lexical units. The **lexical units** in the MAX3 main program (besides comments) are identifiers, delimiters, and strings (these terms will be explained more fully in Section 1.2). For instance, among the identifiers in MAX3 one may list

```
with    MAX3    I    J    else
```

delimiters like

```
,    ;    (    )
```

and the string

```
" The largest is : "
```

Two other kinds of lexical units can appear in an Ada program, numeric literals and character literals. **Numeric literals** represent integers or real values, like

```
12.0    8.5e1    144
```

Character literals may be any of the 95 characters of the expanded character set, enclosed within single quotation marks, like

```
'a'    '5'
```

The body of the procedure MAX3 has two parts. The first part is the **declarative part** between the identifier "is" and the identifier "begin." The second part is a **sequence-of-statements part,** between the identifier "begin" and the identifier "end."

The declarative part accounts for and makes available the logical entities to be used by the procedure. For instance, one has to account for the GET and

PUT procedures used with integers in the sequence-of-statements part of the MAX3 program. This accounting is accomplished by the following two lines in the declarative part of the procedure MAX3:

```
package INT_IO is new INTEGER_IO(INTEGER);
use INT_IO;
```

As will be explained in Section 1.5, these two lines create a suitable package named INT_IO from the package INTEGER_IO, which is part of the package TEXT_IO. The package INT_IO will make available a number of versions of the GET and PUT procedures for reading and writing integers (the GET and PUT versions depend on the input data format and on where the data is read from).

The program line

```
I, J, K, L : INTEGER;
```

introduces four logical entities of type integer. If more entities are needed, extra declarations can be inserted before the "begin" identifier.

When the program MAX3 starts running, the sequence of statements will be executed beginning with three calls to the procedure GET for reading three integers and placing them in the locations associated with variables I, J, and K. The integers should be typed in free form, that is, without regard to their column position and with spaces around them. Next, some "if" statements are executed. Each **"if" statement** starts with the identifier "if" and ends with the identifiers "end if" followed by the delimiter ";". The "if" statements are **compound statements** because they may contain other statements. In this case they contain some **assignment statements** like

```
L := I ;
```

whose effect is to place the value of I in the location of L. As one may guess, the assignment statements and calls to procedures are **simple statements,** because they contain no other statements. The remaining statements are calls to procedures of the packages TEXT_IO and INT_IO.

All Ada statements are terminated by a semicolon, and one can have several statements per line. The statements are generally executed in sequence. The sequential execution of statements may be interrupted by certain statements like "return" or by the appearance of errors or unusual events. Ada reacts to these errors or unusual events by the *raising of exceptions*. Full details about exceptions will be provided in Chapter 11, but some introductory explanations are given in Section 1.5.

ADA "WHILE" LOOP

A second complete Ada program, MAXALL, is exhibited next in order to introduce what is known as a **while loop** and to show a more crowded appearance of the code. The program is to print the largest of a stream of several integers. The stream of positive integers is assumed to end with −1.

MAXALL Program

```
with TEXT_IO; use TEXT_IO;

procedure MAXALL is

    package INT_IO is new INTEGER_IO(INTEGER); use INT_IO;

    I, MAX_NO : INTEGER ;

begin

    MAX_NO := 0; GET(I);

    while I /= -1  loop

    if I > MAX_NO then MAX_NO := I; end if;

    GET(I);

                end loop;

    PUT(" The largest is : "); PUT(MAX_NO); NEW_LINE;

end MAXALL;
```

In the program MAXALL the statements between the identifier "loop" and the identifiers "end loop" are executed just as long as the expression following the identifier "while" is true—in this case as long as I is not equal to −1. The sequence /= (slash followed by the equal sign) means "not equal." It is a compound delimiter. Again the integers are entered in free form, maybe several per line.

The reader might be puzzled by the elaborate process needed to read or write simple entities like integers. At this stage the best strategy is to suspend judgment until a more detailed discussion of packages is possible. Until then, a healthy imitation of the related examples is recommended.

As might be expected, in most interactive implementations the assumption is made that the input is from the keyboard and the output is sent to the terminal (unless other files are explicitly mentioned). To actually run these programs, one needs to make use of an editor for typing in the code, and one must obtain, from the local installation, the necessary commands to invoke the Ada compiler and linker.

1.2   MORE ABOUT LEXICAL UNITS

Any Ada program can be viewed as a sequence of lexical units. While several lexical units can appear on a single line, no lexical unit is allowed to span more than one line. As mentioned already, the lexical units are identifiers, numeric literals, character literals, strings, delimiters, and comments. Identifiers and numeric literals must be separated from other identifiers or numeric literals by at least a space or must appear on different lines.

Identifiers in Ada are sequences of letters, digits, and underscores, provided that the first character of the sequence is a letter and each underscore is surrounded by letters or digits. Identifiers are considered identical if any of the letters are changed from uppercase to lowercase or vice versa.

EXAMPLE   Some identifiers in Ada are

```
I    Q12_PqR    General_Ledger    ACCOUNT_123
ZZZZ    Check_CREDIT_APPROVAL    INTEREST
```

Here are some incorrect examples of identifiers:

`1Expect`	The sequence of characters starts with a digit
`MORENO_`	The underscore is not surrounded by a letter or a digit
`TOO_ _MANY`	The underscore is not surrounded by a letter or a digit

Some of the identifiers are **reserved words** having a special meaning in the Ada language and may not be used as names for other entities. Ada has 63 reserved words, which are exhibited in Figure 1.1.

Numeric literals represent integers and real numbers, as discussed previously. Underscores can be embedded among digits in numeric literals in order to improve readability. A real literal contains a decimal point, while an integer literal does not. Integer literals can have an exponential part as long as the exponent is not negative. Some examples follow.

Integer literals   0   5   13   21e+3   21_345   34   21e+2
Real literals   1.3   2.0e−12   1_2_3_45.08E;+7   1_123.456

Numeric literals can be expressed in terms of any base from 2 to 16. If the base of the numeric literal is not 10, then the base (in decimal) and the character "#" must precede the actual literal. For instance, 2#1110 represents the decimal integer 14 written in base 2. The exponent part, if present, has to be written in

FIGURE 1.1   ADA Reserved Words

abort	declare	generic	of	select
accept	delay	goto	or	separate
access	delta		others	subtype
all	digits	if	out	
and	do	in		task
array		is	package	terminate
at			pragma	then
	else		private	type
	elsif	limited	procedure	
	end	loop		use
begin	entry		raise	
body	exception		range	
	exit	mod	record	when
			rem	while
		new	renames	with
case	for	not	return	
constant	function	null	reverse	xor

decimal notation. For instance, the decimal number 56 can be written in base 2 as $2\#111e+3$. If the base exceeds 10, then the letters A through F are used for the six digits greater than 9.

As already mentioned, character literals are formed by enclosing any of the 95 ASCII graphic characters within single quotation marks. For example,

```
'a'    'A'    '2'    ','    '5'
```

are character literals.

Character literals should not be confused with **strings,** which are formed by enclosing zero or more characters within double quotation marks (quotes). For example,

```
"a"    "Just a regular string"    " 1,234 ; "
," 2.1 cents "
```

are strings. The **null string** (no characters) is represented by a sequence of two double quotes " ". If one needs the double quote within a string, then the double quote has to be typed twice in order to appear once within a string.

Long strings can be split into smaller pieces spanning more than one line with the help of the **catenation symbol,** denoted by &. For example,

```
" if you need a really long string like a heading " &
```

```
" you can use the symbol ""&"" to catenate - i.e., " &
" glue together - the pieces from several lines "
```

Note how we used two double quotes " "&" " within the string in order to have just a single double quote appear in the printout.

One may be able to use (again, depending on a particular Ada implementation) characters that are not in the basic character set. In this case any character not in the basic character set will be converted to an equivalent representation within the basic character set by using identifiers of a package called ASCII (listed in Appendix C). The use of packages will be described in Chapter 7.

As mentioned before, comments start with two dashes (maybe after some statements appearing on the same line) and end with the end of the line. However, Ada statements may not follow a comment on the same line.

1.3 INTRODUCTION TO TYPES AND OBJECTS

INTEGER AND ENUMERATION TYPES AND ASSOCIATED OBJECTS

With few exceptions every identifier (when it is not an Ada key word) must be explicitly accounted for and its properties must be known before it can be used in a sequence-of-statements part. Identifiers are accounted for mainly by declarations appearing in a declarative part. Roughly speaking, then, a **declaration** spells out what kind of entity the declared identifier is. For instance, in the previous two programs we declared variables like I, J, and K, and these declarations were necessary in order for us to manipulate integers with them. Another kind of entity that may be denoted by an identifier is the type. **Types** play a central role in Ada, and they are somewhat like templates or models of data.

The general form of type declarations is

```
type type_name is type_definition;
```

The underlined words are Ada reserved words. The type_name is an identifier chosen by the programmer.

Types are used to define a collection of values and the operations allowed on these values. This subsection will be concerned with two important Ada types: integer types and enumeration types. Integer types and enumeration types are called **discrete types.**

For **integer types** the type_definition part of the declaration is a **range constraint,** which is formed by the Ada reserved word "range" followed by the lower value of the range, two periods, and the upper value of the range. The lower value cannot exceed the upper value. Here are some examples of integer type declarations:

```
type AGE is  range 0 .. 200 ;

type DAY_OF_MONTH is range 1 .. 31 ;

type ACCOUNT_NO is range 0 .. 9999 ;

type TEMPERATURE is range -140 .. 2100 ;

type FEVER is range 95 .. 109 ;
```

For integer types the possible values are given by the range constraint. For instance, the allowed values for the integer type AGE are the integers between 0 and 200 (inclusive). The operations allowed for integer types are the usual ones: assignments, comparisons, and arithmetic operations like addition (+), subtraction (−), multiplication (∗), division (/), and exponentiation (∗∗).

For **enumeration types** the type_definition part of the declaration consists of a sequence of enumeration literals separated by commas and enclosed in parentheses. **Enumeration literals** can be either identifiers or character literals. The following examples present some declarations of enumeration types.

```
type DAY is (MON,TUE,WED,THU,FRI,SAT,SUN) ;

type ACCOUNT is (MARGIN,HEDGE) ;

type SECURITY is (DISCOUNT,COUPON) ;

type SWITCH is (ON,OFF);
```

Enumeration types have their set of values defined by the explicit listing of these values in the type declaration. For instance, the allowed values for the enumeration type SECURITY are two: the enumeration literal DISCOUNT and the enumeration literal COUPON.

Among the operations defined for enumeration types one should mention "<" (less than). A value of an enumeration type is less than another of the same type if the first value appears in the list of enumeration literals before the second one. The operation ">" is defined in a similar manner.

Ada has a small supply of predefined types. **Predefined types** do not need to be declared in the declarative part of a subprogram. Among them, one finds the predefined integer type INTEGER, the predefined enumeration type CHARACTER, the predefined enumeration type BOOLEAN, and the predefined type STRING (the STRING type belongs to a kind of type that will be introduced in Chapter 2). A short description of the values and operations for these predefined types follows.

The values that can be taken by the INTEGER type are implementation-dependent. That is, every vendor of an Ada compiler decides what the exact range is, but one would expect a range of at least 64k (maybe from −32k to +

32k − 1). The operations allowed on this predefined type are the same as the operations for any other integer type.

The type CHARACTER has as values the ASCII character set. Some of the operations allowed for this type (and, in general, for any enumeration type) include comparisons and assignments.

For the BOOLEAN type the values are FALSE and TRUE.

The predefined type STRING has as its values sequences of characters enclosed within double quotes. The operations that can be applied to these values are comparisons with other strings, assignments, and catenation with both strings and characters.

Once types are declared, one can declare entities associated with them, called **objects.** There are two kinds of Ada objects: constants and variables. After a **variable** of certain type is declared, it can hold any value allowed by the type. The value held by a variable may be changed—for instance, by assigning a new value to it. **Constants** of a certain type be given any value allowed by the type when it is declared, but no change of the value is allowed later. For instance, in the program MAX3 the variables I, J, K, and L are declared as being of the predefined type INTEGER. These variables are compared in the program and used in assignment statements. As we mentioned earlier, these operations are allowed for integer type variables.

Here are some examples of variable declarations:

```
AGE_EMPL_1 : AGE ;

MORE_AGE, EVEN_MORE_AGE : AGE ;

TRANS_DAY : DAY_OF_MONTH ;

SETTLEMENT_DATE, NOTICE_DAY : DAY_OF_MONTH ;

EMPL_ACC, EMPL_ACC_TEMP : ACCOUNT_NO ;

PATIENT_1_TEMP : FEVER ;

BOILING_TEMP : TEMPERATURE;

DAY_1, DAY_2 : DAY ;
```

We note again that every type mentioned in an object declaration should be declared (unless the type is predefined) before the object is.

Here are some examples of constant declarations:

```
MINIMUM_AGE : constant AGE := 18;

DRINKING_AGE : constant AGE := 21;
```

```
MONTHLY_STATEMENTS_DAY : constant DAY_NO :=1;

NORMAL_TEMP : constant FEVER := 98 ;

PAY_DAY : constant DAY := FRI ;
```

The declarations of objects (variables and constants) in the examples follow a certain pattern. For variables the form is

```
identifier_list : type_name ;
```

For constants the declaration form is

```
identifier_list: constant type_name :=
    numeric_literal;
```

The identifier_list is a sequence of identifiers, separated by commas, representing the object names. The type_name is a predefined type or a type introduced by the programmer. Other forms for object declarations connected with different kinds of constraints will be discussed in the next chapter.

One may naturally ask why concepts like types or range constraints are useful. Among the many reasons that they are useful is that the definition of types introduces a number of restrictions on the possible values and on the manipulation of these values. The restrictions are built in by the Ada compiler (and enforced by it), and they help in preventing the manipulation of invalid data.

USING CHARACTER AND STRING TYPES

The following program shows how the program MAX3 can be rewritten so that it chooses, from any three characters, the one that is last according to the ASCII sequence of enumeration literals.

CHAR_MAX3 Program

```
with TEXT_IO; use TEXT_IO;

-- The package TEXT_IO is made  available for the program

-- CHAR_MAX3. Now one can use subprograms supplied byf TEXT_IO

-- like  NEW_LINE, GET, PUT, etc.

procedure CHAR_MAX3 is

    I, J, K, L: CHARACTER;
```

```
                -- The four variables I, J, K, and L are declared as
                -- character type variables.
begin
-- Now the declarations are over and statements will follow.
        GET(I); GET(J); GET(K);
        -- Make  use  of  the  GET subprogram of the TEXT_IO package.
        -- Three characters are read and placed in locations associated
        -- with the variables I, J,and K.
        if I > J
            then
                L := I;                 -- The largest among I and J
        else                            -- is placed in the location
                L := J;                 -- associated with L.
        end if;
        if L < K
            then                        -- The character placed in L is
                L := K;                 -- replaced by the character in K
        end if ;                        -- only if L < K  in the ASCII
                                        -- sequence.
        -- The largest character is now in L.
        NEW_LINE;
        -- Make use of the subprogram NEW_LINE of TEXT_IO.
        PUT( " The largest is : " );
        -- Print or display the message:      The largest is :
        PUT ( L );
        -- And next to it print the character found in L.
```

```
      NEW_LINE;

end CHAR_MAX3;

-- The procedure ends here
```

Unlike the corresponding program for integers, there is no need to make use of an extra package part of TEXT_IO in order to read (GET) or write (PUT) characters. The characters are read in sequence. After each GET has been executed, the column position in the input file will be incremented by one. Therefore no spaces should be typed between the three characters read (something like ZAP would be the input if one wanted to display the last character among 'Z', 'A', and 'P').

The meaning of the assignment statement

```
    L := K;
```

is the same for both integer and character types. The current value of the variable appearing to the left of the compound symbol : = is replaced by the value obtained from the evaluation of the expression (here it is a variable) found to the right of it. Literals (numeric and character) and variables are simple kinds of expressions called **primaries,** and they may serve as building blocks for more complex expressions. But Ada is quite strict and generally does not allow types to be mixed in expressions or on both sides of an assignment statement.

EXAMPLE   If we declare

```
    M,N : INTEGER;

    X,Y : CHARACTER;
```

then we can have the following assignment statements:

```
    M := M + N ;

    M := N * 3 ;

    X := 'c';

    X := Y ;
```

But the following statements are not valid because types are mixed:

```
    M := M + X;

    N := 'A';

    X := 5;
```

The predefined type STRING will be discussed in detail in the next chapter dealing with array types. In this chapter, though, we must be able to declare some STRING type variables and use them with TEXT_IO procedures like GET or PUT. For example,

```
F_NAME : STRING(1 . . 25);
```

is a STRING type variable holding 25 characters, with the first character in position 1 and the last character in position 25. The length of the string is 25. Another example of a STRING type variable is

```
STREET_ADDRESS : STRING(1 . . 20);
```

When GET and PUT procedures are used with STRING type variables, characters are read or written starting with the next column position for a number of columns equal to the length of the string. For instance,

```
GET(F_NAME) ;
```

will read the next 25 characters. If the last column position was, say, 13, then characters from column 14 to 38 inclusive will be read. Similarly, a statement like

```
PUT (STREET_ADDRESS) ;
```

will write the 20 characters of the variable STREET_ADDRESS, starting with the next available column.

One can control the position of the integers read or written by using another GET or PUT procedure that allows the programmer to specify the width (number of digits) of the number. If we have the declaration

```
I : INTEGER ;
```

then a statement such as

```
GET(I,5);
```

means to read an integer from the next five column positions. If the last column position was 8, then the integer should be read from columns 9 to 13, inclusive.

The following Ada program, named HEAVY, illustrates these concepts. Each input line contains a person's name in the first 20 columns and his or her weight (in pounds) in the next 5 columns. The last line is assumed to contain the letter X in the first column followed by spaces. The program will display the name of the heaviest person.

HEAVY Program

```
with TEXT_IO; use TEXT_IO;

procedure HEAVY is

    package INT_IO is new INTEGER_IO(INTEGER); use INT_IO;
```

```
        WEIGHT, MAX_WEIGHT : INTEGER;

        H_NAME, MAX_H_NAME : STRING (1 .. 20 );

    begin

        MAX_WEIGHT := 0; GET(H_NAME);

        -- Read the first twenty characters of the line. If there is

        -- no SKIP_LINE statement, the next GET statement will read

        -- starting with column 21.

        while H_NAME /= "X                      "

        -- Lines are read and processed as long as  there  is  no

        -- line starting  with  an X followed by 19 spaces.


            loop

            GET(WEIGHT,5);

            -- Read an integer from the next five columns, that is,

            -- columns 21 through 25 and place it in the location

            -- associated with WEIGHT.

            if WEIGHT > MAX_WEIGHT

                then

                MAX_WEIGHT := WEIGHT;

                MAX_H_NAME := H_NAME;

                -- This assignment statement works for strings

                -- of equal length.

            end if;

            SKIP_LINE;

            -- This subprogram of TEXT_IO works with the input

            -- file  only.  It  skips to the beginning of the  next

            -- line.
```

```
          GET(H_NAME);

       end loop;

     NEW_LINE;

     PUT(" The heaviest person is : ");

     PUT(MAX_H_NAME);

     NEW_LINE;

end HEAVY;
```

If we use the following sample input lines,

```
JOHNSON K. Mary      00145
J.K. Peterson        00175
Paul Amaretto        00155
X
```

then the program will display this result:

```
J.K. Peterson
```

INTEGER AND ENUMERATION TYPE ATTRIBUTES

Ada types and objects may have certain predefined characteristics called **attributes.** The integer and enumeration types, for example, have a common set of attributes, among them FIRST and LAST. These attributes give the minimum and the maximum value found in the set of values associated with the type. The following list gives some examples.

Attribute	Description
INTEGER'FIRST	Gives the smallest integer value supported by the predefined type INTEGER
INTEGER'LAST	Gives the largest integer value supported by the predefined type INTEGER
AGE'FIRST	Gives the smallest value allowed for the type AGE (introduced in the examples on pages 10–11); here the value is 0
AGE'LAST	Gives 200 (see page 10)
ACCOUNT_NO'FIRST	Gives 0 (see page 10)
ACCOUNT_NO'LAST	Gives 9999 (see page 10)

`DAY'FIRST`	Gives MON (see page 10)
`DAY'LAST`	Gives SUN (see page 10)

As the list shows, FIRST and LAST attributes are invoked by writing the type name followed by the apostrophe and the attribute name.

We are going to mention four more attributes of the discrete types: POS, SUCC, PRED and VAL. These attributes are invoked by supplying, in addition to the type name and the attribute name, a value (or an expression resulting in a value) to be placed within parentheses.

The POS attribute returns the position number of the value considered relative to the minimum value of the type. Here are some examples.

POS Attribute	Value
`AGE'POS(2)`	2
`DAY'POS(TUE)`	1
`SWITCH'POS(ON)`	0

The SUCC attribute returns the successor value of the same type.

SUCC Attribute	Value
`INTEGER'SUCC(7)`	8
`CHARACTER'SUCC('f')`	g
`AGE'SUCC(2)`	3
`DAY'SUCC(TUE)`	WED
`SWITCH'SUCC(ON)`	OFF
`AGE'SUCC(200)`	An error exception will occur
`DAY'SUCC(SUN)`	An error exception will occur

The PRED attribute returns the predecessor value of the same type.

PRED Attribute	Value
`INTEGER'PRED(8)`	7
`CHARACTER'PRED('g')`	'f'
`AGE'PRED(3)`	2
`DAY'PRED(TUE)`	MON
`SWITCH'PRED(OFF)`	ON
`AGE'PRED(0)`	An error exception will occur
`DAY'PRED(MON)`	An error exception will occur

The VAL attribute returns the value whose position is given by the supplied positive number.

VAL Attribute	Value
CHARACTER'VAL(71)	'F'
AGE'VAL(3)	2
DAY'VAL(2)	TUE
SWITCH'VAL(1)	ON
DAY'VAL(8)	An error exception will occur

The program UP_MONDAY in the next subsection provides examples of the actual use of discrete type attributes.

USING INTEGER AND ENUMERATION TYPES

The next Ada program, called UP_MONDAY, relates to a saying on Wall Street: Up on Monday, down on Tuesday. That is, if the market goes up on Monday, it is likely to see a reversal (go down) on Tuesday. The program reads information from each line as a pair of words, the first word representing the trading day (Monday through Friday) and the second word representing the change from the previous day (up, down, unchanged). We assume that the end of data is signaled by a day of Sunday, a nontrading day. An unspecified number of trading days are supplied. The program is supposed to check that every Tuesday line is preceded by a Monday line (holidays sometimes fall on Mondays, sometimes on Tuesdays—like election days—and one has to check that this sequence is not spoiled). No other checks are made, even though they might be required in a more realistic setting. The program assumes that at least two lines are entered.

UP_MONDAY Program

```
with TEXT_IO; use TEXT_IO;

procedure UP_MONDAY is

    type DAY is (MON,TUE,WED,THU,FRI,SAT,SUN) ;

    type CHANGE is (DOWN,UNCHANGED,UP);

    -- Two enumeration types are declared. The first

    -- one has values MON through SUN, and the second

    -- has values DOWN, UNCHANGED, and UP.

    package DAY_IO is new ENUMERATION_IO(DAY);
```

```
      use DAY_IO;

      -- These two lines are needed in order

      -- to read and/or write the values of the type DAY.

      -- One can now use free-form GET and PUT for the

      -- type  DAY. The values of the type DAY can

      -- be spelled with uppercase or lowercase letters

      -- without affecting the result - which is true

      -- for any enumeration type.

      package CHANGE_IO is new ENUMERATION_IO(CHANGE);

      use CHANGE_IO;

      -- As just explained, these two lines are needed

      -- for doing input and output (I/O) with values of

      -- type CHANGE.

      CURRENT_DAY, PREVIOUS_DAY : DAY ;

      -- Two variables of type DAY are declared.

      CURRENT_CHANGE, PREVIOUS_CHANGE : CHANGE ;

      -- Two variables of type CHANGE are declared.

      package INT_IO is new INTEGER_IO(INTEGER);

      use INT_IO;

      TOTAL_UP_MONDAY, TOTAL_UP_MON_AND_DOWN_TUE : INTEGER ;

      -- Two variables of the predefined type INTEGER.

begin

      TOTAL_UP_MONDAY := 0;

      TOTAL_UP_MON_AND_DOWN_TUE := 0;

      GET(PREVIOUS_DAY);

      GET(PREVIOUS_CHANGE);
```

```
-- The first line was just read, and the DAY and CHANGE
-- values are placed in the PREVIOUS variables.
SKIP_LINE;
GET(CURRENT_DAY);
while  CURRENT_DAY /= SUN

    loop

    GET(CURRENT_CHANGE);

    if PREVIOUS_DAY = MON and PREVIOUS_CHANGE = UP

      -- an equivalent condition using attributes is

      --          PREVIOUS_DAY        =       DAY'FIRST       and

      --          PREVIOUS_CHANGE     =       CHANGE'FIRST

        then

        TOTAL_UP_MONDAY := TOTAL_UP_MONDAY + 1;

        if  CURRENT_DAY = TUE and CURRENT_CHANGE = DOWN

        -- here  an equivalent condition using  attributes is

        -- CURRENT_DATE   = DAY'SUCC(PREVIOUS_DAY)      and

        -- CURRENT_CHANGE = CHANGE'SUCC(PREVIOUS_CHANGE)

        -- Another example is :

        -- DAY'PREV(CURRENT_DATE)      = PREVIOUS_DAY     and

        -- DAY'PREV(CURRENT_CHANGE) = PREVIOUS_CHANGE

            then

            TOTAL_UP_MON_AND_DOWN_TUE :=

                TOTAL_UP_MON_AND_DOWN_TUE + 1 ;

        end if;

    end if;

    PREVIOUS_DAY := CURRENT_DAY;
```

```
                    PREVIOUS_CHANGE := CURRENT_CHANGE;

                    SKIP_LINE;

                    GET(CURRENT_DAY);

          end loop;

          NEW_LINE;

          PUT( " The total of up days on Mondays is : ");

          PUT(TOTAL_UP_MONDAY);

          NEW_LINE;

          PUT(" The total of up on Mondays and down on Tuesdays is ");

          PUT(TOTAL_UP_MON_AND_DOWN_TUE);

    end UP_MONDAY;
```

Note that any GET statement that does not encounter a value of the expected type will cause an error exception to be raised.

The UP_MONDAY program makes use of the logical operator "and" to build a complex expression (actually, a BOOLEAN expression, because its resulting value has the type BOOLEAN) from two simpler relations. While the meaning of the expression is quite clear, the following section (1.4) will provide some additional details.

The next program exhibits the handling of both integer and enumeration types. It deals with inventory control. The program reads information about items in inventory. Every line gives information for just one item. The expected format is as follows:

Column	Data
Columns 1–4	Item number
Columns 5–24	Item description
Columns 25–27	Quantity on hand
Columns 28–30	Quantity on order
Columns 31–50	Warehouse location

The last line is assumed to have 9999 for its item number.

For every line read, the quantity on hand is added to the quantity on order, and a message is printed warning the user about the need to reorder if the sum is below 10. After all the lines are read, the item number and the item description having the highest inventory level are displayed together with its warehouse location and the total number of items that need reordering.

INVENTORY Program

```
with TEXT_IO; use TEXT_IO;

procedure INVENTORY is

      package INT_IO is new INTEGER_IO(INTEGER);

      use INT_IO;

      type QUANTITY is range 0 .. 999;

      type ITEM_NO is range 0 .. 9999;

      TOTAL_QUANTITY_PER_ITEM ,TOTAL_REORDERED_ITEMS : QUANTITY;

      HIGH_QUANTITY_PER_ITEM : QUANTITY ;

      package QUANT_IO is new INTEGER_IO (QUANTITY);

      use QUANT_IO;

      package ITEM_IO is new INTEGER_IO(ITEM_NO);

      use ITEM_IO;

      QUANT_ON_HAND, QUANT_ON_ORDER : QUANTITY;

      ITEM_NO_IN, HIGH_ITEM_NO_IN : ITEM_NO ;

      REORDER_POINT: constant QUANTITY := 10;

      ITEM_DESCRIPTION, HIGH_ITEM_DESCRIPTION : STRING(1 .. 20);

      type   WAREHOUSE    is
      (ILLINOIS,NEW_YORK,TEXAS,CALIFORNIA,FLORIDA);

      HIGH_WAREHOUSE,WAREHOUSE_IN : WAREHOUSE;

      package WAREHOUSE_IO is new ENUMERATION_IO(WAREHOUSE);

      use WAREHOUSE_IO;

begin

      TOTAL_REORDERED_ITEMS := 0;
```

```
HIGH_QUANTITY_PER_ITEM := 0;

GET ( ITEM_NO_IN, 4);

-- Here the package ITEM_IO is used.

while ITEM_NO_IN /= 9999

      loop

      GET (ITEM_DESCRIPTION);

      GET (QUANT_ON_HAND, 3);

      -- Here the package QUANT_IO is needed.

      GET (QUANT_ON_ORDER,3);

      GET (WAREHOUSE_IN);

      TOTAL_QUANTITY_PER_ITEM := QUANT_ON_HAND +

                                       QUANT_ON_ORDER ;

      if    HIGH_QUANTITY_PER_ITEM <

            TOTAL_QUANTITY_PER_ITEM

            then

            HIGH_QUANTITY_PER_ITEM := TOTAL_QUANTITY_PER_ITEM ;

            HIGH_ITEM_NO_IN := ITEM_NO_IN ;

            HIGH_ITEM_DESCRIPTION := ITEM_DESCRIPTION;

            HIGH_WAREHOUSE := WAREHOUSE_IN;

      end if;

      if TOTAL_QUANTITY_PER_ITEM  <  REORDER_POINT

            then

            NEW_LINE;

            PUT(ITEM_DESCRIPTION);

            PUT(" *** This item has to be reordered *** ");

            NEW_LINE;
```

```
            TOTAL_REORDERED_ITEMS := TOTAL_REORDERED_ITEMS + 1;

        end if;

        SKIP_LINE;

        GET (ITEM_NO_IN);

    end loop;

    NEW_LINE;

    PUT( " The highest inventory level is for ");

    PUT(HIGH_ITEM_NO_IN);

    PUT(HIGH_ITEM_DESCRIPTION);

    NEW_LINE;

    PUT(" Located in ");

    PUT(HIGH_WAREHOUSE);

    NEW_LINE;

    PUT(" The total number of items needed to be " &

       " reordered is ");

    PUT( TOTAL_REORDERED_ITEMS, 4);

end INVENTORY;
```

1.4 INTRODUCTION TO EXPRESSIONS

So far we encountered expressions appearing to the right of the compound symbol ":=" in assignment statements and following the reserved word "if" in "if" statements. These expressions were quite simple and consisted mainly of primaries, which in our examples were literals, constants, and variables.

Expressions represent formulas that compute values. For literals, constants, and variables (the primaries just mentioned), the value computed by the formulas is just the value associated with the given literal or identifier. The primaries, however, can be combined to form more complex expressions representing more complicated formulas. The primaries are combined with the help of operators.

Operators are applied to operands. If an operator needs only one operand in order to be applied, it is called a **unary operator.** For instance, "not" is a unary (logical) operator. Also "+" and "−" as signs (positive and negative) are unary (arithmetic) operators. If an operator needs two operands in order to be applied, it is called a **binary operator.** For instance, "+" (for addition) and "*" (for multiplication) are (arithmetic) binary operators. The reserved word "and" is a (logical) binary operator.

There is a priority list for operators, and the higher-priority operators are applied before lower-priority operators. If several operators have the same priority, then they are applied from left to right. These priorities can be overruled by the use of parentheses. In this case expressions within parentheses are computed first. Here is a complete list of predefined operations that have meaning for integer types, starting with the highest-priority operators.

**, abs	Exponentiation, absolute value
*, /, mod, rem	Multiplication, division, modulus, remainder
+, −	Sign (unary)
+, −	Addition, subtraction (binary)
=, /=, <, <=, >, >=, in, not in	

The final line in the list contains the lowest-priority operators that can be applied to integers. These operators are defined as follows:

=	Equality
/=	Inequality
>	Greater than
>=	Greater than or equal to
<	Less than
<=	Less than or equal to
in	Membership test
not in	Membership test

The operators "in" and "not in" are called **membership operators;** the remaining ones are called **relational operators.** Relational and membership operations are the only operations that can be performed on enumeration types.

The membership operators can have complex forms. In this chapter we will make use of a particularly simple form, with the left operand a variable and the right operand a range.

Note the operators >= (greater than or equal to) and <= (less than or equal to). They should not be confused with the sequence of characters =< or =>. The symbol => is used to point at possible choices in *case statements,* as will be discussed in Chapter 4.

The list that follows gives various examples of expressions. These examples use the following declarations:

```
type DAY is (MON,TUE,WED,THU,FRI,SAT,SUN) ;
I,J : INTEGER;
CURRENT_DAY,PREVIOUS_DAY: DAY;
```

Now here is a list of some valid expressions and their descriptions.

Expression	Description
I ** 5	The content of I is raised to the power 5.
3 + I * J	The value in I is multiplied by the value in J, and the result is added to 3.
5 / 3	The integer 5 is divided by 3; the result is 1, and the fractional part is dropped.
-I + J = 100 * I	First, 100 * I is evaluated; then − I; then −I + J; then the equality test is performed.
I in 1 . . J	A membership test is performed. If the value of I happens to be among the integers 1 through J, then the test returns the predefined Boolean value TRUE; otherwise, it returns the value FALSE.
I rem 5	Returns the integer remainder, which takes the sign of the dividend. If I is 23, then the returned value is 3. If I is −23, the returned value is −3.
23 rem -5	Returns the value 3.
I mod 5	Mod returns a value whose sign is the sign of the divisor, and in absolute value is equal to the absolute value of rem. If I is 23, the returned value is 3.
I mod -5	The returned value is negative. If I is 23, the returned value is −3.

```
CURRENT_DAY <
    PREVIOUS_DAY
```
If the value of CURRENT_DAY appears before the value of PREVIOUS_DAY in the list of values defined for the type DAY, then the returned value is TRUE; otherwise, it is FALSE.

```
CURRENT_DAY not in
    Mon . . PREVIOUS_DAY
```
The membership test returns the predefined Boolean value TRUE if the value of CURRENT_DAY is outside the range of values from Mon through the value of PREVIOUS_DAY.

We remind you that types are generally not mixed in expressions. For integer and enumeration types, however, attributes can be applied to one type to generate values of another type. For instance,

```
I + DAY'POS(CURRENT_DAY)
```

is a valid expression because the value supplied by the attribute POS is of integer type. Also, the expression

```
CURRENT_DAY <= DAY'VAL(I)
```

is valid, provided that the value of I is an integer from 1 to 7, because the value supplied by the attribute VAL is of type DAY. Of course, one can build complex and lengthy expressions as long as they are properly formed. Here is a valid complex expression:

```
I + J ** 2 - 7 / I * J ** 4 + J / I ** 3 * J rem I
```

Note that whenever the relational or membership operators are applied, the resulting type is BOOLEAN. Expressions whose resulting type is BOOLEAN can be further combined by using logical operators like "not," "and," and "or," as well as some other logical operators that will be covered in Chapter 4.

The logical operator "not" is unary and has the same high priority as "**" and "abs." The logical operators "and" and "or" are binary operators, and their priority is lowest, even lower than the priority of the relational operators.

Now let us review the application of these logical operators. The result of the expression

A and B

is TRUE if and only if the result of the evaluation of A is TRUE and the result of the evaluation of B is FALSE. The result of the evaluation of

A or B

is FALSE if and only if both A and B are found to be FALSE. The result of the evaluation of

not A

is TRUE if A is FALSE, and it is FALSE if A is TRUE.

In Ada we distinguish between dynamic and static expressions. If the evaluation of an expression can be completed before the sequence-of-statements part is executed, then the expression is **static.** Otherwise, the expression is **dynamic.**

The short program DAY_CONVERSION that follows, as well as the program in Section 1.5, demonstrates the use of some of the concepts discussed in this section. The input consists of just two items: a Julian day (days counted starting with the first of January) followed by the weekday of the first of January. Since the days can come from different years, one can have different weekdays on the first of January. The output should list the weekday corresponding to the Julian day and whether or not it falls on a weekend.

DAY_CONVERSION Program

```
with TEXT_IO; use TEXT_IO;

procedure DAY_CONVERSION is

    type DAY is (MON,TUE,WED,THU,FRI,SAT,SUN) ;

    package INT_IO is new INTEGER_IO(INTEGER);

    use INT_IO;

    package DAY_IO is new ENUMERATION_IO(DAY);

    use DAY_IO;

    JULIAN_DAY : INTEGER ;

    CURRENT_DAY,FIRST_JAN_DAY: DAY;

    CURRENT_DAY_POS : INTEGER;

begin

    GET(JULIAN_DAY,3);

    GET(FIRST_JAN_DAY);

    CURRENT_DAY_POS :=  JULIAN_DAY mod 7  +

                        DAY'POS(FIRST_JAN_DAY) ;
```

```
      if CURRENT_DAY_POS > 7

          then

          CURRENT_DAY_POS := CURRENT_DAY_POS - 7;

      end if;

      CURRENT_DAY := DAY'VAL(CURRENT_DAY_POS);

      NEW_LINE;

      PUT(" This julian day falls on a ");

      PUT(CURRENT_DAY);

      if CURRENT_DAY not in Mon .. Fri

      then

          PUT("  is a weekend");

      else

          PUT(" is a working day ");

      end if;

  end DAY_CONVERSION;
```

1.5 INTRODUCTION TO PACKAGES, SUBPROGRAMS, AND EXCEPTIONS

Ada programs are made up of one or more **program units.** Ada program units can be compiled separately, a clear advantage for developing large software programs. Subprograms are one example of program units. Other program units are tasks (to be discussed in Chapter 10) and packages. We will briefly discuss packages and subprograms in this section.

PACKAGES

One of the novelties of Ada is the concept of package. **Packages** are collections of resources usable by other programs. These resources might be types, objects, subprograms, other packages, and various operations defined on chosen types. In addition, the package designer has complete control over what an outsider may use and know about the package resources.

Ada provides a number of predefined packages (the TEXT_IO package, for instance). The predefined packages can be made available to any Ada program. We used statements like

```
with TEXT_IO ;
use TEXT_IO;
```

to actually make the resources of the package TEXT_IO available within an Ada program, which is what the **"with" clause** does. The **"use" clause** is a convenience allowing the names declared in TEXT_IO to be used as if they were declared within the program itself.

Ada has also generic facilities for subprograms and packages. Ada **generic facilities** allow the programmer to create subprograms or packages that are well defined for solving a certain problem yet general enough to cover a number of variations. For use within an Ada program generic subprograms and packages must be **instantiated;** that is, a unique copy incorporating the desired particular variation must be created. In this chapter we have used instantiation of generic packages in order to create a package handling the input/output for a particular type of integer or enumeration type. For instance, in several programs of this chapter we had a statement like

```
package INT_IO is new INTEGER_IO(INTEGER);
```

In this statement the generic package is INTEGER_IO, the particular copy instantiated is called INT_IO, and the type for which the generic package is customized is the predefined integer type INTEGER.

SUBPROGRAMS

Subprograms have a specification part and a body part. None of the programs in this chapter have a separate specification part, that is, a specification part that is separately compiled. In our programs the body acts as its own specification. We will cover the use of specification parts in detail in Chapter 5.

There are two kinds of subprograms in Ada: **procedures** and **functions.** They both define a collection of actions, and they represent the main avenue for expressing algorithms. In addition, functions are required to return a value as the expected result of certain computations, and they may appear in expressions.

Procedures are invoked in other programs by using their name followed by appropriate arguments within parentheses and then a semicolon. Procedure calls are considered statements by themselves.

There are many examples of procedure calls in this chapter's programs. For instance,

```
NEW_LINE;
```

is a procedure call invoking NEW_LINE. The procedure has no parameters, and therefore no arguments are supplied. The procedure

```
GET(I);
```

invokes GET and supplies I as the argument.

A function is invoked when its name appears in an expression with proper arguments. For instance, the package TEXT_IO has a function named LINE_LENGTH that returns the length (an integer, representing the number of print positions) of the line. An expression like

```
LINE_LENGTH < 80
```

in any of the programs of this chapter will invoke the function LINE_LENGTH.

EXCEPTIONS

Whenever an Ada program is executed, there is the possibility that an error of some kind will happen. For example, the input data may not match the expected type, a division by zero may be attempted, and so on.

These errors may be handled in Ada through the raising of exceptions. Unless some specific statements are written to handle the exception, the **raising of an exception** in an Ada main program usually means that the execution of the main program is abandoned, and, of course, the program is not able to perform its intended job.

Ada has some predefined exceptions. Among the predefined exceptions, one is likely to encounter CONSTRAINT_ERROR (for instance, when a range is violated) and NUMERIC_ERROR (for instance, division by zero).

Besides dealing with run-time errors, Ada exceptions can deal with a number of other kinds of exceptional situations. What constitutes an exceptional situation depends mainly on the particular application.

The concepts of subprograms, packages, and exceptions have been sketchily presented. Full details about subprograms, packages, and exceptions will be given in Chapters 5, 7, and 11, respectively. For the moment we will be content with this sketchy information but use it to show how we can define and use procedures as part of an Ada program.

PROGRAM USING PROCEDURES

The following program, called INVENTORY_REPORT, has input lines that use the same layout as the program INVENTORY presented in Section 1.3. But there is an additional constraint imposed on the input: Lines are sorted by warehouse location, and within a location they are sorted by item number. The sorting by warehouse location is not done in alphabetical order but is done according to the position it has in the enumeration list (for instance, FLORIDA is after NEW_YORK). One can have more than one line per item number in each warehouse location if there are several physical locations in a state.

The required output is as follows: For each item number in a location a line should be displayed listing the item number, the item description, the total quantity on hand, and the total quantity on order. For each warehouse location a line should be displayed listing the total number of items in inventory, the total quantity on hand, and the total quantity on order (for all items). Also, a last line should be printed listing a grand total of the quantity on hand and on order, and a message should be displayed if any line is out of sequence. Out-of-sequence lines should not be processed. As before, the last line should have an item number of 0.

INVENTORY_REPORT Program

```
with TEXT_IO; use TEXT_IO;

procedure INVENTORY_REPORT is

    package INT_IO is new INTEGER_IO(INTEGER);

    use INT_IO;

    type QUANTITY is range 0 .. 999;

    type ITEM_NO is range 0 .. 9999;

    CURR_QUANT_ON_HAND, CURR_QUANT_ON_ORDER : QUANTITY;

    PREV_QUANT_ON_HAND, PREV_QUANT_ON_ORDER : QUANTITY;

    CURR_ITEM, PREV_ITEM : ITEM_NO;

    TOT_QUANT_ON_HAND_LOC, TOT_QUANT_ON_ORDER_LOC : QUANTITY ;

    TOT_QUANT_ON_HAND_ITEM, TOT_QUANT_ON_ORDER_ITEM :  QUANTITY ;

    TOT_QUANT_ON_HAND, TOT_QUANT_ON_ORDER :  QUANTITY ;

    package QUANT_IO is new INTEGER_IO (QUANTITY);

    use QUANT_IO;

    package ITEM_IO is new INTEGER_IO(ITEM_NO);

    use ITEM_IO;

    CURR_ITEM_DESCRIPTION, PREV_ITEM_DESCRIPTION : STRING(1 .. 20);

    type   WAREHOUSE   is

    (ILLINOIS,NEW_YORK,TEXAS,CALIFORNIA,FLORIDA);
```

```
          package WAREHOUSE_IO is new ENUMERATION_IO(WAREHOUSE);

          use WAREHOUSE_IO;

          CURR_WAREHOUSE,PREV_WAREHOUSE : WAREHOUSE;

procedure NEW_ITEM_PROC is

-- The objects declared for the procedure INVENTORY_REPORT will

-- be known and will be usable    within   the   body   of   the

-- procedure NEW_ITEM_PROC. This process will be explained in

-- Chapter 7, Section 7.3.

begin

-- This procedure is invoked when a new item is processed and

-- the old item has to be displayed together with associated

-- totals.

     NEW_LINE;

     PUT(PREV_ITEM);

     PUT(PREV_ITEM_DESCRIPTION);

     PUT(TOT_QUANT_ON_HAND_ITEM,5);

     PUT(TOT_QUANT_ON_ORDER_ITEM,5);

     TOT_QUANT_ON_HAND_LOC :=  TOT_QUANT_ON_HAND_LOC +

                                 TOT_QUANT_ON_HAND_ITEM;

     TOT_QUANT_ON_ORDER_LOC := TOT_QUANT_ON_ORDER_LOC +

                                 TOT_QUANT_ON_ORDER_ITEM;

     TOT_QUANT_ON_HAND_ITEM := 0;

     TOT_QUANT_ON_ORDER_ITEM := 0;

     PREV_ITEM :=CURR_ITEM;

     PREV_ITEM_DESCRIPTION := CURR_ITEM_DESCRIPTION;

     PREV_QUANT_ON_HAND := CURR_QUANT_ON_HAND ;
```

```
        PREV_QUANT_ON_ORDER := CURR_QUANT_ON_ORDER ;

end NEW_ITEM_PROC;


procedure NEW_LOC_PROC is

begin

-- This procedure is invoked when a new location is read and

-- the old location has to be displayed together with associated

-- totals.

        NEW_LINE;

        PUT(PREV_WAREHOUSE,20);

        PUT(TOT_QUANT_ON_HAND_LOC,7);

        PUT(TOT_QUANT_ON_ORDER_LOC,7) ;

        TOT_QUANT_ON_HAND :=  TOT_QUANT_ON_HAND +

                              TOT_QUANT_ON_HAND_LOC;

        TOT_QUANT_ON_ORDER := TOT_QUANT_ON_ORDER +

                              TOT_QUANT_ON_ORDER_LOC;

        TOT_QUANT_ON_HAND_LOC  := 0;

        TOT_QUANT_ON_ORDER_LOC := 0;

        PREV_ITEM := CURR_ITEM;

        PREV_ITEM_DESCRIPTION := CURR_ITEM_DESCRIPTION;

        PREV_QUANT_ON_HAND := CURR_QUANT_ON_HAND ;

        PREV_QUANT_ON_ORDER := CURR_QUANT_ON_ORDER ;

        PREV_WAREHOUSE := CURR_WAREHOUSE;

end NEW_LOC_PROC;


begin

-- First, we initialize some totals.
```

```
TOT_QUANT_ON_HAND_LOC := 0;

TOT_QUANT_ON_ORDER_LOC := 0;

TOT_QUANT_ON_HAND_ITEM := 0;

TOT_QUANT_ON_ORDER_ITEM := 0;

TOT_QUANT_ON_HAND :=0 ;

TOT_QUANT_ON_ORDER :=0 ;

GET(CURR_ITEM);

if CURR_ITEM /= 0

-- The very first line will be used to initialize

-- the "previous item".

    then

    GET(CURR_ITEM_DESCRIPTION);

    PREV_ITEM_DESCRIPTION := CURR_ITEM_DESCRIPTION;

    GET(CURR_QUANT_ON_HAND);

    PREV_QUANT_ON_HAND := CURR_QUANT_ON_HAND ;

    GET(CURR_QUANT_ON_ORDER);

    PREV_QUANT_ON_ORDER := CURR_QUANT_ON_ORDER ;

    GET(CURR_WAREHOUSE);

    PREV_WAREHOUSE := CURR_WAREHOUSE;

end if;

CURR_ITEM := PREV_ITEM;

SKIP_LINE;

while    CURR_ITEM /= 0

    loop

    if CURR_WAREHOUSE = PREV_WAREHOUSE  and

        CURR_ITEM = PREV_ITEM
```

```
    then

        -- Note that the test is true for the line read

        -- in. Below we accumulate totals for identical

        -- items placed in the same warehouse.

        TOT_QUANT_ON_HAND_ITEM :=

            TOT_QUANT_ON_HAND_ITEM + CURR_QUANT_ON_HAND ;

        TOT_QUANT_ON_ORDER_ITEM :=

            TOT_QUANT_ON_ORDER_ITEM   + CURR_QUANT_ON_ORDER ;

elsif CURR_WAREHOUSE = PREV_WAREHOUSE   and

        CURR_ITEM > PREV_ITEM

        then

        -- We have a new item in the same warehouse

        NEW_ITEM_PROC;

elsif CURR_WAREHOUSE > PREV_WAREHOUSE

        then

        NEW_ITEM_PROC;

        NEW_LOC_PROC;

else

        PUT(" This line is bad and will be skipped ");

end if;

SKIP_LINE;

GET(CURR_ITEM);

if CURR_ITEM /= 0

        then

        -- we only want to read the rest of the

        -- line if we have a regular item line
```

```
                        GET(CURR_ITEM_DESCRIPTION);

                        GET(CURR_QUANT_ON_HAND);

                        GET(CURR_QUANT_ON_ORDER);

                        GET(CURR_WAREHOUSE);

                end if;

        end loop;

        -- We reached the end of the input data, but we

        -- did not display the last total for the last

        -- item in the last warehouse. We now take care of

        -- these last two lines.

        NEW_ITEM_PROC;

        NEW_LOC_PROC;

        NEW_LINE;

        PUT(" THE GRAND TOTAL IS ");

        PUT(TOT_QUANT_ON_HAND);

        PUT(TOT_QUANT_ON_ORDER);

end INVENTORY_REPORT ;
```

The program INVENTORY_REPORT made use of the "elsif" reserved word as part of an "if" statement. The meaning of it is as follows: First, the condition following the reserved word "if" is evaluated. If the condition is true, then the statements following the reserved word "then" are executed. Otherwise, the condition following the reserved word "elsif" is evaluated. And if it is true, the statements following the "elsif . . . then" are executed. Otherwise, the following condition is evaluated. And the process continues until one condition following an "elsif" reserved word is true or the reserved word "else" is reached, in which case the statements following the reserved word "else" are executed.

The example that follows will help clarify the use of the option "elsif" in "if" statements. We assume that variable I is of INTEGER type.

```
if I > 3

        then
```

```
        I := I * I;

elsif   I > 1

        then

        I := I * 3 ;

elsif I > -3

        then

        I := 0 ;

else

        I := I / 3 ;

end if;
```

In this example, if I is 4, then the first condition (I > 3) is true. Therefore the value of I will become 4 * 4 = 16. The other conditions (and they are true in this case because 4 > 1 and 4 > −3) are not evaluated because a previous condition evaluated was true. We only reach the condition I > 1 if the condition I > 3 is false. We only reach the condition I > −3 if the previous conditions, I > 3 and I > 1, are false. We only execute the statements following the reserved word "else" if all conditions, I > 3, I > 1, and I > −3, are false.

EXERCISES FOR CHAPTER 1

1. Change the program MAXALL of Section 1.1 so that the largest and next-to-largest numbers are found.

2. Modify the program CHAR_MAX3 of Section 1.3 so that the first letter (according to alphabetical order) of several letters read will be displayed. The end of the sequence of letters is signaled by the character '!'.

3. Rewrite the program HEAVY of Section 1.3 for an additional field in column 21: a one-character string representing the sex ('M' for male and 'F' for female). The required output is the name and the weight of the heaviest male, the name and the weight of the heaviest female, and the name and the weight of the lightest female.

4. Modify the program UP_MONDAY of Section 1.3 so that the program lists, in addition to the previous output, the number of trading Mondays not followed by a trading Tuesday and the number of trading Tuesdays not preceded by a trading Monday.

5. Change the program INVENTORY of Section 1.3 so that you can display the answer to the following question: Are there more items in the warehouse in Texas than in the warehouse in California?

6. Modify the program DAY_CONVERSION of Section 1.4 so that you can answer the following question: Are there more lines that supply days falling on Mondays than on Tuesdays?

7. Rewrite the program INVENTORY_REPORT of Section 1.5 assuming that there is only one warehouse location. The items in the warehouse are sorted, and one could have several lines with the same item numbers (this program should be easier to write than the program in Section 1.5 because there is one less level to keep track of).

REAL, ARRAY, AND RECORD TYPES

2.1   REAL TYPES

Real types provide a finite set of values approximating the real numbers. There are infinitely many real numbers, and they can be arbitrarily close to each other; but a computer can only supply a finite number of bits to represent a real number. For this reason the computer cannot provide an exact representation of every real number, and therefore Ada defines a **model set of real numbers** for every type declaration involving reals.

As with integer types, there is a predefined real type called FLOAT. For instance,

```
RATE: FLOAT;
```

declares the variable RATE as being real of type FLOAT. However, with the use of this declaration, the user is relying on the accuracy of the real type defined on a particular piece of hardware.

To shift the control of the accuracy from the hardware to the software level (this shift improves the portability of the program), Ada has a mechanism, described in the following subsections, for defining the error bounds of a particular real type. Two kinds of real types can be defined in Ada: floating-point types and fixed-point types. **Floating-point types** handle real values with relative accuracy, while **fixed-point types** handle real values with absolute accuracy. Therefore the Ada accuracy mechanism is different for each kind of real type. Integer and real types (floating-point and fixed-point) are called **numeric types.**

FLOATING-POINT TYPES

The declaration of the floating-point types follows the pattern

```
type type_name is digits
    static_integer_expression;
```

If a range is specified, the pattern is

```
type type_name is digits static_integer_expression
    range L . . R;
```

The "digits static_integer_expression" part of the declaration is called an **accuracy constraint.** Recall that a static integer expression is an expression whose value can be computed before the program starts running. The part "range L . . R" is called a **range constraint.** The value of L is the left side of the range, and the value of R is the right side of it.

Here are some examples of floating-point type declarations:

```
type DISTANCE is digits 8;

type SECURITY_PRICE is digits 10 range 0.0 . .
    10000.00;
```

The first declaration introduces the type DISTANCE with a relative accuracy of 8 decimal digits. Since every decimal digit accounts for about 3.32 binary digits, the accuracy, restated in binary, is 8 * 3.32, or 27 binary digits (this number will be denoted as B).

For a given accuracy (in binary) B, the model numbers are defined to have an exponent from $-4 * B$ to $+4 * B$, and the model numbers always contain zero. The general form of the model numbers is

```
sign * binary_mantissa * 2.0 ** exponent
```

where the binary_mantissa has B binary digits after the decimal point (27 for our example). The same number can have many possible representations of the general form. For instance, the number 0.5 (0.1 in binary) can be written as

```
1/2 * 2 ** 0
1/4 * 2 ** 1
```

and so on.

Model numbers are **normalized.** That is, from the many possible representations of a binary number using the general form, the number with a binary_ mantissa of at least 0.1 (0.5 in decimal) is chosen.

The smallest positive number closest to zero for the model numbers is

```
2.0 ** (-4 * B -1)
```

which is 0.1 in binary (0.5 in decimal) times 2 raised to the maximum negative exponent:

```
0.5 * 2 ** (-4 * B )
```

For our B = 27 the number is 2.0 ** (− 109). This number, uniquely defined for every floating-point type, is the value returned by the attribute

```
DISTANCE'SMALL
```

And if F is any floating-point type, the notation is

```
F'SMALL
```

The largest positive model number for our DISTANCE type has a mantissa in binary of

```
0.11 . . . (27 ones) . . . 11
```

which can be written as 1 − 0.00 . . . (26 zeros) . . . 01. The exponent is 4 * 27 = 108. Then the number is

```
( 1 - 2 ** ( -27) ) * 2.0 ** ( 4 * 27 )
```

and is the value returned by the Ada attribute

```
DISTANCE'LARGE
```

In general, the value returned is

```
( 1 - 2 ** ( - B) ) * 2.0 ** ( 4 * B )
```

and can be obtained by invoking

```
F'LARGE
```

for any floating-point type F.

Another important value when dealing with model numbers is the difference between 1.0 and the next model number. For the type DISTANCE the difference is between

```
0.1 * 2 ** ( 1 )
```

and

```
0.100 . . . (25 zeros) . . . 001 * 2 ** ( 1 )
```

which is 2 ** (1 −27). This value is returned by the attribute

DISTANCE'EPSILON

In general, for any floating-point type denoted by F, the difference between 1.0 and next highest model number is

    2 ** (1 - B)

and is obtained by invoking

F'EPSILON

As we said earlier, floating-point types offer relative accuracy. While the number of significant digits for any related computation is kept constant (8 decimals, which translates to 27 binary digits for DISTANCE), the difference between two consecutive values varies. It is smallest around zero, when the difference is equal to

    2 ** (-1 - 4 * B)

It is $2 ** (3 * B + 2)$ times bigger around 1, when it is

    2 ** (1 - B)

And the difference between the largest and the next largest model number is 2 ** (3 * B). Figure 2.1 illustrates these concepts.

During computations one may obtain a value that is not a model number. If the resulting value falls in between two model numbers, the implementation is free to choose any of the two closest model numbers.

When the accuracy constraint and the range constraint are both present, the model numbers inside the range are retained and the others discarded. Note that the left side and the right side of the range must be static real expressions.

Here is a list of operators and their priority for floating-point types (starting with the highest priority):

abs , **	Absolute value, exponentiation
* , /	Multiplication, division
+ , -	Sign (unary)

FIGURE 2.1   Floating-Point Model Numbers

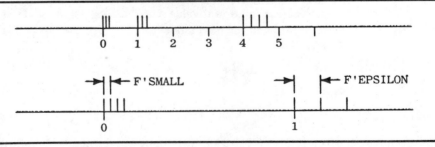

```
+ , -                    Addition, subtraction (binary)
= , /= , < , <= , > , >= , in , not in
```

Note that "**" (exponentiation) is allowed provided that the floating-point real is raised to an integer type value. Also, the result of any of the arithmetic operations on floating-point type values is a value of the same type.

FIXED-POINT TYPE

A real type can be declared to have an absolute accuracy by using the fixed-point representation. The form of the fixed-point declaration is

```
type type_name is delta delta_expression range
    L , , R ;
```

Here are some examples:

```
type AMOUNT is delta 0.001 range 0.00 , ,
    10000.00;
type PRICE is delta 0.0025 range 0.00 , , 200.00;
type LEVEL is delta 0.25 range -100.00 , ,
    5000.00;
```

Note that the range constraint is required for the fixed-point declaration, while it is not required for floating-point types.

The model numbers for fixed-point reals are evenly spaced (hence we have absolute accuracy), and the guaranteed difference between two neighboring numbers is at least equal to the value of the delta_expression (which is the expression following the reserved word "delta"). The delta_expression should be a static expression that evaluates to a positive real. Quite possibly, the implementation of the model numbers on a particular system will choose a different delta, perhaps a more convenient one, named actual_delta. In this case the actual_delta cannot exceed the specified delta, and the difference between any two consecutive model numbers has to be (the same) multiple of actual_delta.

A possibly unexpected feature of fixed-point types is that L and R, the left and right static real expressions, do *not* have to be among the model numbers. The only requirement is that the model numbers start (for L) and end (for R) within a delta_expression of L and R, respectively. Thus, for example, in the declaration of LEVEL given previously, if we have an L of −100.00, there is no guarantee that −100.00 is actually among the model numbers. The only guarantee is that the lowest model number is within 0.25 of −100.00.

The lowest model number can be found and used, though, by invoking the attribute F'FIRST, where F is the fixed-point type. In our example LEVEL'-

FIRST has to lie within 0.25 of −100.00. Similarly, the highest model number is returned by F'LAST. For the type LEVEL the attribute LEVEL'LAST will return a model number within 0.25 of 5000.00.

Other fixed-point attributes are quite straightforward. If F is a fixed-point type, then F'DELTA returns the value of the delta_expression. For our types defined earlier we have

```
PRICE'DELTA
```

which returns the value 0.0025, and

```
AMOUNT'DELTA
```

which returns the value 0.001.

Some other attributes for fixed-point types (using the same notation) are as follows:

Attribute	Description
F'SMALL	The smallest positive model number associated with the type
F'LARGE	The largest positive model number associated with the type

The handling of fixed-point types raises some questions regarding rounding errors. Since the fixed-point types are the preferred types in business applications, how can one make sure that rounding errors do not give results unacceptable for, let us say, an accountant? What if the sum of two pennies gives three? One way to diminish the chance of this error's happening is to choose a finer delta_expression than required, maybe a delta of 0.0001 when dealing with pennies.

Another question deals with input/output. As for the integer types and the enumeration types, some packages (part of TEXT_IO) are needed in order to read and write fixed-point values of a certain type. The same is true of floating-point types. The use of such packages is demonstrated in the program PAYROLL that is presented a little later.

Operations with fixed-point types include multiplication (*) and division (/) of two fixed-point values of the same type, which yield a number of the type called **universal fixed** of arbitrary fine accuracy. This universal fixed type number has to be explicitly converted to the desired type by using the type name followed by the expression within parentheses. For example, suppose we have the declaration

```
AMT_IN, AMT_OUT, AMT_RATIO : AMOUNT;
```

and we need the ratio AMT_IN / AMT_OUT, which gives a value of type universal fixed. The proper way to obtain this ratio in Ada is

```
AMT_RATIO := AMOUNT ( AMT_IN / AMT_OUT ) ;
```

There is no need for this kind of explicit conversion for addition and subtraction. Therefore we can have

```
AMT_IN = AMT_IN + AMT_OUT ;
```

No exponentiation is allowed for fixed-point type objects (variables and constants).

Here is a list of operators and their priority for fixed-point types (starting with the highest priority):

abs	Absolute value
*, /	Multiplication, division
+, -	Sign (unary)
+, -	Addition, subtraction (binary)
=, /=, <, <=, >, >=, in, not in	

For both floating-point and fixed-point types, the resulting values (after expression evaluations) have to satisfy whatever range constraints are specified for the type.

PROGRAM USING REAL TYPES

The following simplified PAYROLL problem exercises some of the new concepts related to real types. The program reads information about employees. Each line contains information about just one employee, in the following format:

Column	Data
Columns 1–9	Social Security number
Columns 10–30	Name
Columns 31–35	Weekly hours worked, with two decimal places (such as 42.35)
Columns 36–40	Hourly pay (in dollars and cents, such as 12.45)
Columns 41–42	Number of dependents (an integer, such as 5)

The last line should contain a Social Security number of 999999999.

For every employee read a line will be displayed listing the employee name, the Social Security number, the gross pay, and the net pay. We arrive at the net pay this (simplified) way: FICA (Social Security) tax is 7.0% of gross pay. Taxable income is the gross pay minus $10 per dependent. The federal tax is 25% of the taxable income, and the state tax is 5% of the taxable income. The net pay is gross pay less FICA tax, federal tax, and state tax.

PAYROLL Program

```
with TEXT_IO; use TEXT_IO;

procedure PAYROLL is

     Package INT_IO is new INTEGER_IO(INTEGER);

     use INT_IO;

     type PAY is delta 0.001 range 0.00 .. 10000.00 ;

     HOURS_WORKED, HOURLY_RATE : PAY ;

     GROSS_PAY, NET_PAY, TAX_INCOME : PAY;

     NO_DEPENDENTS : INTEGER ;

     SOC_SEC_NO : STRING ( 1 .. 9 );

     EMP_NAME   : STRING ( 1 .. 21);

     FICA_RATE : constant PAY := 0.07;

     FED_RATE  : constant PAY := 0.25;

     STATE_RATE: constant PAY := 0.05;

     package PAY_IO is new FIXED_IO (PAY);

     -- Here we make available the GET and PUT procedures

     -- for reading and writing objects of type PAY.

     -- Look below for their use and format.

     use PAY_IO;

begin

     GET(SOC_SEC_NO);

     while SOC_SEC_NO /= "999999999"

          loop

          GET(EMP_NAME);

          GET(HOURLY_RATE,5);        -- The input value should  be
                                     -- typed with a decimal point.
```

```
GET(HOURS_WORKED,5);        -- The  input value should be
                            -- typed with a decimal point.
GET(NO_DEPENDENTS,2);
GROSS_PAY := PAY ( HOURLY_RATE * HOURS_WORKED );
-- Remember: The multiplication gives a result in fixed
-- universal, and it has to be converted to Pay.
if PAY ( NO_DEPENDENTS * 10 ) < GROSS_PAY
    then
    TAX_INCOME :=  GROSS_PAY -
                   PAY ( NO_DEPENDENTS * 10 ) ;
else
    TAX_INCOME := 0.00 ;
end if;
NET_PAY := GROSS_PAY - PAY ( GROSS_PAY * FICA_RATE )
            - PAY ( TAX_INCOME * FED_RATE )
            - PAY ( TAX_INCOME * STATE_RATE ) ;
NEW_LINE;
PUT(SOC_SEC_NO);
PUT(EMP_NAME);
PUT(GROSS_PAY,7,2);
-- This statement is a version of the GET part of
-- the package PAY_IO, with 7 positions allocated
-- for the part  before  the decimal  point , and
-- 2 positions for the part after the decimal point.
PUT(NET_PAY,7,2);
SKIP_LINE;
```

```
            GET(SOC_SEC_NO);

      end loop;

   end PAYROLL ;
```

Note that explicit conversions are allowed among numeric types. Conversions are done by writing the type name of the target value type followed, within parentheses, by the expression itself. Here are some examples using the declarations of the PAYROLL program:

Declaration	Result
INTEGER (GROSS_PAY)	The GROSS_PAY is *rounded* to the nearest integer
FLOAT (21)	The integer 21 is converted to the pre-defined type FLOAT
PAY (NO_DEPENDENTS)	The integer NO_DEPENDENTS is converted to a model number of the fixed-point type PAY

The integer, enumeration, and real types are called **scalar types** because the values of these types have no components. In the following sections we are going to introduce types whose objects consist of several logical parts. These types are array types and record types.

2.2 ARRAY TYPES

An **array** is a collection of logically related components. Every **component** has the same type, and each component has a unique position in the array relative to other components. The position of the component is given by one or more **indices.** If there is one index, we have a one-dimensional array. If there are two or more indices, then we have a multidimensional array. Ada has no predefined limit for the number of dimensions an array should have. Array concepts are illustrated in Figure 2.2. Figure 2.2A shows a one-dimensional array of type STATE_RATE. Figure 2.2B shows a two-dimensional array of type SHIPPING_RATES. These arrays are taken from the program given later in this section.

Ada has two varieties of array types: constrained and unconstrained. In **unconstrained types** the array bounds (first and last position of each index) are not specified when the type is declared. Instead, the bounds can be supplied in various declarations of objects (variables and constants), and actual values for bounds can be supplied even later, when the program is running.

FIGURE 2.2 Arrays

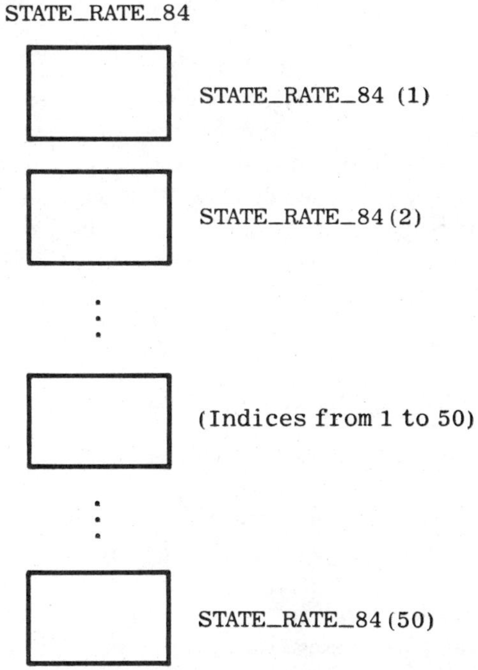

STATE_RATE_84

STATE_RATE_84 (1)

STATE_RATE_84 (2)

⋮

(Indices from 1 to 50)

⋮

STATE_RATE_84 (50)

A. Variable STATE_RATE_84 of Type STATE_RATE

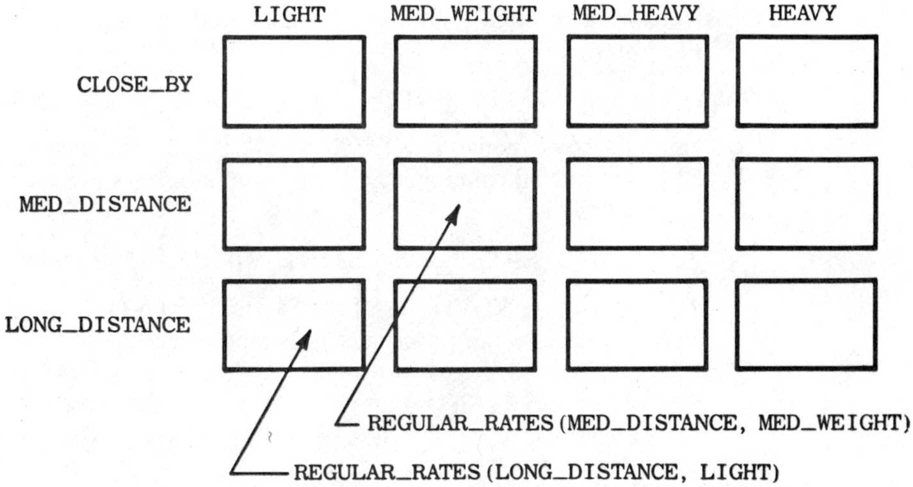

	LIGHT	MED_WEIGHT	MED_HEAVY	HEAVY
CLOSE_BY				
MED_DISTANCE				
LONG_DISTANCE				

REGULAR_RATES (MED_DISTANCE, MED_WEIGHT)

REGULAR_RATES (LONG_DISTANCE, LIGHT)

B. Variable REGULAR_RATES of Type SHIPPING_RATES

For the **constrained array** the bounds of the array have to be known by the time objects of that type (variables and constants) are declared. As a consequence, constrained array variables of the same type have the same bounds, while unconstrained array variables of the same type may have different bounds.

Array **bounds** are given as expressions whose values are discrete types (integer or enumeration types). If the expressions are all static—that is, a value can be derived before the program starts running—then the array is called **static.** An array is a **dynamic array** if at least one of the bounds is given by a dynamic expression—that is, the value of the expression will be determined while the program is running. Both constrained array and unconstrained array variables can be dynamic arrays.

These concepts will be further clarified shortly by several examples.

CONSTRAINED ARRAYS

The form of the declaration for constrained array types is

```
type type_name is array index_constraint of
    type_of_components ;
```

The index_constraint is a sequence of ranges separated by commas and enclosed within parentheses. The ranges must be discrete; that is, the left and right bounds of the range must consist of expressions of type integer or enumeration.

EXAMPLE Here we give some examples of constrained array types and object declarations. For instance,

```
type STATE_RATES is array ( 1 . . 50) of FLOAT;
```

Here the type_name is STATE_RATES, and the index_constraint is (1 . . 50), defining 50 components. Each component has the type FLOAT. The range is 1 through 50.

```
STATE_RATES_84, STATE_RATES_85 : STATE_RATES ;
```

The variables STATE_RATES_84 and STATE_RATES_85 are of type STATE_RATES, and each has 50 components.

```
N : INTEGER;
type CLASS_STUDENT_ID is array (1 . . N ) of
        INTEGERS;
SECTION_A, SECTION_B : CLASS_STUDENT_ID ;
```

Note that SECTION_A and SECTION_B are examples of dynamic arrays. The others are static arrays.

```
type WAREHOUSE is (CHICAGO,NEW_YORK,FRESNO,
    BOSTON);
```

An enumeration type is declared here, which will be the range of the index constraint for the array type LOCATIONS.

```
type LOCATIONS is array (WAREHOUSE ) of FLOAT;
CURR_LOCATION, PREV_LOCATION: LOCATIONS;
type DISTANCE_CLASS is (CLOSE_BY,MED_DISTANCE,
    LONG_DISTANCE);
type WEIGHT_CLASS is
        (LIGHT, MED_WEIGHT, MED_HEAVY, HEAVY);
type PRICES is delta 0.0001 range 0.000 . .
    5000.000;
type SHIPPING_RATES is array ( DISTANCE_CLASS,
    WEIGHT_CLASS ) of PRICES;
```

The array type SHIPPING_RATES has two ranges, which are part of the index_constraint. It is a two-dimensional array. As a final example, we give

```
REGULAR_RATES ,PREMIUM_RATES : SHIPPING_RATES;
```

A component of any array object can be referred to by following the name of the object with the desired index value enclosed within parentheses. Here are some examples.

STATE_RATES (48)	Component 48 of the array STATE_RATES; it is of type FLOAT
CURR_LOCATION (CHICAGO)	Component CHICAGO of the array CURR_LOCATION; it is of type FLOAT
REGULAR_RATE (CLOSE_BY, HEAVY)	Component with a DISTANCE_ CLASS of CLOSE_BY and a WEIGHT_CLASS of HEAVY; it is of type PRICES

The index values can be arrived at by the evaluation of any expression, as long as the resulting value has the required type and it falls within the proper range.

The discrete_range (a range with values of either integer or enumeration type) can have no values at all, in which case the range is said to be null and the array has no components. For instance, assume that the value of N in the previous examples is initialized as

```
N : INTEGER := -1 ;
```

Then the arrays SECTION_A and SECTION_B have a null range.

We are going to illustrate the use of arrays in a program called SHIP_RATE. But before we give the program, we must introduce a new Ada statement that helps in the efficient manipulation of arrays. It is a second kind of loop statement (the first kind was the "while" loop) called a "for" loop.

"FOR" LOOPS

The general form of the **"for" loop** statement is

```
for loop_parameter in discrete_range
    loop
    sequence_of_statements
        end loop;
```

Another option of the loop uses the reserved words

```
in reverse
```

instead of the reserved word "in".

The loop_parameter is a variable whose type is the same as the type of the discrete_range. Therefore its possible values are restricted to the values present in the range. The loop_parameter is not declared and is undefined outside the loop statement. The declaration of the loop_parameter is accomplished by its mere appearance in the loop statement; this kind of declaration is called an **implicit declaration.** Implicit declarations are an exception to the rule stating that all variables must be declared in the declarative part of the subprogram.

The sequence_of_statements part of the "for" loop is executed once for each value contained in the discrete_range of the loop. Each execution of the sequence_of_statements inside the "for" loop is done with the loop_parameter set to a value of the discrete_range, as follows: in increased order (starting with the lower-bound value of the range) if only the reserved word "in" is present; in decreased order (starting with the upper-bound value of the range) if the reserved words "in reverse" are present. The sequence_of_statements is not executed if the range is a null range.

As one may expect, the loop_parameter cannot appear to the left of ":=" in an assignment statement and cannot otherwise be modified within a loop. That is, the loop_parameter is committed to the loop execution with certain values and in a certain sequence; modifying its value means overruling this commitment.

EXAMPLE   Let us look at some examples of "for" loops. For instance,

```
J := 0 ;

for I in  1 .. 20
```

```
        loop

        J = J + I;

end loop;
```

Here J is assumed to be of INTEGER type. This loop should place the sum of integers from 1 to 20 in J. Because the expressions used in the discrete range are of type INTEGER, I is of type (implicitly declared) INTEGER.

Another example is

```
for I in 0 .. -1

        loop

        J := J * 2 ;

end loop;
```

Here we have a null range, and the statement

```
J := J * 2;
```

is not executed.

As a final example, consider

```
GET(K,3);

J := 0;

for I in - K ** 3 .. K ** 2

        loop

        J = I ** 2 + J / 2 ;

end loop;
```

We assume here that K is an INTEGER type variable. Note that the range is null if K is negative.

As we mentioned before, one can write programs using "while" loops only. For the program SHIP_RATE given later, however, the use of "for" loops greatly improves the readability of the code. In particular, "for" loops are well suited for serially processing array components, because the emphasis is on applying similar statements to each of the components. In this case the loop_parameter provides a convenient and well-controlled way to index and manipulate the desired components.

PROGRAMS USING ARRAYS

In the following program a shipping table is initialized by the first three lines, and the remaining lines contain information about the items to be shipped. The table has three rows and four columns. The rows represent the three distance classes, and the columns represent the four weight classes. Each of the first three lines contains four real numbers representing the charge per pound for shipping items falling within each of the 12 possible categories. The other lines have the following information: item number, item weight, and the distance the item is shipped. The last line has an item number of 9999999. Each of the input numbers is assumed to have seven positions available. At least three lines are assumed to be present. The program is supposed to display, for each item, the price charged for its shipping.

SHIP_RATE Program

```
with TEXT_IO; use TEXT_IO;

procedure SHIP_RATE is

    Package INT_IO is new INTEGER_IO(INTEGER);

    use INT_IO;

    type ALLOWED_WEIGHT is digits 10 range 0.00 .. 7000.00 ;

    -- One should check the particular Ada implementation

    -- for the maximum number of allowed digits.

    type ALLOWED_DISTANCE is digits 10 range 0.00 .. 8000.00 ;

    -- We just declared two floating-point types with a range

    -- constraint and an accuracy constraint of ten decimal digits.

    Package DISTANCE_IO is new FLOAT_IO(ALLOWED_DISTANCE);

    use DISTANCE_IO;

    Package WEIGHT_IO is new FLOAT_IO(ALLOWED_WEIGHT);

    use WEIGHT_IO;

    -- We just made available the packages necessary to read

    -- and write some floating-point types.

    type DISTANCE_CLASS is (CLOSE_BY,MED_DISTANCE,LONG_DISTANCE);
```

```
-- Here an enumeration type is declared. It will be used

-- for indexing several arrays below.

CURR_DIST_CLASS : DISTANCE_CLASS ;

-- Here is a variable declaration of enumeration

-- type DISTANCE_CLASS.

type            WEIGHT_CLASS        is

            ( LIGHT, MED_WEIGHT, MED_HEAVY, HEAVY);

\ CURR_WEIGHT_CLASS : WEIGHT_CLASS;

type DIST_CATEGORIES is array ( DISTANCE_CLASS ) of

        ALLOWED_DISTANCE;

  -- A one-dimensional array type is declared, indexed by

  -- the enumeration type DISTANCE_CLASS.

ACT_DIST_LIM : constant DIST_CATEGORIES :=

        ( 100.00, 400.00, 8000.00 ) ;

-- This declaration means that ACT_DIST_LIM ( CLOSE_BY )

-- is 100.00, .. , ACT_DIST_LIM (LONG_DISTANCE) is 8000.00.

-- Array values can be constructed by listing the

-- values to be assigned to each of its  components

-- within parentheses. These values are called

-- array aggregates. They can be used for assignments to

-- constants, as in ACT_DIST_LIM, or to variables.

-- There   are  some  other  possible  forms  for  defining

-- aggregates; they will be discussed in Chapter 4.

type  WEIGHT_ARRAY  is  array  (  WEIGHT_CLASS  )  of

        ALLOWED_WEIGHT;

ACT_WEIGHT_LIM   : constant WEIGHT_ARRAY :=

        ( 10.00, 20.00, 40.00, 5000.00 ) ;
```

```
        -- A constant array of type WEIGHT_ARRAY is declared, with

        -- upper limits of each of the weight classes again using

        -- array aggregates.

        type PRICES is delta 0.0001 range 0.000 .. 5000.000;

        -- A fixed-point type is declared.

        Package PRICES_IO is new FIXED_IO(PRICES);

        use PRICES_IO;

        -- We just made available a package necessary to read and

        -- write values of the fixed-point type PRICES.

        type SHIPPING_RATES is array ( DISTANCE_CLASS,  WEIGHT_CLASS )
                of PRICES;

         -- This type is a two-dimensional array with three rows and

         -- four columns, indexed by two enumeration types.

        CURR_RATES : SHIPPING_RATES ;

        ITEM_NO : INTEGER ;

        ITEM_DISTANCE : ALLOWED_DISTANCE ;

        ITEM_WEIGHT : ALLOWED_WEIGHT ;

        ITEM_COST    : PRICES ;

begin

        for JUNK_DIST in DISTANCE_CLASS

                -- An equivalent way of writing the above

                -- line is

                --    for JUNK_DIST in DISTANCE_CLASS'FIRST ..

                --                      DISTANCE_CLASS'LAST

                -- another way is

                --    for JUNK_DIST in CLOSE_BY .. LONG_DISTANCE
```

```
                --    which is not as general (why ? )

    loop

    for JUNK_WEIGHT in WEIGHT_CLASS

            loop

            GET( CURR_RATES ( JUNK_DIST, JUNK_WEIGHT ), 7);

    end loop;

    SKIP_LINE;

end loop;

                -- The table was just initialized. Note that

                -- the variables JUNK_DIST and JUNK_WEIGHT were

                -- not explicitly declared as being of

                -- type DISTANCE_CLASS and WEIGHT_CLASS,

                -- respectively. Remember that these loop

                -- parameters (JUNK_DIST and JUNK_WEIGHT )

                -- are implicitly declared and have the type

                -- of the specified range.

GET(ITEM_NO,7);

while ITEM_NO /= 9999999

        loop

        GET(ITEM_WEIGHT,7);

        -- Using the float I/O package WEIGHT_IO.

        GET(ITEM_DISTANCE,7);

        -- Using the float I/O package DISTANCE_IO.

        SKIP_LINE;

        for JUNK_DIST in reverse DISTANCE_CLASS

                loop
```

```
    if ITEM_DISTANCE < ACT_DIST_LIM ( JUNK_DIST )

        then

            CURR_DIST_CLASS := JUNK_DIST;

        end if;

end loop;

for JUNK_WEIGHT  in reverse WEIGHT_CLASS

    loop

    if ITEM_WEIGHT < ACT_WEIGHT_LIM ( JUNK_WEIGHT )

        then

        CURR_WEIGHT_CLASS := JUNK_WEIGHT;

    end if;

end loop;

ITEM_COST :=

        PRICES ( CURR_RATES ( CURR_DIST_CLASS, CURR_WEIGHT_CLASS )

        * PRICES ( ITEM_WEIGHT ) ) ;

        NEW_LINE;

        PUT(ITEM_COST,7,2);

        SKIP_LINE;

        GET(ITEM_NO);

    end loop;

end SHIP_RATE;
```

The next program illustrates the use of dynamic arrays. The program, named GRADES, is supposed to display the score of multiple-choice tests. The first line of the input contains an integer between 20 and 50 that represents how many questions there were on the test. The following line contains the answer key.

For instance, if 34 questions were given in the test, the second line will have a sequence of 34 correct answers. Each answer is a digit between 1 and 5, and there are no spaces between answers. Each of the following lines represents a set of answers for a given student.

The student ID is in the first ten columns, and his or her answers start in column 11. The program is supposed to print the number of correct answers for every student. The input ends with a 9999999999 student ID.

GRADES Program

```
with TEXT_IO; use TEXT_IO;

procedure GRADES is

    Package INT_IO is new INTEGER_IO(INTEGER);

    use INT_IO;

    type CHOICES is range 1 .. 5 ;

    type POSSIBLE_QUESTIONS is range 1 .. 50 ;

    -- CHOICES and POSSIBLE_QUESTIONS are integer types.

    package CHO_IO is new INTEGER_IO(INTEGER);

    use CHO_IO;

    package POSS_IO is new INTEGER_IO(POSSIBLE_QUESTIONS);

    use POSS_IO;

    NO_QUESTIONS : POSSIBLE_QUESTIONS := 50 ;

    type ANSWERS is array ( 1 .. NO_QUESTIONS ) of CHOICES;

    KEY_ANSWERS, STUDENT_ANSWERS : ANSWERS ;

    GOOD_ANSWERS : INTEGER ;

    STUDENT_ID : STRING ( 1 .. 10 );

begin

    GET(NO_QUESTIONS);

    -- We have two dynamic arrays: KEY_ANSWERS and

    -- STUDENT_ANSWERS. Their number of  elements  is decided

    -- at running time,  in this case by reading in the
```

```
-- number of questions.

-- The package POSS_IO is needed here.

SKIP_LINE;

for I in 1 .. NO_QUESTIONS

    loop

    GET ( KEY_ANSWERS (I), 1);

    -- The package CHO_IO is needed here

end loop;

SKIP_LINE;

GET ( STUDENT_ID ) ;

while STUDENT_ID /= "9999999999"

    loop

    GOOD_ANSWERS := 0;

    for J in 1 .. NO_QUESTIONS

        loop

        GET ( STUDENT_ANSWERS(J), 1);

        if STUDENT_ANSWERS (J) = KEY_ANSWERS (J)

            then

            GOOD_ANSWERS := GOOD_ANSWERS + 1 ;

        end if;

    end loop;

    NEW_LINE;

    PUT ( " The number of good answers is " );

    PUT ( GOOD_ANSWERS, 5);

    PUT ( " for the ID ");

    PUT ( STUDENT_ID );

    SKIP_LINE;
```

```
        GET ( STUDENT_ID) ;

    end loop;

end GRADES;
```

UNCONSTRAINED ARRAYS

The unconstrained array type definition has the form

```
type type_name is array (one_or_more_indices ) of
    type_of_component ;
```

The one_or_more_indices part is a sequence of the form

```
type_mark range<>
```

separated by commas. Type_marks are either type names or (as will be seen later in this chapter) subtype names.

Here are some examples:

```
type MATRIX is array ( INTEGER range <>, INTEGER
    range <>) of FLOAT;
type VECTOR is array ( INTEGER range <> ) of
    FLOAT;
```

For the predefined type STRING we use

```
type STRING is array ( NATURAL range<>) of
    CHARACTER;
```

where NATURAL is a predefined type having positive integers as values. The pair of characters <> is called a **box** and represents an undefined range.

Objects of unconstrained array types must supply bounds (index constraints) when declared. For instance,

```
Z : MATRIX ( 1 .. (N-1)/2, N .. N + 10 );
Y : MATRIX ( -3 .. 3, -2 .. 2 ) ;
YY : MATRIX ( 0 .. 7, -1 .. 3 );
```

Note that for the declaration of Z and Y the bounds are different but their types are the same. Here are a few more examples:

```
X : STRING ( 5 .. L ** 2 ) ;
V : VECTOR ( -7 .. 1 ) ;
VV : VECTOR ( -7 .. 2 ) ;
```

Unconstrained arrays are quite a flexible tool in the design of subprograms. We will provide details of their use in Chapter 5.

ARRAY ATTRIBUTES

For the type of an array denoted by A, the following list gives some attributes that can be used with objects of type A. If the type A is a constrained type, then the attributes can be applied to the type too. These attributes cannot be used with unconstrained array types, but they may be used with objects of unconstrained array types.

Attribute	Description
A'FIRST	Gives the lower bound of the range of the first index. For any array of type SHIPPING_RATES appearing in the program SHIP_RATE, SHIPPING_RATES'FIRST will return the value CLOSE_BY. Equivalently, one can use CURR_RATES'FIRST.
A'LAST	Gives the upper bound of the range of the first index. For the same example SHIPPING_RATES'LAST will return the value LONG_DISTANCE.
A'LENGTH	Gives the size of the first index. For SHIPPING_RATES'LENGTH the value is 3.
A'RANGE	Gives all the values in the range A'FIRST . . A'LAST. For SHIPPING_RATES'RANGE we have CLOSE_BY . . LONG_DISTANCE.

The attributes listed next apply to any index of a multidimensional array. The N denotes a static integer type expression.

Attribute	Description
A'FIRST(N)	Gives the lower bound for the Nth index of the array type A. For instance, SHIPPING_RATES'FIRST(2) returns LIGHT. A'FIRST and A'FIRST(1) are identical.
A'LAST(N)	Gives the upper bound for the Nth index of the array type A. For instance, SHIPPING_RATES'LAST(2) returns HEAVY. A'LAST and A'LAST(2) are identical.
A'LENGTH(N)	Gives the size of the Nth index. For instance, SHIPPING_RATES'LENGTH(2) is 4. A'LENGTH(1) and A'LENGTH are identical.

A'RANGE(N) Gives the range A'FIRST(N) . . A'LAST(N), which is actually a subtype, as will be explained later in this chapter. For example, SHIPPING_RATES'RANGE(2) returns the range LIGHT . . HEAVY. A'RANGE(1) and A'RANGE are identical.

2.3 OPERATIONS FOR ARRAY TYPES

EQUALITY AND INEQUALITY

The equality and inequality operators are defined for any two objects of the types introduced in Chapter 1 and in this chapter. For arrays equality means that all their *matching components* are equal according to the equality defined for the component types. The matching of components is done as follows: The lower bounds of the index ranges are defined to match, and successive corresponding index positions are defined to match. If there is no matching component in either of the arrays, or if there is a matching component with unequal values, then the arrays are unequal. Also, if two arrays of the same type have matching components, then one can be assigned to the other.

EXAMPLE The following examples deal with the variables V and VV, of type VECTOR, and Y and YY, of type MATRIX, defined in the previous section.

```
V := ( 1.0 ,1.0, 1.0, 1.0, 1.0, 1.0, 1.0, 1.0, 1.0 ) ;

VV := ( 1.0 ,1.0, 1.0, 1.0, 1.0, 1.0, 1.0, 1.0,
        1.0, 1.0) ;
```

Here V and VV have the same type, but the components do not match: VV has more components than V. Therefore the arrays V and VV are not equal and no assignment is possible.

```
Y := ( ( -2.0, -2.0, -2.0, -2.0, -2.0, -2.0, -2.0 ),
        ( -2.0, -2.0, -2.0, -2.0, -2.0, -2.0, -2.0 ),
        ( -2.0, -2.0, -2.0, -2.0, -2.0, -2.0, -2.0 ),
        ( -2.0, -2.0, -2.0, -2.0, -2.0, -2.0, -2.0 ),
        ( -2.0, -2.0, -2.0, -2.0, -2.0, -2.0, -2.0 )) ;

YY := Y;
```

Since the two arrays YY and Y have matching components and have the same type, the array assignment is valid. Now the two arrays are equal. If, in addition, we have the assignment

```
YY ( 0, 3 ) := 0.0 ;
```

then Y and YY are *not* equal. Notice how the arrays were initialized by using aggregates.

OTHER RELATIONS

There are some other possible relations that apply to array types. But these other ordering operators apply only to one-dimensional arrays whose components are enumeration or integer (that is, discrete) types. The operators that can apply in this case are

```
< <= > >=
```

and the ordering follows the lexicographical rule: The first component has the highest priority, the second component has the next highest priority, and so on. Furthermore, if two one-dimensional array objects have the same type and have components of a discrete type, then in a comparison to decide which is the greater, the first components will be compared first. If there is inequality, then the greater object is the one that has the greater first component. Otherwise, the process is repeated for the second component and the others until a decision is reached. A null array has no components and is always less than an array with at least one component.

Here are some examples:

```
type POSSIBLE_RANGE is range -1000 .. INTEGER'LAST;

type DAY is (MON,TUE,WED,THU,FRI,SAT,SUN);

type EVENTS is array ( POSSIBLE_RANGE range <> ) of DAY;

LAST_5_IN_NY : EVENTS ( 1 .. 5) := (MON,TUE,TUE,SAT,FRI);

LAST_3_IN_LA : EVENTS ( 8 .. 10 ) := (MON,MON,SAT);
```

EXAMPLE   With these declarations then the relation

```
LAST_5_IN_NY < LAST_3_IN_LA
```

is valid and returns the Boolean value FALSE, because the second component of LAST_5_IN_NY, which is LAST_5_IN_NY (2) and is TUE, is greater than the second component of LAST_3_IN_LA, which is LAST_3_IN_LA (9) and is MON.

However, if we further have

```
LAST_3_IN_LA (9) := TUE ;
```

then the relation will return the Boolean value TRUE, because the first two components in the two array variables are equal, but for the third component we have LAST_5_IN_NY (3), which is TUE and is less than LAST_3_IN_LA (10), which is SAT.

CATENATION

There is another operation defined for objects of one-dimensional unconstrained array types. It is called **catenation** and is denoted by "&". Let us denote the array type by T and its component type by C, and let us assume a type declaration of the form

```
type T is array ( INDEX range <>) of C;
```

The result of a catenation operation is an array whose first component is always INDEX'FIRST.

The two operands can both be of type T, or one can be of type C and the other of type T. The resulting array has as its components the components of the first operand followed by the components of the second operand. If one of the operands is of type C, then it is treated as an array with one component.

EXAMPLE   It is valid to have

```
LAST_5_IN_NY & LAST_3_IN_LA
```

resulting in a one-dimensional array whose first component has an index of −1000, with a total of eight components and the component values given by the aggregate

```
(MON,TUE,TUE,SAT,FRI,MON,MON,SAT)
```

Also, one can have

```
FRI & LAST_5_IN_NY
```

resulting in the aggregate

```
(FRI,MON,TUE,TUE,SAT,FRI)
```

with the first component having an index of −1000.

STRING APPLICATIONS

As we mentioned in the previous section, the type STRING is defined as an unconstrained array type in the form

```
type STRING is array ( NATURAL range <>) of
  CHARACTER;
```

The bounds are supplied at the time that objects are declared.

Here are some examples of object declarations of STRING type:

```
FIELD1 : STRING ( I .. I+7 );

FIELD2 : STRING ( I - 7 .. I - 1 );

FIELD3 : STRING (20 .. 27) := "NEW-YORK";

FIELD4 : STRING (40 .. 49) ;
```

FIELD3 is a statically initialized string variable. Again note that FIELD1 and FIELD2 have different bounds, even though they have the same type. Remember that this situation is not possible for constrained array objects. The additional restriction is that, of course, whenever the bounds take some actual values, either before the program starts running or while the program runs, those values must be positive integers.

All the array attributes apply to objects of type STRING even though (because STRING is an unconstrained array type) they are not defined for the type STRING itself. Thus

```
FIELD2'LENGTH
```

should return the value 7, and

```
FIELD3'FIRST
```

should return the value 20. Because the type of the components of STRING is characters, one can have assignment statements like

```
FIELD3(21) := 'G' ;
```

And an equivalent way of initializing FIELD3 is

```
FIELD3 : STRING (20 . . 27 ) := ('N','E','W',
'-','Y','O','R','K');
```

The relational operators <, <=, >=, and > and the catenation operator "&" are clearly defined for objects of type STRING.

EXAMPLE   Given

```
FIELD4 := ''CALIFORNIA'';
```

then the relation

FIELD4 < FIELD3

will return the Boolean value TRUE. The result of

FIELD3 & FIELD4

will be a string of length 18 with the first component having an index of 1.

SLICES

For one-dimensional arrays Ada allows the naming and the referencing of a sequence of consecutive components, which is called a **slice.** A slice is actually a piece of a previously defined one-dimensional array.

EXAMPLE   One can name a slice as follows:

V (-5 . . -2)   V is a variable defined earlier as V : VECTOR (−7 . . 1)

V (LL . . RR)   This name is valid if LL and RR are integers in the proper range (here, −7 . . 1)

The slice V (−5 . . −2) has four components. The first one is V (−5 . . −2) (−5), which is identical to V(−5). The fourth component of the slice is V(−5 . . −2) (−2), which is identical to V (−2).

Assignments of slices are allowed, and they are useful for a compact manipulation of a sequence of assignment statements. For instance, it is valid to have

V (-7 . . -4) := V (-5 . . -2) ;

This statement means that the slice V(−7 . . −4), with four components indexed from −7 to −4, will take the value of the slice V (−5 . . −2), which has four components indexed from −5 to −2.

Care should be taken, however, in the interpretation of this statement. It means that, first, the components of the slice V (−5 . . −2) are extracted. Then they are placed in the matching components of V (−7 . . −4). Therefore to try to propagate the first component (that is, to repeat placing it in the other components) of the array V by the following statement is wrong:

V (-6 . . 1) := V (-7 . . 0) ;

No propagation results here because the first component of the slice V (−7 . . 0), which is V (−7), is placed in V (−6). Then the second component of the slice V (−7 . . 0), which is (the previous, not the current) V (−6), is placed in V (−5); and so on. If V (−7 . . 0) is "NEW_YORK", then after assignment, V (−7 . . 1) is "NNEW_YORK" and not "NNNNNNNNN".

2.4 RECORD TYPES

Arrays represent collections of components of the same type. **Records,** in contrast, represent collections of named components that may be of different types. The record type declaration has the form

```
type record_type_name is

record

        component_list

end record;
```

The component_list in its simplest form is a list of declarations. If the record has no components, the list is represented by the reserved word "null." The record type declarations can also contain a *discriminant part* and/or a *variant part*. We will cover records with discriminants later in this section; we will discuss variants in Chapter 4.

FEATURES OF RECORD TYPES

Here is one record type declaration:

```
type EMPLOYEE is

    record

            FIRST_NAME      : STRING (1 .. 20);

            LAST_NAME       : STRING (1 .. 20);

            HOME_ADDRESS    : STRING (1 .. 30);

            SOC_SEC_NO      : STRING (1 .. 9);

            HOURLY_RATE     : FLOAT ;

            HOURS_WORKED    : INTEGER range 1 .. 168;

    end record;
```

The record_type_name here is EMPLOYEE, and its components are the variables listed after the reserved word "record," starting with FIRST_NAME and ending with HOURS_WORKED.

Here are some more record type declarations:

```
type DAY is (MON,TUE,WED,THU,FRI,SAT,SUN);

type DAY_NO is 1 .. 31;

type MONTH is (JANUARY,FEBRUARY,MARCH,APRIL,MAY,JUNE,

          JULY,AUGUST,SEPTEMBER,OCTOMBER,NOVEMBER,DECEMBER);

type YEAR is 1900 .. 2050 ;

type DATE is

    record

           WEEK_DAY    : DAY;

           MONTH_NAME : MONTH;

           DAY_NO      : DAY;

           YEAR_NO     : YEAR;

    end record;
```

Some declarations of record type objects are

```
CURR_EMPLOYEE, PREV_EMPLOYEE: EMPLOYEE ;

ACTUAL_DATE, SETTLEMENT_DATE : DATE;
```

A component of a record object is referenced by using the **selected-component notation.** That is, the object name is followed by a period and the component name.

EXAMPLE   The line

```
ACTUAL_DATE.WEEK_DAY
```

selects the component WEEK_DAY of the variable ACTUAL_DATE of type DATE. The component itself is of type DAY. The notation

```
CURR_EMPLOYEE.HOME_ADDRESS
```

selects the component HOME_ADDRESS of the variable CURR_EMPLOYEE of type EMPLOYEE.

Just as we use array aggregates, we can use record aggregates (actually, positional record aggregates) to supply values to record type objects. The positional record aggregates consist of a complete sequence of values separated by commas and enclosed within parentheses. For instance, we can declare

```
STARTING_DATE : constant DATE :=
    (MON,AUGUST,20,1984);
```

Here we declared the constant STARTING_DATE, and its value was set to the aggregate (MON,AUGUST,20,1984).

The objects of the same record type (without a discriminant or a variant part) have the same components.

Two objects of the same record type can be compared for equality or inequality. Two objects are equal if every two components with the same name are equal; otherwise, the objects are not equal. However, two null records of the same type are always equal. Other relational operators like $<$, $<=$, $>=$, and $>$ are not defined for record types.

The assignment statement can also be used for two objects of the same record type. It means that every component value of the right-hand side replaces the value of the component with the same name on the left-hand side. For instance,

```
ACTUAL_DATE := SETTLEMENT_DATE;
```

is a valid assignment statement. It means

```
ACTUAL_DATE.WEEK_DAY    := SETTLEMENT_DATE.WEEK.DAY;

ACTUAL_DATE.MONTH_NAME := SETTLEMENT_DATE.MONTH_NAME;

ACTUAL_DATE.DAY_NO      := SETTLEMENT_DATE.DAY_NO ;

ACTUAL_DATE.YEAR_NO     := SETTLEMENT_DATE.YEAR_NO ;
```

Component declarations of record types can be other records or arrays. For instance, one can define a record type like

```
type MORE_INFO is

    record

        NEW_EMPLOYEE : EMPLOYEE;

        DATE_HIRED   : DATE;

    end record;
```

Thus if one has the declaration

```
EMPL : MORE_INFO;
```

then EMPL.DATE_HIRED.DAY_NO refers to the component DAY_NO of record component DATE_HIRED of record variable EMPL of type MORE_INFO. There are no predefined record types in Ada.

In this section we will not discuss attributes that apply to record types. We merely mention that there are attributes that return relative offsets of components, the location of the first and last bits of a component, and some other attributes that are hardware-dependent.

PROGRAM USING RECORD TYPES

The following program uses record types. It displays the name of the last hired employee. The input consists of LAST_NAME (columns 1–20) and the hiring date as YEAR_NO (columns 21–22), MONTH_NO (columns 23–24), and DAY_NO (columns 25–26). The end-of-input line is signaled by an employee name of "12345678901234567890".

LAST_HIRED Program

```
with TEXT_IO ; use TEXT_IO ;

procedure LAST_HIRED is

type DATE is

    record

            YEAR_NO  : INTEGER range 50 .. 99 ;

            MONTH_NO : INTEGER range 1 .. 12 ;

            DAY_NO   : INTEGER range 1 .. 31 ;

    end record ;

type EMPLOYEE is

    record

            LAST_NAME    : STRING ( 1 .. 20 ) ;

            HIRING_DATE : DATE ;

    end record ;

CURR_EMPL, LAST_EMPL : EMPLOYEE ;
```

```
package INT_IO is new INTEGER_IO(INTEGER);
use INT_IO ;
begin
    LAST_EMPL := ("JUST AN EARLY DATE  ",(50,1,1)) ;
    -- Here we are initializing with a very early date.
    GET(CURR_EMPL.LAST_NAME);
    while CURR_EMPL.LAST_NAME /= "12345678901234567890"
        loop
        GET(CURR_EMPL.HIRING_DATE.YEAR_NO,2);
        GET(CURR_EMPL.HIRING_DATE.MONTH_NO,2);
        GET(CURR_EMPL.HIRING_DATE.DAY_NO,2);
        if CURR_EMPL.HIRING_DATE.YEAR_NO >
                LAST_EMPL.HIRING_DATE.YEAR_NO        or
                CURR_EMPL.HIRING_DATE.YEAR_NO        =
                LAST_EMPL.HIRING_DATE.YEAR_NO        and
                ( CURR_EMPL.HIRING_DATE.MONTH_NO     >
                LAST_EMPL.HIRING_DATE.MONTH_NO       or
                CURR_EMPL.HIRING_DATE.MONTH_NO       =
                LAST_EMPL.HIRING_DATE.MONTH_NO       and
                CURR_EMPL.HIRING_DATE.DAY_NO         =
                LAST_EMPL.HIRING_DATE.DAY_NO   )
            then
                LAST_EMPL := CURR_EMPL ;
        end if;
        SKIP_LINE ;
        GET(CURR_EMPL.LAST_NAME);
```

```
    end loop;

    NEW_LINE ; PUT ( " The last hired is " ) ;

    PUT(LAST_EMPL.LAST_NAME) ;

end LAST_HIRED ;
```

Figure 2.3 illustrates the contents of the objects declared in LAST_HIRED just before the last line is read, using the sample input data listed in the figure.

MANY-FEATURED PROGRAM

Now we present another Ada program, one that uses many of the concepts introduced in the first two chapters. In particular, it makes use of record types.

Each line of input has information about subcontractors, defined as follows:

Column	Data
Columns 1–9	Contractor ID
Columns 10–30	Contractor name
Columns 31–36	Starting period, in the format YYMMDD (such as 840431)
Columns 37–42	Ending period, in the format YYMMDD
Columns 43–48	Daily fee (in dollar and cents)

FIGURE 2.3 Input Data and Object Contents for Program LAST_HIRED

Input Data

```
STEVEN K. KNIGHT      820317
B.B. HANSEN           820425
LOU HARRIS            820901
12345678901234567890
```

Objects Contents	CURR_EMPL.LAST_NAME	CURR_EMPL.HIRING_DATE
CURR_EMPL	Lou Harris	820901

	LAST_EMPL.LAST_NAME	LAST_EMPL.HIRING_DATE
LAST_EMPL	STEVEN K. KNIGHT	820317

The contractors are paid a daily fee, except that the fee is 100% higher if they work on a Saturday and 200% higher if they work on a Sunday.

The program should display, for every contractor, the name, the ID, the exact number of days worked, the amount due, and the due date, which is five working days after the working period date. The due date should have the format

```
week_day,month_day day_no,year
```

such as Tuesday,August 21,1984. The last line is assumed to have an ID of "999999999". The program has to check that each date is valid (no day number 31 in April, for instance).

DATE_CONVERSION Program

```
with TEXT_IO; use TEXT_IO;

procedure DATE_CONVERSION is

     type DAY is (MONDAY,TUESDAY,WEDNESDAY,THURSDAY,FRIDAY,

          SATURDAY,SUNDAY);

     type DAY_INT is range 1 .. 31;

     type JULIAN_DAYS is range 1 .. 366 ;

     type MONTH is (JANUARY,FEBRUARY,MARCH,APRIL,MAY,JUNE,

               JULY,AUGUST,SEPTEMBER,OCTOMBER,NOVEMBER,DECEMBER);

     type YEAR is range 00 .. 2050 ;

     type MONTH_INT is range 1 .. 12;

     type DATE is

          record

               WEEK_DAY : DAY;             -- Example: TUESDAY.

               MONTH_NAME : MONTH;         -- Example: JULY.

               MONTH_NO : MONTH_INT;       -- Example: 7.

               DAY_NO   : DAY_INT;         -- Example: 15.

               YTD_DAYS : JULIAN_DAYS;     -- Days are from 1 to 366.

               TOTAL_DAYS : INTEGER ;      -- Total are counted from

                                           -- base date.
```

```
            YEAR_NO  : YEAR;

    end record;

BASE_DATE : constant DATE := ( MONDAY,JANUARY,1,1,1,1,1984);

            -- For this program we assume that only dates

            -- after January 1 ,1984 are supplied. For other

            -- dates change the constant to an earlier

            -- convenient date, such as the 1800s.

BASE_LEAP : constant INTEGER :=

            INTEGER(BASE_DATE.YEAR_NO)  / 4 +

            INTEGER(BASE_DATE.YEAR_NO)  / 400 -

            INTEGER(BASE_DATE.YEAR_NO)  / 100;

            -- This constant represents how many leap years

            -- elapsed from year 0 to BASE_DATE.YEAR_NO.

            -- Note the static expression used to evaluate it

            -- and the necessary conversion.

INPUT_DATE, HOLD_DATE: DATE;

NO_OF_SATURDAYS,NO_OF_SUNDAYS : INTEGER;

type CONTRACTOR is

    record

        ID_NO   :   STRING ( 1 .. 9) ;

        CO_NAME :   STRING ( 1 .. 21 );

    end record ;

type INFO_LINE is

    record

        CURR_CONTRACTOR : CONTRACTOR ;

        DAYS_WORKED     : INTEGER ;
```

```
                    DUE_DATE          : DATE ;

            end record;

        PROC_LINE : INFO_LINE;

        type DAYS_IN_MONTH is array (MONTH_INT,BOOLEAN) of DAY_INT;

        ACTUAL_DAYS_IN_YEAR : constant DAYS_IN_MONTH :=

                ( (31,31),(28,29),(31,31),(30,30),

                    (31,31),(30,30),(31,31),(31,31),

                    (30,30),(31,31),(30,30),(31,31) ) ;

                -- We just declared a constant array indexed by

                -- month_int with values from 1 to 12

                -- and by Boolean with values (just two)

                -- from false to true; false means that there is

                -- no leap year.

        type FEE is delta 0.0001 range 0.000 .. 500_000.000;

                        -- A fixed point type is declared.

                        -- One has to also check whether the

                        -- Ada implementation allows for this

                        -- many digits.

        Package FEE_IO is new FIXED_IO(FEE);

        use FEE_IO;

        CONTR_DAILY_FEE, CONTR_TOTAL_FEE : FEE;

        Package INT_IO is new INTEGER_IO(INTEGER);

        use INT_IO;

        GOOD_DAY, GOOD_YEAR ,LEAP_YEAR : BOOLEAN;

        Package DAY_IO is new ENUMERATION_IO(DAY);

        use DAY_IO;
```

```
Package MONTH_IO is new ENUMERATION_IO(MONTH);

use MONTH_IO;

Package YEAR_IO is new INTEGER_IO(YEAR);

use YEAR_IO;

Package MONTH_INT is new INTEGER_IO(MONTH_INT);

use MONTH_INT;

Package DAY_INT_IO is new INTEGER_IO(DAY_INT);

use DAY_INT_IO;

INPUT_LEAP   : INTEGER ;

XTRA_DAYS    : INTEGER ;

procedure COUNT_DAYS_AND_CHECK is

        -- This procedure will fill in the remaining components

        -- of a record type variable INPUT_DATE. The components

        -- already present are DAY_NO, MONTH_NO, and YEAR_NO

        -- Remember from Section 1.5 that objects declared for

        -- the DATE_CONVERSION procedure  will be known and

        -- can be used by this  procedure.

begin

        -- Is this a valid year ? if not GOOD_YEAR:=FALSE;

    if INPUT_DATE.YEAR_NO < 1900

        then

        INPUT_DATE.YEAR_NO := INPUT_DATE.YEAR_NO + 1900;

    end if;

    if INPUT_DATE.YEAR_NO < BASE_DATE.YEAR_NO

        then

        GOOD_YEAR := FALSE;
```

```
        else

            GOOD_YEAR := TRUE;

        end if;

            -- We don't check for the month number. If it is
            -- outside the range 1 .. 12, an error condition will be
            -- raised when the month number is assigned.
            -- Is this data a valid day? If not GOOD_DAY := FALSE;
            -- But first, let us check to see whether this is a
            -- leap year. Refer also to the program DAY_CONVERSION of
            --   Section 1.4.

        if    INPUT_DATE.YEAR_NO rem 4 = 0      and

              INPUT_DATE.YEAR_NO rem 100 /= 0    or

              INPUT_DATE.YEAR_NO rem 400 = 0

              then

              LEAP_YEAR := TRUE;

        else

              LEAP_YEAR := FALSE;

        end if;

            -- Now LEAP_YEAR can be used to refer to the proper
            -- row in ACTUAL_DAYS_IN_YEAR array.

        if    INPUT_DATE.DAY_NO >

              ACTUAL_DAYS_IN_YEAR( INPUT_DATE.MONTH_NO ,LEAP_YEAR)

              then

              GOOD_DAY := FALSE;

        else

              GOOD_DAY := TRUE;
```

```
end if;

        -- Now find out YTD_DAYS for this date.
if GOOD_DAY

    then

    INPUT_DATE.YTD_DAYS := JULIAN_DAYS(INPUT_DATE.DAY_NO);

    -- Conversion needed above.

    if INPUT_DATE.MONTH_NO > 1

        then

        for I in 1 .. INPUT_DATE.MONTH_NO - 1

            loop

            INPUT_DATE.YTD_DAYS := INPUT_DATE.YTD_DAYS +

            JULIAN_DAYS(ACTUAL_DAYS_IN_YEAR

                ( I, LEAP_YEAR )) ;

        end loop;

    end if;

end if;

        -- Find out how many days elapsed from the

        -- base date to the input date. First find out

        -- how many leap years there were until the

        -- input year.
INPUT_LEAP := INTEGER(INPUT_DATE_YEAR_NO) / 4 +

            INTEGER(INPUT_DATE_YEAR_NO) / 400 -

            INTEGER(INPUT_DATE_YEAR_NO) / 100 ;

INPUT_DATE.TOTAL_DAYS := 365 * INTEGER(( INPUT_DATE.YEAR_NO -

        BASE_DATE.YEAR_NO   )) +

            INTEGER(INPUT_DATE.YTD_DAYS)   +   INPUT_LEAP
```

```
                    - BASE_LEAP;

            -- Find the week day and the month name.

      INPUT_DATE.MONTH_NAME := MONTH'VAL(INPUT_DATE.MONTH_NO);

            -- Remember how VAL attribute works for

            -- the enumeration types.

      INPUT_DATE.WEEK_DAY := DAY'VAL (

         (INPUT_DATE.TOTAL_DAYS + DAY'POS(BASE_DATE.WEEK_DAY)-2)

            mod 7  + 1                         )   ;

            -- This expression is somewhat complex.

            -- First, the position of the base date weekday

            -- is  evaluated  (it is 2  for  Tuesday,  for

            -- instance) and is added to the total days

            -- less  2.   The  modulus  7  of  this  number

            -- plus 1 represents the relative position

            -- of the input date weekday (an integer between

            -- 1 and 7). Trying a few actual dates

            -- might   help   you   to   understanding   tthe

            -- expression.

   end COUNT_DAYS_AND_CHECK;

   begin

   GET(PROC_LINE.CURR_CONTRACTOR.ID_NO);

   while PROC_LINE.CURR_CONTRACTOR.ID_NO /= "999999999"

      loop

      GET(PROC_LINE.CURR_CONTRACTOR.CO_NAME);

      GET(INPUT_DATE.YEAR_NO,2);

      GET(INPUT_DATE.MONTH_NO,2);
```

```
GET(INPUT_DATE.DAY_NO,2);

-- Starting date is read as YYMMDD.

-- Note how three different packages are needed for the three

-- GET statements.

COUNT_DAYS_AND_CHECK;

-- The procedure COUNT_DAYS_AND_CHECK is invoked,

-- and we proceed with the reading of the ending

-- period only if the starting period was a valid date.

if GOOD_YEAR and GOOD_DAY

     then

     HOLD_DATE := INPUT_DATE;

     -- We just  saved  the  starting  period.   A  record

     -- assignment statement is used.

     GET(INPUT_DATE.YEAR_NO,2);

     GET(INPUT_DATE.MONTH_NO,2);

     GET(INPUT_DATE.DAY_NO,2);

     COUNT_DAYS_AND_CHECK;

     if GOOD_YEAR and GOOD_DAY

          then

          -- Compute number of days worked.

          PROC_LINE.DAYS_WORKED :=INPUT_DATE.TOTAL_DAYS -

               HOLD_DATE.TOTAL_DAYS + 1;

          GET(CONTR_DAILY_FEE,6);

          -- Now count how many Saturdays there are.

          NO_OF_SATURDAYS := PROC_LINE.DAYS_WORKED / 7;

          if DAY'POS(HOLD_DATE.WEEK_DAY) +
```

```
          INFO_LINE.DAYS_WORKED mod 7 - 1  > 5

          then

          NO_OF_SATURDAYS := NO_OF_SATURDAYS + 1;
end if;
-- Now count how many Sundays there are.
NO_OF_SUNDAYS := PROC_LINE.DAYS_WORKED / 7;
if DAY'POS(HOLD_DATE.WEEK_DAY) +

        PROC_LINE.DAYS_WORKED mod 7 - 1  > 6

   then

   NO_OF_SUNDAYS := NO_OF_SUNDAYS + 1;
end if;
-- Now find out the exact due date.
-- Banks care about this date. Five working days
-- generally means a week - maybe one or two
-- fewer days if the ending period falls on weekends.
if INPUT_DATE.WEEK_DAY = SATURDAY

     then

     PROC_LINE.DUE_DATE.TOTAL_DAYS :=

            INPUT_DATE.TOTAL_DAYS + 6;

     PROC_LINE.DUE_DATE.WEEK_DAY := FRIDAY;
elsif INPUT_DATE.WEEK_DAY = SUNDAY

     then

     PROC_LINE.DUE_DATE.TOTAL_DAYS :=

                INPUT_DATE.TOTAL_DAYS + 5;

     PROC_LINE.DUE_DATE.WEEK_DAY := FRIDAY;
else
```

```
      PROC_LINE.DUE_DATE.TOTAL_DAYS :=

                  INPUT_DATE.TOTAL_DAYS + 7;

      PROC_LINE.DUE_DATE.WEEK_DAY   :=

                  INPUT_DATE.WEEK_DAY ;

end if;

XTRA_DAYS := PROC_LINE.DUE_DATE.TOTAL_DAYS -

                  INPUT_DATE.TOTAL_DAYS ;

-- Now we check to find out whether the due date

-- falls on a new month or  a new year.

if INPUT_DATE.DAY_NO + DAY_INT(XTRA_DAYS) <

   ACTUAL_DAYS_IN_YEAR (INPUT_DATE.MONTH_NO,LEAP_YEAR)

   then

   PROC_LINE.DUE_DATE.DAY_NO :=

                  INPUT_DATE.DAY_NO + XTRA_DAYS;

   PROC_LINE.DUE_DATE.MONTH_NAME :=INPUT_DATE.MONTH_NAME;

   PROC_LINE.DUE_DATE.YEAR_NO :=INPUT_DATE.YEAR_NO;

else

   PROC_LINE.DUE_DATE.DAY_NO :=

      INPUT_DATE.DAY_NO + DAY_INT(XTRA_DAYS) -

      ACTUAL_DAYS_IN_YEAR (INPUT_DATE.MONTH_NO,LEAP_YEAR);

   if INPUT_DATE.MONTH_NAME < DECEMBER

      then

      PROC_LINE.DUE_DATE.MONTH_NAME :=

            MONTH'SUCC(INPUT_DATE.MONTH_NAME);

      PROC_LINE.DUE_DATE.YEAR_NO :=INPUT_DATE.YEAR_NO;

   else
```

```
                              PROC_LINE.DUE_DATE.MONTH_NAME := JANUARY;

                              PROC_LINE.DUE_DATE.YEAR_NO :=

                                             INPUT_DATE.YEAR_NO + 1;

                end if;

           end if;

           -- Compute amount due.

           CONTR_TOTAL_FEE := FEE( CONTR_DAILY_FEE *

                FEE ( PROC_LINE.DAYS_WORKED *

                (1 + NO_OF_SATURDAYS + 2 * NO_OF_SUNDAYS ) ) ;

                 -- Remember that the result of multiplication

                 -- of fixed point  reals of type FEE is

                 -- not of type FEE.

           -- Finally print the results.

           PUT(PROC_LINE.CURR_CONTRACTOR.ID_NO);

           PUT(PROC_LINE.CURR_CONTRACTOR.CO_NAME);

           PUT(" Days worked ");

           PUT(PROC_LINE.DAYS_WORKED,5);

           NEW_LINE;

           PUT(" Amount due :");PUT(CONTR_TOTAL_FEE,10,2);

           PUT(" Due date :");

           PUT(PROC_LINE.DUE_DATE.WEEK_DAY);PUT(",");

           PUT(PROC_LINE.DUE_DATE.MONTH_NAME);

           PUT(PROC_LINE.DUE_DATE.DAY_NO,5);PUT(",");

           PUT(PROC_LINE.DUE_DATE.YEAR_NO,5);

      else

      PUT(" Bad ending period ");
```

```
            end if;

        else

            PUT(" Bad starting period ");

        end if;

        SKIP_LINE;

        GET(PROC_LINE.CURR_CONTRACTOR.ID_NO);

    end loop;

    end DATE_CONVERSION;
```

RECORD DISCRIMINANTS

Ada has a facility called record discriminants useful for defining a family of record types. A **discriminant** is a named component of each object of the record type, and its name should appear before the names of the components listed in the record type definition.

The declaration of a record type with discriminants has the form

```
type record_type_name ( discriminant_declarations ) is

    record

        component_list

    end record;
```

The discriminant_declarations end with semicolons, and each declaration is quite similar to the declaration of any discrete type object. The discriminant itself is the sequence of discriminant_declarations enclosed within parentheses.

EXAMPLE   Here is an example of a record type declaration with discriminants:

```
type PAGES is array (NATURAL range <>,NATURAL
    range <>) of CHARACTERS ;
```

Natural has as its values integers greater than 0. It is a predefined subtype, as we will see in the next section.

Another example is

```
type LINE_NUMBERS is array (NATURAL range <>)
    of INTEGER;
```

We just declared two unconstrained array types whose objects will be used in the next example.

```
type PAGE_FORMAT ( NO_OF_LINES :   POSITIVE   :=55 ;

                   NO_OF_COLUMNS: POSITIVE   :=80  )      is

    record

        STD_HEADER : STRING ( 1 .. NO_OF_COLUMNS );

        STD_BODY   :   PAGES   ( 1  ..   NO_OF_LINES,

                                 1  ..   NO_OF_COLUMNS);

        STD_LINES  :   LINE_NUMNBERS ( 1 .. NO_OF_LINES );

        STD_FOOTER : STRING ( 1 .. NO_OF_COLUMNS );

    end record;
```

The type PAGE_ FORMAT is a record type with a discriminant. The discriminant part has two discriminant declarations. The first one is

```
NO_OF_LINES : POSITIVE :=55
```

separated by a semicolon from the second one, which is

```
NO_OF_COLUMNS: POSITIVE :=80
```

Both discriminant declarations are given a default initial value. Default initial values must be provided for all or none of the discriminants of a discriminant part.

Within a record type definition the discriminant names (for our example NO_OF_COLUMNS, NO_OF_LINES) can be used as a bound in an index constraint. In our example bounds were supplied by using NO_OF_COLUMNS for the components STD_HEADER, STD_BODY, and STD_FOOTER. The identifier NO_OF_LINES supplied bounds for the components STD_BODY and STD_LINES.

A discriminant name can only be used by itself; that is, it cannot be used in a larger expression. For instance, it is not valid to have a component of the PAGE_FORMAT declared as

```
STD_COLUMN : STRING ( 1 , , NO_OF_COLUMNS - 1) ;
```

The name of a discriminant may also be used with variant parts (to be discussed in Chapter 4). Or it may be used to specify a discriminant value in an object declaration of another (nested) record with discriminants.

The use of a discriminant with PAGE_FORMAT helped us define a family of possible PAGE_FORMAT's, with the actual NO_OF_LINES and NO_OF_COLUMNS being supplied at the time objects of this type are declared. A possible object declaration is

```
TITLE_PAGE : PAGE_FORMAT ( 25, 45 );
```

Here an object of type PAGE_FORMAT is declared, where the NO_OF_LINES is 25 and the NO_OF_COLUMNS is 45. Other object declarations are

```
REGULAR_PAGE : PAGE_FORMAT (45,70);

MARGIN_WIDTH : constant INTEGER := 10 ;

APPENDIX_PAGE,  INDEX_PAGE :

       PAGE_FORMAT ( 40,  MARGIN_WIDTH +30 );
```

The actual discriminant values supplied when we declare these objects are called **discriminant specifications**. A complete list of discriminant specifications separated by commas and enclosed within parentheses is called a **discriminant constraint**. For the INDEX_PAGE declared above the discriminant constraint is

```
(50, MARGIN + 30)
```

and there are two discriminant specifications. The first one is 50, and the second one is MARGIN + 30. As indicated here, discriminant constraints can be expressions. We will make extensive use of records with discriminants in several programs, starting in Chapter 4.

Figure 2.4 illustrates the declarations related to the PAGE_FORMAT.

If there are default initial values for the discriminant of a type, then a discriminant constraint is not necessary. For instance, it is valid to have the object declaration

```
ANY_PAGE : PAGE_FORMAT;
```

because the discriminant values are given by the initial values (55,80). Otherwise, one has to supply discriminant constraints for every object declaration.

Discriminants cannot be directly assigned a value. For instance, it is not valid to have

```
ANY_PAGE.NO_OF_LINE := 2;
```

However, we can modify the discriminants by assigning a value to every component of the object, as in the following list:

```
ANY_PAGE := (2,2,          NO_OF_LINES and NO_OF_
                           COLUMNS are assigned the value
                           2
```

FIGURE 2.4   Record Type with Discriminants for PAGE_FORMAT

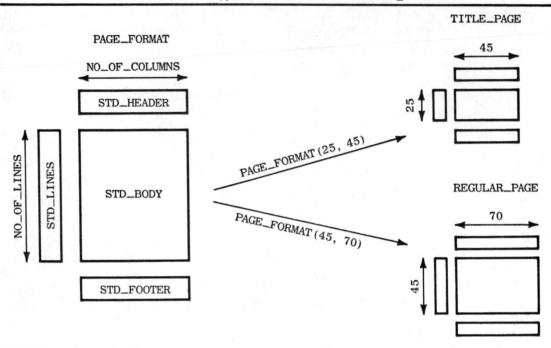

`"AA",`	STD_HEADER is assigned "AA"
`(('X','Y'),`	STD_BODY is assigned 'X','Y' in the
`('M','N')),`	first row and 'M','N' in the second row
`(1,2),`	STD_LINES is assigned 1,2
`"VV" );`	STD_FOOTER is assigned "VV"

In all other respects discriminants behave like ordinary components. One should note as well that if the discriminant constraints are present, then the values of the discriminants cannot be modified further. Therefore the assignment statement that was valid for ANY_PAGE—because it had no discriminant constraints—is not valid for, say, TITLE_PAGE, because it has discriminant constraints.

As indicated by the aggregate assignment to ANY_PAGE, in many situations the positional specifications of aggregates may be hard to read. We will introduce an alternative way, which is easier to read, to denote aggregates in Chapter 4.

Objects of the same record type with discriminants can be compared for equality or inequality, which means equality (or inequality) of each component.

Thus for the declarations above, REGULAR_PAGE cannot be equal to INDEX_PAGE as long as REGULAR_PAGE.STD_BODY has a different number of rows and/or columns from those of INDEX_PAGE.STD_BODY.

2.5 SUBTYPES AND DERIVED TYPES

Recall that types define collections of values together with operations allowed on these values. So far we covered the following Ada types: enumeration types, integer types, real types, array types, and record types. Ada has two more types: *access types* (to be covered in the next chapter) and *private types* (to be covered in Chapter 7). In addition, Ada makes use of *subtypes* and *derived types,* which will be presented in this section.

SUBTYPES

One might be interested in restricting the possible values of a type but keeping the same set of possible operations. This objective can be achieved in Ada by defining a **subtype** of the given type. The restriction is called a **constraint,** and the given type is called the **base type.** A type is considered a subtype of itself, and therefore a type is its own base type. There are four kinds of constraints in Ada: range_constraint, accuracy_constraint, index_constraint, and discriminant_constraint. Examples of each have been given in connection with various type declarations in the first two chapters. The examples of this section will show the same Ada constraints in connection with Ada subtypes.

The form of a subtype declaration is as follows:

```
subtype subtype_name is type_mark;
```

If there is a constraint, the declaration is

```
subtype subtype_name is type_mark constraint;
```

The type_mark is either a type_name or another subtype_name. The constraint is one of the four kinds listed above.

EXAMPLE   Here is a possible subtype declaration with a range constraint:

```
subtype POSITIVE is INTEGER range 1 . . INTEGER'LAST;
```

This predefined subtype of the INTEGER type has as values the integers from 1 to the last integer allowed by the implementation. All the operations on INTEGER are also allowed for the subtype POSITIVE. A range constraint is present. If the result of, say, a subtraction of two positive numbers is negative, then a constraint error exception will be raised.

The bounds of the range constraint in a subtype definition can be complex static or dynamic expressions, as the next example shows:

```
subtype MARGIN is INTEGER range LEFT_MARGIN + 5
   . . RIGHT_MARGIN ;
```

Here the left bound (LEFT_MARGIN + 5) is either a static or a dynamic expression that should not exceed the right bound at running time.

EXAMPLE   For the type

```
type DAY is (MONDAY,TUESDAY,WEDNESDAY,THURSDAY,
   FRIDAY,SATURDAY,SUNDAY);
```

one can define the subtypes

```
subtype WEEKEND is DAY range SATURDAY . . SUNDAY ;
subtype WORKDAY is DAY range MONDAY . . FRIDAY ;
CURR_DAY : WORKDAY;
```

These types are subtypes of the enumeration type DAY. The same operations and attributes apply to the type DAY and its subtypes. If values outside the range are assigned, then a constraint error exception will be raised (for instance, CURR_DAY: = SATURDAY;).

Accuracy constraints apply to real types, both floating-point and fixed-point. Here are some examples for floating-point types:

```
type HIGH_PRECISION is digits 15 ;
subtype LESS_PRECISION is HIGH_PRECISION digits 8 ;
subtype TIGHT_RANGE is HIGH_PRECISION range -2.00 . .
   2.00 ;
```

The subtype LESS_PRECISION has as its values the values of HIGH_PRECISION with only eight digits of accuracy. The number of digits in the subtype definition must be a positive integer less than or equal to the number of digits of the base type. Thus it is not valid to have

```
subtype BAD_FLOAT is HIGH_PRECISION digits 16;
```

But it is valid to have

```
subtype GOOD_FLOAT is HIGH_PRECISION digits 14;
```

Here are some examples of accuracy constraints used with fixed-point subtype declarations:

```
type FEE is delta 0.0001 range 0.00 .. 500_000.00 ;

subtype CHECK is FEE delta 0.005 range 0.01 .. 5000.00 ;

subtype PAYOFF is FEE delta 0.002 ;

subtype SMALL_FEE is FEE range 0.01 .. 5000.00 ;

subtype PETTY_CASH is SMALL_FEE range 0.01 .. 200.00;
```

Note that the delta value of the subtype cannot exceed the delta value of the base type. Note also that for a fixed-point subtype the range constraint can be missing, the range constraint being the range of the base type. A range constraint is mandatory, however, for a fixed-point type declaration. Also, the range of the subtype has to be compatible with any previous ranges. A declaration of a subtype of SMALL_FEE such as

```
subtype BAD_PETTY_CASH is SMALL_FEE range 0.01
   .. 50000.00 ;
```

is not valid because the upper bound of the subtype exceeds the range of the type_mark.

Index constraints, as discussed in Section 2.2, are used to supply discrete bounds to array types. The index constraint can only be imposed on a type or a subtype that does not already have an index constraint. The index constraints are supplied in the definition of the constrained array type, and therefore one cannot define subtypes (besides the type itself) for them.

EXAMPLE If we declare the constrained array type

```
type RATES is array (I .. J, K .. L ) of FLOAT;
```

then a declaration like

```
subtype BAD_RATES is RATES(I+1 .. J -1, K .. L) ;
```

is not valid because a set of index constraints—here they are (I. . J,K . . L)—was given before the set of index constraints (I+1 . . J−1, K . . L) was supplied by the subtypes. However, if we have an unconstrained array declaration such as

```
type MATRIX is array (INTEGER range <>,INTEGER
   range <>) of INTEGER ;
```

then the subtype declaration

```
subtype POS_MATRIX is MATRIX(I+1 , , J-1,
  K , , L);
```

is valid

The fourth kind of constraint that can be used in subtype declarations is the discriminant constraint. It is used in record declarations. As with index constraints, a discriminant constraint can only be imposed on a type or a subtype that does not already have a discriminant constraint.

EXAMPLE   Let us consider the type PAGE_FORMAT, introduced in the previous section and declared as

```
type PAGE_FORMAT ( NO_OF_LINES :  POSITIVE  :=55 ;

                   NO_OF_COLUMNS: POSITIVE  :=80  )      is

  record

        STD_HEADER : STRING ( 1 .. NO_OF_COLUMNS );

        STD_BODY   :   PAGES   ( 1   ..   NO_OF_LINES,

                                 1   ..   NO_OF_COLUMNS);

        STD_LINES  :   LINE_NUMNBERS ( 1 .. NO_OF_LINES );

        STD_FOOTER : STRING ( 1 .. NO_OF_COLUMNS );

  end record;
```

We can define a subtype of this record type declaration with discriminants because the type itself does not introduce constraints. (Refer to the previous section for the remaining declarations.) Then it is valid to have

```
subtype DRAFT_PAGES is PAGE_FORMAT ( 50,80 );
```

where 50 and 80 are the two discriminant constraints.

More examples of subtype declarations using discriminant constraints will be given in Chapter 4, after records with variants are introduced.

DERIVED TYPES

While subtypes belong to their base type and their values are values of the base type, **derived types** may be introduced when a new set of values, independent of the original set used in the definition, is needed. The general form of derived type declarations is

```
type derived_type_name is new type_mark;
```

Or if a constraint is present, the declaration is

```
type derived_type_name is new type_mark
    constraint;
```

The constraints that can be used for derived types have the same form as the form used by subtypes.

The type_mark in the declarations can be either a type name or a subtype name. The base type of the type mark is called the **parent type** of the derived type name, and the set of possible values of the derived type is a copy of the set of possible values of the parent type. The operations, attributes, literals, and aggregates (if any) of the parent type are duplicated for the derived type. Also, explicit conversions of values from the parent type to the derived type and vice versa are possible.

EXAMPLE   Let us consider some possible derived types. For instance, in

```
type ACCOUNT is new INTEGER;
```

the parent type is INTEGER. The values of the derived type ACCOUNT are copies of integers. The operations on ACCOUNT objects represent a duplicate of the operations for INTEGERS.

In the declaration

```
ACC1, ACC2 : ACCOUNT ;
```

ACC1 and ACC2 are objects of type ACCOUNT. In

```
NUM1, NUM2 : INTEGER ;
```

NUM1 and NUM2 are objects of type INTEGER. For the assignment statement

```
ACC1 := ACC1 + 7;
```

the operation addition for type ACCOUNT is used on the variable ACC1 of type ACCOUNT and the literal 7, of type universal integer (for universal integers no explicit conversion is needed when used with integer types).

The assignment statement

```
NUM1 := ACC1 + NUM2 ;
```

using derived types is not valid because one cannot use the addition operation on two different types.

For the assignment statement

```
NUM1 := ACC1 + ACCOUNT(NUM2);
```

first, the explicit conversion of the integer type variable NUM2 into a value of type ACCOUNT is performed. Then addition of two values of type ACCOUNT is done. From the context one can see that the operation is of the type ACCOUNT. Then a value of type ACCOUNT is assigned to a variable of type INTEGER, and this assignment is not valid.

Further examples of valid assignment statements using derived types are

```
NUM1 := INTEGER(ACC1 + ACCOUNT(NUM2));
NUM1 := INTEGER(ACC1) + NUM2;
```

A more detailed discussion of conversion rules will be presented in Chapter 6.

Now let us look at some examples of derived types using constraints. For

```
type ITEM is new INTEGER range 1 . . 9999 ;
```

ITEM is a derived type using a range constraint. In

```
type FEE is delta 0.0001 range 0.00 . .
   500_000.00 ;
```

FEE is a derived type using an accuracy constraint. For

```
type PAYCHECK is new FEE delta 0.001 ;
I,J : INTEGER;
type IT_MATRIX is new MATRIX ( I, J );
```

PAYCHECK is a derived type using an index constraint. MATRIX was defined earlier in this section. Finally,

```
type PRINT_PAGE is new PAGE_FORMAT ( 59,132);
```

is a derived type using a discriminant constraint.

Note that whenever a constraint is used in the definition of a derived type, Ada introduces a derived type whose values are copies of the parent type. The defined derived type is then acting as a subtype whose values are chosen from the copies of the parent type. For example, the declaration

```
type XYZ is new FEE delta 0.01;
```

is equivalent to

```
type ABC is new FEE;
subtype XYZ is ABC delta 0.01 ;
```

Derived types are useful for enforcing logical or mental distinctions by defining entirely different types for different abstract concepts and therefore preventing their inadvertent mix. For instance, if one defines the types

```
type BODY_TEMPERATURE is new FLOAT ;
type BLOOD_COUNT is new FLOAT ;
CURR_TEMP : BODY_TEMPERATURE ;
CURR_BLOOD_COUNT : BLOOD_COUNT ;
```

then one cannot mix CURR_TEMP and CURR_BLOOD_COUNT by mistake. The compiler will detect this kind of error and prevent the execution of the program. The usefulness of derived types and the automatically enforced discipline associated with them are more likely to be appreciated when one is dealing with large programs and hundreds of objects.

EXERCISES FOR CHAPTER 2

1. In this exercise you will write a program that will calculate and display yields, given prices for discounted securities. The formula is

$$y = (\text{rv} - \text{price}) / \text{price} * b / \text{dsm}$$

where we have the following definitions:

y	Annual yield (as a decimal, such as 9.85) on the investment with the security held to maturity
rv	Redemption value per \$100 par value (usually 100 but it could be 95, for instance)
price	Quote price of the security divided by 100 (for instance, 0.9805)
b	Number of days in the year (365 or 366)
dsm	Number of days from the settlement date to the maturity date

Each input line gives information about one discount security, in the following format:

Maturity date	Columns 1–20
rv	Columns 21–28 (two decimal places)
price	Columns 29–36 (four decimal places)
b	Columns 37–39 (integer)
dsm	Columns 40–42

Here is some sample input:

Column	123456789012345678901234567890123456789012
Content	December 27 1984 100.0 0.9875366055

The last line of input contains a maturity date of "X   ".
The program should display, for every security, its yield together with its maturity date. The highest- and lowest-yielding security should be displayed after all securities are processed. No date validation should be attempted.

2. Modify the program SHIP_RATE of Section 2.2 so that the ACT_ DIST_LIM and ACT_WEIGHT_LIM are not constants. Instead, ACT_ DIST_LIM and ACT_WEIGHT_LIM should be loaded from the first two lines. Also, the bounds should be checked to see that they appear in ascending sequence. The other input lines are not changed. Some consistency checks should be implemented when the CURR_RATES are loaded, in the following sense: The further an item is shipped, the more it should cost.

3. Modify the program GRADES of Section 2.2 so that a frequency distribution table of the proportion of correct answers for each question is displayed.

4. For this payroll problem, assume that each of the 50 states and the federal government use a different tax rate. The tax brackets are identified by the lower bound of the bracket, and each bracket has a corresponding tax rate. Tax rate information is loaded before the employee payroll records are processed. For each state the tax rate information has the following format: One line has the state ID (AL for Alabama, for instance) in the first two columns and has a two-digit integer counting the number of tax brackets in the third and fourth columns. The next several lines (depending on how many tax brackets there are) have, at most, five pairs of bracket lower bounds and bracket rates. Both the bracket bounds and the rates are assumed to use eight columns each. After this information is provided for all 50 states and the federal government (identified by FG), individual payroll records are input, using the following format:

Columns 1–9	Social Security number
Columns 10–30	Employee name
Columns 31–38	Employee weekly pay (which must be converted to annual salary in order to use tax rates)
Columns 39–40	Number of dependents

The last line of input is identified by a Social Security number of 999999999. The taxable income is the gross income less $25 per dependent. State and federal taxes apply to the taxable income; the FICA tax of 7% applies to the gross income. The net income is given by the gross income less FICA, state, and federal taxes. Write a program that displays, for every employee, the employee's name and his or her net income.

5. Modify the program for Exercise 1, assuming that the settlement date and the maturity date are supplied in the format YYMMDD. The field dsm is replaced by

Settlement date	Columns 40–45
Maturity date	Columns 46–51

The date of the first 20 columns is used for identifying the security only. The two new dates have to be validated, and they cannot fall on a weekend. Use the program DATE_CONVERSION of Section 2.4 for help in checking the dates.

ACCESS TYPES

3.1 Introduction to Access Types
3.1 Recursive Access Type Declarations

3.1 INTRODUCTION TO ACCESS TYPES

So far variables declared in the declarative part of a subprogram existed and were used at any time the subprogram was executed. In this section we introduce a new type, called **access type,** whose objects are created or destroyed while the subprogram is executed.

Values of type access provide access to other objects. The type of objects that can be accessed by every access type is made known when the access type is declared. The form of the access type declaration is

```
type access_type_name is access type_mark;
```

If constraints are present, the form is

```
type access_type_name is access type_mark
              constraint;
```

The type_mark is a type name or a subtype name. The only constraints allowed are index or discriminant constraints.

EXAMPLE
```
type NAME_STRINGS IS NEW STRING (1 .. 30);
type ACC_NAMES is access NAME_STRINGS;
```

Here ACC_NAMES is an access type. The values for the type ACC_NAMES provide access to (or point to) objects of type NAME_STRINGS. The type NAME_STRINGS is assumed to be declared before the type ACC_NAMES is.

FEATURES OF ACCESS TYPES

Every access type has the value NULL among its values. An object of type access whose value is NULL points to no object at all. After an object of type access is declared, the value assigned to it is NULL. Note that this is the only instance where an implicit value is assigned to an Ada object.

EXAMPLE

```
AC_NAME_1 , AC_NAME_2 : ACC_NAMES ;
```

is a declaration of two access variables of type ACC_NAMES, and their value is NULL. This value is implicitly assigned to AC_NAME_1 and AC_NAME_2 by the compiler before the program starts running.

New objects of access types can be created while the program is running by using **allocators** such as "new" followed by the type name or the subtype name and, optionally, by a constraint. The values of these new objects can be assigned to other variables of the same type.

EXAMPLE

```
ACC_NAME_1 := new ACC_NAMES;
```

Here an object of type ACC_NAMES has been created. The value of this object has been assigned to ACC_NAME_1. Now the value of ACC_NAME_1 points to (accesses) a string of 20 characters.

The main operations for objects of type access are assignments and relations such as equality ($=$) and inequality ($/=$). Therefore it is valid to have

```
ACC_NAME_2 := ACC_NAME_1;
```

which means that the pointer accessing a string with 20 positions, which is placed in ACC_NAME_1, will be placed in the variable ACC_NAME_2. Now both variables will access the same string.

A test like

```
ACC_NAME_2 = ACC_NAME_1
```

returns the Boolean value TRUE only if both variables access the same object. Otherwise, it returns the value FALSE.

Dot notation is used to refer to the actual objects pointed to by the access type. That is, the access type name is followed by the dot and the reserved word "all." For instance,

```
ACC_NAME_2.all
```

is a STRING object of type ACC_NAMES. A valid statement, then, is

```
ACC_NAME_2.all := "12345678901234567890";
```

There is no restriction regarding the type of objects accessed by the accessed types. They can be enumeration, integer, array, record, access, or, as we will see later, private types.

EXAMPLE   We can have the following declarations:

```
type EMPLOYEE is

    record

            EMPL_NAME  : STRING (1 .. 20);

            HRS_WORKED : INTEGER ;

    end record;

type E_ACCESS is access EMPLOYEE;

I : E_ACCESS;
```

Here I has, as values, a pointer to objects of type EMPLOYEE. The I.all refers to the whole record objects, while I.EMPL_NAME refers to its string type component.

PROGRAM USING ACCESS TYPES

We present next a program using access type variables. The program is a modification of the program MAX3 of Chapter 1, which finds the largest among three integers. Given three employees and their hours worked, the hardest-working employee name should be listed. There are three input lines, one line for each employee.

ACCESS_MAX3 Program

```
with TEXT_IO; use TEXT_IO;

procedure ACCESS_MAX3 is

    package INT_IO is new INTEGER_IO(INTEGER);

    use INT_IO;

    type EMPLOYEE is
```

```
        record

            EMPL_NAME  : STRING (1 .. 20);

            HRS_WORKED : INTEGER ;

        end record;

    type E_ACCESS is access EMPLOYEE;

    I,J,K,L : E_ACCESS;

begin

    I := new EMPLOYEE;

    -- An object accessing  EMPLOYEE is created. Its value is

    -- assigned to I. Note that I.EMPL_NAME is not initialized.

    J := new EMPLOYEE;

    K := new EMPLOYEE;

    GET(I.EMPL_NAME);GET(I.HRS_WORKED);

    SKIP_LINE;

    GET(J.EMPL_NAME);GET(J.HRS_WORKED);

    SKIP_LINE;

    GET(K.EMPL_NAME);GET(K.HRS_WORKED);

    NEW_LINE;

    if I.HRS_WORKED > J.HRS_WORKED

        then

        L  :=  I  ;

        --  Two employees's hours worked were compared. Then

        --  L  will  point  to  the employee whose hours

        --  worked are higher.

    else

            L :=   J  ;
```

```
end if ;

if L.HRS_WORKED < K.HRS_WORKED

      then

      L := K;

end if;

PUT( " The hardest working is ")

PUT(L.EMPL_NAME);

PUT(" and he worked ");

PUT(L.HRS_WORKED,5);

PUT(" hours ");

-- Mark for insertion of statement (to be explained in the

-- next subsection).

end ACCESS_MAX3;
```

Figures 3.1A and 3.1B illustrate the values of the pointer L for two sets of data.

FIGURE 3.1   Values of Pointer L

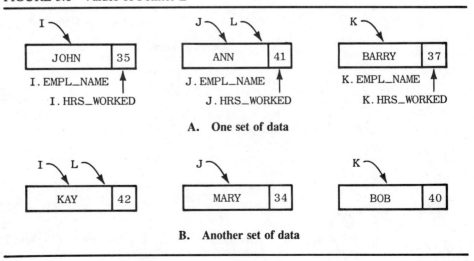

A.   One set of data

B.   Another set of data

DEALLOCATION

As indicated in the program ACCESS_MAX3, an access value obtained by an allocator such as "new" can be assigned to several access variables. Namely, in the program ACCESS_MAX3 the record with the hardest-working person was pointed at by two access variables: one of the three I, J, K variables and L. As long as the object created is accessible (is pointed at) by an access variable, the object remains allocated and in existence. The object becomes inaccessible when no access variable can point to it.

What happens with the storage of an object that cannot be retrieved anymore? Some implementations make the storage available for new uses (that is, they *reclaim* the storage the object occupies); others do not. For instance, let us return to the program ACCESS_MAX3 and make the objects not listed (that is, not exceeding the largest number of hours worked) inaccessible. We can make them inaccessible by adding the following "if" statement after the "mark" comment in the program:

```
If L = I

    then

    J := NULL ; K := NULL;

    -- Objects that used to be pointed at by J and K become

    -- inaccessible (they cannot be retrieved anymore).

    -- Their    storage    may    or    may    not    be

    -- automatically reclaimed by the particular

    -- Ada implementation.

elsif L = J

    then

    I :=NULL; K := NULL ;

else

    I := NULL ; J := NULL;

end if;

-- Now only one object can be accessed (retrieved).

-- It can be accessed by L and one other access variable.
```

Because the storage of objects controlled by allocators like "new" varies during program execution, Ada has means for explicit deallocation. **Deallocation** is the opposite of allocation, and it means making the storage previously allocated available for other uses. The explicit deallocation of individual access objects can be achieved by using procedures such as FREE, which is part of the predefined (generic) procedure UNCHECKED_DEALLOCATION. Of course, one has to be quite careful whenever explicit deallocation of access variables is done in order to avoid leaving access variables that point to an object that does not exist anymore.

USING ACCESS TYPES EFFICIENTLY

In some situations the use of access types improves the clarity and efficiency of a program. As an example, we are going to present a variation of the program SHIP_RATE of Section 2.2. The following modifications are made: There are several tables (instead of just one table, as in SHIP_RATE) to be loaded from the input file. Each table is loaded together with its particular distance and weight categories, and it is identified by a ten-character string. More precisely, a table is initialized by a sequence of four input lines, with the first line having the following layout:

Column	Data
Columns 1–10	Table type, such as OVERNIGHT, meaning overnight delivery.
Columns 11–34	Three eight-digit numbers representing upper bounds on the distance categories, in increasing order. For instance,

                100.00   500.00   5000.00

	means that the first distance category (corresponding to CLOSE_BY) is between 0 and 100.00 miles; the third one is between 500 and 5000 miles.
Columns 35–66	Four eight-digit numbers in an ascending sequence representing upper bounds on the weight categories.

The next three lines contain four real numbers each and represent the charges per pound for items falling within a certain weight and distance class (same layout as in SHIP_RATE). After the last table there is a line with XXXXXXXXX as table type. An unknown number of tables is supplied (not exceeding 20, however). The other input lines have the same layout as in SHIP_RATE, with the addition of a ten-character field identifying the table type.

ACCESS_SHIP_RATE Program

```
with TEXT_IO; use TEXT_IO;
procedure ACCESS_SHIP_RATE is

    Package INT_IO is new INTEGER_IO(INTEGER);
    use INT_IO;
    type ALLOWED_WEIGHT is digits 10 range 0.00 .. 7000.00 ;
    type ALLOWED_DISTANCE is digits 10 range 0.00 .. 8000.00 ;
    Package DISTANCE_IO is new FLOAT_IO(ALLOWED_DISTANCE);
    use DISTANCE_IO;
    Package WEIGHT_IO is new FLOAT_IO(ALLOWED_WEIGHT);
    use WEIGHT_IO;
    type DISTANCE_CLASS is (CLOSE_BY,MED_DISTANCE,LONG_DISTANCE);
    CURR_DIST_CLASS : DISTANCE_CLASS ;
    type           WEIGHT_CLASS        is
                ( LIGHT, MED_WEIGHT, MED_HEAVY, HEAVY);
    CURR_WEIGHT_CLASS : WEIGHT_CLASS;
    type DIST_CATEGORIES is array ( DISTANCE_CLASS ) of
        ALLOWED_DISTANCE;
    type   WEIGHT_ARRAY   is   array   (   WEIGHT_CLASS   )   of
            ALLOWED_WEIGHT;
    type PRICES is delta 0.0001 range 0.000 .. 5000.000;
    Package PRICES_IO is new FIXED_IO(PRICES);
    use PRICES_IO;
    type SHIPPING_RATES is array ( DISTANCE_CLASS,  WEIGHT_CLASS )
        of PRICES;
        -- The record below contains complete information
```

```
              -- about a shipping table.
      type SHIP_TBL is
          record
                CATEGORY : STRING ( 1 .. 10 );
                ACT_DIST_LIM : DIST_CATEGORIES ;
                ACT_WEIGHT_LIM  :  WEIGHT_ARRAY ;
                CURR_RATES : SHIPPING_RATES ;
          end record;
      type REGULAR_REC is
          record
                ITEM_NO : INTEGER ;
                ITEM_DISTANCE : ALLOWED_DISTANCE ;
                ITEM_WEIGHT :   ALLOWED_WEIGHT ;
                ITEM_COST   :   PRICES ;
                ITEM_SERVICE : String ( 1 .. 10 );
          end record;
INPUT_REC : REGULAR_REC;
type SHIP_POINTER is access SHIP_TBL;
type FULL_TBL is array ( 1 .. 20 ) of SHIP_POINTER;
ACT_TBL : FULL_TBL;
      -- Up to 20 pointers can be allocated.
TBL_CNT,CRT_CNT : INTEGER := 0;
begin
      TBL_CNT := TBL_CNT + 1 ;
      ACT_TBL (TBL_CNT) := new SHIP_TBL ;
      -- An object of type SHIP_POINTER was created, and
```

```
-- its value is placed in ACT_TBL (TBL_CNT).

-- Extra code is inserted here to process the first

-- line  supplying  the category and the upper bounds  of  a

-- table.

GET ( ACT_TBL(TBL_CNT).CATEGORY );

-- Read the table type of the first table supplied.

while  ACT_TBL(TBL_CNT).CATEGORY /= "XXXXXXXXXX"

     loop

     for JUNK_DIST in DISTANCE_CLASS

          loop

          GET(ACT_TBL(TBL_CNT).ACT_DIST_LIM(JUNK_DIST),8);

     end loop;

     -- The distance upper bounds were just loaded.

     for JUNK_WEIGHT in WEIGHT_CLASS

          loop

          GET(ACT_TBL(TBL_CNT).ACT_WEIGHT_LIM(JUNK_WEIGHT),8);

          -- The weight upper bounds were just loaded.

     end loop;

     SKIP_LINE;

     -- The extra code ends here. Now code similar to

     -- the code in SHIP_RATE follows.

     for JUNK_DIST in DISTANCE_CLASS

       loop

       for JUNK_WEIGHT in WEIGHT_CLASS

          loop

          GET(ACT_TBL(TBL_CNT).CURR_RATES(JUNK_DIST,JUNK_WEIGHT),7)
```

```
        end loop;

          SKIP_LINE;

      end loop;

      TBL_CNT := TBL_CNT + 1;

      ACT_TBL (TBL_CNT) := new SHIP_TBL ;

      -- Another access value pointing at a

      -- shipping table is allocated.

      GET ( ACT_TBL(TBL_CNT).CATEGORY );

  end loop;

GET(INPUT_REC.ITEM_NO,7);

while INPUT_REC.ITEM_NO /= 9999999

    loop

    GET(INPUT_REC.ITEM_WEIGHT,7);

    GET(INPUT_REC.ITEM_DISTANCE,7);

    GET(INPUT_REC.ITEM_SERVICE);

    SKIP_LINE;

    -- Extra code is inserted here to  search for the

    -- ITEM_SERVICE.

    CRT_CNT := 0;

    for I in 1 .. TBL_CNT

        loop

        if INPUT_REC.ITEM_SERVICE = ACT_TBL(TBL_CNT).CATEGORY

            then

            CRT_CNT := I;

        end if;

    end loop;
```

```
-- The extra code for search ends here. The statements
-- below are executed only if ITEM_SERVICE
-- is in one of the tables.
if CRT_CNT /= 0
    then
    for JUNK_DIST in reverse DISTANCE_CLASS
        loop
        if INPUT_REC.ITEM_DISTANCE >
            ACT_TBL(CRT_CNT).ACT_DIST_LIM ( JUNK_DIST )
            then
            CURR_DIST_CLASS := JUNK_DIST;
        end if;
    end loop;
    for JUNK_WEIGHT  in reverse WEIGHT_CLASS
        loop
        if INPUT_REC.ITEM_WEIGHT >
            ACT_TBL(CRT_CNT).ACT_WEIGHT_LIM ( JUNK_WEIGHT )
            then
            CURR_WEIGHT_CLASS := JUNK_WEIGHT;
        end if;
    end loop;
    INPUT_REC.ITEM_COST :=
        PRICES ( ACT_TBL(CRT_CNT).CURR_RATES(CURR_DIST_CLASS,
                CURR_WEIGHT_CLASS) *
                PRICES ( INPUT_REC.ITEM_WEIGHT ) ) ;
    NEW_LINE;
```

```
        PUT(INPUT_REC.ITEM_COST,7,2);

    end if;

    SKIP_LINE;

    GET(INPUT_REC.ITEM_NO);

  end loop;

end ACCESS_SHIP_RATE;
```

Figure 3.2 illustrates a possible ACT_TBL set up for only three table types and an arbitrary item to be shipped.

CONSTRAINTS

As we mentioned earlier, the only kind of constraints allowed when one is declaring access type variables are discriminant and index constraints. For instance, one can have the declarations

```
type NAME_POINTER is access STRING ( 21 . . 55 );
```

Here a discriminant constraint is present in an access type declaration.

If the type accessed in a declaration is an unconstrained type, then a constraint must be present at the time an object of the specified type is created by the allocator "new."

EXAMPLE Suppose one has the following declarations:

```
type LINE_POINTER is access STRING;
CURR_LINE : LINE_POINTER;
```

Then it is not valid to have the statement

```
CURR_LINE := new STRING ;
```

because STRING is an unconstrained array type, and an index constraint must be present when an object of this type is created by the allocator "new." Instead, one can have

```
CURR_LINE := new STRING ( 8 . . 89 ) ;
```

with the constraints supplied.

FIGURE 3.2 ACT_TBL with Three Tables and a Sample Input Line

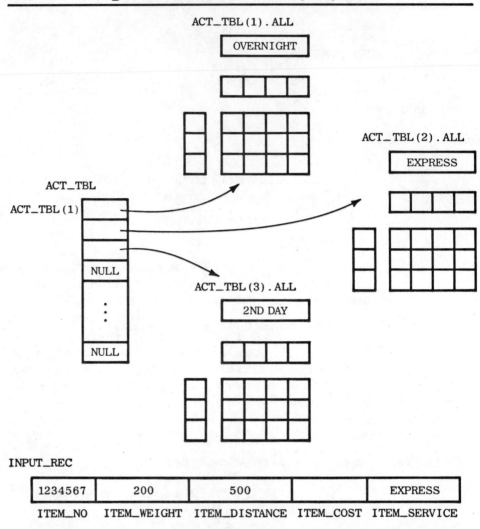

INPUT_REC

1234567	200	500		EXPRESS
ITEM_NO	ITEM_WEIGHT	ITEM_DISTANCE	ITEM_COST	ITEM_SERVICE

Other examples are

```
type  JOB_DESCRIPTION  is array (NATURAL range <>)

        of STRING  (1  .. 10);

type EMPLOYEE  ( JOB_NO : POSITIVE )  is

    record
```

```
        L_NAME : STRING ( 1 .. 30 ) ;

        JOBS_HELD : JOB_DESCRIPTION ( 1 .. JOB_NO) ;

    end record;

  type EMP_POINTER is access EMPLOYEE ;
```

Here an access type has been declared without constraints. And in

```
  type EMP_CONSTR_POINTER is access
     EMPLOYEE ( 20 ) ;
```

an access type has been declared with discriminant constraints.
Finally, consider

```
  JOHN_PAUL : EMP_POINTER ;
  MARY_LOU : EMP_CONSTR_POINTER ;
```

With this kind of declaration every time an object of type JOHN_PAUL is created, one has to supply discriminant constraints. For instance, one can have

```
  JOHN_PAUL := new EMPLOYEE ( 5 );
```

However, no discriminant constraints are supplied when we have the creation of objects of type MARY_LOU:

```
  MARY_LOU := new EMPLOYEE ;
```

Once the constraints appear in the type declaration, it is not valid to supply another set of related constraints when the objects are created.

The program ACCESS_SHIP_RATE could have been written by using dynamic arrays instead of access types. The use of access types is justified if the resulting program is clearer, more general, and more reliable or if it manages the storage better. These advantages become more evident when the problem to be solved can be naturally expressed in a recursive form, as we will see in the next section.

3.2 RECURSIVE ACCESS TYPE DECLARATIONS

There is no restriction on the type of the objects that can be designated by a value of an access type. Therefore one of the components referred to by a certain access type variable can itself be an access type variable of identical type. In this case Ada requires an incomplete type declaration of the type referred to, followed by the corresponding access type declaration, followed by the complete declaration of the type referred to.

INCOMPLETE TYPE DECLARATIONS

An **incomplete type** declaration in Ada has the form

```
type identifier optional_discriminant_part;
```

EXAMPLE   An example of an incomplete type declaration is

```
type PAYROLL_REC ;
```

Some other unrelated declarations can be used here. To continue the example:

```
type PAY_ACCESS is access PAYROLL_REC;
```

Here PAY_ACCESS is the corresponding access type variable for PAYROLL_REC. Some other unrelated declarations can be used here, too. To continue the example:

```
type PAYROLL_REC is

    record

            EMP_NAME : STRING ( 1 .. 20 );

            EMP_ID   : STRING ( 1 .. 9 );

            EMP_PAY  : FLOAT ;

            EMP_NEXT : PAY_ACCESS ;

    end record ;
```

Here a component of the type referred to by the PAY_ACCESS type variables is itself a PAY_ACCESS type variable. The next lines are

```
CURR_PTR, PREV_PTR : PAY_ACCESS;

HOLD_REC : PAYROLL_REC ;
```

Now here are some examples of valid statements that can create objects of type PAY_ACCESS:

```
CURR_PTR := new PAYROLL_REC;
```

This line creates an object of type PAYROLL_REC referred to by CURR_PTR.

FIGURE 3.3   Objects of Type PAY_ACCESS

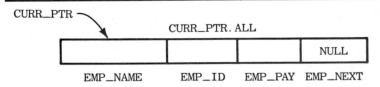

A.   After CURR_PTR := NEW PAYROLL_REC is first executed

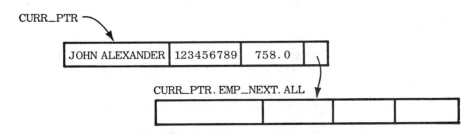

B.   After CURR_PTR.EMP_NEXT := NEW PAYROLL_REC is first executed

Figure 3.3A illustrates the contents of various components after this statement is executed. Other examples are

```
CURR_PTR.EMP_NAME := "JOHN ALEXANDER      ";

CURR_PTR.EMP_ID    := "123456789";

CURR_PTR.EMP_PAY   := 758.00 ;

CURR_PTR.EMP_NEXT := new  PAYROLL_REC ;
```

Figure 3.3B illustrates the contents of various components pointed at by CURR_PTR, after these statements are executed.
   The next line is

```
PREV_PTR := CURR_PTR;
```

Here we prepare to assign a new value to the variable CURR_PTR. First, we save its value so that the first record will be retrievable. The next lines are

```
CURR_PTR := CURR_PTR.EMP_NEXT ;

CURR_PTR.EMP_NAME := "EUGENE SORENSEN      ";

CURR_PTR.EMP_ID    := "222222222";
```

```
CURR_PTR.EMP_PAY   := 800.00 ;

CURR_PTR.EMP_NEXT := new  PAYROLL_REC ;

HOLD_REC  :=  (   "MARY MURPHY        ", "555555555",

          850.00,NULL);
```

Note that the variable HOLD_REC of type PAYROLL_REC was initialized by using a positional record aggregate. The final line is

```
CURR_PTR.EMP_NEXT.all := HOLD_REC ;
```

The record referred to by the access type variable CURR_PTR.EMP_NEXT.all was initialized with the content of HOLD_REC. It would be invalid, though, to have

```
CURR_PTR.EMP_NEXT := HOLD_REC ;
```

because a record type variable cannot be assigned to an access type variable.

Note also that the record created first can be accessed by PREV_PTR, the second record created can be accessed by PREV_PTR.EMP_NEXT and CURR_PTR, and the third one can be accessed by CURR_PTR.EMP_NEXT.

The final setup is illustrated in Figure 3.4.

MUTUAL DEPENDENCIES

Loosely speaking, types like PAY_ACCESS are called **recursive type** declarations because they refer to themselves in their definition. One can, as well, introduce access types that refer to each other, thus establishing **mutual dependencies.**

EXAMPLE   The following lines introduce mutual dependencies:

```
type CEREAL;

type PACK_BOX;
```

First, we use two incomplete type declarations. Next, we have

```
type  CEREAL_PTR   is access CEREAL;

type  PACK_BOX_PTR is access PACKAGE_BOX;
```

These two lines give two access types referring to the incomplete types. To continue:

FIGURE 3.4   Final Setup for Objects of Type PAY_ACCESS

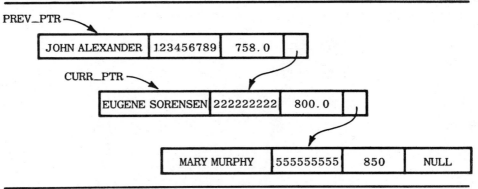

```
type CEREAL is

    record

            SUGAR_CONT      : FLOAT;

            SALT_CONT       : FLOAT;

            FIBER_CONT      : FLOAT;

            VITAMIN_C_CONT  : FLOAT;

            ADV_TYPE        : STRING ( 1 .. 10 ) ;

            PACKING_INSTR   : PACK_BOX_PTR;

    end record;

type PACKAGE_BOX is

    record

            SHIP_VOLUME   : FLOAT;

            SHIP_WEIGHT   : FLOAT;

            SHIP_CONTENT  : CEREAL_PTR;

    end record;
```

The mutual dependency was defined as follows: The type CEREAL refers to PACKAGE_BOX through the access type variable PACKING_INSTR, and the type PACKAGE_BOX refers to the type CEREAL through the access type SHIP_CONTENT. The next lines of the example are

```
CURR_CEREAL : CEREAL_PTR ;

CURR_BOX    : PACK_BOX_PTR ;
```

Some statements that use these mutual dependencies are the following:

```
CURR_CEREAL := new CEREAL ;

CURR_CEREAL.all := (0.08, 0.005, 0.02, 0.003 ,

                    "DAVY CROCK", NULL ) ;
```

Here the record CURR_CEREAL.all is initialized. To continue:

```
CURR_BOX    := new PACKAGE_BOX ;

CURR_BOX.all := ( 25.00, 16.50, NULL ) ;
```

The two access type variables refer to objects that do not point to each other yet, as Figure 3.5 illustrates. We continue with the statements

```
CURR_CEREAL.PACKING_INSTR := CURR_BOX ;

CURR_BOX.SHIP_CONTENT     := CURR_CEREAL ;
```

Now the mutual dependencies are established, as shown in Figure 3.6.

PROGRAM USING RECURSIVE TYPES

We illustrate the concepts of recursive type definitions and mutual dependencies in the next program. This program is a modification of the program GRADES of Section 2.2. There are several possible tests, each one identified by a five-character subject ID (for instance, MATH1). The information necessary for

FIGURE 3.5   CURR_CEREAL and CURR_BOX Before Mutual Dependencies
              Are Established

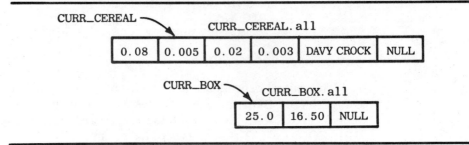

FIGURE 3.6   CURR_CEREAL and CURR_BOX After Mutual Dependencies
Are Established

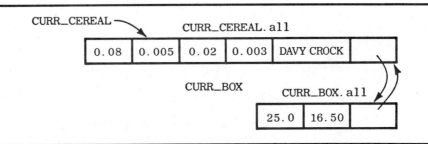

grading each test is supplied by a pair of lines with the following layout: The first
of the pair uses

Columns 1–5   Subject ID (MATH1, ENGL5, and so on)

Columns 6–7   Number of questions in the test (between 20 and 500)

The second of the pair is a sequence of digits taking values between 1 and 5.
There are as many digits as indicated by the number of questions in the first line
of the pair. The end of the key answers to the tests is signaled by a line with
XXXXX as the subject ID.

The remaining lines represent sets of answers for a given student. The
student ID is in the first ten columns, and the subject ID is in the next five
columns. The answers start in column 16. As in the original GRADES version,
the input ends with a 9999999999 student ID. The required output is the same:
For each student line read, a line with the student's name and the number of
correct answers is displayed.

ACCESS_GRADES Program

```
with TEXT_IO; use TEXT_IO;

procedure ACCESS_GRADES is

    Package INT_IO is new INTEGER_IO(INTEGER);

    use INT_IO;

    type CHOICES is range 1 .. 5 ;

    type POSSIBLE_QUESTIONS is range 20 .. 50 ;

    Package CHO_IO is new INTEGER_IO(CHOICES);

    use CHO_IO;
```

```
type POSS_IO is new INTEGER_IO(POSSIBLE_QUESTIONS);

use POSS_IO;

DNO_QUESTIONS : POSSIBLE_QUESTIONS := 50 ;

type ANSWERS is array ( 1 .. DNO_QUESTIONS ) of CHOICES;

type TEST_KEY;

-- An incomplete type declaration is needed for the recursive

-- type definition.

type TEST_KEY_PTR is access TEST_KEY;

type TEST_KEY is

    record

            SUBJ          : STRING ( 1 .. 5 );

            NO_QUESTIONS : POSSIBLE_QUESTIONS;

            KEY_ANSWERS  : ANSWERS;

            NEXT_TEST    : TEST_KEY_PTR;

        end record;

CURR_TEST, START_TEST : TEST_KEY_PTR;

GOOD_ANSWERS : INTEGER ;

type IN_REC is

    record

            STUDENT_ID : STRING ( 1 .. 10 );

            SUBJECT_ID : STRING ( 1 .. 5 );

            STUDENT_ANSWERS : ANSWERS ;

        end record;

    CURR_REC : IN_REC;

begin

    CURR_TEST := new TEST_KEY;
```

```
GET(CURR_TEST.SUBJ);

while CURR_TEST.SUBJ /= "XXXXX"

    loop

    -- Here we are building   a   list   of   tests   (known

    -- sometimes   as a one-way link list ).   The

    -- top of the list is pointed at by START_TEST.

    GET(CURR_TEST.NO_QUESTIONS,2);

    DNO_QUESTIONS := CURR_TEST.NO_QUESTIONS ;

    SKIP_LINE;

    for I in 1 .. CURR_TEST.NO_QUESTIONS

        loop

            GET ( CURR_TEST.KEY_ANSWERS (I), 1);

    end loop;

    if START_TEST = NULL

        then

        -- START_TEST  is NULL only  the  first time it is

        -- read. The first test read is placed

        -- in the list.

        START_TEST := CURR_TEST ;

    else

        CURR_TEST.NEXT_TEST := START_TEST;

        START_TEST := CURR_TEST;

        -- Every new test becomes the top

        -- of the list until the next test is

        -- processed.

    end if;

    SKIP_LINE;
```

```
            CURR_TEST := new TEST_KEY ;

            GET(CURR_TEST.SUBJ);

    end loop;

    SKIP_LINE;

    GET ( CURR_REC.STUDENT_ID ) ;

    while CURR_REC.STUDENT_ID /= "9999999999"

        loop

        GET ( CURR_REC.SUBJECT_ID);

        CURR_TEST := START_TEST;

        while CURR_TEST /= NULL or

            CURR_TEST.SUBJ /= CURR_REC.SUBJECT_ID

            loop

                -- Look for the test subject in the list.

                CURR_TEST := CURR_TEST.NEXT_TEST;

        end loop;

        if CURR_TEST.SUBJ = CURR_REC.SUBJECT_ID

            then

            -- If  the  test  id true,  then  the  subject  was

            -- found, otherwise there is no such subject in

            -- the list.

            GOOD_ANSWERS := O;

            for J in 1 .. CURR_TEST.NO_QUESTIONS

                loop

                GET (CURR_REC.STUDENT_ANSWERS(J), 1);

                if CURR_REC.STUDENT_ANSWERS (J) =

                    CURR_TEST.KEY_ANSWERS (J)
```

```
                            then

                                GOOD_ANSWERS := GOOD_ANSWERS + 1 ;

                    end if;

                end loop;

                NEW_LINE;

                PUT ( " The number of good answers is " );

                PUT ( GOOD_ANSWERS, 5);

                PUT ( " for the ID ");

                PUT ( CURR_REC.STUDENT_ID );

                NEW_LINE;

            else

                PUT(" No such subject:");PUT(CURR_REC.SUBJECT_ID);

            end if;

            SKIP_LINE;

            GET ( CURR_REC.STUDENT_ID) ;

        end loop;

end ACCESS_GRADES;
```

Figure 3.7 illustrates the subject list with only three subjects, MATH1, ENGL1, and COMP1, and a sample CURR.REC.

PROGRAM USING MUTUAL DEPENDENCIES

In the next program we provide an example of mutual dependencies using access types. The program will display the ranking of horses in a scheduled race.

The input consists of pairs of horse and jockey information lines. Horse information consists of the following:

Column	Data
Columns 1–10	Horse name
Columns 11–13	Best time ever in the race (in seconds)
Columns 14–15	Number of wins in the last ten races

FIGURE 3.7   Sample Test List and Student Answers Line

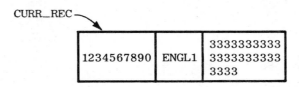

Jockey information consists of the following:

Column	Data
Columns 1–10	Jockey name
Columns 11–13	Jockey weight (in pounds)
Columns 14–15	Number of wins in the last ten races

The rank is computed (quite arbitrarily) as follows:

$$rank = horse\_time - 5 * horse\_wins - 5 * jockey\_wins + 2 * jockey\_weight$$

There are an unknown number of entries in the race, and the last line is signaled by a horse name of CALIGULA. A list of horses, their riders, and their rankings must be provided in ascending order.

RACES Program

```
with TEXT_IO; use TEXT_IO;

procedure RACES is
```

```
Package INT_IO is new INTEGER_IO(INTEGER);

use INT_IO;

type HORSE;

type JOCKEY;

-- Incomplete type definitions are needed to introduce

-- two mutually dependent types.

type HORSE_PTR is access HORSE;

type JOCKEY_PTR is access JOCKEY;

type HORSE is

    record

        H_NAME : STRING ( 1 .. 10 );

        WIN_TIME : INTEGER ;

        WIN_RACE : INTEGER ;

        RIDER :  JOCKEY_PTR ;

        -- The RIDER points to objects of type Jockey.

        PAIR_RANK : INTEGER ;

        NXT_HORSE : HORSE_PTR ;

    end record;

type JOCKEY is

    record

        J_NAME : STRING ( 1 .. 10 );

        J_WEIGHT : INTEGER;

        J_WINS   : INTEGER;

        -- J_WINS points to objects of type HORSE.

        H_TO_RIDE : HORSE_PTR;

    end record;

CURR_HORSE_PTR, TOP_HORSE_PTR, ANY_HORSE_PTR ,
```

```
            PREV_HORSE_PTR : HORSE_PTR ;

      CURR_JOCKEY_PTR : JOCKEY_PTR ;


begin

      CURR_HORSE_PTR := new HORSE;

      GET(CURR_HORSE_PTR.H_NAME);

      while CURR_HORSE_PTR.H_NAME /= "CALIGULA "

            loop

            GET(CURR_HORSE_PTR.WIN_TIME,3);

            GET(CURR_HORSE_PTR.WIN_RACE,2);

            SKIP_LINE;

            CURR_JOCKEY_PTR := new JOCKEY;

            GET(CURR_JOCKEY_PTR.J_NAME);

            GET(CURR_JOCKEY_PTR.J_WEIGHT,3);

            GET(CURR_JOCKEY_PTR.J_WINS,2);

            SKIP_LINE;

            CURR_HORSE_PTR.RIDER := CURR_JOCKEY_PTR;

            CURR_JOCKEY_PTR.H_TO_RIDE := CURR_HORSE_PTR;

            -- These assignments establishe a mutual dependency.

            CURR_HORSE_PTR.PAIR_RANK :=CURR_HORSE_PTR.WIN_TIME-

                  5 * ( CURR_HORSE_PTR.WIN_RACE +

                        CURR_JOCKEY_PTR.J_WINS ) +

                  2 * CURR_JOCKEY_PTR.J_WEIGHT ;

            -- After the ranking is computed, the pair

            -- is placed in the list in  ascending order.

            ANY_HORSE_PTR := TOP_HORSE_PTR ;

            while ANY_HORSE_PTR.PAIR_RANK <
```

```
                CURR_HORSE_PTR.PAIR_RANK

                        or

            ANY_HORSE_PTR  /= NULL

            loop

            PREV_HORSE_PTR := ANY_HORSE_PTR;

            ANY_HORSE_PTR := ANY_HORSE_PTR.NXT_HORSE ;

        end loop;

        if ANY_HORSE_PTR = TOP_HORSE_PTR

            then

            CURR_HORSE_PTR.NXT_HORSE := TOP_HORSE_PTR ;

            TOP_HORSE_PTR := CURR_HORSE_PTR ;

        else

            PREV_HORSE_PTR.NXT_HORSE := CURR_HORSE_PTR ;

            CURR_HORSE_PTR.NXT_HORSE := ANY_HORSE_PTR ;

        end if;

        GET(CURR_HORSE_PTR.H_NAME);

end loop;

ANY_HORSE_PTR := TOP_HORSE_PTR ;

-- Now we display the list in ascending order by rank.

while ANY_HORSE_PTR /= NULL

    loop

    PUT(ANY_HORSE_PTR.H_NAME);

    CURR_JOCKEY_PTR := ANY_HORSE_PTR.RIDER ;

    PUT(CURR_JOCKEY_PTR.J_NAME);

    PUT(ANY_HORSE_PTR.PAIR_RANK);

    ANY_HORSE_PTR := ANY_HORSE_PTR.NXT_HORSE;

    end loop;

end RACES;
```

FIGURE 3.8   Sample Race Setup for Three Horses and Three Jockeys

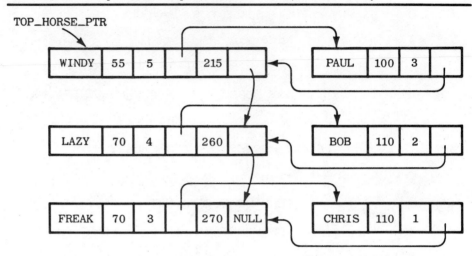

A possible setup of a race with three horses and three jockeys is illustrated in Figure 3.8.

The full power of recursive type definitions and mutual dependencies can be appreciated only after one has knowledge of recursive calls. Recursive calls will be covered in Chapter 5.

EXERCISES FOR CHAPTER 3

1.   Modify the program ACCESS_SHIP_RATE so that totals for items shipped by type of shipping service (table type) are kept. After all items are processed, the totals together with the corresponding table types should be listed.

2.   Modify the program ACCESS_GRADES so that a list of students and their scores is kept in ascending sequence for each subject (make use of access types). After all students are read, a listing of the students by subject and their scores in increasing order should be displayed.

3.   Modify the program RACES so that an extra component is present for objects of type JOCKEY pointing to an object of the same type. This component should be used to keep the objects of type JOCKEY sorted by J_WEIGHT. A listing of riders and their horses should be given as output, first according to the rank and then according to the rider's weight.

CHAPTER FOUR

OTHER ADA STATEMENTS AND RECORDS WITH VARIANTS

4.1   SIMPLE AND COMPOUND ADA STATEMENTS

As mentioned in Chapter 1, Ada statements have two forms: simple statements and compound statements. We can recognize simple statements by inspection: **Simple statements** contain no other statements. **Compound statements** contain other statements.

So far we have used just two simple statements: assignment statements and procedure call statements. The compound statements we used in the first three chapters are "if" statements and two varieties of loop statements ("for" and "while" loop statements).

In this section we will cover several new simple statements: null statements, exit statements, and go to statements. The return statement, another simple statement, will be explained in the next chapter in connection with subprograms. The remaining simple statements of the Ada language are abort statements, delay statements, entry call statements (to be covered in Chapter 10 on concurrency), raise statements (to be covered in Chapter 11 on exceptions), and code statements related to implementation of low-level (perhaps assembly language level) statements.

We will also introduce in this section two new compound statements: the case statements and block statements. We will cover as well a third (and last)

131

variation of the loop statement. To complete the account, the Ada language has two more compound statements: accept statements and select statements. They will be covered in Chapter 10.

CASE STATEMENTS

The **case statement** provides for the selection of just one alternative out of several, depending on the value of a discrete expression. The form of this statement is

```
case expression is

    when choice => sequence_of_statements

    -- maybe one or more other choices here

    when choice => sequence_of_statements

end case ;
```

The expression following the reserved word "case" must be of discrete type—that is, the value returned by the expression after evaluation must be an integer or enumeration type value. Depending on its values, one of the sequence_of_statements following a choice will be executed, namely, the one following the choice matching the value of the expression at a particular time during the program execution.

The choice expression following the reserved word "when" must be a static expression of discrete type or a discrete range. One can use the choice "others" as the last alternative to cover all values not given in previous choices. Also, several choices in sequence separated by a '!' are allowed. In this situation if any of the choices of the sequence match the value of the expression following the reserved word "when," then the corresponding sequence_of_statements is executed.

EXAMPLE   Suppose SOME_CHAR is declared, of type CHARACTER. Then we can have the following case statement:

```
case SOME_CHAR is

    when 'A' .. 'Z' => PUT(" Uppercase letter ");

    when 'a' .. 'z' => PUT(" Lowercase letter ");

    when '0' .. '9' => PUT(" Digit  " );

    when '+' ! '-'  => PUT( " Signs " );
```

```
when others      => PUT(" Other characters ");

end case ;
```

The expression following the reserved word "case" is the primary SOME_CHAR, which is of the predefined enumeration type CHARACTER (it clearly is a discrete type). The choices present here are as follows:

Choice	Description
'A' . . 'Z'	A static range
'a' . . 'z'	A static range
'0' . . '9'	A static range
'+'	A character literal (primary)
'−'	A character literal (primary)
Others	Covers all the other values that the variable SOME_CHAR can take and are not among the values present in the other choices

Note that

```
when '+' ¦ '-' => PUT( `` Signs '' );
```

means that whenever SOME_CHAR is '+' or '−', the message " Signs " will be displayed.

Given any two choices of the same case statement, one cannot have a value present in both choices. For instance, the statement

```
case SOME_CHAR is

    when 'A' .. 'M' => PUT(" First half ");

    when 'L' .. 'Z' => PUT(" Second half ");

end case;
```

is not valid because the two static ranges 'A' . . 'M' and 'L' . . 'Z' have the values 'L' and 'M' in common.

Of course, one can use an "if" statement whenever a case statement is used. For instance, the first case statement in the example is equivalent to

```
if SOME_CHAR in 'A' .. 'Z'

    then
```

```
                    PUT(" Uppercase letter ");
       elsif SOME_CHAR in  'a' .. 'z'

            then

            PUT(" Lowercase letter ");
       elsif SOME_CHAR in '0' .. '9'

            then

            PUT(" Digit   " );
       elsif SOME_CHAR = '+' or SOME_CHAR = '-'

            then

            PUT( " Signs " );
       else

                PUT(" Other characters ");

       end if ;
```

At times (as our examples illustrate), the case statement is more readable than an "if" statement, particularly when several discrete alternatives are to be implemented.

Note that the choices present in a case statement must cover all the possible values of the static expression following the reserved word "case." Therefore, for instance, to drop the alternative selected by the choice "others" in the above case statement would be incorrect.

LABELS

Ada allows for labels to precede any simple or compound statement. A **label** consists of an identifier enclosed within double angle brackets. For instance, we might use

```
<<JUST_IN_CASE>> if I < 0
        then I := -I ; end if;
```

Here the label <<JUST_IN_CASE>> is identifying an "if" statement. Ada allows several labels to precede a statement. It is valid then to have

```
<<GOOD>> <<BON>> <<GUT>> K := K + 1;
```

Even though there is no visible (explicit) declaration of Ada labels, they are implicitly declared at the end of the declarative part of the innermost enclosing subprogram body. The other implicitly declared object encountered so far was the loop_parameter of the "for" loop statement. The loop_parameter, however, was implicitly declared as a variable local to the loop statement. Thus the loop_parameter is known in a more restricted manner than a label in two ways. First, the label is known throughout the innermost subprogram body, while the loop_parameter is known within the loop statement only. Second, the implicit label declaration takes effect before any statement of the subprogram is executed, while the loop_parameter comes into existence only when the loop statement is executed. As will be discussed in Chapters 7 and 10, labels can be used as well in package bodies and task bodies.

GOTO STATEMENTS

The transfer of control to a labeled statement can be achieved in Ada with a **goto statement.** The general form of the goto statement is

```
goto label_name;
```

For instance,

```
goto GOOD;
```

is a valid goto statement.

The Ada goto statement is quite restricted in scope. It must not transfer control out of or into a subprogram. It is not allowed to transfer control from outside into a compound statement (an "if" statement, a case statement, or a loop statement, for instance). It must not transfer control from other program units (packages or tasks). Within an "if" or case statement it cannot transfer control from one alternative to another. Finally, there are other restrictions related to the handling of exceptions and of tasks; these restrictions will be discussed in Chapters 10 and 11.

EXAMPLE   The following program lines illustrate some of these restrictions. All variables are assumed to be declared of the predefined type INTEGER.

```
<<JOHN>> if  I = J

    then

        <<MARY>> K :=2;

        case J - 3 is

            when 1 .. 5  => L := 5;
```

```
                              <<LOU>> K := L*2;

               when 6 .. 10 => L := 10;

               -- A goto LOU statement here would be

               -- wrong because control would be transferred

               -- from one alternative of the case

               -- statement to another.

               when 0 | 13  => L := 1 ;

               when others  => l. := 0 ;

          end case;

     else

          <<BOB>> J := abs ( I );

          if  J = L

               then

               L := L * L ; I:= I +1 ;

               -- A goto BOB statemnt would be valid here:

               -- It branches out of the inner "if", and the

               -- same alternative goto JOHN would still be

               -- valid as well. A statement like

               -- goto MARY would be incorrect because it

               -- would transfer control from one alternative

               -- to another of the "if" statement.

               -- Goto LOU would not be valid because

               -- it transfers control within a compound

               -- statement.

          end if;

     end if;
```

One of the reasons a goto statement is provided in Ada is to facilitate the translation of programs written in other languages into Ada. The use of goto statements, however, should be carefully controlled and justified.

NULL STATEMENTS

Ada has a **null statement,** which has the effect of passing control to the following statement. The null statement is simply

```
null;
```

A possible use of this statement is in case statements (remember that choices have to cover all possible values in the case expression) to prescribe some actions for choices that would not be of interest. For instance, assuming again integer type variables, we might have

```
case I is

    when 1          => J := 1;

    when 3          => J := 2;

    when 5 ! 8      => J := 3;

    when others     => null;

end case;
```

LOOP STATEMENTS WITHOUT ITERATION

In Chapter 1 we introduced "while" loops, and in Chapter 2 we introduced "for" loops. Here we will introduce the simplest form of the loop statement, which expresses an **endless loop.** Its form is

```
loop
        -- Some statements are given here.
end loop;
```

This form of the loop statement will be executed forever unless a statement within the loop explicitly transfers control outside it. Among the Ada statements that can transfer control outside a loop statement are goto and, as will be described shortly, the exit statement.

NAMED LOOP STATEMENTS

Every loop statement can be named. The name, if present, has to be given at the beginning and the end of the loop statement. The loop name is an identifier followed by a colon. For instance, we can have (again assuming that we have integer type variables)

```
ONE_LOOP:       loop

                    -- Some Ada statements are given here.

                end loop ONE_LOOP;
```

If we have a "while" loop, we may use

```
TWO_LOOP:    while I > 0

                loop

                J := J + I ;

                I := I -1 ;

             end loop TWO_LOOP;
```

If we have a "for" loop, we may use

```
THREE_LOOP:     for I in 3 .. 10

                J := J + I;

             end loop THREE_LOOP;
```

The loop name (for instance, THREE_LOOP) is implicitly declared, just as Ada labels are. Thus the loop name (called a loop identifier) is declared at the end of the innermost enclosing subprogram body (or task or package body, as will be discussed in Chapters 7 and 10). Note that the loop identifier (THREE_LOOP) and the loop parameter (it is I in the previous example), even though they are implicitly declared, come into existence at different times during the execution of a program. Also, the loop parameter is known within the loop statement only.

EXIT STATEMENTS

The **exit statement** in Ada is used in connection with the possible termination of an enclosing loop. The forms of this statement are

```
exit;
exit when condition;
```

If loop identifiers are present, the forms are

```
exit loop_name ;
exit loop_name when condition;
```

The condition mentioned in the exit statement is evaluated, and if it is found TRUE, then the loop is exited. If the condition is not present, then the loop is exited unconditionally.

Whenever a loop_name is not present and the loop is exited, the innermost loop enclosing the exit statement is left. If there are several nested loops, and if each loop has a loop_name, one can control the level to which the exit statement will transfer control by specifying the desired loop_name.

EXAMPLE The following program lines illustrate some uses of the exit statement. Again all variables are assumed to be of type INTEGER.

```
AA: for I in 1 .. 10

    loop

    case J is

        when 1  =>

            L := 0 ;

        BB: for  K in 11 .. 20

            loop

            L := I * K + L ;

            exit when L > K * K ;

            -- The loop named BB is enclosed in

            -- the loop named AA. Since

            -- there is no loop name mentioned in the

            -- exit statement, the BB loop

            -- will  be exited if the condition L > K*K

            -- is true, and the next statement

            -- to be executed is then L := L * L.
```

```
                        -- Thus we have an exit statement within

                        -- a for loop statement.

                        end loop BB;

            when 5 : 8  =>

                L := I ;

                CC: while L < 89

                    loop

                    exit AA when L = 55;

                    -- The loop named

                    -- CC is enclosed in the loop named AA.

                    -- The loop name mentioned in the  exit

                    -- statement is AA. So the AA loop

                    -- will  be exited if the condition L = 55

                    -- is true, and the next statement

                    -- to be executed is K := L / 100. If

                    -- the exit statement is never executed

                    -- and the loop statement is completed,

                    -- the next statement to be executed is

                    -- L := L * L.

                    -- Thus we have here an exit statement

                    -- within a while loop statement.

                    -- Note that the exit statement can be

                    -- placed   anywhere   within   a   loop

                    -- statement.

                    L:= 2 * I + L ;

                    end loop CC;
```

```
        when others  =>

            L := 0 ;

            DD: loop

                L := L + I + J ;

                exit DD when L > 144 ;

                -- Note that it would not be vaild to

                -- have "exit BB when L > 144"

                -- because the loop named DD is not

                -- within the loop BB.

                -- Here we  have  an exit statement  within a

                --  basic (endless) loop statement.

                end loop;

        end case;

        L := L * L ;

        exit when L > 8000 ;

        end loop AA;

K := L / 100 ;
```

BLOCK STATEMENTS

The final compound statement we will introduce in this section is **the block statement.** Its complete form is

```
block_identifier:

declare

-- Some declarations are made here.

begin

-- Some statements are supplied here.

end block_identifier;
```

Both the block_identifier and the declarative part are optional.

EXAMPLE   A block without an identifier is

```
declare

    I:  INTEGER ;

begin

    I := J ; J   := K ; K := I ;

end ;
```

A block without a declarative part is

```
begin

    I := 100 ;

end ;
```

A block with an identifier and a declarative part is

```
EXTRA:

declare

    I: INTEGER := 100 ;

begin

    if I > J then J := J + I ; end if ;

end EXTRA;
```

The objects declared in a given block (like I in the block identified by EXTRA) are *local* to the block. That is, they are not known to the rest of the subprogram containing the block.

A block is executed sequentially. First, its declarative part is "elaborated" (this term is the preferred Ada term used in connection with the processing of declarations and is covered in more detail in Chapter 6). Then the statements of the block are executed. The needed storage for block statements is allocated when the declarations are elaborated, and this allocation occurs every time (perhaps several times) the block is executed.

One of the natural uses of block statements is in connection with handling of exceptions, as will be discussed in Chapter 11.

PROGRAM USING CASE AND EXIT STATEMENTS

We conclude this section with an example of a program using case and exit statements. We will make use of a new subprogram of the TEXT_IO package, the procedure GET_LINE, which reads a line, places the line in a string type variable, and returns a count of the number of characters read. The string name and the integer counting the number of characters read are the two arguments that have to be supplied to the procedure GET_LINE.

The program reads lines, each line having names and telephone numbers. The names are listed first, separated by a comma from the telephone numbers. The telephone numbers have ten digits and/or letters in a variety of formats: They can be a sequence of ten digits (including area codes; for instance, 2125551212); or they can have imbedded dashes (like 212-555-1212); or they can have some letters instead of some of the digits (like 212jkl1A1B, which is 2125551212).

The names can be listed in two possible ways. In one way the first name is followed by at least a space, and (optionally) by the middle initial and a period, and at least a space, and, finally, the last name. The second format starts with the last name, followed by a comma and (optionally) a middle initial and a period, another space, and the first name. First names, last names, and middle initials are made up of letters, either uppercase or lowercase. Apostrophes and dashes may be embedded in the names (for instance, Robbe-Grillet or O'Hara).

Here are some sample input lines:

```
John S. Burundi,213-9AB-COOL
Christensen, Paul, 3129129292
Kandisky, F. Richard, 914-abcabcd
```

The last line of the input contains the characters "XX".

The output should list valid names and phone numbers as follows: first names and last names in uppercase letters and phone numbers using digits only and two imbedded dashes. Each of these items should be separated by a space. If either the names or the phone numbers are not valid (too few digits or special characters as part of the names, for instance), the input line should be displayed without changes together with a message like "invalid name or phone number."

Here are some sample output lines using the names given previously:

```
JOHN BURUNDI 213-922-2665
RICHARD KANDISKY 914-222-2223
```

Remember that letters are associated with digits, starting with the digit 2, which corresponds to ABC, and ending with the digit 9, which corresponds to WXY.

NAME_PHONE Program

```
with TEXT_IO; use TEXT_IO;

procedure NAME_PHONE is

    LINE_LN : NATURAL ;

        -- Remember that NATURAL is a predefined

        -- subtype of INTEGER base type. It takes values from

        -- 0 to INTEGER'LAST.

    F_NAME_LN, L_NAME_LN, PHONE_LN: NATURAL ;

        -- These variables represent the number of characters

        -- in the first name, middle initial, last name,

        -- and phone number.

    INP_LINE: STRING ( 1 .. LINE_LN );

        -- Remembere that LINE_LN :=0 ; makes INP_LINE

        -- an array with a NULL range.

    WRK_LINE: STRING ( 1 .. LINE_LN );

        -- This string is used for making changes in the

        -- original line.

    F_NAME: STRING ( 1 .. F_NAME_LN ) ;

        -- The first name will be moved here if it is valid.

    L_NAME : STRING ( 1 .. L_NAME_LN ) ;

        -- The last names will be placed here.

    PHONE_NO: STRING ( 1 .. PHONE_LN ) ;

        -- The phone numbers will be placed here.
```

```
NO_COMMAS: INTEGER;

        -- This variable holds the number commas which are
        -- found per line.

BAD_DATA : BOOLEAN;

        -- This variable has the value true if invalid data is
        -- supplied for a particular line.

STRT_POS, END_POS: NATURAL;

        -- These variables hold the starting and ending
        -- position of names or phone numbers.

DIGIT_CT, CURR_DIG: INTEGER ;

        -- These variables are counting.
        -- All procedures below refer to WRK_LINE.

procedure LOW_TO_UPPER_N_CT_COMMAS is

begin

        -- Now make every lowercase letter an uppercase letter and
        -- count how many commas there are. One comma means
        -- that the first name is first; two commas mean that the
        -- last name is first, anything else is a mistake.
        NO_COMMAS := 0;
        For I in 1 .. LINE_LN
            loop
            case WRK_LINE (I) is
                when 'a' .. 'z' => WRK_LINE (I) := CHARACTER'VAL (
                    CHARACTER'POS('A') - CHARACTER'POS('a')  +
                    CHARACTER'POS( WRK_LINE (I))     ) ;
                    -- The conversion of a letter from lower
```

```
                        -- case to uppercase is done here. The

                        -- difference between the relative position

                        -- of 'A' and 'a' is the difference between

                        -- any other lowercase letter and the

                        -- corresponding uppercase letter. Remember

                        -- that strings are arrays of the predefined

                        -- enumeration type CHARACTER .

            when ','        => NO_COMMAS := NO_COMMAS + 1 ;

            when others     => NULL;

            end case ;

        end loop;

end LOW_TO_UPPER_N_CT_COMMAS;

procedure IGNORE_LEADING_SPACES is

        -- This procedure sets the value of STRT_POS to the

        -- position of the first nonspace character.

begin

        for I in 1 .. LINE_LN

            loop

            STRT_POS := I;

            exit when WRK_LINE (I) /= ' ';

        end loop;

end IGNORE_LEADING_SPACES ;

procedure  FIND_NEXT_SP_OR_COMMA is

        -- This procedure sets END_POS to the position of the last

        -- non space or non comma character after  STRT_POS.

begin
```

```
      END_POS := STRT_POS;

      for I in STRT_POS .. LINE_LN

            loop

            exit when WRK_LINE (I) = ' ' or WRK_LINE (I) = ',' ;

            END_POS := I;

      end loop;

end   FIND_NEXT_SP_OR_COMMA ;

procedure PLACE_SPACES is

      -- This procedure changes  the characters between STRT_POS

      -- and END_POS into spaces and chnages the first

      -- encountered comma, if any, into a space.

      -- It stops with the first encountered non space

      -- character after END_POS.

begin

      for I in STRT_POS .. END_POS

            loop

            WRK_LINE (I) := ' ' ;

      end loop;

      for I in END_POS + 1 .. LINE_LN

            loop

            if WRK_LINE (I) = ','

                  then

                  WRK_LINE (I) := ' ' ;

                  exit;

                  end if;

            exit when WRK_LINE (I) /= ' ';
```

```
        end loop;

    end PLACE_SPACES;

    procedure IS_CORRECT_NAME is

        -- This procedure makes sure that, a dash or an

        -- apostrophe in a name is embedded. If it is not,

        -- BAD_DATA is set to TRUE.

    begin

        for I in STRT_POS .. END_POS

            loop

            case WRK_LINE (I) is

                when 'A'.. 'Z'    => NULL;

                when  '-' | '''   => if I = STRT_POS or I = END_POS

                            -- Dashes and apostrophes are allowed,

                            -- but embedded only.

                                        then

                                        BAD_DATA := TRUE;

                                        exit;

                                        -- This line is an

                                        -- unconditional exit.

                                        end if;

                when others      => BAD_DATA := TRUE;

                                        exit;

            end case;

            end loop;

    end IS_CORRECT_NAME;

    procedure  XTR_N_VAL_FIRST_NAME is
```

```
     -- This procedure validates the first name and extracts it
     -- into F_NAME. BAD_DATA is set to TRUE if there is any
     -- invalid character in the first name.
begin
     IGNORE_LEADING_SPACES;
     FIND_NEXT_SP_OR_COMMA;
     IS_CORRECT_NAME;
     L_NAME_LN := END_POS - STRT_POS + 1;
     L_NAME := WRK_LINE ( STRT_POS .. END_POS ) ;
     -- Here we use a slice assignment above.
     PLACE_SPACES;
end XTR_N_VAL_FIRST_NAME;
procedure   XTR_N_VAL_MDL_INIT is
     -- This procedure looks for a middle initial followed
     -- by a period and a space or a comma. If it is found, it
     -- will replace them by spaces; otherwise, nothing will
     -- be changed in WRK_LINE.
begin
     IGNORE_LEADING_SPACES;
     if WRK_LINE (STRT_POS) in 'A' .. 'Z' and
        WRK_LINE (STRT_POS + 1 ) = '.'     and
        ( WRK_LINE ( STRT_POS + 2 ) = ' ' or
          WRK_LINE ( STRT_POS + 2 ) = ',' )
              then
              FIND_NEXT_SP_OR_COMMA;
              PLACE_SPACES;
```

```
          end if;

end   XTR_N_VAL_MDL_INIT ;

procedure XTR_N_VAL_LAST_NAME is

     -- This procedure does a job similar to the job of

     -- XTR_NVAL_FIRST_NAME, except that it applies to last names.

begin

     IGNORE_LEADING_SPACES;

     FIND_NEXT_SP_OR_COMMA;

     IS_CORRECT_NAME;

     F_NAME_LN := END_POS - STRT_POS + 1;

     F_NAME := WRK_LINE ( STRT_POS .. END_POS ) ;

     -- Here we use a slice assignment above.

     PLACE_SPACES;

end XTR_N_VAL_LAST_NAME;

procedure XTR_N_VAL_PHONE is

     -- This procedure checks phone numbers. If the phone number

     -- is correct, it is converted into an all-digit format

     -- and placed in PHONE_NO.

begin

     IGNORE_LEADING_SPACES;

     FIND_NEXT_SP_OR_COMMA;

     DIGIT_CT :=  0 ;

     for I in STRT_POS .. END_POS

         loop

         case WRK_LINE (I) is

             when '0'.. '9'  => DIGIT_CT := DIGIT_CT + 1 ;
```

```
when   '-'        => if I = STRT_POS or I = END_POS
-- Dashes are allowed, but imbedded only.

                        then

                        BAD_DATA := TRUE;

                        exit;

                        -- This is an

                        -- unconditional exit.

                        end if;

when 'A' .. 'C'  => WRK_LINE (I) := '2' ;

when 'D' .. 'F'  => WRK_LINE (I) := '3' ;

when 'G' .. 'I'  => WRK_LINE (I) := '4' ;

when 'J' .. 'L'  => WRK_LINE (I) := '5' ;

when 'M' .. 'O'  => WRK_LINE (I) := '6' ;

when 'P' ! 'R' ! 'S'  => WRK_LINE (I) := '7' ;

when 'T' .. 'V'  => WRK_LINE (I) := '8' ;

when 'W' .. 'Y'  => WRK_LINE (I) := '9' ;

when others      => BAD_DATA := TRUE;

                        exit;

end case;

if not BAD_DATA

    then

            DIGIT_CT := DIGIT_CT + 1;

        end if;

    end loop;

if DIGIT_CT /= 10

    then
```

```
                BAD_DATA := TRUE;

        end if;

        if not BAD_DATA

                then

                PHONE_LN := 12;

                CURR_DIG  := 3 ;

                for I in STRT_POS .. END_POS

                    loop

                    if WRK_LINE (I) in '0' .. '9'

                        then

                        PHONE_NO ( CURR_DIG ) := WRK_LINE (I) ;

                        CURR_DIG := CURR_DIG + 1 ;

                    end if;

                end loop;

                PHONE_NO ( 1 .. 3 ) := PHONE_NO ( 3 .. 5);

                -- Here are more slice assignments.

                PHONE_NO ( 4) := '-' ;

                PHONE_NO ( 5 .. 7 ) := PHONE_NO ( 6 .. 8 );

                PHONE_NO ( 8) := '-' ;

        end if;

        PLACE_SPACES;

end XTR_N_VAL_PHONE;

procedure DISP_ERROR is

        -- This procedure displays an error

        -- message and the error line.

    begin
```

```
     PUT(" This line is invalid: ");

     PUT( INP_LINE );

     NEW_LINE;

end DISP_ERROR;

begin

     GET_LINE ( INP_LINE, LINE_LN ) ;

          -- Now we read a line with names and a phone number.

          -- A basic loop follows.

     while INP_LINE /= "XX"

     loop

     WRK_LINE := INP_LINE;

     LOW_TO_UPPER_N_CT_COMMAS;

     BAD_DATA := FALSE;

     case NO_COMMAS is

          when 1      =>
          -- This choice is taken if the first name is
          -- followed by the last name.

                    XTR_N_VAL_LAST_NAME;

                    XTR_N_VAL_FIRST_NAME;

                    XTR_N_VAL_MDL_INIT;

                    XTR_N_VAL_PHONE;

          when 2      =>
          -- This choice is taken when the last name is
          -- followed by a comma and then the first name.

                    XTR_N_VAL_FIRST_NAME;

                    XTR_N_VAL_MDL_INIT;
```

```
                         XTR_N_VAL_LAST_NAME;

                         XTR_N_VAL_PHONE;

            when others => BAD_DATA := TRUE;

            end case;

     if BAD_DATA then

            DISP_ERROR;

            else

            PUT ( F_NAME ); PUT ( ' ');

            PUT ( L_NAME ); PUT ( ' ');

            PUT ( PHONE_NO ) ;

            NEW_LINE;

     end if ;

     GET_LINE ( INP_LINE, LINE_LN ) ;

     end loop;

  end NAME_PHONE;
```

4.2   NAMES, VALUES, AND EXPRESSIONS

This section introduces new aspects of concepts heavily used in previous chapters: names, values, and expressions.

NAMES

Ada **names** were used in previous chapters as identifiers, such as *variables, constants, types, subtypes,* and *subprograms.* New kinds of identifiers were introduced in this chapter: *labels, block names,* and *loop names.* To complete the listing of possible Ada identifiers, we mention *tasks* and their entries and exceptions (these terms will be discussed in Chapters 10 and 11).

Besides identifiers, Ada has some other kinds of names, like *attributes, selected components, slices, indexed components* (the last three were introduced in Chapter 2), *character literals,* and *operator symbols.* Here we will briefly describe additional features of selected and indexed components.

The **indexed components** were used in Chapter 2 to denote an array component; as we will see in Chapter 10, they can also be used to denote an entry in a family of entries. The general form for an indexed-component name is

```
name_or_function_call ( one_or_more_expressions )
```

The one_or_more_expressions are separated by commas, and each expression will be evaluated to a specific value for the component. The use of function calls in indexed components will be presented in the next chapter.

We mention here that components of multidimensional arrays and components of arrays of arrays are different and have distinct notations. For instance, if we have the declarations

```
type X is array ( 1 .. 10, 1 .. 10 ) of INTEGER ;

type Y is array ( 1 .. 10) of INTEGER;

type YY is array ( 1 .. 10 ) of Y;

A: X ;

B: YY;
```

then A is a two-dimensional array. To refer to a component, one supplies two index values (or more general expressions) like A (2, 5). Array B, however, is an array of arrays, and B (2)(5) denotes the fifth component of the array B (2).

Turning our attention now to **selected-component** names, we give their general form:

```
name_or_function_call.selector ;
```

The selector can be an identifier, a character literal, an operator symbol (as will be shown in Chapter 5), or the reserved word "all."

We used selected components to denote record components (in Chapter 2) or objects designated by access values (in Chapter 3). To complete the listing of possible selected components, we should mention entities declared in the visible part of a package (as will be discussed in Chapter 7), entries of a task (Chapter 10), or entities declared in an enclosing subprogram body, package body, task body, block, or loop.

EXAMPLE　The following program lines show the use of selected components in an enclosing block:

```
AA: declare

    I: INTEGER ;

    begin
```

```
        I := 10;

    BB: declare

        I, J: INTEGER;

    begin

            J := AA.I ; BB.I := J ** 2 ;

            AA.I := J mod 5 + BB.I / 5 ;

    end BB;

end AA;
```

Here AA.I and BB.I are two selected-component names; the name part is the block identifier (AA or BB), and the selector part is the identifier I (variable name). The notation AA.I and BB.I within the block BB was necessary in order to specify which variable I we intended to use: the one declared in AA or the one declared in BB. There are some visibility rules that apply in this case, and they will be explained in Chapters 6 and 7.

VALUES

We turn now to Ada values. Recall that a type in Ada can be described as a collection of values and operations on these values. Ada **values** are represented by values of types that have no components (for instance, we encountered enumeration, integer, and real types) or values of types that have components (such as record types and array types).

Enumeration, integer and real types are called scalar types, and, as one may guess, their values are called **scalar values**. The values of composite types (that is, types whose values have components) are called **composite values** or **aggregates**. They were first introduced in Chapter 2 in connection with array and record types, and the variety of aggregate we used there is called a **positional aggregate**.

We used literals for naming scalar values: numeric literals and enumeration literals (character literals are among these). Literals were used as well to describe composite values (character strings, for instance) or to denote access values ("null"). Numeric literals are of type universal_integer or universal_real. Numeric literals have an important feature: Their type has values of arbitrary precision, and they should be the preferred way of introducing constants (as opposed to defining numeric constants of a particular—and nonuniversal—type).

We introduce now a new kind of aggregate for composite values: the **named-component aggregate**. In a named-component aggregate each component value is preceded by the name or the index value of the component and the compound symbol "=>". The advantage of this notation is that one can supply the values of the components in any order.

EXAMPLE Suppose we have the following declarations:

```
type WEIGHT_CLASS  is array ( 1 .. 5 ) of FLOAT;

type EMPL_REC is

    record

            F_NAME: STRING (1 .. 10 );

            SOS_ID: STRING (1 .. 9) ;

            SALARY: FLOAT ;

    end record ;

CURR_EMPL: EMPL_REC;

WEIGHT_TABLE: WEIGHT_CLASS ;
```

Then we can define aggregates in a variety of ways:

```
( "NICHOL      ","123456789",550.25)
```

This aggregate is a positional one.

```
( F_NAME => "NICHOL     ",

  SOS_ID => "123456789" ,

  SALARY => 550.25 )
```

This aggregate is a named-component aggregate.

```
( SALARY => 550.25, F_NAME => "NICHOL     " ,

SOS_ID   => "123456789" )
```

Here the named components are in arbitrary order, and

```
CURR_EMPL :=

( SALARY => 550.25, F_NAME => "NICHOL     " ,

SOS_ID   => "123456789" );
```

is a valid assignment.

Also, regarding the variable WEIGHT_TABLE, we can have the following equivalent aggregates:

(1.0, 3.0, 5.0, 8.0, 13.0)

which is a positional aggregate. Or

```
( 1 => 1.0, 2 => 3.0, 3 => 5.0, 4 => 8.0, 5 => 13.0 )

( 3 => 5.0 ,

    1 => 1.0, 2 => 3.0, 4 => 8.0, 5 => 13.0 )
```

These two aggregates are named-component aggregates.

One can also use a range to define an aggregate, such as

```
( 1 .. 5 => 3.5 )
```

which is equivalent to

```
( 3.5, 3.5, 3.5, 3.5, 3.5 )
```

Furthermore, it is valid to use the reserved word "others" for the last choice, referring to the values of the components not mentioned in the other choices. For instance, we can use

```
( 2 .. 4 => 0.5, others => 1.0 )
```

which is equivalent to

```
( 1.0, 0.5, 0.5, 0.5, 1.0 )
```

The choice "others" has to be the last listed choice in the aggregate.

One can assign the same value to several components by using the symbol "¦" to separate the component names receiving the common value. For instance,

```
( 1 ¦ 3 ¦ 5 => 3.0, others => 5.0 )
```

is a valid named-component aggregate, and it is equivalent to

```
( 3.0, 5.0, 3.0, 5.0, 3.0 )
```

Ada allows the use of an **ambiguous aggregate**, that is, an aggregate that can be a value for two distinct types. For instance, if we have, in addition to the type WEIGHT_CLASS, a type DIST_CLASS, declared as

```
type DIST_CLASS is array ( 0 .. 7 ) of FLOAT;
```

and we have the aggregate

```
( 1 => 13.0, 3 ¦ 5 => 8.0, others => 0.0 )
```

then this aggregate can be a value of the type DIST_CLASS or of the type WEIGHT_CLASS. The ambiguity is removed if we qualify the aggregate (or any expression for that matter) with the type name. That is, we write

```
DIST_CLASS '( 1 => 13.0, 3 : 5 =>
   8.0, others => 0.0 )
```

if we refer to a value of the type DIST_CLASS. And we write

```
WEIGHT_CLASS' ( 1 => 13.0, 3 : 5 => 8.0,
   others => 0.0 )
```

if we refer to a value of the type WEIGHT_CLASS.

The format for qualifying a value is similar to the use of attributes: The type (or subtype) name is followed by an apostrophe (when aggregates are involved) and the value itself. Section 6.1 gives more details regarding the handling of ambiguous values and qualifiers.

EXPRESSIONS

Now we turn our attention to Ada expressions. As we mentioned in Chapter 1, the most basic kind of expression is called a **primary.** An aggregate is a primary, as are qualified values like the examples above. Other Ada primaries we have encountered are numeric literals, character strings, null, names, and allocators. The list of possible primaries is completed if we add function calls (more details about function calls will be given in the next chapter), type conversions, and finally, any expression within parentheses. These primaries can be used as building blocks for more complex expressions.

For the definitions and examples that follow, we assume that all variables are of INTEGER type.

A **factor** is any primary, a primary raised to a power (like I ** J), the absolute value of a primary (abs I), or a primary preceded by the reserved word "not" (not 0).

A **term** is any factor or a factor followed by one of the operators *, /, mod, or rem, followed by another factor (I * J, for instance).

A **simple expression** is any term optionally preceded by a sign (+ or −) or any term followed by one of the operators +, −, or &, and followed by another term (I + J, for instance).

A **relation** is any simple expression; a simple expression followed by one of the relational operators =, /=, <, <=, >, >=, then followed by another expression (for instance, I <= J); or a simple expression followed by the reserved words "in" or "not in," followed by a range, a type, or a subtype (for instance, I in 1 . . 7).

Finally, an **expression** is any relation; or any relation followed by one of the logical operators "or," "and," or "xor," and followed by another relation (for instance, I < J and J > K); or any relation followed by the reserved words "and then," followed by a relation (for instance I < J and then I = 0); or any relation followed by the reserved words "or else," followed by another relation (for instance, I = J or else J = 3). The operator "and then" is called a *short-circuit conjunction,* and the operator "or else" is called a *short-circuit* (inclusive) *disjunction.* Later we will explain both of these operators in detail.

EXAMPLE   Here are some examples to help clarify the hierarchical setting of the concepts primary, factor, term, simple expression, relation, and expression.

A primary is

```
( I ** J * K + L > M or N = P )
```

An expression (but not a relation) is

```
I ** J * K + L > M or N = P
```

A relation (but not a simple expression) is

```
I ** J * K + L > M
```

A simple expression (but not a term) is

```
I ** J * K + L
```

A term (but not a factor) is

```
I ** J * K
```

A factor (but not a primary) is

```
I ** J
```

Figure 4.1 illustrates this hierarchy.

The logical operator "xor" (exclusive or) has not been used before. The values returned by expressions using this logical operator are as follows: If I and J are two BOOLEAN variables, then

```
I xor J
```

is an expression that is FALSE whenever both I and J have the same value; the expression is TRUE otherwise.

We mentioned earlier the **short-circuit control** forms of the logical operators "and" and "or," which are "and then" and "or else." These short-circuit control forms require the compiler to evaluate the left-hand side first. The right-hand side is next evaluated only if the value of the left-hand side does not determine the value of the whole expression.

FIGURE 4.1   Hierarchy of Expressions

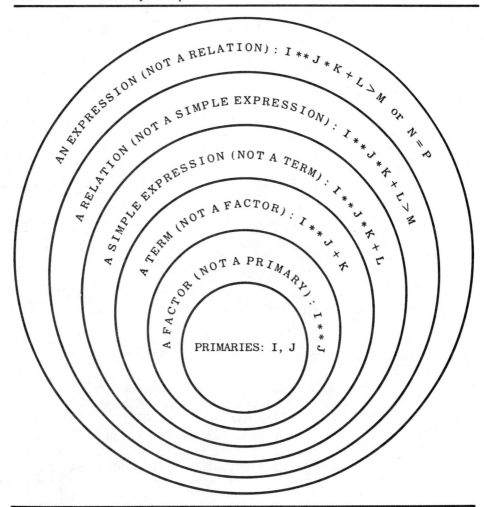

EXAMPLE   The following procedure illustrates the usefulness of the short-circuit control forms. We have rewritten the procedure FIND_NEXT_SP_OR_COMMA part of the program PHONE_NAME by using the short-circuit form "and then."

```
procedure  FIND_NEXT_SP_OR_COMMA is

I: INTEGER ;

begin

    END_POS := STRT_POS;
```

```
I := STRT_POS;

while I <= LINE_LN and then WRK_LINE (I) /= ' ' and then

        WRK_LINE (I) /= ','

    loop

    I := I + 1;

end loop;

END_POS := I - I / ( LINE_LN + 1 ) ;

-- The part I / ( LINE_LN + 1 ) is used in order to

-- subtract 1 from I in case I ends up equal to

-- LINE_LN + 1.

end   FIND_NEXT_SP_OR_COMMA ;
```

The expression

```
I <= LINE_LN and then WRK_LINE (I) /= ' ' and
then WRK_LINE (I) /= ','
```

is evaluated as follows: First, the relation I <= LINE_LN is evaluated. Only if it is TRUE will the expression WRK_LINE (I) /= ' ' be evaluated. And if it is TRUE, then the last relation WRKLINE (I) /= ',' will be evaluated.

Note that if we replace the short-circuit form "and then" by the logical operator "and," we can have an index value out of range. If I becomes LINE_LN + 1, then there is no component WRK_LINE (LINE_LN + 1).

Apart from the short-circuit form, there is no particular order assumed when two operands of an operator are to be evaluated. Remember that "and" has a higher priority than "or" when both are present in the same expression. The priority of "and then" is the priority of the operator "and." The operators "or else" and "xor" have the same priority as "or."

A final remark: The logical operators can be applied to one-dimensional arrays whose components are of type BOOLEAN. The operations are applied individually to each component. For instance, suppose we have the following declarations:

```
type SWITCHES is array ( 1 .. 7 ) of BOOLEAN;
CURR_STATUS, PREV_STATUS: SWITCHES ;
```

Then we can have the following statements:

```
PREV_STATUS := ( 1 , , 4 ! 7 => TRUE,
   others => FALSE );CURR_STATUS := PREV_STATUS
   xor PREV_STATUS ;
```

These statements are equivalent to

```
CURR_STATUS := ( 1 , , 7 => FALSE );
CURR_STATUS := ( 4 , , 7 => TRUE, others =>
   FALSE );
```

We can also have

```
CURR_STATUS := CURR_STATUS or PREV_STATUS;
```

This statement is equivalent to

```
CURR_STATUS := ( 1 , , 7 => TRUE );
```

Figure 4.2 summarizes the Ada operators, the types to which they apply, and the type of the result.

4.3   RECORDS WITH VARIANTS

Variant records are special kinds of records with discriminants. They offer the programmer the possibility of specifying an alternative list of components to be included in the record object. The variant part of the record, if it is present, is placed immediately before the reserved words "end record," and it has the form

```
case discriminant_name is

    when one_or_more_choices => component_list

        -- several variants like the line above can be present

end case;
```

If there are several choices following the reserved word "when," they are separated by a vertical bar "!".

The choices can be a (static) simple_expression, a discrete range, the reserved word "others," or a component_simple_name (that is, a component introduced as an identifier only, with no indexed components, for instance). The reserved word "others" can only appear as the choice for the last alternative. Because record variables can be components of other records (nested records),

FIGURE 4.2   Ada Operators

OPERATOR	OPERATION	OPERAND TYPE		RESULT TYPE
		LEFT OPERATOR	RIGHT OPERATOR	
Unary				
+	Identity	Numeric		Same numeric type
−	Negation	Numeric		Same numeric type
abs	Absolute value	Numeric		Same numeric type
not	Logical negation	Boolean		Same Boolean type
		Boolean array		Same Boolean array
Binary				
+	Addition	Numeric	Same numeric type	Same numeric type
−	Subtraction	Numeric	Same numeric type	Same numeric type
&	Catenation	One-dimensional array type	Same one-dimensional array type	Same one-dimensional array type
		One-dimensional array type	Same array element type	Same one-dimensional array type
		Array element type	Same one-dimensional array type	Same one-dimensional array type
		Element type	Element type	Any array type
mod	Modulus	Integer	Integer	Integer
rem	Remainder	Integer	Integer	Integer
*	Multiplication	Integer	Integer	Integer
		Float	Float	Float
		Fixed	Integer	Same fixed type
		Integer	Fixed	Same fixed type
		Fixed	Fixed	Universal fixed
/	Division	Integer	Integer	Integer
		Float	Float	Float
		Fixed	Integer	Same fixed type
		Fixed	Fixed	Universal fixed
**	Exponentiation	Integer	Natural	Same numeric type
		Float	Integer	Same float type
=	Equality	Scalar	Same	Same
		Composite	Same	Same
		Access	Same	Same

FIGURE 4.2 (Continued)

| OPERATOR | OPERATION | OPERAND TYPE | | RESULT TYPE |
		LEFT OPERATOR	RIGHT OPERATOR	
/=	Inequality	Scalar	Same	Same
		Composite	Same	Same
		Access	Same	Same
< ,< =	Less than, less than or equal	Scalar	Same	Same
> , > =	Greater than, greater than or equal	Discrete array type	Same	Same
in, not in	Membership test	Value of right operand type	Range, type, or subtype	Boolean
and	Conjunction	Boolean	Boolean	Boolean
		Boolean array	Same	Same
or	Inclusive disjunction	Boolean	Boolean	Boolean
		Boolean array	Same	Same
xor	Exclusive disjunction	Boolean	Boolean	Boolean
		Boolean array	Same	Same
and then	Short-circuit and	Boolean	Boolean	Boolean
or else	Short-circuit or	Boolean	Boolean	Boolean

one can have nested variant parts. The choices should cover all possible values of the discriminant_name, and no two choices are allowed to have a common value.

The component_list is any list of record components (that is, a sequence of declarations of record components). A "null" component should be present if the component list is empty.

EXAMPLE   The following program lines show declarations of a record type with a variant part.

```
type LABOR is ( SALARIED, HOURLY, SUBCONTRACTOR );

type EMPLOYEE ( LAB_KIND: LABOR := SALARIED ) is

    -- Remember (see Chapter 2) that LAB_KIND: LABOR
```

```
     -- is the discriminant part. This discriminant part has
     -- no default initial value. The discriminant name is
     -- LAB_KIND.
record
     F_NAME: STRING ( 1 .. 10 );
     L_NAME: STRING ( 1 .. 15 );
     SOS_ID: STRING ( 1 .. 9 ) ;
     case LAB_KIND is
          when SALARIED => YEARLY_SAL: FLOAT;
                           Y_T_DATE_TOTAL: FLOAT;

          when HOURLY    => HOURLY_PAY: FLOAT ;
                           HOURS_WORKED: FLOAT ;
                           OVERTIME_HRS: FLOAT ;
          when SUBCONTRACTOR => DAILY_FEE: FLOAT;
                           Y_T_DATE_DAYS :NATURAL;
     end case;
end record;
```

Now we give declarations of variables of type EMPLOYEE.

```
SAL_EMPLOYEE: EMPLOYEE ( SALARIED );
CURR_EMPLOYEE: EMPLOYEE ;
     -- This declaration  is valid because a
     -- discriminant constraint has been supplied by
     -- the default initial value.
CLERICAL_EMPL: EMPLOYEE ( HOURLY );
```

Here are two examples of the assignment of an aggregate of type EMPLOYEE:

```
CURR_EMPLOYEE := ( LAB_KIND => SALARIED, F_NAME =>

    "ROBERT    ", L_NAME => "MUNHAUSEN        " ,

    SOS_ID => "555554444", YEARLY_SAL => 25_000.00 ,

    Y_T_DATE_TOTAL => 13_000.00 ) ;
```

Changing the discriminant of a record object is valid if all the other components are given new values. For instance, we can have

```
CURR_EMPLOYEE := ( LAB_KIND      => HOURLY,

                   F_NAME        => "HARDY12345",

                   L_NAME        => "LAURENTINI54321",

                   SOS_ID        => "123456789" ,

                   HOURLY_PAY    => 9.75 ,

                   HOURS_WORKED  => 45.5 ,

                   OVERTIME_AMT  => 4.0              ) ;
```

The following program illustrates the use of records with discriminants and, in particular, of records with a variant part. The program reads information about student grades at the end of a semester. The valid grades are A, A−, B+, B, B−, C+, C, C−, D+, D, F, NC (means no credit), W (withdrawal), I (incomplete), and P (pass).

For each degree student the program should display the student's cumulative grade point average according to the following grade point values: A is 4.0, A− is 3.7, B+ is 3.3, . . . , D is 1.0, and F is 0. The following rules apply: A grade of C− or better is required for a course taken in a student's major area; otherwise, the course has to be repeated, and a message should be printed to signal this situation. For major or minor subjects a grade of P is not allowed. There are no restrictions regarding the grades of a nondegree student, and no grades are supplied for an auditing student. A degree student is placed on probation if his or her grade point average is below 1.5. For a nondegree student the grade point should be printed, and for an auditing student the total number of credit hours audited should be printed as well. Upper-level courses (course numbers above 100) cannot be taken by auditing students.

The information for each student is supplied in two steps. The first step supplies the following data: the number of courses taken by the student (columns 1–2) followed by the type of student: degree, nondegree, or auditor (in columns 3–15). This information is followed by the student ID (columns 16–24) and the student name (columns 25–39). If the student is a degree student, then columns 40–43 give the major ID and columns 44–47 give the minor ID.

In the second step the information related to courses is supplied. Course IDs, course numbers, and credit hours carried by each course are listed for auditors. Course IDs, course numbers, credit hours, and grades are listed for degree and nondegree students. This information requires 10 columns per course for auditors and 12 columns per course for degree and nondegree students.

The end of the input stream is signaled by a student taking 99 courses.

GR_POINT_AVE Program

```
with TEXT_IO; use TEXT_IO;

procedure GR_POINT_AVE is

type COURSE_INFO is

    record

        CR_ID    : STRING ( 1 .. 4 );

        -- An example is "ENGL".

        CR_NO    : STRING ( 1 .. 4 );

        -- An example is "117 ".

        CR_CRDT  : NATURAL ;

        -- An example is 3.

    end record;

type COURSE_LIST is array ( NATURAL range <> ) of    COURSE_INFO;

type COURSE_N_GRADE_INFO is

    record

        DESCR   : COURSE_INFO;

        CR_GRADE : STRING ( 1 .. 2 );

        -- An example is "A-".
```

```
        end record;
type TRANSCRIPT is array ( NATURAL range <> )
                        of   COURSE_N_GRADE_INFO;
type STUD_KIND is ( DEGREE, NON_DEGREE, AUDITOR );
package ST_TYPE_IO is new ENUMERATION_IO ( STUD_KIND );
use ST_TYPE_IO;
package INT_IO is new INTEGER_IO ( INTEGER );
use INT_IO;
type STUDENT ( ST_TYPE :STUD_KIND := DEGREE ;
                NO_COURSES: NATURAL ) is

    record
         ST_ID   : STRING ( 1.. 9 )  ;
         ST_NAME : STRING ( 1 .. 15 ) ;
         case ST_TYPE is
              when DEGREE  =>
                   ST_MAJOR: STRING ( 1 .. 4 ) ;
                   ST_MINOR: STRING ( 1 .. 4 ) ;
                   ST_COURSES: TRANSCRIPT ( 1 .. NO_COURSES ) ;
              when NON_DEGREE =>
                   ST_COURSES: TRANSCRIPT ( 1 .. NO_COURSES ) ;
              when AUDITOR =>
                   CRS_AUDITED: COURSE_LIST ( 1 .. NO_COURSES) ;
         end case;
    end record;
CURR_STUD: STUDENT;
CURR_COURSE_INFO: COURSE_INFO := ( "      "," "      " ,0 );
```

```
CURR_NO_COURSES: NATURAL ;

CURR_COURSE_N_GRADE: COURSE_N_GRADE_INFO := ( ( "     "," ",
              0 ) ," ");

CURR_ST_TYPE   : STUD_KIND ;

GRADE_POINT, GRADE_POINT_AVE : FLOAT;

package FLOAT_IO is new FLOAT_IO ( FLOAT );

use FLOAT_IO;

VALID_GRADE, AVE_FLAG: BOOLEAN;

NO_IN_GRADE_POINT, NO_CREDITS: NATURAL;

SEC_CHAR: CHARACTER ;

-- This variable holds the second character of

-- a  grade (a + or  - or C).

procedure CHECK_GRADE is

begin

    -- This procedure checks whether the grade of the course is

    -- valid. If it is a grade that can be used for the grade point

    -- average, then the grade point value will be placed in

    -- GRADE_POINT and the AVE_FLAG is set to TRUE.

    VALID_GRADE := TRUE ;

    SEC_CHAR :=  CURR_STUD.ST_COURSES(I).CR_GRADE(2);

    AVE_FLAG := TRUE ;

    case CURR_STUD.ST_COURSES(I).CR_GRADE(1) is

        when "A"  => case SEC_CHAR is

                        when ' ' => GRADE_POINT := 4.0 ;

                        when '-' => GRADE_POINT := 3.7 ;

                        when others => VALID_GRADE := FALSE;
```

```
                   end case ;
  when "B"  => case SEC_CHAR is

                 when '+' => GRADE_POINT := 3.3 ;

                 when ' ' => GRADE_POINT := 3.0 ;

                 when '-' => GRADE_POINT := 2.7 ;

                 when others => VALID_GRADE := FALSE;

               end case ;

  when "C"  => case SEC_CHAR is

                 when '+' => GRADE_POINT := 2.3 ;

                 when ' ' => GRADE_POINT := 2.0 ;

                 when '-' => GRADE_POINT := 1.7 ;

                 when others => VALID_GRADE := FALSE;

               end case ;

  when "D"  => case SEC_CHAR is

                 when '+' => GRADE_POINT := 1.3 ;

                 when ' ' => GRADE_POINT := 1.0 ;

                 when others => VALID_GRADE := FALSE;
               end case ;

   when "F"  => case SEC_CHAR is

                  when ' ' => GRADE_POINT := 0.0 ;

                  when others => VALID_GRADE := FALSE;

                end case ;

   when "N"  => case SEC_CHAR is

                  when 'C' => AVE_FLAG := FALSE ;

                  when others => VALID_GRADE := FALSE;

                end case ;
```

```
               when "W" : "I" : "P"  =>

                         case SEC_CHAR is

                             when ' ' => AVE_FLAG := FALSE ;

                             when others => VALID_GRADE := FALSE;

                         end case ;

          when others => VALID_GRADE := FALSE;

     end case ;

end CHECK_GRADE;

begin

     GET ( CURR_NO_COURSES, 2 );

     while CURR_NO_COURSES /= 99

          loop

          GET ( CURR_ST_TYPE, 13 ) ;

          -- Here we establish one of three possible variations

          -- for CURR_STUD. Now the values of the two

          -- discriminants are known, and the record

          -- CURR_STUD can be initialized.

          case CURR_ST_TYPE is

          when DEGREE => CURR_STUD :=

                    ( ST_TYPE    => CURR_ST_TYPE ,

                      NO_COURSE => CURR_NO_COURSES ,

                      ST_ID      => "123456789" ,

                      ST_NAME    => "123456789012345",

                      ST_MAJOR  => "XXXX" ,

                      ST_MINOR  => "YYYY" ,

                      ST_COURSES ( 1 ) ..
```

```
                              ST_COURSES ( CURR_NO_COURSES) =>

                                   CURR_COURSE_N_GRADE );


        when NON_DEGREE =>  CURR_STUD :=

                   ( ST_TYPE   => CURR_ST_TYPE ,

                     NO_COURSE => CURR_NO_COURSES ,

                     ST_ID     => "123456789" ,

                     ST_NAME   => "123456789012345",

                     ST_COURSES ( 1 ) ..

                         ST_COURSES ( CURR_NO_COURSES) =>

                              CURR_COURSE_N_GRADE );

        when AUDITOR =>  CURR_STUD :=

                   ( ST_TYPE   => CURR_ST_TYPE ,

                     NO_COURSE => CURR_NO_COURSES ,

                     ST_ID     => "123456789" ,

                     ST_NAME   => "123456789012345",

                     CRS_AUDITED ( 1 ) ..

                        CRS_AUDITED (CURR_NO_COURSES) =>

                             CURR_COURSE_INFO ) ;

end case;

GET(CURR_STUD.ST_ID);

GET(CURR_STUD.ST_NAME);

case CURR_ST_TYPE is

     when DEGREE =>

             GET(CURR_STUD.ST_MAJOR);

             GET(CURR_STUD.ST_MINOR);
```

```
                    SKIP_LINE;

                    for I in 1 .. CURR_NO_COURSES

                     loop

                     GET(CURR_STUD.ST_COURSES(I).DESC.CR_ID);

                     GET(CURR_STUD.ST_COURSES(I).DESC.CR_NO);

                     GET(CURR_STUD.ST_COURSES(I).DESC.CR_CRDT,2);

                     GET(CURR_STUD.ST_COURSES(I).CR_GRADE,2);

                    end loop;

            when NON_DEGREE =>

                    SKIP_LINE;

                    for I in 1 .. CURR_NO_COURSES

                     loop

                     GET(CURR_STUD.ST_COURSES(I).DESC.CR_ID);

                     GET(CURR_STUD.ST_COURSES(I).DESC.CR_NO);

                     GET(CURR_STUD.ST_COURSES(I).DESC.CR_CRDT,2);

                     GET(CURR_STUD.ST_COURSES(I).CR_GRADE,2);

                    end loop;

            when AUDITOR =>

                    SKIP_LINE;

                    for I in 1 .. CURR_NO_COURSES

                     loop

                     GET(CURR_STUD.CRS_AUDITED(I).CR_ID);

                     GET(CURR_STUD.CRS_AUDITED(I).CR_NO);

                     GET(CURR_STUD.CRS_AUDITED(I).CR_CRDT,2);

                    end loop;

        end case;
```

```
-- At this point the information for a student

-- has been stored in CURR_STUD.

-- Next we check whether the grades are valid

-- and start computing the grade point average

-- if the student is not an auditor.

case CURR_ST_TYPE is

    when DEGREE =>

        GRADE_POINT_AVE   := 0.0 ;

        NO_IN_GRADE_POINT := 0 ;

        for I in 1 .. CURR_NO_COURSES

            loop

            CHECK_GRADE;

            -- The course has a grade from F to A

            if VALID_GRADE and AVE_FLAG

                then

                GRADE_POINT_AVE   :=

                        GRADE_POINT_AVE + GRADE_POINT ;

                NO_IN_GRADE_POINT :=

                        NO_IN_GRADE_POINT + 1 ;

            -- Is this a course in the major area ?

            -- If yes then the grade should be above

            -- C- ( i.e. exceed GRADE_POINT of 1.7)

            if  CURR_STUD.ST_MAJOR =

                CURR_STUD.ST_COURSES(I).DESC.CR_ID

                and then

                GRADE_POINT < 1.7
```

```
                    then

                    PUT(" The course must be repeated");

                    PUT(I) ;

                    NEW_LINE;

                end if;

        end if;

        -- Remember that there  are no grades of

        -- "P " for a major or a minor.

        if (CURR_STUD.ST_MAJOR =

                CURR_STUD.ST_COURSES(I).DESC.CR_ID

                or   CURR_STUD.ST_MINOR =

                CURR_STUD.ST_COURSES(I).DESC.CR_ID)

                and CURR_STUD.ST_COURSES(I).CR_GRADE

                = "P "

                then

                PUT( " No pass fail option ");

                PUT( I );

        end if;

        end loop;

        if NO_IN_GRADE_POINT > 0

            then

            GRADE_POINT_AVE  :=

                    GRADE_POINT_AVE /

                        FLOAT(NO_IN_GRADE_POINT);

            PUT (GRADE_POINT_AVE ,5,3 ) ;

            if GRADE_POINT_AVE < 1.7
```

```
                 then

                     PUT ( " Probation " );

                 end if;

             PUT(CURR_STUD.ST_NAME);

             NEW_LINE ;

         end if;

when NON_DEGREE =>

     GRADE_POINT_AVE   := 0.0 ;

     NO_IN_GRADE_POINT := 0 ;

     for I in 1 .. CURR_NO_COURSES

         loop

         CHECK_GRADE;

         -- The course has a grade from F to A

         if VALID_GRADE and AVE_FLAG

             then

             GRADE_POINT_AVE   :=

                     GRADE_POINT_AVE + GRADE_POINT ;

             NO_IN_GRADE_POINT :=

                     NO_IN_GRADE_POINT + 1 ;

         end if;

     end loop;

     if NO_IN_GRADE_POINT > 0

         then

         GRADE_POINT_AVE   :=

             GRADE_POINT_AVE /

                     FLOAT(NO_IN_GRADE_POINT);
```

```
                        PUT (GRADE_POINT_AVE ,5,3 ) ;

                end if;

                PUT(CURR_STUD.ST_NAME);

                NEW_LINE ;

           when AUDITOR =>

                NO_CREDITS := 0 ;

                for I in 1 .. CURR_NO_COURSES

                    loop

                    if CURR_STUD.CRS_AUDITED(I).CR_NO > 99

                        then

                        PUT( " Course no not allowed " );

                    else

                            NO_CREDITS := NO_CREDITS +

                            CURR_STUD.CRS_AUDITED(I).CR_CRDT ;

                    end if;

                end loop;

                PUT(NO_CREDITS,3);

                PUT(CURR_STUD.ST_NAME);

                NEW_LINE ;

            end case;

            GET ( CURR_NO_COURSES, 2 );

        end loop;

    end GR_POINT_AVE;
```

EXERCISES FOR CHAPTER 4

1. Modify the program NAME_PHONE as follows: The first character of the first and last names should be printed by using uppercase letters, and the remaining characters should be printed by using lowercase letters.

2. Suppose integer and real type literals are supplied as input, one literal per line. Use the procedures developed in the program NAME_PHONE to check the validity of each literal, and print a message (valid or invalid) next to each numeric literal. (Literals were introduced in Chapter 1.)

3. Write a program that will read dates and print them in a standardized format. The date can have a variety of formats but will not take more than one line. The first item to be read is either the day or the month, and the last item to be read is the year. Each of the three items is preceded by at least a space. The year can be optionally preceded by a comma and at least a space. Months can be shortened to not fewer than three characters; and if they are shortened, a period must be placed after the last character present in the month name. Both uppercase and lowercase letters are allowed in a month name. Days can be optionally followed by the suffix *th;* or if day numbers are 1, 2, 3, and so on, then the format can be 1st, 2nd, 3rd, and so forth, with both uppercase and lowercase letters. If the day precedes the month, then the word *of* can be placed between the day and the month. If the month precedes the day, then the word *the* can be placed between the month and the day. Days must be in the range 1 through 31, and years should have exactly four digits. Some possible valid dates follow:

```
15th of November, 1975
Nov. 17, 1984
Sept. 12 1985
1st JULY 1985
DEcemb. the 2nd 1987
```

Here are some invalid ones

3 Jun 1985	No period after Jun
4th of July 87	Year has only two digits
Sept. the 4th ,1988	No space preceding the year

For each line read, the program should print the word "valid" or the word "invalid" together with the actual date read. The last line contains a period in the first column. When you write this program, you may wish to use some of the procedures appearing in the program NAME_PHONE.

4. Write a program to compute employer pension contributions for HOURLY and SALARIED employees (but not for SUBCONTRACTOR). For the types LABOR and EMPLOYEE as defined in Section 4.3, the input lines have the following format:

Columns 1–15	LAB_KIND
Columns 16–25	F_NAME
Columns 26–40	L_NAME
Columns 41–49	SOS_ID

Then, depending on the labor kind, the name is followed by two real numbers, three real numbers, or a real and an integer. One line is used for each employee, and the first line has a count of how many employees will be input. The pension contribution is computed as follows: It is 10% of the Y_T_DATE_TOTAL for SALARIED employees and 8% of the gross income of HOURLY employees, which is computed as

```
HOURLY_PAY * ( HOURS_WORKED + 1.5 *
    OVERTIME_HRS )
```

The contribution is limited to $5000 per employee, and an employee may show up as SALARIED and HOURLY as well (he or she might change positions several times within the company). There is no particular order assumed for the input lines. The program should list the name and the employer pension contribution for each employee.

5. Students quite often complain about their final grade and ask about the computation of the grade. To check the accuracy of a final grade, modify the input for the GR_POINT_AVE program as follows: The information for degree and nondegree students is supplied in three steps. The first two steps are identical to the original two steps. In the third step information about each test used in the computation of the final grade is given. For each course taken by the student that gives a letter grade (A through F), there is a line with the following format:

Column	Data
Columns 1–4	Course ID
Columns 5–8	Course number
Columns 9–10	Number of tests
Columns 11–12	Weight of the first test (15 means 15% of the final grade)
Columns 13–14	Letter grade of the first test (A, A−, . . . , F)
Columns 15–18, 19–22, and so on	Information for the second test, the third test, and so on

The program GR_POINT_AVE should now perform an additional task: Every final grade should be checked against the grade computed as a weighted average from the test information lines, and a message should be printed indicating whether the final grade is correct. For instance, for the output

```
Final grade B
```

the test information line is

```
30A 20B 20B 30C
```

and the weighted average is

```
( 30 * 4.0 + 20 * 3.0 + 20 * 3.0 + 30 * 2.0 )
/ 4 = 3.0    (means B)
```

For this example the final grade is correct. (If the weighted average is in the middle of two letter grades, the final grade is the higher letter grade.)

CHAPTER FIVE

SUBPROGRAMS: PROCEDURES AND FUNCTIONS

5.1 Procedures
5.2 Functions
5.3 Application Using Functions and Procedures
5.4 Overloading of Subprograms
5.5 Recursive Calls of Subprograms

5.1 PROCEDURES

As we mentioned in Chapter 1, Ada programs are made up of one or more *program units*. In this chapter we will discuss a form of program unit called a **subprogram.** We made use of one kind of subprogram, called a **procedure,** to write the programs presented in the first four chapters. There is also a second kind of subprogram called a *function,* which we will discuss in the next section.

The procedures we have used all had the same form. They all defined a **subprogram body:**

```
procedure procedure_identifier is

maybe_some_declarations

begin

sequence_of_statements

end procedure_identifier;
```

A brief example is

```
procedure NOTHING is

begin

NULL;

end NOTHING;
```

The previous procedures did not have a **formal part,** which introduces a list of *parameter specifications* within parentheses. If a formal part is present, though, it must immediately follow the procedure_identifier. The parameter specifications must be separated by semicolons. An uncomplicated way of introducing a parameter specification is to list some variables followed by a colon and their type or subtype.

EXAMPLE   The following lines illustrate a subprogram body with a formal part.

```
procedure SOMETHING ( I,J : INTEGER ;

                            K : STRING ) is

LOC : INTEGER := 4;

begin

LOC := I * J * LOC ;

if LOC > 100 then

    PUT ( " Product exceeds limit " ) ;

end if;

if K ( 1 .. 5 ) = K ( 6 .. 10 ) then

    PUT ( " Repeated String " );

end if;

end SOMETHING;
```

In the procedure SOMETHING we have a formal part, namely,

```
( I,J : INTEGER ; K : STRING )
```

Here there are two parameter specifications. The first one is

```
I,J : INTEGER
```

and the second one, after the semicolon, is

```
K : STRING
```

In the first parameter specification the list of variables is

```
I,J
```

The list is made up of the two variables separated by a comma. The type or subtype is INTEGER. In the second parameter specification the list is made up of just one variable (namely, K) and the type_ mark (which is the way type or subtypes are named, as discussed in Chapter 2) in STRING.

FORMAL PARAMETERS

Variables that appear in these lists are called **formal parameters.** Thus I, J, and K are formal parameters. They are known within the body of the procedure only. The type of the formal parameter is the type indicated by the type_mark following the colon in the parameter specification.

The execution of procedures is terminated if the "end" reserved word is reached. The procedures used in previous chapters finished their execution in this way. A procedure can be terminated, however, in any other place within its sequence-of-statements part by using the statement

```
return;
```

For instance, we can change the procedure SOMETHING by providing another possible exit point, as follows:

```
procedure SOMETHING2 ( I,J : INTEGER ;

                          K : STRING ) is

LOC : INTEGER := 4;

begin

if I > 10 then

    return;

end if;

LOC := I * J * LOC ;

if LOC > 100 then

    PUT ( " Product exceeds limit " ) ;
```

```
end if;

if K ( 1 .. 5 ) = K ( 6 .. 10 ) then

      PUT ( " Repeated String " );

end if;

end SOMETHING2;
```

Actually, a more complete definition of a parameter specification includes the mode of the formal parameters. The **mode** is any of these three possibilities:

in   in out   out

If none of these words are present, the assumption (the default value) is "in." In the procedure SOMETHING, therefore, all formal parameters, I, J, and K, are of the mode "in."

Ada does not allow the modification of the value of a formal parameter of mode "in." Therefore a statement like

```
I := I * J ;
```

would be invalid within the body of SOMETHING2, because the value of I would be changed.

Some formal parameters can be given initial values by following the type_ mark with the compound symbol ":=" and an expression. This initializing is allowed only if the mode of the formal parameters in the corresponding list is "in."

We illustrate these new concepts in the next version of the procedure SOMETHING3.

```
procedure SOMETHING3 ( I,J : in out INTEGER ;

                K : in STRING := "CREATURES " ) is

LOC : INTEGER := 4;

begin

if I > 10 then

      return;

end if;

LOC := I * J * LOC ;

if LOC > 100 then
```

```
      PUT ( " Product exceeds limit " ) ;

end if;

if K ( 1 .. 5 ) = K ( 6 .. 10 ) then

      PUT ( " Repeated String " );

end if;

end SOMETHING3;
```

In the procedure SOMETHING3 the variables I and J are of mode "in out." The variable K has the mode "in," and it has a default initial value.

There is another variable declared within the procedure, namely, LOC. This variable is known within the procedure only (as was the case for formal parameters). In addition, no matching with outside variables is possible.

INVOKING PROCEDURES

A procedure can be invoked in a number of ways. The chosen way for the programs presented up to this point was to place the body of the procedure to be invoked within the Ada program invoking the procedure. This method works if the body of the procedure to be invoked appears in the invoking program before the call.

If the procedure is invoked by an Ada program and the body of the procedure follows the call, then a subprogram declaration for the procedure has to be present in the declarative part of the invoking program. The declaration of a subprogram is merely the subprogram specification followed by a semicolon (the specification part of a procedure is the reserved word "procedure" followed by the procedure_identifier and the formal part, if present).

Whether or not a procedure has to be declared, it can be invoked by listing its name in the calling program. If the procedure invoked has a formal part, the name is followed by a list of actual parameters within parentheses.

In the execution of a procedure the actual parameters and the formal parameters are matched, the declarations within the procedure are elaborated, and then the sequence of statements is executed, using the actual parameter values. The execution is terminated when the end statement or the return statement is reached (assuming no exception is raised). We invoked procedures in many of the programs of the previous chapters, arranging their bodies carefully so that we would not need additional procedure declarations.

The following program examples illustrate how one can invoke procedures with a formal part and how one might use a procedure declaration. In addition, a formal parameter of mode "out" is defined.

ENVELOP Procedure

```
with TEXT_IO; use TEXT_IO;

procedure ENVELOP is

II, JJ : INTEGER ;

KK : STRING ( 1 .. 10 );

LL : STRING ( 1 .. 10 );

    procedure SOMETHING4 ( I,J : in out INTEGER ;
                    K : in STRING := "CREATURES " ;
                    L : out STRING ) is

    LOC : INTEGER := 4;

    begin

    if I > 10 then

        return;

    end if;

    I := I * J * LOC ; LOC := I ;

    if LOC > 100 then

        PUT ( " Product exceeds limit " ) ;

    end if;

    if K ( 1 .. 5 ) = K ( 6 .. 10 ) then

        PUT ( " Repeated String " ); L := K ;

        else

        L ( 1 .. 10 ) := K ( 1 .. 5 ) & K ( 1 .. 5 );

    end if;

    end SOMETHING4;

procedure INVOKES is

begin
```

```
SOMETHING4( II, JJ, KK, LL) ;

        -- The procedure SOMETHING4 is invoked here. The actual

        -- parameters are II, JJ, KK, and LL.

end INVOKES;

begin

        II := 5 ; JJ := 8 ;

        KK := "XXXXXYYYYY";

        INVOKES;

end ENVELOP;
```

Here is the same procedure ENVELOP with a declaration needed for SOMETHING4:

ENVELOP, Using a Procedure Declaration

```
with TEXT_IO; use TEXT_IO;

procedure ENVELOP is

II, JJ : INTEGER ;

KK : STRING ( 1 .. 10 );

LL : STRING ( 1 .. 10 );

    procedure SOMETHING4 ( I,J : in out INTEGER ;

                K : in STRING  := "CREATURES " ;

                L : out STRING ) ;

    -- Here we have the declaration of the procedure SOMETHING4.

    -- It is needed because the procedure INVOKES will

    -- invoke the procedure SOMETHING4 before the body

    -- of SOMETHING4 is defined.

procedure INVOKES is

begin
```

```
        SOMETHING4( II, JJ, KK, LL);
    end INVOKES;
        procedure SOMETHING4 ( I,J : in out INTEGER ;
                        K : in STRING   := "CREATURES " ;
                        L : out STRING  ) is
        LOC : INTEGER := 4;
        begin
        if I > 10 then
            return;
        end if;
        LOC := I * J * LOC ; I := LOC;
        if LOC > 100 then
            PUT ( " Product exceeds limit " ) ;
        end if;
        if K ( 1 .. 5 ) = K ( 6 .. 10 ) then
            PUT ( " Repeated String " ); L := K ;
            else
            L ( 1 .. 10 ) := K ( 1 .. 5 ) & K ( 1 .. 5 );
        end if;
        end SOMETHING4;
begin
    II := 5 ; JJ := 8 ;
    KK := "XXXXXYYYYY";
    INVOKES;
end ENVELOP;
```

MATCHING FORMAL AND ACTUAL PARAMETERS

As we discussed earlier, an association is formed between the formal parameters and the actual parameters when a procedure is invoked. In the procedure IN-VOKES, when the call SOMETHING4 is executed, the association is formed between the actual parameters II, JJ, KK and the formal parameters I, J, K. The types of the formal and the actual parameters have to match exactly: The type of II has to be the type of I, the type of JJ has to be the type of J, and the type of KK has to be the type of K.

The mode of the formal parameters dictates the treatment of the values of the matched formal and actual parameters. If the mode is "in" (as for the formal parameter K), then the value of the actual parameter KK is passed to the subprogram (here the value "XXXXXYYYYY" is passed to the subroutine SOMETHING4). It can be used (but not modified) by the subprogram, and no value is passed back to the corresponding actual argument. That is, the value of the actual parameter acts as a constant within the invoked subprogram.

If the mode of the formal parameter is "out," then the formal parameter makes no use of the value of the matching actual parameter when the procedure is invoked. However, the value of the formal parameter at the time the execution of the procedure is terminated is placed in the corresponding actual parameter. In the procedure SOMETHING4 the formal parameter L has the mode "out," and its value will be placed in LL when the procedure is finished (in this case the value "XXXXXXXXXX" will be placed in LL).

If the mode of the formal parameter is "in out," then the formal parameter will start the invoked procedure with the value of the corresponding actual parameter. In the procedure ENVELOP the actual parameters II and JJ have the values 5 and 8. When SOMETHING4 is invoked, the values I and J will start with 5 and 8.

The values of the formal parameters of mode "in out" can be changed within the procedure. When the procedure terminates, their values will be placed in the corresponding actual parameters. When SOMETHING4 is executed, the formal parameter I is given a new value, 160. And when the procedure terminates, the new value 160 will be placed in the actual parameter II. The value of the formal parameter J (it is unchanged and is still 8) is placed in the actual parameter JJ. Assignments to formal parameters of mode "in out" are clearly permitted.

Of course, formal parameters can be of any of the types already introduced: array, record, or access. Formal parameters can also be of private types, as will be seen in Chapter 7.

If the execution of the subprogram is terminated in an abnormal way (say an exception is raised), the final value of the actual parameter is undetermined.

An actual parameter can be a variable or the value of an expression. If the matching formal parameter is of mode "in out" or "out," then the actual parameter can only be an expression or a type conversion of the variable name. For instance, one can invoke the procedure SOMETHING4 as

```
SOMETHING4 ( II, JJ, ''ABCDEABCDE'', LL );
```

because the formal parameter K is of mode "in." However, it would not be valid to have

```
SOMETHING4 ( 4, JJ, ''ABCDEABCDE'', LL );
```

because I has the mode "in out," and the matching actual parameter has to be a variable name or a type conversion of a variable name.

NAMED PARAMETER ASSOCIATION

When we invoked the procedure SOMETHING4, we used the positional notation to pass the actual parameters. In this case each formal parameter is matched with the actual parameter that is placed in the same position of the actual parameter list.

Ada allows the programmer to explicitly name the corresponding formal parameters in a procedure call. The programmer lists the formal parameter followed by the compound symbol " => " and then the actual parameter. Here are some equivalent ways of invoking the procedure SOMETHING4:

```
SOMETHING4 ( II, JJ, KK, LL );
SOMETHING4 ( I => II, J => JJ, K => KK, L =>
   LL );
SOMETHING4 ( J => JJ, K => KK, I => II, L =>
   LL );
```

The last two calls use a **named parameter association.** For a named parameter association the order in which the parameters are listed is not important.

One may combine the named parameter association and positional parameters in the same call. In this situation the positional parameters have to be listed first. Once a named parameter is used, all the other parameters have to use the named parameter association. For example,

```
SOMETHING4 ( II, JJ, L => LL, K => KK ) ;
```

is valid. However,

```
SOMETHING4 ( II, L => LL, K => KK, JJ ) ;
```

is not a valid call because a positional notation follows a named parameter notation.

One need not supply an actual argument for a formal parameter having a default initial value. For instance, it is valid to have the following procedure call:

```
SOMETHING4 ( I => II, L => LL, J => JJ ) ;
```

The formal parameter K has no matching actual parameter, and the default initial value of "CREATURES " will be used.

CONSTRAINTS ON FORMAL PARAMETERS

Constraints on formal parameters must be obeyed by the actual parameters as follows: If the mode of the formal parameter is "in" or "in out" and it is a scalar type, then any range constraint has to be satisfied by the value of the actual parameter before the call is executed. If the mode is "out" or "in out," then the value of the formal parameter has to satisfy any constraint on the actual parameters (again assuming a scalar type).

If the type of the parameter is array or record (or a private type with discriminants, as discussed in Chapter 7), regardless of the mode (it can be "in," "out," or "in out"), then the constraints on the formal parameter must be satisfied by the actual parameter before the call is executed.

Some of the rules regarding constraints are illustrated in the procedure MAIN_CALL given next.

MAIN_CALL Procedure

```
procedure MAIN_CALL is

type REAL_TABLES is array ( POSITIVE range <> )  of FLOAT;

SOME_TABLE : REAL_TABLE ( 1 .. 12 )

            := ( 1 .. 12 => 5.0 )  ;

            -- Here we have an index constraint.

CURR_TABLE : REAL_TABLE ( 1 .. 10 )

            := ( 1 .. 10 => 5.0 ) ;

            -- Here is another index constraint.

type REC_DISCR ( STR_LENGTH : range  1 .. 255 := 80 ) is
    record

        LINE_CONT : STRING ( 1 .. STR_LENGTH ) ;

    end record;

LONG_LINE : REC_DISCR ( 90 );

-- Here we have a discriminant constraint.
```

```
REG_LINE   : REG_DISCR ( 75 );

-- Here is another discriminant constraint.

type DIGIT_COUNT  is range 0 .. 9 ;

subtype FEW_CHOICES  is DIGIT_COUNT range 1 .. 5 ;

II : DIGIT_COUNT;

JJ : FEW_CHOICES;

procedure CONSTR_PARAM (

        I : DIGIT_COUNT ;

        J : in out  DIGIT_COUNT ;

        X : in out REAL_TABLE  ;

        FOR_LINE : in out REC_DISCR  ) is

begin

    J := I + 2;

    X := X + X;

    FOR_LINE ( 20 .. 30 ) := FOR_LINE ( 40 .. 50 ) ;

end CONSTR_PARAM ;

begin

    REG_LINE (1 .. 10 ) := "0123456789";

    for L in 11 .. 75

        loop    REG_LINE ( L ) := ' ' ;   end loop ;

    LONG_LINE := ( 1 .. 90 => 'A' );

    II := 5 ;   JJ := 3 ;

CONSTR_PARAM ( 2, JJ, CURR_TABLE, REG_LINE );

--This is a valid call. All constraints are satisfied.

CONSTR_PARAM ( 13, JJ, CURR_TABLE, REG_LINE );

-- A range constraint is violated here: 13, the
```

```
-- actual parameter value, exceeds 10, the upper

-- limit of the formal parameter I range.

-- A CONSTRAINT_ERROR is raised.

CONSTR_PARAM ( II, JJ, CURR_TABLE, REG_LINE );

-- A range constraint is violated here. The end

-- result of the formal parameter J is the

-- the value 6. It is copied back into JJ,

-- which cannot have a value exceeding 5 .

-- A CONSTRAINT_ERROR is raised.

CONSTR_PARAM ( 3, JJ, CURR_TABLE, LONG_LINE );

-- Here a discriminant constraint for the formal

-- parameter  is  not  satisfied  by  the

-- actual parameter.

-- A CONSTRAINT_ERROR is raised.

CONSTR_PARAM ( 3, JJ, SOME_TABLE, REG_LINE );

-- Here an index constraint for the formal parameter

-- is not satisfied by the actual parameter.

-- A CONSTRAINT_ERROR is raised.
```

```
end MAIN_CALL;
```

5.2 FUNCTIONS

We now turn our attention to the other form of an Ada subprogram: the function. A **function**, unlike procedures, has to return a value. Also, when invoked, functions represent primary expressions, while procedure calls represent statements by themselves. The function body has the following form:

```
function identifier_or_operator_symbol

      maybe_a_formal_part
```

```
              return type_or_subtype is

maybe_some_declarations

begin

sequence_of_statements

-- The sequence_of_statements part has to include a

-- a return statement.

end procedure_identifier;
```

As for procedures, the part preceding the reserved word "is" is the subprogram (function) specification. If an operator is used to name the function, it must be a character string. If a formal part is present, it has the same format as the procedure formal part, except that the only mode allowed for formal parameters is the mode "in."

A function body must have a return statement, and a function terminates only when a return statement is executed. The return statement used with functions has a different form, because the expression following the reserved word "return" is mandatory. The form is

```
return expression;
```

and the value of the expression in a return statement is the value returned by the function.

EXAMPLE   Here is an example of a function body together with a function call:

```
with TEXT_IO; use TEXT_IO;

procedure CALL_OF_FUNCTION is

II : INTEGER;

JJ : FLOAT := 5.0 ;

function DOUBLE ( I : INTEGER := -1 ;

                  J : FLOAT   := 1.0 )

        return FLOAT is

K : INTEGER := 5;

begin
```

```
if I > 0

    then

        return FLOAT ( 2 * K * I );

    else

        return 2.0 * J ;

    end if;

end DOUBLE;

begin

    for M in 1 .. 10

        loop

        II := ( -1 ) ** M ;

        JJ := DOUBLE ( II, JJ);

        if II > JJ then

            PUT ( " First argument exceeds the second " );

        end if;

    end loop;

end CALL_OF_FUNCTION;
```

The function has DOUBLE as its identifier; when invoked, the function DOUBLE exits through one of its two return statements. The function DOUBLE returns a value of type FLOAT. The formal part is present and has a list of two formal parameters: I, which is of type INTEGER, and J, which is of type FLOAT. Their mode is "in" (remember that no other mode is allowed for functions), and they both have a default initial value.

Because both formal parameters in the previous example have default initial values, one can have the following valid assignment statements:

```
JJ := DOUBLE;       The returned value is 2.0
JJ := DOUBLE        The default I := -1 will be used and returns
   ( J => JJ           double the value of JJ
   );
```

```
            JJ := DOUBLE       The default JJ := 1.0 will be used and returns
              (   I  =>  II        ten times the value of II
              );
```

In Section 4.2 we mentioned, without giving details, that functions can return arrays. In this case functions can be used as names of indexed components. The following example illustrates this point.

EXAMPLE   In the following program lines a function is used as the name of indexed components.

```
with TEXT_IO; use TEXT_IO ;

procedure GET_MULTIPLE_TABLE is

type TABLE is array ( POSITIVE range <> ) of INTEGER;

type TWO_DIM_TABLE is array ( POSITIVE range <>,

                           POSITIVE range <> ) of INTEGER;

II, JJ : INTEGER;

CURR_TWO_TABLE : TWO_DIM_TABLE ( II, II );

Package INT_IO is new INTEGER_IO(INTEGER);

use INT_IO;

function FILL_TABLE ( I, J : INTEGER )

      return TABLE  is

FUN_TABLE : TABLE ( I );

    -- This function places alternating values J and -J  in the

    -- table FUN_TABLE, starting with J if J is odd.

begin

    for L in 1 .. I

        loop

        FUN_TABLE ( L ) := ( -1 ) ** ( I + J ) * J ;

    end loop;
```

```
        return FUN_TABLE ;

end FILL_TABLE;

begin

        GET ( II );   GET ( JJ );

        for LL in 1 .. II

                loop

                -- If JJ is positive then place the table returned

                -- by FILL_TABLE on the main diagonal of CURR_TWO_TABLE

                if JJ > 0

                        then

                        CURR_TWO_TABLE ( LL, LL ) :=

                                        FILL_TABLE ( II,JJ ) ( LL );

                -- Here  is  the  indexed  component.  The

                -- function  call  FILL_TABLE ( II, JJ )

                -- returns an array,  and LL is the value of

                -- the desired component.

                -- Note  as  well  that  the  function  is

                -- evaluated every time the assignment is

                -- executed (not a very efficient way in this

                -- case).

                end if;

        end loop;

end GET_MULTIPLE_TABLE;
```

When we introduced the general form for selected components in Section 4.2, we noted that a function name can represent the name part returning a record. Then the selected component may have the form

```
function_name.component_identifier
```

An example of this situation is illustrated in the next section by the function FIND_COUP_DATE.

5.3 APPLICATION USING FUNCTIONS AND PROCEDURES

In this section we will apply the newly introduced concepts in a program called ACCR_INTEREST. The program computes accrued interest on coupon-bearing U.S. government securities (no long or short coupons). The formula for computing accrued interest is

```
Accrint = Rate / 2 * nofdays / totaldays *
    parvalue
```

where we use the following definitions:

Rate	Annual coupon rate (a decimal, such as 12.5)
nofdays	Accrued days (from the last coupon interest payment)
totaldays	Length (in days, between the last and the next coupon interest payment)
parvalue	Face value of the security (taken to be $100.00)

The coupons are redeemed twice a year. The input consists of lines containing the following items:

Column	Item	Description
Columns 1–7	Rate	Given in decimals.
Columns 8–13	Mat-_date	The maturity date in the format YYMMDD (thus 950515 means May 15, 1995). Note that coupon payments are scheduled on May 15 and November 15 of each year for this particular Mat_date.
Columns 14–19	Setl_date	The settlement date, which cannot be a weekend or a national holiday. It has to precede the maturity date.

There is a list of holiday dates, one per line, which is supplied before the security items are provided. The holiday dates have the format YYMMDD, and the very first line counts the number of holidays for the year. The end-of-input line is marked by a negative coupon rate.

ACCR_INTEREST Program

```
procedure ACCR_INTEREST is

    -- Some of the types and constants for this program have
    -- been used in the program DATE_CONVERSION of Chapter 2.

    type DAY is (MONDAY,TUESDAY,WEDNESDAY,THURSDAY,FRIDAY,
        SATURDAY,SUNDAY);

    subtype WEEKEND is DAY range SATURDAY..SUNDAY ;

    type DAY_INT is range 1 .. 31;

    type JULIAN_DAYS is range 1 .. 366 ;

    type MONTH is (JANUARY,FEBRUARY,MARCH,APRIL,MAY,JUNE,
            JULY,AUGUST,SEPTEMBER,OCTOMBER,NOVEMBER,DECEMBER);

    type YEAR is range 0 .. 2050 ;

    type MONTH_INT is range 1 .. 12;

    Package DAY_IO is new ENUMERATION_IO(DAY);

    use DAY_IO;

    Package MONTH_IO is new ENUMERATION_IO(MONTH);

    use MONTH_IO;

    Package YEAR_IO is new INTEGER_IO(YEAR);

    use YEAR_IO;

    Package MONTH_INT is new INTEGER_IO(MONTH_INT);

    use MONTH_INT;

    Package DAY_INT_IO is new INTEGER_IO(DAY_INT);

    use DAY_INT_IO;

    type DATE is

        record

                WEEK_DAY : DAY;
```

```
            MONTH_NAME : MONTH;

            MONTH_NO : MONTH_INT;

            DAY_NO   : DAY_INT;

            YTD_DAYS : JULIAN_DAYS;

            TOTAL_DAYS : INTEGER ;

            YEAR_NO  : YEAR;

    end record;

BASE_DATE·· constant DATE := ( MONDAY,JANUARY,1,1,1,1,1984);

            -- For this program we assume that only dates

            -- after Jan. 1, 1984 are supplied. If earlier

            -- dates are used, change the constant to an

            -- earlier convenient date, in the 1800.

BASE_LEAP : constant INTEGER :=

            INTEGER(BASE_DATE.YEAR_NO)  / 4 +

            INTEGER(BASE_DATE.YEAR_NO)  /  400 -

            INTEGER(BASE_DATE.YEAR_NO)  /  100;

            -- This constant represents the number of leap years

            -- occurred from year 0 to BASE_DATE.YEAR_NO.

type DAYS_IN_MONTH is array (MONTH_INT,BOOLEAN) of DAY_INT;

ACTUAL_DAYS_IN_YEAR : constant DAYS_IN_MONTH :=

    ( (31,31),(28,29),(31,31),(30,30),

      (31,31),(30,30),(31,31),(31,31),

      (30,30),(31,31),(30,30),(31,31) ) ;

    -- We just declared a constant array indexed by

    -- MONTH_INT, with values from 1 to 12,

    -- and by Boolean, with values (just two)
```

```
        -- from FALSE to TRUE; FALSE false means that there

        -- is no leap year.

type RATE is digits 13 ;

ACCRUED_INT : RATE;

type COUPON_SECURITY is

    record

            COUP_RATE : RATE ;

            MAT_DATE  : DATE;

            SETL_DATE : DATE ;

    end record;

ACT_SECUR : COUPON_SECURITY ;

NEXT_DATE, PREV_COUP_DATE : DATE ;

Package RATE_IO is new FLOAT_IO(RATE);

use RATE_IO;

Package INT_IO is new INTEGER_IO(INTEGER);

use INT_IO;

LEAP_YEAR : BOOLEAN;

NOFDAYS, INTERVDAYS : NATURAL ;

INPUT_LEAP  : INTEGER ;

NO_OF_HOLIDAYS, NO_GOOD_HOLIDAYS : NATURAL;

type HOLIDAYS  is array ( 1 .. NO_OF_HOLIDAYS) of DATE;

ACT_HOLIDAYS : HOLIDAYS ;

GOOD_MAT_DATE, GOOD_SETL_DATE : BOOLEAN;

GOOD_HOLIDAY, GOOD_NEXT_DATE : BOOLEAN ;

-- Note that the function   IS_VALID_DATE and the procedure

-- FILL_IN_DATE    are     based    on    the    procedure
```

```
        -- COUNT_DAYS_AND_CHECK of program DATE_CONVERSION in

        -- Chapter 2. Also note that the declarations

        -- above are known (are visible) within each of the

        -- subprograms below

function IS_VALID_DATE ( FORM_DATE : DATE )

                return BOOLEAN is

            -- This function returns the value TRUE if the

            -- date FORM_DATE.MONTH_NO, FORM_DATE.DAY_NO,

            -- FORM_DATE.YEAR_NO represents a valid date.

            -- Otherwise, it returns  the value FALSE.

            -- There is just one formal parameter of type record.

begin

            -- Is this year a valid year? If not, the function

            -- returns the value FALSE.

        if FORM_DATE.YEAR_NO < BASE_DATE.YEAR_NO

            then

            return FALSE;

        end if;

            -- We do not check on the month.

            -- Is this day a valid day? If not, the function

            -- returns the value FALSE.

            -- But first, we check to see whether this year

            -- is a leap year.

        if  FORM_DATE.YEAR_NO rem 4 = 0     and

            FORM_DATE.YEAR_NO rem 100 /= 0  or

            FORM_DATE.YEAR_NO rem 400 = 0
```

```
        then

            LEAP_YEAR := TRUE;

    else

            LEAP_YEAR := FALSE;

    end if;

            -- Now LEAP_YEAR can be used to refer to the proper

            -- row in the ACTUAL_DAYS_IN_YEAR array

    if    FORM_DATE.DAY_NO >

          ACTUAL_DAYS_IN_YEAR( FORM_DATE.MONTH_NO ,LEAP_YEAR)

          then

            return FALSE ;

    else

            return TRUE;

    end if;

end IS_VALID_DATE;

procedure FILL_IN_DATE

          ( PROC_F_DATE : in out DATE ;

            GOOD_DATE   : in out BOOLEAN ) is

          -- This procedure will supply some components

          -- of PROC_F_DATE assuming that the other components,

          -- FORM_DATE.MONTH_NO, FORM_DATE.DAY_NO, and

          -- FORM_DATE.YEAR_NO, represent a valid date. If these

          -- other components do not represent a valid date, then

          -- GOOD_DATE is set to FALSE.

          -- There are two formal parameters in the formal part:

          -- PROC_F_DATE of type record and GOOD_DATE of type
```

```
                -- Boolean.
    begin
        -- If the year is in the form YY, it is set to a
        -- four-digit representation.
        if PROC_F_DATE.YEAR_NO < 50
            then
            PROC_F_DATE.YEAR_NO :=
                PROC_F_DATE.YEAR_NO + 2000 ;
        elsif PROC_F_DATE.YEAR_NO < 99
            then
            PROC_F_DATE.YEAR_NO :=
                PROC_F_DATE.YEAR_NO + 1900 ;
        else
            NULL;
        end if;
        GOOD_DATE := IS_VALID_DATE ( PROC_F_DATE );
                -- Now find out YTD_DAYS for this date
        if GOOD_DATE
            then
            PROC_F_DATE.YTD_DAYS := JULIAN(PROC_F_DATE.DAY_NO);
            if PROC_F_DATE.MONTH_NO > 1
                then
                for I in 1 .. PROC_F_DATE.MONTH_NO - 1
                    loop
                    PROC_F_DATE.YTD_DAYS := PROC_F_DATE.YTD_DAYS +
                    JULIAN(ACTUAL_DAYS_IN_YEAR ( I, LEAP_YEAR ));
```

```
            end loop;

        end if;

end if;

        -- Find out how many days have elapsed from the

        -- base date to the input date. First, though find

        -- how many leap years there were until the

        -- input year.

        INPUT_LEAP := INTEGER(PROC_F_DATE.YEAR_NO) / 4 +

                    INTEGER(PROC_F_DATE.YEAR_NO) / 400 -

                    INTEGER(PROC_F_DATE.YEAR_NO) / 100 ;

        PROC_F_DATE.TOTAL_DAYS := 365 *

            INTEGER( PROC_F_DATE.YEAR_NO -

            BASE_DATE.YEAR_NO    )  +

            INTEGER(PROC_F_DATE.YTD_DAYS)    +

            INPUT_LEAP - BASE_LEAP;

            -- Find the week day and month name.

        PROC_F_DATE.MONTH_NAME := MONTH'VAL(PROC_F_DATE.MONTH_NO);

            -- Remember how the VAL attribute works for

            -- the enumeration types.

        PROC_F_DATE.WEEK_DAY := DAY'VAL (

          (PROC_F_DAYS.TOTAL_DAYS + DAY'POS(BASE_DATE.WEEK_DAY)-2)

            mod 7 + 1                        )  ;

            -- This expression above is somewhat complex.

            -- The position of the base date weekday

            -- is  evaluated  (it is 2  for Tuesday,  for

            -- instance ) and is added to the total days
```

```
                    -- less    2.   The   modulus   7   of   this   number
                    -- plus 1 represents the relative position
                    -- of the input date weekday (an integer between
                    -- 1 and 7). Try a few actual dates
                    -- to help in understanding this expression.
end FILL_IN_DATE ;
function FIND_COUP_DATE ( FORM_MAT_DATE, FORM_SETL_DATE : DATE )
                    return DATE is
          -- This procedure will return a record type value .
          -- The coupons are paid twice a year;   one coupon
          -- payment date is on the month and day listed in the
          -- maturity date, and the other is six month later.
WORK_DATE_1 , WORK_DATE_2 : DATE;
GOOD_WORK_DATE : BOOLEAN;
begin
     WORK_DATE_1 := FORM_MAT_DATE ;
     WORK_DATE_1.YEAR_NO    := FORM_SETL_DATE.YEAR_NO ;
     FILL_IN_DATE ( WORK_DATE_1, GOOD_WORK_DATE ) ;
          -- Why do we not use FORM_MAT_DATE as an actual
          -- parameter for the function FILL_IN_DATE? We do not
          -- because the mode of the corresponding formal
          -- parameter is "in out", which implies that the value
          -- of the formal parameter of FIND_COUP_DATE may be
          -- changed. This change is not allowed for function
          -- parameters .
     WORK_DATE_2 := WORK_DATE_1;
```

```
-- WORK_DATE_1 and WORK_DATE_2 will contain

-- the  two closest coupon payment dates to

-- the settlement day. We return the closest

-- date preceding the settlement date.

if WORK_DATE_1.YTD_DAYS < FORM_SETL_DATE.YTD_DAYS

    then

    if WORK_DATE_1.MONTH_NO < 7

        then

        WORK_DATE_2.MONTH_NO := WORK_DATE_2.MONTH_NO + 6 ;

    else

        WORK_DATE_2.MONTH_NO := WORK_DATE_2.MONTH_NO - 6 ;

        WORK_DATE_2.YEAR_NO := WORK_DATE_2.YEAR_NO + 1 ;

    end if;

else

    if WORK_DATE_1.MONTH_NO > 6

        then

        WORK_DATE_2.MONTH_NO := WORK_DATE_2.MONTH_NO - 6 ;

    else

        WORK_DATE_2.MONTH_NO := WORK_DATE_2.MONTH_NO + 6 ;

        WORK_DATE_2.YEAR_NO := WORK_DATE_2.YEAR_NO - 1 ;

    end if;

end if;

FILL_IN_DATE( WORK_DATE_2, GOOD_WORK_DATE ) ;

if WORK_DATE_1.TOTAL_DAYS < WORK_DATE_2.TOTAL_DAYS

    then

    if FORM_SETL_DATE.TOTAL_DAYS > WORK_DATE_2.TOTAL_DAYS
```

```
                    then

                            return WORK_DATE_2 ;

                else

                            return WORK_DATE_1 ;

                end if;

        else

            if FORM_SETL_DATE.TOTAL_DAYS > WORK_DATE_1.TOTAL_DAYS

                then

                    return WORK_DATE_1 ;

            else

                    return WORK_DATE_2 ;

            end if;

        end if;

end FIND_COUP_DATE;

        -- Note that the function body of IS_VALID_DATE precedes the

        -- body of FILL_IN_DATE, which makes use of it.  Hence  there

        -- is no need for a function declaration for IS_VALID_DATE.

        -- The same things holds for the procedure FIND_COUP_DATE: It

        -- makes use of the procedure FILL_IN_DATE and FILL_IN_DATE

        -- does not need a separate declaration because its body

        -- precedes the body of FIND_COUP_DATE.

begin

GET(NO_OF_HOLIDAYS);

        -- Next, read all holiday dates into the array.

NO_GOOD_HOLIDAYS := 0;

for I in 1 .. NO_OF_HOLIDAYS
```

```
      loop

      NO_GOOD_HOLIDAYS := NO_GOOD_HOLIDAYS + 1 ;

      GET(ACT_HOLIDAYS (NO_GOOD_HOLIDAYS).YEAR_NO,2) ;

      GET(ACT_HOLIDAYS (NO_GOOD_HOLIDAYS).MONTH_NO,2) ;

      GET(ACT_HOLIDAYS (NO_GOOD_HOLIDAYS).DAY_NO,2) ;

      FILL_IN_DATE ( ACT_HOLIDAYS(NO_GOOD_HOLIDAYS),

                        GOOD_HOLIDAY );

      -- The FILL_IN_DATE procedure is invoked here with

      --  ACT_HOLIDAYS(NO_GOOD_HOLIDAY) and GOOD_HOLIDAY as

      -- actual parameters.

      if not GOOD_HOLIDAY

            then

            -- Only proper dates will be placed in

            -- in the table.

            NO_GOOD_HOLIDAYS := NO_GOOD_HOLIDAYS - 1 ;

      end if;

      SKIP_LINE;

end loop;

-- Read lines until  a negative coupon rate is reached.

GET(ACT_SECUR.COUP_RATE, 7 );

while ACT_SECUR.COUP_RATE <= 0.0

      loop

      GET(ACT_SECUR.MAT_DATE.YEAR_NO,2);

      GET(ACT_SECUR.MAT_DATE.MONTH_NO,2);

      GET(ACT_SECUR.MAT_DATE.DAY_NO,2);

      GET(ACT_SECUR.SETL_DATE.YEAR_NO,2);
```

```
GET(ACT_SECUR.SETL_DATE.MONTH_NO,2);

GET(ACT_SECUR.SETL_DATE.DAY_NO,2);

FILL_IN_DATE ( ACT_SECUR.MAT_DATE, GOOD_MAT_DATE );

        -- The FILL_IN_DATE procedure is invoked here with

        --   ACT_SECUR.MAT_DATE and GOOD_MAT_DATE as

        -- actual parameters.

FILL_IN_DATE ( ACT_SECUR.SETL_DATE, GOOD_SETL_DATE );

        -- The FILL_IN_DATE procedure is invoked here with

        --   ACT_SECUR.SETL_DATE and GOOD_SETL_DATE as

        -- actual parameters. There should be

        -- no settlement date after the maturity date.

        -- If there is, then set GOOD_MAT_DATE to FALSE.

  if ACT_SECUR.MAT_DATE.TOTAL_DAYS <=

    ACT_SECUR.SETL_DATE.TOTAL_DAYS

        then

        GOOD_MAT_DATE := FALSE;

  end if;

        -- There is no settlement day on a weekend. The value

        -- of GOOD_SETL_DATE  should be FALSE on a weekend.

  if ACT_SECUR.SETL_DATE.WEEK_DAY in WEEKEND

    then

        GOOD_SETL_DATE := FALSE;

  end if;

        -- There is no settlement day on a holiday. Check to

        -- see whether the settlement date is on a holiday,

        -- and set GOOD_SETL_DATE to FALSE if it is.
```

```
for I in 1 .. NO_GOOD_HOLIDAYS

    loop

    exit when not GOOD_SETL_DATE;

    if ACT_HOLIDAYS ( I ).TOTAL_DAYS =

        ACT_SECUR.SETL_DATE.TOTAL_DAYS

        then

        GOOD_SETL_DATE := FALSE;

    end if;

end loop;

if GOOD_MAT_DATE and GOOD_SETL_DATE

    then

    -- Find the previous coupon payment day.

    PREV_COUP_DATE := FIND_COUP_DATE ( ACT_SECUR.MAT_DATE ,

                        ACT_SECUR.SETL_DATE );

    -- The function FIND_COUP_DATE has been invoked with

    -- actual    num its ACTSECUR.MAT_DATE and

    -- ACT_SECUR.SETL_DATE. It returns a value

    -- of type DATE. It is valid as well to use

    -- a selected component notation here:

    --   FIND_COUP_DATE ( ACT_SECUR.MAT_DATE ,

    --                   ACT_SECUR.SETL_DATE ).MONTH_NO

    --    or

    --   FIND_COUP_DATE ( ACT_SECUR.MAT_DATE ,

    --               ACT_SECUR.SETL_DATE ).WEEK_DAY

    NEXT_DATE.DAY_NO := PREV_COUP_DATE.DAY_NO;

    -- Find the next coupon payment date.
```

```
    -- A better way to do so would be to write a procedure

    -- that returns both the PREV_COUP_DATE and

    -- the NEXT_DATE. See Exercise 3 at the

    -- end of the chapter.

    if PREV_COUP_DATE.MONTH_NO < 7

        then

        NEXT_DATE.MONTH_NO := PREV_COUP_DATE.MONTH_NO + 6;

        NEXT_DATE.YEAR_NO  := PREV_COUP_DATE.YEAR_NO ;

    else

        NEXT_DATE.MONTH_NO := PREV_COUP_DATE.MONTH_NO - 6;

        NEXT_DATE.YEAR_NO  := PREV_COUP_DATE.YEAR_NO + 1 ;

    end if;

    FILL_IN_DATE ( NEXT_DATE, GOOD_NEXT_DATE );

    -- Compute the accrued interest

    NOFDAYS := ACT_SECUR.SETL_DATE.TOTAL_DAYS -

                    PREV_COUP_DATE.TOTAL_DAYS ;

    INTERVDAYS := NEXT_DATE.TOTAL_DAYS -

                    ACT_SECUR.SETL_DATE.TOTAL_DAYS ;

    ACCRUED_INT := ACT_SECUR.COUP_RATE / 2.0 *

                    RATE  ( NOFDAYS ) / RATE (INTERVDAYS);

    PUT ( " The accr. interest for the security maturing " ) ;

    PUT(ACT_SECUR.MAT_DATE.YEAR_NO,2);

    PUT(ACT_SECUR.MAT_DATE.MONTH_NO,2);

    PUT(ACT_SECUR.MAT_DATE.DAY_NO,2);

    NEW_LINE;

    PUT (" Is : ") ; PUT ( ACCRUED_INT, 8, 2 );
```

```
        NEW_LINE;

    else

        -- Some of the dates are wrong  for this line.

        PUT ( " Wrong maturity or settlement date " );

    end if;

    SKIP_LINE;

    GET(ACT_SECUR.COUP_RATE, 7 );

end loop;

end ACCR_INTEREST;
```

5.4 OVERLOADING OF SUBPROGRAMS

In Ada one can use the same identifier to name different subprograms. The identifier is then called **overloaded.** Of course, any call to an overloaded subprogram has to be able to distinguish among the different subprograms. Otherwise, the call is said to be **ambiguous.**

We have used quite a few overloaded subprograms—everytime we used statements like GET or PUT. We used the GET (PUT) statement (same identifier) to read (write) strings and values of type integer, float, and enumeration.

Here is a list of the GET and PUT subprogram specification parts of the generic package TEXT_IO (we label these procedures as Proc_1 through Proc_7 for easy reference)

```
procedure GET ( ITEM : out CHARACTER );   -- Proc_1

procedure GET ( ITEM : out STRING );      -- Proc_2

procedure PUT ( ITEM : in CHARACTER );    -- Proc_3

procedure PUT ( ITEM : in STRING );       -- Proc_4
```

For the package INTEGER_IO, where NUM is an integer type and FIELD is a natural integer subtype, we used

```
procedure GET (ITEM  : out NUM ;

              WIDTH : in FIELD := 0 ) ;      -- Proc_5
```

For the package FLOAT_IO some initialized integer type variables are used in subprogram specifications, and NUM (different from the same name used in the INTEGER_IO package) is a FLOAT type. Some specifications for the PUT and GET procedures follow:

```
DEFAULT_FORE : FIELD := 2;

DEFAULT_AFT  : FIELD := NUM'DIGITS - 1;

DEFAULT_EXT  : FIELD := 3;

procedure PUT ( ITEM : in NUM ;

                FORE : in FIELD := DEFAULT_FORE ;

                AFT  : in FIELD := DEFAULT_AFT ;

                EXP  : in FIELD := DEFAULT_EXP ); -- Proc_6

procedure GET ( ITEM : out NUM ;

                WIDTH: in FIELD := 0 ) ;        -- Proc_7
```

EXAMPLE Here we offer a number of illustrations of the use of these overloaded procedures. We assume the following variable declarations:

```
I  : INTEGER ;
CH : CHARACTER ;
F  : FLOAT ;
```

The calls are listed next; we assume all the procedures given earlier are available.

Call	Description
PUT('A');	This call makes use of the procedure Proc_3. The type of 'A' is CHARACTER, and this procedure is the only PUT procedure with a CHARACTER type formal parameter.
GET(CH);	This call makes use of the procedure Proc_1. The type of CH is CHARACTER, and this procedure is the only GET procedure with a CHARACTER type formal parameter.

`GET(STR);`	This call makes use of the procedure Proc_2. The type of STR is STRING, and this procedure is the only GET procedure with a STRING type formal parameter.
`PUT( "Tomorrow" );`	This call makes use of the procedure Proc_4. The type of "Tomorrow" is STRING, and this procedure is the only PUT procedure with a STRING type formal parameter.
`GET(I);`	This call makes use of the procedure Proc_5. The type of I is INTEGER, and this procedure is the only GET procedure with an INTEGER type formal parameter. The second argument is missing, and it is assumed to pass the default value for width.

`PUT( F,`
`    FORE => 7,`
`    AFT => 3,`
`    EXP => 3 );`
	This call makes use of the procedure Proc_6. The type of F is FLOAT and this procedure is the only PUT procedure with a FLOAT type formal parameter. The named component notation is used.

`GET ( F ,7 )`	This call makes use of the procedure Proc_7. The type of F is FLOAT and this procedure is the only GET procedure with a FLOAT type formal parameter.

Overloading of subprograms is natural if one is to use names meaningful for the user of programs. Moreover, one can use operators like +, −, *, /, and ** as function designators (function names) for types that do not support the operations but can be defined in a manner that reminds the designer of the original meaning. For instance, exponentiation is not defined if both operands are of type FLOAT. One can overload the operator "**" by writing a function with a designator "**" with a formal part consisting of two FLOAT type parameters. One can define as well, for instance, a new type COMPLEX that is intended to imitate the properties of the complex numbers. For this new type one can introduce a multiplication operation that would overload the "*" operator symbol. Multiplication of matrices is another example of possible overloading of the operator symbol "*".

EXAMPLE   We provide some examples here of overloading of operators for the type DATE used in the program ACCR_INTEREST. The body of the function IS_

VALID_DATE and the body of the procedure FILL_IN_DATE, together with the declarative part of the procedure ACCR_INTEREST, are assumed to precede the functions that are described here. The packaging of these subprograms will be done in Chapter 7.

```
function "<=" ( X, Y : DATE := BASE_DATE )

                return BOOLEAN is


--    This function assumes that the dates supplied have the

--    components MONTH_NO, YEAR_NO, and DAY_NO present.


      LOCAL_GOOD_X, LOCAL_GOOD_Y : BOOLEAN

      LOCAL_X, LOCAL_Y : DATE;

begin

      LOCAL_X := X; LOCAL_Y := Y ;

      -- Variables X and Y are formal parameters of mode "in".

      -- They cannot be used in the call to FILL_IN_DATE because

      -- their component values might be modified.

      FILL_IN_DATE ( LOCAL_X, LOCAL_GOOD_X );

      FILL_IN_DATE ( LOCAL_Y, LOCAL_GOOD_Y );

      if LOCAL_GOOD_X and LOCAL_GOOD_Y and

            LOCAL_X.TOTAL_DAYS <= LOCAL_Y.TOTAL_DAYS

            then

            return TRUE;

      else

            return FALSE;

      end if;

      -- An alternative way to define the same function

      -- is to simply compare the relevant  components.
```

```
        -- For example we might use

        -- if  X.YEAR_NO < Y.YEAR_NO or X.YEAR_NO = Y.YEAR_NO

        --      and X.MONTH_NO < Y.MONTH_NO or

        --      X.YEAR_NO = Y.YEAR_NO and X.MONTH_NO = Y.MONTH_NO

        --      and X.DAY_NO <= Y.DAY_NO

        --    then return TRUE; else return FALSE ; end if ;

        -- The chosen alternative does the extra validity check.
end "<=";

-- The second operand of this function assumes the YEAR_NO,

-- MONTH_NO, and DAY_NO elapsed from the X date (rather than

-- rhe year 0, for all the other dates).

function "+" ( X, Y : DATE )

            return DATE is

        LOCAL_GOOD_Z, LEAP_Z : BOOLEAN ;

        LOCAL_Z  : DATE;

begin

        LOCAL_Z.DAY_NO := X.DAY_NO + Y.DAY_NO;

        LOCAL_Z.MONTH_NO := X.MONTH_NO + Y.MONTH_NO ;

        LOCAL_Z.YEAR_NO := X.YEAR_NO + Y.YEAR_NO ;

        if LOCAL_Z.MONTH_NO > 12

        then

            LOCAL_Z.YEAR_NO := LOCAL_Z.YEAR_NO + 1 ;

            LOCAL_Z.MONTH_NO := LOCAL_Z.MONTH_NO - 12 ;

end if;

-- Check to see whether the new year is a leap year.

if  LOCAL_Z.YEAR_NO rem 4 = 0     and
```

```
             LOCAL_Z.YEAR_NO rem 100 /= 0   or

             LOCAL_Z.YEAR_NO rem 400 = 0

          then

             LEAP_Z := TRUE;

       else

             LEAP_Z := FALSE;

       end if;

             -- Now LEAP_Z can be used to refer to the proper

             -- row in the ACTUAL_DAYS_IN_YEAR array.

       if    LOCAL_Z.DAY_NO >

             ACTUAL_DAYS_IN_YEAR( LOCAL_Z.MONTH_NO ,LEAP_Z)

             then
             LOCAL_Z.DAY_NO := LOCAL_Z.DAY_NO -

                  ACTUAL_DAYS_IN_YEAR( LOCAL_Z.MONTH_NO ,LEAP_Z);

             LOCAL_Z.MONTH_NO := LOCAL_Z.MONTH_NO + 1 ;

             if LOCAL_Z.MONTH_NO > 12

                  then

                  LOCAL_Z.YEAR_NO := LOCAL_Z.YEAR_NO + 1 ;

                  LOCAL_Z.MONTH_NO := LOCAL_Z.MONTH_NO - 12 ;

             end if;

       end if;

       FILL_IN_DATE ( LOCAL_Z ,LOCAL_GOOD_Z);

       return LOCAL_Z;

   end "+";
```

Now if we assume that these functions are part of the declarative part of a subprogram that contains the declarations

```
ACT_X, ACT_Y, ACT_Z : DATE;
```

and each of these variables has a valid date, then we can have

```
if ACT_X <= ACT_Y

    then

        ACT_X := ACT_X + ACT_Z;

else

        ACT_Y := ACT_Y + ACT_Z;

end if;
```

Here the operators "<=" and "+", used in connection with ACT_X, ACT_Y, and ACT_Z, are overloaded, and the compiler should be able to use the proper function after the inspection of the operands.

5.5 RECURSIVE CALLS OF SUBPROGRAMS

Functions and procedures in Ada may be **recursive**; that is, they can invoke themselves. This feature is a powerful one that can generate, at times, a large number of statements to be executed with a few lines of code. The recursive feature makes it difficult, though, to trace recursive programs. There are, however, some simple examples of recursive programs, such as the following function for computing the factorial of a positive integer.

```
function FACTORIAL ( I : NATURAL )

            return NATURAL is

    begin

        if I = 0

            then

            return 1;

        else

            return I * FACTORIAL ( I - 1 ) ;

            -- Here the function FACTORIAL invokes

            -- itself, with I - 1 as an actual parameter.
```

```
        end if;

    end FACTORIAL;
```

Assuming that II is a NATURAL type variable, then one can invoke the function FACTORIAL as follows:

```
    II := FACTORIAL ( 5 ) ;
```

The value returned by the function is 120 (5*4*3*2*1). The call invokes the function FACTORIAL with the actual parameter 5 (of mode "in," which is the mode of all function parameters). The function FACTORIAL is then executed, starting with the value 5, and reaches the statement

```
    return I * FACTORIAL ( I - 1 ) ;
```

which requires the execution of another call of the function FACTORIAL, this time with the actual parameter $I - 1$, in this case 4.

Note that the call that started with the value 5 is not completed yet, because the expression

```
    I * FACTORIAL ( I -1 )
```

is not evaluated yet. What happens to the uncompleted call using 5 as an actual parameter while the call using 4 as an actual parameter is executed? The environment of the uncompleted call is saved (point of interruption, values of the variables, parameters, and so on) on a last-in, first-out basis, until the expression

```
    I * FACTORIAL ( I -1 )
```

can be evaluated, that is, until FACTORIAL ($I - 1$) returns a value.

If we trace what happens next, we see that the calls using 4, then 3, then 2, then 1, as actual parameters will be saved for the same reason: The expression

```
    I * FACTORIAL ( I -1 )
```

needs the value of FACTORIAL ($I - 1$) in order to be evaluated. When, finally, the call to FACTORIAL (0) is invoked, there is a pile of five uncompleted calls; at the top (and last in) is FACTORIAL (1), and at the bottom (first in) is FACTORIAL (5). The call FACTORIAL (0) is next completed and returns the value 1. Then, in turn, FACTORIAL (1) is completed (the last call saved is the first one to be completed), and it returns the value 1. Next, the FACTORIAL (2) call will be completed, and it will return the value 2. Then, in sequence, FACTORIAL (3), FACTORIAL (4), and, finally, FACTORIAL (5) will be completed, the last call returning the value 120.

All Ada subprograms are also **reentrant.** We explain the term *reentrant* by describing what it is *not*. A subprogram that has one kind of behavior at one time and a different behavior at another time, with exactly the same actual parameters and exactly the same values of the variables known outside the subprogram, is not reentrant. For instance, suppose we have a subprogram that, the first time it is invoked, sets some variables to some values known only within the subprogram (as opposed to variables that can be known outside the subprogram as well), and these values are used to follow a different logical flow when the subprogram is invoked the second time. This subprogram is not reentrant.

Ada, because it elaborates the declarative part each time the subprogram is invoked, does not allow this kind of behavior (however, each "elaboration" takes some extra time for each subprogram call). Among other advantages, this reentrant feature allows, for instance, the use of only one copy of the subprogram for several different Ada programs, which may all call the subprogram at the same time.

Now we use recursive subprograms in a meaningful and powerful manner in connection with recursive definitions of access types. We will write a modification of the program ACCESS_GRADES of Chapter 3. There is no change in the required input. As in the ACCESS_GRADES program, the information necessary for grading each test is supplied by a pair of lines with the following layout: The first of the pair uses

Columns 1–5   Subject ID (such as MATH1 and ENGL5)
Columns 6–7   Number of questions in the test (between 20 and 50)

The second of the pair is a sequence of digits between 1 and 5. There are as many digits as indicated by the number of questions in the first line of the pair. The end of the key answers to the tests is signaled by a line with XXXXX as the subject ID.

The remaining input lines represent sets of answers for a given student. The student ID is in the first ten columns, and the subject ID is in the next five columns. The answers start in column 16. The input ends with a 9999999999 student ID. Note that a student can take several tests in several different subjects, and there is no predefined order for the student input lines. There is a limit of 25 different tests that can be taken by any student (corresponding to about seven subject matters per semester). Figure 3.7 gave a sample test list, and in Figure 5.1 we supply some sample student IDs and test answers.

FIGURE 5.1 Sample Student Input Lines (Five Tests)

```
1234567890COMP112345123455555111115
1111199999ENGL133333555553333355553333
1111111111ENGL112345678901234567890123
1188888888MATH122222222233333333333322
2222222222ENGL155555555555555555555555
9999999999
```

The required output is quite different from the output for the ACCESS_GRADES program. For each student line read, a corresponding student record is updated by adding the subject and the test score. After all students are read, a list in ascending order by student ID is printed. Each item of the list contains the information related to one student: the student's ID and the subjects taken, together with the test scores.

The student records are organized in a manner sometimes called a **binary tree.** This binary tree organization is illustrated in Figure 5.2, which shows the final setup of the tree for the sample data of Figure 5.1.

We choose to identify a student record by the student ID component (we assume that the student ID is unique for each student). One advantage (among others) of the binary tree organization is that if the student IDs are uniformly random, the adding, retrieval, and updating of student records is fast and straightforward.

RECUR_PROC_GRADES Program

```
with TEXT_IO; use TEXT_IO;

procedure RECUR_PROC_GRADES is

    Package INT_IO is new INTEGER_IO(INTEGER);

    use INT_IO;

    type CHOICES is range 1 .. 5 ;

    type POSSIBLE_QUESTIONS is range 20 .. 50 ;
```

FIGURE 5.2 Sample Binary Tree

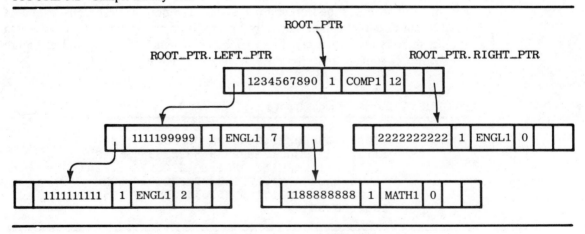

```
Package CHO_IO is new INTEGER_IO(CHOICES);

use CHO_IO;

Package POSS_IO is new INTEGER_IO(POSSIBLE_QUESTIONS);

use POSS_IO;

DNO_QUESTIONS : POSSIBLE_QUESTIONS;

type ANSWERS is array ( 1 .. NO_QUESTIONS ) of CHOICES;

type TEST_KEY;

        -- Here we have an incomplete type declaration,

        -- unchanged from the one inACCESS_GRADES.

type TEST_KEY_PTR is access TEST_KEY;

type TEST_KEY is

    record

            SUBJ          : STRING ( 1 .. 5 );

            NO_QUESTIONS : POSSIBLE_QUESTIONS;

            KEY_ANSWERS  : ANSWERS;

            NEXT_TEST    : TEST_KEY_PTR;

    end record;

CURR_TEST, START_TEST : TEST_KEY_PTR;

GOOD_ANSWERS : INTEGER ;

type IN_REC is

    record

            STUDENT_ID : STRING ( 1 .. 10 );

            SUBJECT_ID : STRING ( 1 .. 5 );

            STUDENT_ANSWERS : ANSWERS ;

    end record;

CURR_REC : IN_REC;
```

```
                       -- There is no change up to this point from the

                       -- ACCESS_GRADES program of Chapter 3.

                       -- Now the declarations for the binary tree are

                       -- added.

          type T_PAIR is

                       -- This type is a pair of  subject matter and

                       -- corresponding score. If the course is ENGL

                       -- then several tests for this course

                       -- might be ENGL1, ENGL2, and ENGL3.

              record

                  SUBJ_MAT : STRING ( 1 .. 5 );

                  SCORE    : NATURAL ;

              end record;

      CURR_PAIR : T_PAIR;

      type SEMESTER_TESTS  is array ( 1 .. 25 ) of T_PAIR;

      type BIG_REC is

          record

                  -- NO_TESTS counts how many tests the student took

                  BIG_ST_ID : STRING ( 1 .. 10 );

                  NO_TESTS  : NATURAL ;

                  ST_TESTS  : SEMESTER_TESTS ;

          end record ;

      type TREE_RECORD;

      type TREE_REC_PTR is access TREE_RECORD ;

      type TREE_RECORD is

          record
```

```
            LEFT_PTR  : TREE_REC_PTR ;

            INFO      : BIG_REC ;

            RIGHT_PTR : TREE_REC_PTR ;

        end record;

    ROOT_PTR : TREE_REC_PTR ;

            -- The root of the binary tree ( ROOT_PTR ) is

            -- the only necessary variable for the

            -- identification of the tree.

procedure INSERT_OR_UPDATE_STUDENT

            ( FORM_ST_ID   : STRING  ;

              FORM_T_PAIR  : T_PAIR ;

              CURR_TREE    :  in out TREE_REC_PTR ) is

            -- This procedure inserts or updates a student

            -- record, which is pointed at by an access

            -- variable of type TREE_REC_PTR. CURR_TREE

            -- eventually will point at the student whose

            -- ID is equal to FORM_ST_ID. If none

            -- is found, a new student record is created

            -- and initialized by FORM_ST_ID and FORM_T_PAIR.

begin

    if CURR_TREE = NULL

        -- This statement is true only if the student whose ID is

        -- FORM_ST_ID is not in the tree.

        then

        CURR_TREE := new  TREE_RECORD ;

        CURR_TREE.INFO.BIG_ST_ID := FORM_ST_ID;
```

```
            CURR_TREE.INFO.NO_TESTS   := 1 ;

            CURR_TREE.INFO.ST_TESTS ( 1 ) := FORM_T_PAIR ;

            -- Remember that CURR_TREE.LEFT_PTR and

            -- CURR_TREE.RIGHT_PTR are initialized with NULL

            -- by Ada itself. Now CURR_TREE.all is the

            -- new student record. For the test data in Figure

            -- 5.1 we will reach this point five times.

      elsif FORM_ST_ID < CURR_TREE.INFO.BIG_ST_ID

            -- For the test data supplied, this test will

            -- be true once when 1111199999 is added,

            -- twice when 1111111111 is added, once when

            -- 1188888888 is added, and no times when

            -- 2222222222 is added.

            then

            INSERT_OR_UPDATE_STUDENT ( FORM_ST_ID,

                          FORM_T_PAIR, CURR_TREE.LEFT_PTR ) ;

            -- This statement is a recursive call of the procedure

            -- INSERT_OR_UPDATE_STUDENT. The current environment is

            -- saved, and the procedure is invoked again with the

            -- left pointer of the CURR_TREE. A call is completed,

            -- and the opportunity to unsave a previous call appears

            -- only when CURR_TREE is null or  a student ID equal to

            -- FORM_ST_ID is found.

      elsif FORM_ST_ID > CURR_TREE.INFO.BIG_ST_ID

            -- This test will be true once when 1188888888 is

            -- added and once when 2222222222 is added.
```

```
        then

        INSERT_OR_UPDATE_STUDENT ( FORM_ST_ID,

                     FORM_T_PAIR, CURR_TREE.LEFT_PTR ) ;

        -- This statements is a recursive call of the procedure

        -- INSERT_OR_UPDATE_STUDENT. The current environment is

        -- saved, and the procedure is invoked again with the

        -- right pointer of the CURR_TREE.

    else

        -- Update the record of this student.

        -- For this test data, these statements will

        -- be executed twice for  1111111111 and once for

        -- 2222222222.

        CURR_TREE.INFO.NO_TESTS  := CURR_TREE.INFO.NO_TESTS + 1 ;

        CURR_TREE.INFO.ST_TESTS ( CURR_TREE.INFO.NO_TESTS )

                     := FORM_T_PAIR ;

    end if;

end INSERT_OR_UPDATE_STUDENT;

procedure LIST_STUDENTS ( FORM_TREE :   TREE_REC_PTR ) is

        -- This procedure will list all the students in

        -- the binary tree. Initially, the root of

        -- the tree is supplied.

begin

    if FORM_TREE /= NULL

        -- As long as FORM_TREE is not NULL, the program will

        -- try to list students from  branches  of  FORM_TREE

        -- according  to   the conditions defined below.
```

```
                    then
                    -- The first priority is to list the left branches.
                    LIST_STUDENTS ( FORM_TREE.LEFT_PTR );
                    -- This point in the program is marked by **AA**.
                    -- The second priority is to display INFO of
                    -- the students.
                    PUT ( FORM_TREE.INFO.BIG_ST_ID ) ;
                    for I in 1 .. FORM_TREE.INFO.NO_TESTS
                        loop
                        PUT(FORM_TREE.INFO.ST_TESTS(I).SUBJ_MAT   ) ;
                        PUT(FORM_TREE.INFO.ST_TESTS(I).SCORE   ) ;
                    end loop;
                    -- The last priority is to list the right branches.
                    -- This point in the program is marked by **BB**.
                    LIST_STUDENTS ( FORM_TREE.LEFT_PTR );
                    -- This point in the program is marked by **CC**.
                    -- The priorities followed imply that  all student
                    -- records will be listed in increasing order
                    -- by student ID.
              end if;
        end LIST_STUDENTS;
    begin
        CURR_TEST := new TEST_KEY;
        GET(CURR_TEST.SUBJ);
        while CURR_TEST.SUBJ /= "XXXXX"
            loop
            -- Here we build  a   list  of  tests   (quite
```

```
            -- similar to the one in ACCESS_GRADES in Chapter 3).
            GET(CURR_TEST.NO_QUESTIONS,2);
            DNO_QUESTIONS := CURR_TEST.NO_QUESTIONS ;
            SKIP_LINE;
            for I in 1 .. CURR_TEST.NO_QUESTIONS
                loop
                GET ( CURR_TEST.KEY_ANSWERS (I), 1);
            end loop;
            if START_TEST = NULL
                then
                -- START_TEST is NULL only the first time.
                START_TEST := CURR_TEST;
            else
                CURR_TEST.NEXT_TEST := START_TEST;
                START_TEST := CURR_TEST;
                -- Every new test becomes the top.
            end if;
            SKIP_LINE;
            CURR_TEST := new TEST_KEY ;
            GET(CURR_TEST.SUBJ);
    end loop;
    SKIP_LINE;
    GET ( CURR_REC.STUDENT_ID ) ;
    while CURR_REC.STUDENT_ID /= "9999999999"
        loop
        GET ( CURR_REC.SUBJECT_ID);
        CURR_TEST := START_TEST;
```

```
while CURR_TEST /= NULL or

       CURR_TEST.SUBJ /= CURR_REC.SUBJECT_ID

       loop

       -- Look for the test subject in the list

       CURR_TEST := CURR_TEST.NEXT_TEST;

end loop;

if CURR_TEST.SUBJ = CURR_REC.SUBJECT_ID

       then

       -- If the test is TRUE, the subject was found.

       -- Otherwise,  there  is  no such subject  in  the

       -- list.

       GOOD_ANSWERS := 0;

       for J in 1 .. CURR_REC.NO_QUESTIONS

           loop

           GET ( CURR_REC.STUDENT_ANSWERS(J), 1);

           if CURR_REC.STUDENT_ANSWERS (J) =

               CURR_TEST.KEY_ANSWERS (J)

               then

               GOOD_ANSWERS := GOOD_ANSWERS + 1 ;

           end if;

       end loop;

       -- The test score is computed now. Also we update

       -- the student record. Or, if this is a new

       -- student, we create the student record. But first

       -- we need the actual arguments in place .

       CURR_PAIR.SUBJ_MAT := CURR_REC.SUBJECT_ID ;
```

```
        CURR_PAIR.SCORE := GOOD_ANSWERS;

        INSERT_OR_UPDATE_STUDENT ( CURR_REC.STUDENT_ID,

              CURR_PAIR, ROOT_PTR );

        -- For the first student ROOT_PTR is null

        -- before the procedure is executed,

        -- but the access value returned will point

        -- at the first student ID = "1234567890".

        -- The ROOT_PTR will not change afterward.

     else

        PUT(" No such subject:");PUT(CURR_REC.SUBJECT_ID);

     end if;

     SKIP_LINE;

     GET ( CURR_REC.STUDENT_ID) ;

  end loop;

  -- All student input lines are processed.

  LIST_STUDENTS ( ROOT_PTR ) ;

  -- List students in sequence by student ID together with

  -- the test subjects and test  scores.

end   RECUR_PROC_GRADES  ;
```

To trace the recursive procedures in this program is quite involved. Figures 5.3A and 5.3B illustrate what is happening while the procedure LIST_STUDENTS is executed in order to give you an idea of how the recursive procedure works.

EXERCISES FOR CHAPTER 5

1. Rewrite one or more of the procedures included in the program NAME_PHONE of Chapter 4 so that formal parameters will be present as in the declarations that follow. Note that the bounds of the FORM_LINE are the

FIGURE 5.3   LIST_STUDENTS Subprogram Execution

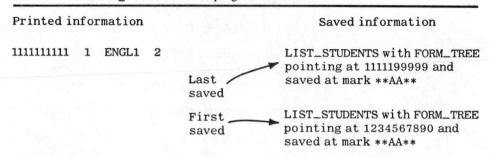

Printed information   Saved information

1111111111   1   ENGL1   2

Last saved ——→   LIST_STUDENTS with FORM_TREE pointing at 1111199999 and saved at mark **AA**

First saved ——→   LIST_STUDENTS with FORM_TREE pointing at 1234567890 and saved at mark **AA**

A. With FORM_TREE Pointing at Student ID 1111111111 Taken at Mark **BB**

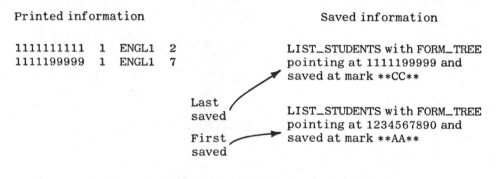

Printed information   Saved information

1111111111   1   ENGL1   2
1111199999   1   ENGL1   7

LIST_STUDENTS with FORM_TREE pointing at 1111199999 and saved at mark **CC**

Last saved

First saved ——→   LIST_STUDENTS with FORM_TREE pointing at 1234567890 and saved at mark **AA**

B. With FORM_TREE Pointing at Student ID 1188888888 Taken at Mark **BB**

bounds of the actual parameters (in this case the use of attributes like FORM_LINE'LAST or FORM_LINE'LENGTH is recommended). The value of the attributes of formal parameters is derived from the value of the attributes of actual parameters.

```
procedure LOW_TO_UPPER_N_CT_COMMAS

        ( FORM_LINE : in out STRING ) ;

procedure IGNORE_LEADING_SPACES

        ( FORM_LINE : in out STRING ;

          FORM_END_POS : out NATURAL );
```

```
        -- Here   the   FORM_END_POS  should  return   the
        -- position of the first non space character
procedure FIND_NEXT_SP_OR_COMMA
        ( FORM_LINE : in out STRING ;
          FORM_START_POS : in out NATURAL ;
          FORM_END_POS   : in out NATURAL ) ;
procedure PLACE_SPACES
        ( FORM_LINE : in out STRING ;
          FORM_START_POS : in out NATURAL ;
          FORM_END_POS   : in out NATURAL ) ;
function IS_CORRECT_NAME
        ( FORM_LINE : STRING ;
          FORM_START_POS : NATURAL ;
          FORM_END_POS   : NATURAL )
               return BOOLEAN ;
procedure XTR_NAME
        -- This procedure will replace
        -- the procedures XTR_N_VAL_FIRST_NAME and
        -- XTR_N_VAL_LAST_NAME.
        ( FORM_LINE : in out STRING ;
          FORM_START_POS : in out NATURAL ;
          FORM_END_POS   : in out NATURAL ;
          XTR_NAME       : out STRING  ) ;
        -- The name extracted is placed in XTR_NAME
procedure XTR_N_VAL_MDL_INIT
        ( FORM_LINE : in out STRING ;
```

```
                              FORM_START_POS : in out NATURAL ;

                              FORM_END_POS   : in out NATURAL ) ;

           procedure XTR_N_VAL_PHONE

                    ( FORM_LINE : in out STRING ;

                      FORM_START_POS : in out NATURAL ;

                      FORM_END_POS   : in out NATURAL ;

                      XTR_PHONE      : out STRING  ) ;
```

2. Write a function that computes the positive square root of a positive real number. You may wish to use Newton's method, where the $(n + 1)$th approximation to the square root of a number X is given by

```
      0.5 * ( Curr_aprox + X / Curr_aprox ) ;
```

and where the Curr_aprox is the nth approximation to the square root. This iterative computation should stop when the difference between two consecutive approximations is less than a predefined small positive number.

3. Replace the function FIND_COUP_DATE appearing in the program ACCR_INTEREST of this chapter by a procedure that will find the coupon dates preceding and following the settlement date. The declaration for the new procedure might be

```
      procedure GET_COUP_DATES

                ( FORM_MAT_DATE  : DATE ;

                  FORM_SETL_DATE : DATE ;

                  FORM_PREV_DATE : out DATE ;

                  FORM_NEXT_DATE : out DATE ) ;
```

Here FORM_PREV_DATE is the coupon payment date immediately preceding the settlement date. FORM_NEXT_DATE is the coupon payment date immediately following the settlement date. Make the required modifications in the program ACCRUED_INTEREST.

4. Replace the procedure CHECK_GRADE appearing in the program GR_POINT_AVE of Chapter 4 by a procedure that has the following declaration:

```
      procedure CHECK_GRADE

                ( FORM_COURSE_GR : STRING ( 1 .. 2 ) ;
```

```
FORM_GR_POINT   : out FLOAT ;

FORM_VALID_GR   : out BOOLEAN ) ;
```

The FORM_VALID_GR should play the role of VALID_GRADE, and FORM_GR_POINT should play the role of GRADE_POINT. Make any other modifications to the program GR_POINT_AVE related to the new procedure.

5. Modify the program RECUR_PROC_GRADES so that after all students are read and placed in the binary tree, each student record is updated to reflect the following policy: If a student takes more than two tests in a subject area, only the best two scores are kept (the remaining scores in the same subject area are discarded). Two tests are in the same subject area if the first four characters of the SUBJ_MAT component are identical.

CHAPTER SIX

DECLARATIVE PARTS AND PRAGMAS

6.1 Elaboration of Declarative Parts
6.2 Type Conversions
6.3 Pragmas
6.4 Review of Main Ada Features

6.1 ELABORATION OF DECLARATIVE PARTS

We have seen that subprograms bodies have a declarative part and a sequence-of-statements part. The **declarative part** associates names with declared entities, and the **sequence-of-statements part** describes the actions to be taken by the subprogram. The order of processing for a subprogram unit is as follows: The declarative part is elaborated, and then the sequence-of-statements is executed.

The **elaboration** of the declarative part involves several steps. First, identifiers are introduced at the point where they are first encountered; this introduction may hide other identical identifiers encountered earlier. Next, the declared entity just introduced is elaborated. For instance, a (static) expression appearing in a declaration part is evaluated as part of the elaboration process. For objects the type is established, and constraints are evaluated. The elaboration of function and procedure declarations involves the elaboration of the parameter declarations in the order in which they appear. The elaboration of a type definition involves the elaboration of a set of values and operations defined for these values. The last step of the elaboration process is the initialization of an object, if it is required.

The lines constituting the declarative part are elaborated in sequence. Unless the body of a subprogram is separately compiled (as we will see in Chapter 9), if a subprogram is declared within a declarative part, then its body has to be present in the same declarative part.

SCOPE AND VISIBILITY OF IDENTIFIERS

The **scope** of an identifier is represented by the portion of Ada code over which the declaration of the identifier is in force. It starts at the point where the identifier is introduced (assuming that it is declared in the declarative part of a block or a subprogram). In subprograms or blocks the scope ends with the end of the subprogram or the block whose declarative part contains the identifier.

The identifier may or may not be **visible** over its whole scope. That is, in some portions of the Ada code, within the scope of the given identifier, the identifier may not be known simply by the use of the identifier. We will provide some examples of this situation later.

No entity (objects, numbers, and so forth) can be used before its elaboration is completed. For this reason we have made sure that whenever a subprogram is invoked, its body appears textually before the invocation point. For the same reason, whenever we have initialized a constant or a variable by using other identifiers, we have made sure that these identifiers were introduced and elaborated earlier.

One may run out of storage during the elaboration of a declarative part. In this case the exception STORAGE_ERROR is raised (we will discuss the raising of exceptions in Chapter 11).

EXAMPLE   The following procedure illustrates some of the concepts mentioned so far.

```
procedure EX is

        I : INTEGER := 0 ;

        J : INTEGER := K + I ;

        -- This declaration is not valid because K has to be

        -- elaborated by the time J is.

        K : INTEGER := 5 ;

        L : SMALL_RANGE ;

        -- This declaration is not valid because the elaboration

        -- of the type SMALL_RANGE has to precede the

        -- elaboration of L.

        type SMALL_RANGE is range 1 .. 5 ;

        procedure IN1 is
```

```
    I : STRING ( 1 .. 5 );

begin

        null;

        -- At least one statement is needed here.

        -- The scope of I (the string type oject) extends

        -- from the declaration point until the line end IN1;

        -- The identifier I (the integer type object) is

        -- not visible within the procedure IN1,  even though

        -- the procedure IN1 is within its scope.

        -- This situation is an example of overloading of the

        -- variable I (as opposed to subprogram overloading

        -- covered in Chapter 5).

        -- If we want to refer to the integer type variable I

        -- within the body of IN1, then we can use the selected

        -- component notation EX.I

    end IN1 ;

    begin

        null;

end EX;
```

Remember that some other entities like loop identifiers and block identifiers are implicitly declared at the end of the innermost enclosing block or subprogram. That is, their elaboration is supposed to take place after the elaboration of the explicit declarations.

OVERLOADING OF VARIABLES AND VALUES AND THE USE OF QUALIFIERS

The procedure EX contained an example of variable overloading. Values can be overloaded too. We gave an example of aggregate overloading in Section 4.2. Here is an example of an enumeration literal overloading:

```
type FEM_NAMES is ( MARY, CHARLIE, LAURIE,
  NANCY ) ;
type MAL_NAMES is ( JOHN, LAURIE, BOB, CHARLIE )
  ;
```

The value (enumeration literal) CHARLIE is overloaded because it denotes two different values belonging to two different types. This overloading is not an error, but one should be careful to refer to the proper CHARLIE by using a **type qualifier,** as follows: Use the qualifier

```
FEM_NAMES' (CHARLIE)
```

to refer to the CHARLIE value of the type FEM_NAMES, and use

```
MAL_NAMES' (CHARLIE)
```

to refer to the CHARLIE value of the type MAL_NAMES.

In general, **qualified expressions** have the form

```
type_or_subtype' (expression)
```

For aggregates the form is

```
type_or_subtype' aggregate
```

Qualified expressions are necessary for expressions or aggregates whenever the type cannot be clearly determined from the context. For instance, an expression like

```
CHARLIE < JOHN
```

is not ambiguous because JOHN is a value of the type MAL_NAMES (here it is FALSE). However, an invalid expression like

```
CHARLIE < LAURIE
```

is ambiguous because it is not clear to which type the two enumeration literals belong. The proper way to write the expression is

```
MAL_NAMES' (CHARLIE) < MAL_NAMES' (LAURIE)
```

If the other alternative is chosen, the form is

```
FEM_NAMES' (CHARLIE) < FEM_NAMES' (LAURIE)
```

6.2 TYPE CONVERSIONS

In the first three chapters we covered all Ada types except the private types (they will be covered in Chapter 7). And in Chapter 2 we briefly described the rules to be followed for type conversions involving numeric types. The rules about mixing types in Ada are strict. However, one has some freedom in using the universal types like the universal integers and the universal real numbers. That is, one can mix universal real and universal integer numbers in expressions without any kind of explicit conversions.

EXAMPLE   Suppose we have the following declarations:

`I : constant := 5 ;`	I is of type universal integer and is initialized by the universal integer literal value 5
`X : constant := 2.71 ;`	X is of type universal real and is initialized by the universal real literal value 2.71

Then the following expressions are valid.

Expression	Result
`5 * I`	Returns a value (25) of type universal integer; no conversion is necessary
`3.0 * X`	Returns a value (8.13) of type universal real; no conversion is necessary
`5.0 * I`	Returns a value (25.0) of type universal real; no conversion is necessary
`I * X`	Returns a value (13.55) of type universal real; no conversion is necessary

In general, explicit type conversions are allowed only among numeric types, derived types, and array types. The general form of the **type conversion** is

```
type_or_subtype ( expression )
```

The exception CONSTRAINT_ERROR is raised by a type conversion whenever the value of the evaluated expression fails to satisfy any of the constraints imposed by the type or the subtype chosen as the target for the conversion.

For numeric types (integer and real types) the expression following the type_or_subtype indication can be of any numeric type. The value of the expression is converted to the base type of the type_or_subtype. The type_or_subtype part is called a type_mark. Conversions from real type values to integers involve rounding.

For array types the conversion is allowed if the index types of each dimension of the type_mark and of the value returned by the expression are the same or are derived from each other, and if the matching component types are the same or are derived from each other.

EXAMPLE   Let us assume that we have the following declarations:

```
type HOURS_WORKED is array ( NATURAL range <> ) of NATURAL;

subtype HRS_WRKD_MONTHLY is HOURS_WORKED ( 1 .. 31 ) ;

subtype HRS_WRKD_WEEKLY is HOURS_WORKED ( 1 .. 7 ) ;

TOTAL_HOURS : HOURS_WORKED ;

MONTHLY_DATA : HRS_WRKD_MONTHLY;

WEEKLY_DATA  : HRS_WRKD_WEEKLY;
```

Then we can have the following array conversions:

```
    HRS_WRKD_MONTHLY( TOTAL_HOURS ( 44 .. 74 ) )
```

Here the bounds 44 . . 74 of the array variable TOTAL_HOURS are converted into bounds 1 . . 31 of an array variable of type HRS_WRKD_MONTHLY.

```
    HOURS_WORKED ( MONTHLY_DATA )
```

Here the bounds 1 . . 31 of the array type variable MONTHLY_DATA supply the bounds 1 . . 31 of an array variable of type HOURS_WORKED.

```
    HRS_WRKD_WEEKLY ( MONTHLY_DATA ( 13 .. 19 ) )
```

Here the bounds 13 . . 19 of the slice of the array MONTHLY_DATA become the bounds 1 . . 7 of an array whose type is HRS_WRKD_WEEKLY.

Conversions involving derived types are allowed when both the type of the type_mark and the type of the value returned by the expression can be derived from each other or have the same parent type.

EXAMPLE   Let us look at some examples of possible conversions making use of derived types. Suppose we have the following declarations:

```
type DAYS is INTEGER range 1 .. 130_000 ;

type JULIAN_DAYS is new DAYS range 1 .. 366 ;

type MONTHLY_DAYS is new DAYS range 1 .. 31 ;

CURR_JUL : JULIAN_DAYS ;

LONG_DAYS : DAYS ;

CURR_MONTH : MONTHLY_DAYS ;
```

Then we can have the following conversions:

```
LONG_DAYS := 5 ;

CURR_MONTH := MONTHLY_DAYS ( LONG_DAYS ) ;

CURR_JUL   := JULIAN_DAYS ( CURR_MONTH ) ;
```

More examples will be provided in the program given in Section 6.4.

Whenever a conversion is allowed from one type to another, the reverse conversion is also allowed. When one is invoking subprograms, the reverse conversion is used when the actual parameter (assumed to be of mode "in out" or mode "out") is supplied as the result of a type conversion.

EXAMPLE   In this example we assume we have the array declarations given in the preceding example. In addition, we have the procedure declaration

```
Procedure ADD_HRS ( FORM_TOT_HRS : in out
    HOURS_WORKED ; I : INTEGER ) ;
```

Then we can invoke it by the statement

```
ADD_HRS ( HOURS_WORKED(WEEKLY_DATA), II ) ;
```

where II is an integer type variable. Here the value of the actual parameter WEEKLY_DATA is converted to a value of type HOURS_WORKED, which is matched with the formal parameter FORM_TOT_HRS. After the execution of the procedure ADD_HRS is completed, the value returned by FORM_TOT_HRS (of type HOURS_WORKED) is converted to a value of type WEEKLY_DATA and placed in the location associated with the variable WEEKLY_DATA. That is, a conversion back to WEEKLY_DATA of the form

```
HRS_WRKD_WEEKLY ( FORM_TOT_HRS ( 1 .. 7 ) )
```

is implicit after the execution of the procedure is completed.

6.3 PRAGMAS

Pragmas in Ada are directives to the Ada compiler. Pragmas have the following form:

```
pragma identifier ;
```

If arguments are present, the form is

```
pragma identifier
        (one_or_more_arguments_separated_by_commas ) ;
```

A pragma is either language-defined (and we are only going to use language-defined pragmas) or implementation-defined. For instance, we may have a pragma without an argument, like

```
PAGE ;
```

The PAGE pragma directs the compiler to start the next line of program text on a new page. Another example of a pragma is

```
pragma LIST ( OFF );
```

(the other possible argument is ON). This pragma directs the compiler to suppress the listing of the compilation until the

```
pragma LIST ( ON ) ;
```

directive is reached. The LIST and PAGE pragmas are allowed anywhere in a program. Other pragmas, however, are allowed only in certain parts of the Ada program.

As we mentioned in the previous chapter, subprograms generate substantial overhead (running time) every time they are invoked. To eliminate the overhead associated with the elaboration of the declarative part and the matching of actual and formal parameters, one can use the pragma INLINE. The effect of this pragma is to expand the subprogram body in line at the point where the subprogram is invoked. All the other benefits associated with the subprogram's use are maintained. The pragma is placed in the declarative part, below the declaration of the subprogram names. For instance, we may have

```
pragma INLINE ( xx, yy, zz );
```

where xx, yy, and zz are subprogram names.

There are pragmas like ELABORATE related to compilation units (compilations units will be discussed in Chapter 9). There are also pragmas related to tasks, like pragma PRIORITY; such pragmas will be covered in Chapter 10. There is also a pragma called INTERFACE that takes a language name (say COBOL) and a program name (written in COBOL, for instance) as arguments.

A complete list of the language pragmas is supplied in Appendix B. Some examples are

```
pragma SUPPRESS ( RANGE_CHECK, ON => INDEX );
```

which gives the permission to omit a given check, and

```
pragma PACK ( ARRAY_NAME );
pragma OPTIMIZE ( TIME ) ;
pragma OPTIMIZE ( SPACE ) ;
```

These last two pragmas will try to optimize the code generated by the compiler with the purpose of choosing representations that speed up the execution of the program (OPTIMIZE (TIME)) or choosing representations that make efficient use of space (OPTIMIZE (SPACE)). There is no language-defined pragma for, say, conditional compilation, but one would expect to find such a pragma among the implementation-defined pragmas.

6.4 REVIEW OF MAIN ADA FEATURES

In this section we present a program that makes use of subprograms, conversion rules, pragmas, records with variants, access types, derived types, subtypes, and a full variety of the Ada statements used so far. It represents a panorama of the features used in the first six chapters of this book.

The program computes interest rates given prices for two kinds of financial instruments. To simplify the problem, we will consider only discounted securities, like U.S. Treasury bills, and securities paying interest at maturity, like certain certificates of deposit (CDs) or commercial paper.

The calculations of yield given price for securities paying interest at maturity use the formula

```
YLD  = ( 1 + DAYS_ISS_MAT / D_IN_YEAR * S_RATE - ( QT_PRICE +

         DAYS_ISS_SET / D_IN_YEAR * S_RATE ) ) /

         ( QT_PRICE + DAYS_ISS_SET / D_IN_YEAR * S_RATE )

       * D_IN_YEAR / DAYS_SET_MAT
```

And the variables used in the formula have the following meaning:

Variable	Meaning
DAYS_ISS_SET	Number of days from the issue date to the settlement date
D_IN_YEAR	Number of days in the year
DAYS_ISS_MAT	Number of days from the issue date to the maturity date
DAYS_SET_MAT	Number of days from the settlement date to the maturity date
QT_PRICE	Quoted price of the security divided by 100
S_RATE	Annual interest rate or coupon rate (as a decimal)
YLD	Annual yield (as a decimal) on the investment, with the security held to maturity or the call date, if priced to the call date

The calculation of the discount rate given the (discounted) price is given by the formula

```
DISC_RATE = ( 100 - DISC_PRICE ) / 100 *
    D_IN_YEAR / DAYS_SET_MAT
```

where DISC_RATE is the discount rate (as a decimal).

To compare the rates (YLD, which is the money market yield) with the discount rate, we use the formula

```
YLD_OF_DISC = DISC_RATE * 100 / DISC_PRICE
```

The program assumes that no settlement date, maturity date, or issue date falls on a weekend or a legal holiday. (See Exercise 1 for this additional check.)

The data for securities, one security per line, has the following format (the last line contains a security name of "5555588888"):

Column	Data
Columns 1–15	Type of security (AT_MATURITY or DISCOUNT)
Columns 16–25	Security name
Columns 26–31	Settlement date in the format YYMMDD
Columns 32–37	Maturity date
Columns 38–48	Day count basis (ACT_360 and so on)

And depending on the security type, for AT_MATURITY the format is as follows:

Column	Data
Columns 49–54	Issue date
Columns 55–60	Stated rate
Columns 61–68	Quoted price (with two decimals)

For DISCOUNT security types the format is

Columns 49–57	Discount price (with two decimals)

For each security the program computes its yield. For discount securities the discount rate is computed first. Securities are placed in a list in ascending order by maturity date.

The yield as a function of maturity date is sometimes referred to as the *yield curve*. After all securities are processed, the yield curve should be tested for convexity (its normal appearance). The convexity test is as follows: For any security its yield should be at least as high as the average of the immediately preceding and immediately following security yield in the list.

The last assumption to be made (this assumption simplifies the problem, but see Exercise 2 for a more realistic treatment) is that the settlement dates are within a few days of each other.

YIELD_COMPUTATION Program

```
with TEXT_IO ; use TEXT_IO ;

procedure YIELD_COMPUTATION is

    type INTEREST is digits 13 ;

    type DISCOUNT_INTEREST is new INTEREST ;

    type AT_MAT_INTEREST is new INTEREST;

        -- We should not  mix discount interest and

        -- other types of interest. They have different

        -- meanings and state different things. The use

        -- of derived types is quite appropriate here.

    WORK_AT_MAT_INT_1, WORK_AT_MAT_INT_2  : AT_MAT_INTEREST ;

            -- Variables   starting   with   work   are   for

            -- housekeeping.

    type INTEREST_KIND is ( COUPON, AT_MATURITY, DISCOUNT ) ;

            -- COUPON yields will not be used; this

            -- enumeration   value   is   given   only   for

            -- completeness.

    package INT_KIND_IO is new ENUMERATION_IO ( INTEREST_KIND );

    use INT_KIND_IO ;

    CURR_INT_KIND : INTEREST_KIND ;

    CURR_SEC_NAME : STRING ( 1 .. 10 ) ;

    type DAY_COUNT_BASIS is ( ACT_ACT, ACT_360, M_30_Y_360 ) ;

            -- ACT_ACT means that for computational purposes

            -- the month has the actual number of days (28-31)
```

```
                    -- and the year the actual number of days (365-366).

                    -- ACT_360 means that for computational purposes

                    -- the month has the actual number of days but

                    -- the year has 360 days. M_30_Y_360 means that the

                    -- month has 30 days and the year has 360.

    package DAY_KIND_IO is new ENUMERATION_IO ( DAY_COUNT_BASIS );

    use DAY_KIND_IO ;

    type PRICES is digits 13 ;

     type DISCOUNT_PRICES is new PRICES     ;

            -- Again, discount prices mean quite different things

            -- from other  kinds of security prices

    type DAY is (MONDAY,TUESDAY,WEDNESDAY,THURSDAY,FRIDAY,

            SATURDAY,SUNDAY);

    subtype WEEKEND is DAY range SATURDAY..SUNDAY ;

    type DAY_INT is range 1 .. 31;

    type JULIAN_DAYS is range 1 .. 366 ;

    type MONTH is (JANUARY,FEBRUARY,MARCH,APRIL,MAY,JUNE,

                JULY,AUGUST,SEPTEMBER,OCTOMBER,NOVEMBER,DECEMBER);

    type YEAR is range 0 .. 2050 ;

    type MONTH_INT is range 1 .. 12;

    Package DAY_IO is new ENUMERATION_IO(DAY);

    use DAY_IO;

    Package MONTH_IO is new ENUMERATION_IO(MONTH);

    use MONTH_IO;

    Package YEAR_IO is new INTEGER_IO(YEAR);

    use YEAR_IO;
```

```
Package MONTH_INT is new INTEGER_IO(MONTH_INT);

use MONTH_INT;

Package DAY_INT_IO is new INTEGER_IO(DAY_INT);

use DAY_INT_IO;

type DATE is

    record

            WEEK_DAY  : DAY;

            MONTH_NAME : MONTH;

            MONTH_NO : MONTH_INT;

            DAY_NO    : DAY_INT;

            YTD_DAYS : JULIAN_DAYS;

            TOTAL_DAYS : INTEGER ;

            YEAR_NO  : YEAR;

    end record;

BASE_DATE : constant DATE := ( MONDAY,JANUARY,1,1,1,1,1984);

            -- For this program we assume that only dates

            -- after Jan. 1 , 1984, are supplied.

BASE_LEAP : constant INTEGER :=

            INTEGER(BASE_DATE.YEAR_NO) / 4 +

            INTEGER(BASE_DATE.YEAR_NO)   /   400 -

            INTEGER(BASE_DATE.YEAR_NO)   /   100;

            -- This constant represents the number of leap years

            -- that have occurred from year 0 to the

            -- BASE_DATE.YEAR_NO.

type DAYS_IN_MONTH is array (MONTH_INT,BOOLEAN) of DAY_INT;

ACTUAL_DAYS_IN_YEAR : constant DAYS_IN_MONTH :=
```

```
        ( (31,28,31,30,31,30,31,31,30,31,30,31) ,

          (31,29,31,30,31,30,31,31,30,31,30,31) ) ;

Package INT_IO is new INTEGER_IO(INTEGER);

use INT_IO;

D_IN_YEAR : NATURAL := 360 ;

DAYS_ISS_SET : NATURAL ;

DAYS_ISS_MAT : NATURAL ;

DAYS_SET_MAT : NATURAL ;

type SECURITY ( INT_PAYM : INTEREST_KIND := DISCOUNT )   is

    record

            SEC_NAME  : STRING ( 1 .. 10 );

            SETL_DATE : DATE ;

            MAT_DATE  : DATE ;

            DAY_KIND  : DAY_COUNT_BASIS ;

            YLD       : INTEREST ;

            case INT_PAYM is

                when AT_MATURITY =>

                        ISSUE_DATE : DATE ;

                        S_RATE     : AT_MAT_INTEREST ;

                        QT_PRICE   : PRICES ;

                when DISCOUNT    =>

                        DISC_PRICE : DISCOUNT_PRICES ;

                        DISC_RATE  : DISCOUNT_INTEREST ;

                when others      => null;

            end case ;

    end record;
```

```
CURR_SECURITY_1 : SECURITY :=

            ( AT_MATURITY, "1234567890",BASE_DATE, BASE_DATE ,

             M_30_Y_360, 10.0, BASE_DATE, 10.0, 100.00 ) ;

            -- This varaible is initialized using a  positional

            -- aggregate , choosing  the AT_MATURITY

            -- discriminant constraint.

CURR_SECURITY_2 : SECURITY :=

          (  INT_PAYM   => DISCOUNT,

             SEC_NAME   => "1234512345",

             SETL_DATE  => BASE_DATE ,

             MAT_DATE   => BASE_DATE ,

             DAY_KIND   => M_30_Y360 ,

             YLD        => 10.00 ,

             DISC_PRICE => 99.00 ,

             DISC_RATE  => 10.00  ) ;

            -- This variable is initialized  using a named

            -- component aggregate,  choosing  the DISCOUNT

            -- discriminant constraint.

Package INTEREST_IO is new FLOAT_IO(INTEREST);

use INTEREST_IO;

Package PRICES_IO is new FLOAT_IO(PRICES);

use PRICES_IO;

Package DISC_IO is new FLOAT_IO(DISCOUNT_INTEREST);

use DISC_IO;

Package AT_MAT_IO is new FLOAT_IO(AT_MAT_INTEREST);

use AT_MAT_IO;
```

```
        LEAP_YEAR : BOOLEAN;

        INPUT_LEAP  : INTEGER ;

        GOOD_MAT_DATE, GOOD_SETL_DATE : BOOLEAN;

        GOOD_ISSUE_DATE : BOOLEAN ;

        BAD_LINE : BOOLEAN ;

                -- If any date on a line

                -- is bad, BAD_LINE is set to TRUE.

        type SEC_NODE;

        type SEC_PTR is access SEC_NODE;

        type SEC_NODE is

            record

                    SEC_INFO : SECURITY ;

                    SEC_NEXT : SEC_PTR ;

            end record;

        CURR_PTR, TOP_PTR, ANY_PTR, PREV_PTR : SEC_PTR ;

        NORM_CURVE : BOOLEAN ;

                -- This variable is set TRUE if the

                -- yield curve appears normal.

        pragma PAGE;

                -- A new page should be started,

                -- commencing with the line below.

    function IS_VALID_DATE ( FORM_DATE : DATE )

                    return BOOLEAN is

                -- This function returns the value TRUE if the

                -- date FORM_DATE.MONTH_NO, FORM_DATE.DAY_NO, and

                -- FORM_DATE.YEAR_NO represents a valid date.
```

```
                    -- Otherwise, it returns  the value FALSE.
    begin

            pragma LIST ( OFF ) ;
                    -- The sequence of statements
                    -- for this subprogram should not be listed.
                    -- The sequence of statements for this procedure
                    -- is identical to the one in the program
                    -- ACCR_INTEREST of Chapter 5. It should
                    -- be inserted here.
            pragma LIST ( ON ) ;
                    -- Resume the listing of the
                    -- source code.
    end IS_VALID_DATE;
    procedure FILL_IN_DATE
            ( PROC_F_DATE : in out DATE ;
            GOOD_DATE : out BOOLEAN ) is
                    -- This procedure will supply the remaining
                    -- components of PROC_F_DATE assuming that the
                    -- other components, FORM_DATE.MONTH_NO,
                    -- FORM_DATE.DAY_NO, and FORM_DATE.YEAR_NO,
                    -- represent a valid date. If the other components
                    -- do not represent a valid date, then GOOD_DATE is
                    -- set to FALSE. There are two formal parameters
                    -- in the formal part:  PROC_F_DATE of type record
                    -- and GOOD_DATE of type BOOLEAN.
    begin
```

```
                  pragma LIST ( OFF ) ;
                      -- The sequence of statements
                      -- for this subprogram should not be listed.
                      -- The sequence of statements for this procedure
                      -- is identical to the one in the program
                      -- ACCR_INTEREST of Chapter 5. It should
                      -- be inserted here.
                  pragma LIST ( ON ) ;
                      -- Resume the listing of the
                      -- source code.
      end FILL_IN_DATE ;
      function "-" ( X, Y : DATE )
                      -- This procedure computes the elapsed days,
                      -- assuming an M_30_Y_360 day count basis.
                      -- An example of an overloaded operator
                      -- is the - used here.
                      return NATURAL is
      begin
          if X.TOTAL_DAYS < Y.TOTAL_DAYS
              then
              return 0 ;
          else
              return 360 * INTEGER ( X.YEAR_NO  - Y.YEAR_NO  ) +
                     30 * INTEGER ( X.MONTH_NO - Y.MONTH_NO ) +
                     INTEGER (  X.DAY_NO   - Y.DAY_NO  ) ;
          end if;
```

```
end "-";

        pragma PAGE ;

            -- Start the sequence of statements

            -- for the program on a new page.

begin

    GET(CURR_INT_KIND);

    GET(CURR_SEC_NAME);

    while CURR_SEC_NAME /= "5555588888"

        loop

        case CURR_INT_KIND is

          when AT_MATURITY =>

            CURR_SECURITY_1.SEC_NAME := CURR_SEC_NAME ;

            -- Get the remaining items off the line.

            GET( CURR_SECURITY_1.SETL_DATE.YEAR_NO,2 ) ;

            GET( CURR_SECURITY_1.SETL_DATE.MONTH_NO,2 ) ;

            GET( CURR_SECURITY_1.SETL_DATE.DAY_NO,2 ) ;

            GET( CURR_SECURITY_1.MAT_DATE.YEAR_NO,2 ) ;

            GET( CURR_SECURITY_1.MAT_DATE.MONTH_NO,2 ) ;

            GET( CURR_SECURITY_1.MAT_DATE.DAY_NO,2 ) ;

            GET( CURR_SECURITY_1.DAY_KIND );

            GET( CURR_SECURITY_1.ISSUE_DATE.YEAR_NO,2 ) ;

            GET( CURR_SECURITY_1.ISSUE_DATE.MONTH_NO,2 ) ;

            GET( CURR_SECURITY_1.ISSUE_DATE.DAY_NO,2 ) ;

            GET( CURR_SECURITY_1.S_RATE, 6  ) ;

            GET( CURR_SECURITY_1.QT_PRICE, 8  ) ;

            -- Check each of the dates to make sure that they
```

```
               -- are valid, and fill in the other components
               -- by invoking FILL_IN_DATE.
               FILL_IN_DATE (CURR_SECURITY_1.SETL_DATE ,
                         GOOD_SETL_DATE) ;
               FILL_IN_DATE (CURR_SECURITY_1.MAT_DATE ,
                         GOOD_MAT_DATE) ;
               FILL_IN_DATE (CURR_SECURITY_1.ISSUE_DATE ,
                         GOOD_ISSUE_DATE) ;
               if not ( GOOD_SETL_DATE and GOOD_MAT_DATE and
                  GOOD_ISSUE_DATE and
                           CURR_SECURITY_1.MAT_DATE.TOTAL_DAYS >
                           CURR_SECURITY_1.SETL_DATE.TOTAL_DAYS
                                    and
                           CURR_SECURITY_1.SETL_DATE.TOTAL_DAYS >
                           CURR_SECURITY_1.ISSUE_DATE.TOTAL_DAYS )
                  then
                     BAD_LINE := TRUE ;
                     PUT ( " Bad line  " ) ;
                     PUT ( CURR_SEC_NAME ) ;
                     NEW_LINE ;
               end if;
               if not BAD_LINE
                  then
                     -- Compute the yield, depending on the
                     -- day count basis.
                     case CURR_SECURITY_1.DAY_KIND is
```

```
when ACT_360     =>

DAYS_SET_MAT := CURR_SECURITY_1.MAT_DATE.TOTAL_DAYS

       -  CURR_SECURITY_1.SETL_DATE.TOTAL_DAYS ;

DAYS_ISS_SET := CURR_SECURITY_1.SET_DATE.TOTAL_DAYS

       -  CURR_SECURITY_1.ISSUE_DATE.TOTAL_DAYS ;

when M_30_Y_360 =>

DAYS_SET_MAT := CURR_SECURITY_1.MAT_DATE -

              CURR_SECURITY_1.SETL_DATE;

DAYS_ISS_MAT := CURR_SECURITY_1.SETL_DATE -

              CURR_SECURITY_1.ISSUE_DATE ;

-- The  operator - is  overloaded.

when  others  =>

      PUT ( " what security is  this ");

      PUT ( CURR_SEC_NAME ) ;

      NEW_LINE;

end case;

-- Here quite a few conversions to the

-- AT_MAT_INTEREST type are necessary.

WORK_AT_MAT_INT_1 :=  CURR_SECURITY_1.S_RATE  /

      AT_MAT_INTEREST ( D_IN_YEAR ) ;

  WORK_AT_MAT_INT_2 :=

  AT_MAT_INTEREST ( CURR_SECURITY_1.QT_PRICE )

  + AT_MAT_INTEREST ( DAYS_ISS_SET ) /

      WORK_AT_MAT_INT_1 ;

CURR_SECURITY_1.YLD := INTEREST (

  ( 1.0 + AT_MAT_INTEREST ( DAYS_ISS_MAT ) /
```

```
                             WORK_AT_MAT_INT_1    -

                             WORK_AT_MAT_INT_2 )    /

                             WORK_AT_MAT_INT_2        *

                             AT_MAT_INTEREST ( D_IN_YEAR ) /

                             AT_MAT_INTEREST (DAYS_SET_MAT ) ) ;

                 -- Create an element to be placed in a list.

                 CURR_PTR := new SEC_NODE ;

                 CURR_PTR.SEC_INFO := CURR_SECURITY_1 ;

             end if;

        when DISCOUNT    =>

             CURR_SECURITY_2.SEC_NAME := CURR_SEC_NAME ;

             -- Get the remaining items off the line.

             GET( CURR_SECURITY_2.SETL_DATE.YEAR_NO,2 ) ;

             GET( CURR_SECURITY_2.SETL_DATE.MONTH_NO,2 ) ;

             GET( CURR_SECURITY_2.SETL_DATE.DAY_NO,2 ) ;

             GET( CURR_SECURITY_2.MAT_DATE.YEAR_NO,2 ) ;

             GET( CURR_SECURITY_2.MAT_DATE.MONTH_NO,2 ) ;

             GET( CURR_SECURITY_2.MAT_DATE.DAY_NO,2 ) ;

             GET( CURR_SECURITY_2.DAY_KIND );

             GET( CURR_SECURITY_2.DISC_PRICE, 8  ) ;

             -- Check each of the dates to make sure that they

             -- are valid, and fill in the other components

             -- by invoking FILL_IN_DATE.

             FILL_IN_DATE (CURR_SECURITY_1.SETL_DATE ,

                     GOOD_SETL_DATE) ;

             FILL_IN_DATE (CURR_SECURITY_1.MAT_DATE ,
```

```
                         GOOD_MAT_DATE) ;

if not ( GOOD_SETL_DATE and GOOD_MAT_DATE

                 and

                 CURR_SECURITY_2.MAT_DATE.TOTAL_DAYS >

                 CURR_SECURITY_2.SETL_DATE.TOTAL_DAYS )

    then

      BAD_LINE := TRUE ;

      PUT ( " Bad line  " ) ;

      PUT ( CURR_SEC_NAME ) ;

      NEW_LINE ;

end if;

if not BAD_LINE

   then

   -- Compute the yield, depending on the

   -- day count basis.

   case CURR_SECURITY_2.DAY_KIND is

     when ACT_360      =>

     DAYS_SET_MAT := CURR_SECURITY_2.MAT_DATE.TOTAL_DAYS

            - CURR_SECURITY_2.SETL_DATE.TOTAL_DAYS ;

     when M_30_Y_360  =>

     DAYS_SET_MAT := CURR_SECURITY_1.MAT_DATE -

                     CURR_SECURITY_1.SETL_DATE;

     -- The operator - is overloaded.

     when  others  =>

             PUT ( " what security is  this ");

             PUT ( CURR_SEC_NAME ) ;
```

```
                NEW_LINE;

        end case;

        -- Again we need conversions to DISCOUNT_INTEREST

        -- and AT_MAT_INTEREST type.

        CURR_SECURITY_2.DISC_RATE := ( 100.0 -

            DISCOUNT_INTEREST (CURR_SECURITY_2.DISC_PRICE )

            / 100.0 * DISCOUNT_INTEREST ( D_IN_YEAR   )

                / DISCOUNT_INTEREST ( DAYS_SET_MAT ) ;

        CURR_SECURITY_2.YLD :=

            AT_MAT_INTEREST ( CURR_SECURITY_2.DISC_RATE )

                * 100.0 /

            AT_MAT_INTEREST ( CURR_SECURITY_2.DISC_RATE ) ;

        -- Create an element to be placed in a list.

        CURR_PTR := new SEC_NODE ;

        CURR_PTR.SEC_INFO := CURR_SECURITY_2 ;

    end if;

when COUPON  => null;

end case;

-- Place a good security in the list.

if not BAD_LINE

    then

    ANY_PTR := TOP_PTR ;

    while ANY_PTR.SEC_INFO.MAT_DATE.TOTAL_DAYS <

        CURR_PTR.SEC_INFO.MAT_DATE.TOTAL_DAYS

            or

            ANY_PTR  /= NULL
```

```
                loop

                    PREV_PTR := ANY_PTR;

                    ANY_PTR := ANY_PTR.SEC_NEXT ;

                end loop;

            if ANY_PTR = TOP_PTR

              then

                    CURR_PTR.SEC_NEXT := TOP_PTR ;

                    TOP_PTR := CURR_PTR ;

                else

                    PREV_PTR.SEC_NEXT := CURR_PTR ;

                    CURR_PTR.SEC_NEXT := ANY_PTR ;

              end if;

        SKIP_LINE;

        GET(CURR_INT_KIND);

        GET(CURR_SEC_NAME);

      end if;

end loop;

-- Is this a normal yield curve?

ANY_PTR     := TOP_PTR ;

NORM_CURVE := TRUE ;

while ANY_PTR /= NULL

      loop

            CURR_PTR := ANY_PTR ;

            ANY_PTR := ANY_PTR.SEC_NEXT;

            if ANY_PTR /= null

                      and then
```

```
                              ANY_PTR.SEC_NEXT /= null

                              and then

                         -- Here the convexity test is applied

                         ANY_PTR.SEC_INFO.YLD < ( CURR_PTR.SEC_INFO.YLD

                              + ANY_PTR.SEC_NEXT.SEC_INFO.YLD ) / 2.0

                                   then

                                   NORM_CURVE := FALSE ;

                                   exit ;

                    end if;

          end loop;

          if NORM_CURVE

               then

               PUT ( " Normal yield curve " ) ;

               else

               PUT ( " Maybe the curve is inverted " ) ;

          end if;

     end YIELD_COMPUTATION;
```

Some sample input data and the list setup are illustrated in Figure 6.1.

EXERCISES FOR CHAPTER 6

1. Make changes to the program YIELD_COMPUTATION so that no settlement date, maturity date, or issue date falls on a weekend or one of seven holidays.

2. Assume that the input lines for the program YIELD_COMPUTATION are sorted by settlement date in ascending order. Change the program YIELD_COMPUTATION so that the test for normality of the yield curve applies to securities having the same settlement date only.

FIGURE 6.1   Sample Input Data and List Setup for the Program
            YIELD_COMPUTATION

Column 1   Column 15   Column 25

DISCOUNT   Trsy 3-14 850107850314ACT_360   00098.25
DISCOUNT   Trsy 3-21 850108850321ACT_360   00098.03
AT_MATURITY   TAX Ex NT 850108850904M_30_Y_360840829003.24100.07
DISCOUNT   5555588888

TOP_PTR

```
┌──────────────────────────┐
│ DISCOUNT                 │
│                          │          Note:   The dates are of type DATE
│      Trsy 3-14           │                  and have many more components
│    19850107              │
│    19850314              │
│       9.99               │
│    ACT_360               │
│    00098.25        ┌─────┤
│       9.85         │     │─→   TOP_PTR.SEC_NEXT
└────────────────────┴─────┘
            ┌──────────────────────────┐
            │ DISCOUNT                 │
            │                          │
            │      Trsy 3-21           │
            │    19850108              │
            │    19850321              │
            │      10.33               │
            │    ACT_360               │
            │    00098.03        ┌─────┤
            │      10.18         │     │─→
            └────────────────────┴─────┘
                      ┌──────────────────────────┐
                      │ AT_MATURITY              │
                      │                          │
                      │      TAX Ex NT           │
                      │    19841228              │
                      │    19850824              │
                      │       3.101              │
                      │    M_30_Y_360            │
                      │    19840829              │
                      │      003.24        ┌─────┤
                      │      100.07        │NULL │
                      └────────────────────┴─────┘
```

3. Modify the program YIELD_COMPUTATION so that the following list is constructed: Every security placed in the list spoils the normality (that is, when the security is removed from the list, the normality of the curve is preserved). Note that the securities placed on the list are good "buy" candidates.

CHAPTER SEVEN

PACKAGES

7.1   PACKAGE SPECIFICATIONS AND PRIVATE TYPES

The first six chapters covered the conventional features of the Ada programming language. Most of these features can be found in equivalent forms in traditional languages like FORTRAN, PL/I, COBOL, BASIC, and Pascal.

The remaining chapters will cover the features constituting a clear departure from these popular languages. We start by covering one of the most useful design tools available in Ada: packages.

PACKAGE SPECIFICATIONS

Packages are Ada program units, like subprograms and tasks (to be introduced in Chapter 10). An Ada package represents a collection of programming resources like types, objects, and subprograms. The collection representing the package has strict rules, however. These rules control what information is made available to the user and how much of its inner workings will be exposed to the user. These rules, though, can be used by the package designer in a flexible manner for forging a desired boundary between the package and its users.

As for procedures and functions, one can have package specifications and package bodies; thus a package is made up of the specification part and the body part.

A package specification followed by a semicolon (this pattern follows the pattern encountered earlier when subprograms were introduced) is called a **package declaration. A package specification** has the form

```
package package_name is

basic_declarations_or_use_clauses_or_representation_clauses

end package_name
```

Note that one needs to add a semicolon after the part

```
    end package_name
```

to have a package declaration. If a private part is present, then the package specification has the form

```
package package_name is

basic_declarations_or_use_clauses_or_representation_clauses

private

basic_declarations_or_use_clauses_or_representation_clauses

end package_name
```

The package_name following the reserved word "end" is optional.

EXAMPLE   Here is an example of a package specification using some of the declarations in the program ACCR_INTEREST of Chapter 5.

```
package DAYS_MODULE is

type DAY is (MONDAY,TUESDAY,WEDNESDAY,THURSDAY,FRIDAY,

      SATURDAY,SUNDAY);

subtype WEEKEND is DAY range SATURDAY..SUNDAY ;

type DAY_INT is range 1 .. 31;

type JULIAN_DAYS is range 1 .. 366 ;

type MONTH is (JANUARY,FEBRUARY,MARCH,APRIL,MAY,JUNE,

          JULY,AUGUST,SEPTEMBER,OCTOBER,NOVEMBER,DECEMBER);
```

```
type YEAR is range 0 .. 2050 ;

type MONTH_INT is range 1 .. 12;

type DATE is

    record

        WEEK_DAY : DAY;

        MONTH_NAME : MONTH;

        MONTH_NO : MONTH_INT;

        DAY_NO   : DAY_INT;

        YTD_DAYS : JULIAN_DAYS;

        TOTAL_DAYS : INTEGER ;

        YEAR_NO  : YEAR;

    end record;

BASE_DATE : constant DATE := ( MONDAY,JANUARY,1,1,1,1,1984);

BASE_LEAP : constant INTEGER :=

    INTEGER(BASE_DATE.YEAR_NO) / 4 +

    INTEGER(BASE_DATE.YEAR_NO) / 400 -

    INTEGER(BASE_DATE.YEAR_NO) / 100;

type DAYS_IN_MONTH is array (MONTH_INT,BOOLEAN) of DAY_INT;

ACTUAL_DAYS_IN_YEAR : constant DAYS_IN_MONTH :=

    ( (31,31),(28,29),(31,31),(30,30),

      (31,31),(30,30),(31,31),(31,31),

      (30,30),(31,31),(30,30),(31,31));

-- Mark here for a possible representation clause

end DAYS_MODULE      -- A ";" here would make this

                     -- specification a package declaration.
```

In the package specification of this example there is no private part, and we made use of **basic declarations** only. Here the basic declarations chosen are declarations of types and associated objects. Among the possible basic declarations, one can use any of the declarations introduced in previous chapters: number and object declarations, type or subtype declarations, and subprogram declarations. For instance, in the package specification CHECK_DATES given later, we encounter examples of functions and subroutines as basic declarations. Other possible basic declarations are task declarations (to be introduced in Chapter 10), exception declarations (to be introduced in Chapter 11), and declarations of other packages (as in the package specification CHECK_DATES_ALT given later). Renaming declarations and deferred-constant declarations are allowed as well. Details about these declarations will be provided later in this chapter.

Representation clauses can be present, too, in a specification package. **Representation clauses** give directions about how types should be represented on the computer. These clauses are sometimes used in order to restrict the choices available to the compiler for a given type implementation. For instance, in the place of the marked comment of the package specification DAYS_MODULE, one can insert the following representation clause:

```
-- Mark here for a possible representation clause

for DAY use ( MONDAY   => 1, TUESDAY => 2, WEDNESDAY => 3,

             THURSDAY => 4, FRIDAY  => 5, SATURDAY => 6 ,

             SUNDAY   => 7 ) ;
```

This representation clause directs the compiler to use the integer codes 1 through 7 for the representation of the value of type DAY. Without this clause the compiler might choose a different set of integer codes to implement this type (for instance, 0 through 6). Representation clauses are important in making a program compatible with, say, files created by other languages.

Finally, package specifications can contain **use clauses.** The general form for the use clause is

```
use package_name ;
```

Several package_names can be supplied separated by commas.

EXAMPLE   Here is an example of a package specification using subprogram declarations of subprograms found in ACCR_INTEREST and containing a "use" clause.

```
with DAYS_MODULE ;

    -- This "with" clause makes the
```

```
       -- declarations    in    the    package    declaration

       -- DAYS_MODULE visible .

package CHECK_DATES is

-- Here comes a "use" clause.

use  DAYS_MODULE;

-- This   use   clause   allows one to   use

-- identifiers in the package specification of DAYS_MODULE

-- without the selected component notation.

-- That is, one can use DATE without using the selected

-- component notation DAYS_MODULE.DATE

-- The identifiers become "directly visible"

-- as it will be explained  in Section 7.3.

function IS_VALID_DATE ( FORM_DATE : DATE )

          return BOOLEAN ;

          -- This function declaration

          -- is a basic declaration.


procedure FILL_IN_DATE

      ( PROC_F_DATE : in out DATE ;

        GOOD_DATE : out BOOLEAN ) ;

          -- This   procedure   declaration   is   a   basic

          -- declaration.

TODAYS_DATE : DATE ;

end CHECK_DATES          -- A ";" would make this package

                          -- specification a package

                          -- declaration.
```

We emphasize that bodies of subprograms or packages are not allowed in a package specification. For instance, it would not be valid to have the body of the procedure FILL_IN_DATE listed in the package specification of CHECK_DATES.

VISIBILITY IN PACKAGE SPECIFICATIONS

Clearly, the package specification just given has no private part. If a private part of the package is present, the declarations following the reserved word "private" make up the so-called private parts of the package. The other declarations make up the visible part of the package. The **visible part** lists the resources that can be made known and available to the user. The **private part** lists resources needed for a proper functioning of the package, but these resources cannot be referenced or made available to the user. The user has no knowledge of the declarations in the private part, even though private types are mentioned in the visible part and are used (somewhat as "black boxes").

The visible part is made available to other program units through a variety of means. A typical method to establish visibility for a package is to have a "with" clause preceding the program unit. The declaration of the package CHECK_ DATES, for instance, is preceded by a "with" clause, in this case

```
with DAYS_MODULE;
```

The "with" clause *exports* (this term is a preferred Ada term for making the declarations of the visible part of the package available and known) the entities of DAYS_MODULE for use within the package CHECK_DATES. It is assumed that the package DAYS_MODULE is separately compiled and available to other Ada program units as well (details and more precise meanings are given in Chapter 9). These entities can be used within the package CHECK_DATES with the help of selected-component notation. For instance, within the package CHECK_DATES identifiers like DAYS_MODULE.BASE_DATE or DAYS_MODULE.BASE_LEAP are valid.

The "use" clause in the package specification CHECK_DATES is convenient because it will simplify the use of visible identifiers of the package DAYS_MODULE. As mentioned above, the visible identifiers can be used without the prefix DAYS_MODULE after the elaboration of the "use" clause. The complex rules regarding the visibility and the scope of identifiers and related interactions with the "use" clause will be covered in more detail in Section 7.3.

Another way to establish visibility of a package is to place its declaration within the package specification making use of it.

EXAMPLE   One can use the following alternative way of defining the package specification of CHECK_DATES (and achieving exactly the same kind of visibility).

```
with TEXT_IO ; use TEXT_IO ;

     -- This line is included because we intend

     -- to initialize TODAYS_DATE byusing a GET procedure.

package CHECK_DATES_ALT is

package DAYS_MODULE is

-- Here the declarations of DAYS_MODULE listed earlier

-- are inserted.

end DAYS_MODULE ;

use DAYS_MODULE ;

-- This "use" clause is used because we want to avoid the

--selected component notation.

function IS_VALID_DATE ( FORM_DATE : DATE )

          return BOOLEAN ;

-- This function declaration is a basic declaration.

procedure FILL_IN_DATE

     ( PROC_F_DATE : in out DATE ;

       GOOD_DATE : out BOOLEAN ) ;

TODAYS_DATE : DATE ;

end CHECK_DATES_ALT

-- A ";" would make this a package declaration.
```

PRIVATE TYPES

Ada **private types** are meant to hide the actual implementation details from the user. Hiding of information is achieved by restricting the operations that can be applied to objects of private type to assignment and testing for equality and/or inequality. Any other desired operations on objects of private types have to be explicitly defined in the visible part of the package.

The declaration of a private type is given in the visible part of the package, and full details about its definition are given in the private part of the package. The form of a private type declaration is

```
type private_type_name is private ;
```

There is an even more restrictive kind of private type, called **limited private type,** whose declaration has the form

```
type lim_private_type_name is limited private ;
```

For a limited private type no predefined operations are allowed; that is, no assignment or test for equality or inequality is permitted. The only possible use of a limited private type is through the functions and procedures provided in the visible part of the package and having limited private type parameters.

EXAMPLE   Here is an example of a package specification with declarations of private types and of limited private types.

```
package ROSTER is

    type STUD_NAME is private ;

            -- This private type declaration is given

            -- in the visible part of the package

            -- specification. Outside users should not be

            -- able to change the names of the students.

            -- We would like to compare, though, different

            -- student names, for equality and inequality

            -- in order to find out, for instance, what other

            -- courses the student took.

    type STUD_GRADE is limited private ;

            -- Nobody  (besides authorized persons as

            -- will be seen shortly) should tamper

            -- with the student grade. Assignment and

            -- comparisons,  in particular,  under

            -- tight control. For this reason we chose
```

```
-- this type as limited private rather than

-- private.

type TEACHER_PASS is private ;

    -- The teacher password is required for computing

    -- grades or listing grades.

procedure GET_PASS ( FORM_PASS : out TEACHER_PASS  ;

                     TEACH_ID  : STRING ( 1 .. 9 ) ;

type COURSE_INFO is

    -- This record is taken from the program

    -- GR_POINT_AVE of Section 4.3.

    record

        CR_ID    : STRING ( 1 .. 4 ) ;

        CR_NO    : STRING ( 1 .. 4 ) ;

        CR_CRDT  : NATURAL ;

    end record ;

type ROSTER_REC is

    record

        ST_NAME   : STUD_NAME ;

        ST_ID     : STRING ( 1 .. 9 ) ;

        ST_CRS    : COURSE_INFO ;

        CRS_GRADE : STUD_GRADE  ;

    end record ;

    -- Only parts of a student record can be made

    -- available users. For instance,

    -- when  grades  are  posted,  the  names  are  not

    -- printed , while  the IDs  are.  But  in
```

```
                    -- order to print grades, one has to supply the

                    -- teacher  password  (see the function  declaration

                    -- below).

            function IS_A_VALID_STUDENT ( FORM_REC : ROSTER_REC )

                    return BOOLEAN :

                    -- Checks to see whether the student is enrolled.

                    -- Only a valid student can be given a grade.

            procedure COMPUTE_GRADE_N_FILL_NAME

                        ( FORM_REC  : in out ROSTER_REC :

                        FORM_PASS : in  TEACHER_PASS ) :

                    -- This procedure fills in the student name

                    -- (a private type value), computes the

                    -- student's final grade, and places it in the

                    -- CRS_GRADE component.

            procedure PRINT_GRADE

                        ( FORM_REC  : in ROSTER_REC :

                        FORM_PASS : in  TEACHER_PASS ) :

                    -- This procedure lists grades if the proper

                    -- teacher password is supplied.

        private

            type STUD_NAME is new STRING ( 1 .. 20 ) :

            type STUD_GRADE is range 0 .. 100 :

            -- The STUD_GRADE  is an integer between 0 and 100,

            -- but the outside user has no control  about it.

            type TEACHER_PASS is range 0 .. 99999 :
```

```
end ROSTER

-- A ";" is needed for a package declaration.
```

EXAMPLE   Now here is an example of the package ROSTER being used by the procedure SAMPLE_ROSTER_USE.

```
with ROSTER ; use ROSTER ;

with TEXT_IO ; use TEXT_IO ;

procedure SAMPLE_ROSTER_USE is

        CURR_ROSTER      : ROSTER_REC ;

        ACT_TEACH_ID     : STRING ( 1 .. 9 ) ;

        ACT_PASS         : TEACHER_PASS ;

        OTHER_ROSTER     : ROSTER_REC ;

begin

        GET(CURR_ROSTER.ST_ID ) ;

        GET(CURR_ROSTER.ST_CRS) ;

        GET(ACT_TEACHER_ID) ;

        GET_PASS ( ACT_PASS, ACT_TEACHER_ID );

             -- The teacher ID is supplied, and the procedure will

             -- return possibly a valid password, which is a value

             -- of a limited private type, placed in ACT_PASS.

             -- The user cannot control and has no knowledge of

             -- the actual value placed in ACT_PASS.

        if IS_A_VALID_STUDENT ( CURR_ROSTER )

             then

             COMPUTE_GRADE_N_FILL_NAME  ( CURR_ROSTER, ACT_PASS ) ;

             PRINT_GRADE    ( CURR_ROSTER, ACT_PASS ) ;
```

```
                    -- The grade is computed ( if the ACT_PASS is valid )

                    -- and placed in CURR_ROSTER.CRS_GRADE, a limited

                    -- private type

        end if ;

        GET(OTHER_ROSTER.ST_ID ) ;

        GET(OTHER_ROSTER.ST_CRS) ;

        if IS_A_VALID_STUDENT ( OTHER_ROSTER )

                    -- One may assume that this function checks

                    -- the student ID against an internally known

                    -- list of valid student IDs and names.

            then

            COMPUTE_GRADE_N_FILL_NAME  ( OTHER_ROSTER, ACT_PASS ) ;

            if OTHER_ROSTER.ST_NAME /= CURR_ROSTER.ST_NAME

            -- A test for equality and inequality is allowed for

            -- private types.

            -- It is not be valid to have a test like

            -- OTHER_ROSTER.CRS_GRADE /= CURR_ROSTER.CRS_GRADE

            -- because it applies to limited private types.

            -- It is not valid to have

            -- OTHER_ROSTER.CRS_GRADE := CURR_ROSTER.CRS_GRADE;

            -- because no assignment statements are allowed for

            -- limited private types. It is valid, however, to have

            -- OTHER_ROSTER.ST_NAME := CURR_ROSTER.ST_NAME ;

                then

                PUT ( " Different names  " );

        end if;
```

```
    end if ;

end SAMPLE_ROSTER_USE ;
```

The outside user of a private type has no knowledge about the implementation of a private type. Even if the user might guess, for instance, that the student name is represented as a string of characters, the user cannot have an assignment like

```
OTHER_ROSTER.ST_NAME := ``12345678901234567890'' ;
```

because the two objects have different types. No type conversion is allowed, either.

Hiding of information, achieved here through the use of private types, was justified in the ROSTER example for security reasons (avoiding tampering with student records was the goal). Hiding of information also makes the writing of application programs independent of private type implementations. For instance, the private type STUD_GRADE is implemented as an integer type ranging from 0 to 100. One can change the implementation to, say, an enumeration type or a string type without making any changes in the applications using the package (but rewriting the subprograms using the private types as formal parameters).

Hiding of information helps in creating and encapsulating new data types, as the following example illustrates.

EXAMPLE   The package declaration GIANT_INT_ARITHMETIC defines arithmetic for integers with many digits.

```
Package GIANT_INT_ARITHMETIC is

    type GIANT_INTEGER is private ;

    function INT_TO_GIANT ( INT_FORM   : INTEGER )

                    return GIANT_INTEGER ;

        -- This function should return a GIANT_INTEGER

        -- with the INT_FORM placed right justified in

        -- the eighth component.

    function GIANT_TO_INT ( GIANT_FORM : GIANT_INTEGER

                    return INTEGER ;

        -- This function tries to convert a
```

```
                    -- giant integer to an integer if it is not

                    -- too big.

          function GIANT_ADD      ( LEFT_FORM, RIGHT_FORM :

                      GIANT_INTEGER ) return GIANT_INTEGER ;

                    -- This function adds two giant integers.

          function GIANT_SUB      ( LEFT_FORM, RIGHT_FORM :

                      GIANT_INTEGER ) return GIANT_INTEGER ;

                    -- This function subtracts two giant integers.

          function GIANT_LT       ( LEFT_FORM, RIGHT_FORM :

                      GIANT_INTEGER ) return BOOLEAN    ;

                    -- This function returns the value TRUE if

                    -- LEFT_FORM is less than RIGHT_FORM.

          function GIANT_GT       ( LEFT_FORM, RIGHT_FORM :

                      GIANT_INTEGER ) return BOOLEAN    ;

                    -- This function returns the value TRUE if

                    -- LEFT_FORM is greater than RIGHT_FORM.

          function GIANT_TO_STRING  ( GIANT_FORM : GIANT_INTEGER )

                      return STRING ;

                    -- This function converts a giant integer

                    -- to a string.

          function STRING_TO_GIANT  ( STRING_FORM : STRING )

                      return GIANT_INTEGER ;

                    -- This function converts a string  to a

                    -- giant integer.

     private

       type GIANT_INTEGER is array ( 1 .. 8 )
```

```
                    of INTEGER ;

          -- This declaration could be changed

          -- in a  number of ways, such as

          --    type GIANT_INTEGER is

          --        record

          --              FIRST_HALF  : INTEGER ;

          --              SECOND_HALF : INTEGER ;

          --          end record ;

end GIANT_INT_ARITHMETIC ;
```

EXAMPLE   Now we will illustrate the use of the package GIANT_INT_ARITHMETIC for manipulating large integers in the subprogram GIANT_INT_USE.

```
with GIANT_INT_ARITHMETIC ; use GIANT_INT_ARITHMETIC ;

with TEXT_IO ; use TEXT_IO ;

procedure GIANT_INT_USE is

I, J : INTEGER := 55 ;

I_BIG, J_BIG : GIANT_INTEGER ;

I_STRING, J_STRING : STRING ( 1 .. 13 ) := "1234567890123" ;

begin

      I_BIG := INT_TO_GIANT ( I ) ;

      J_BIG := INT_TO_GIANT ( J ) ;

          -- Here we use two conversions from integer to

          -- giant.

      I_BIG := GIANT_ADD ( I_BIG, J_BIG ) ;

          -- Here two giant integers are added.

      I     := GIANT_TO_INT ( I_BIG ) ;
```

```
        -- Here we convert back to integer.

I      := I ** 2 ;

I_BIG := INT_TO_GIANT ( I ) ;

J_BIG := STRING_TO_GIANT ( J_STRING ) ;

        -- Here we converst from string to giant.

J_BIG := GIANT_SUB ( J_BIG, I_BIG )  ;

        -- This line subtracts two giant integers.

if    GIANT_LT ( I_BIG, J_BIG )

        -- This line is a less-than test for giant integers.

        then

                I_BIG := STRING_TO_GIANT ( I_STRING ) ;

        else

                I_BIG := GIANT_ADD ( J_BIG, J_BIG ) ;

        end if ;

if   GIANT_GT ( I_BIG, J_BIG )

        -- This line is a greater-than test for giant
        -- integers.

        then

                I_STRING := GIANT_TO_STRING ( I_BIG ) ;

                -- Here we convert to string from giant.

        else

                I_STRING := GIANT_TO_STRING ( J_BIG ) ;

    end if ;

    PUT ( I_STRING ) ;

end GIANT_INT_USE ;
```

The package specification GIANT_INT_ARITHMETIC described operations on an *abstract data type*. The abstract data type is encapsulated in the package: The user of the package does not know how the abstract data type is implemented.

USES OF PACKAGES

The specifications introduced so far illustrate some of the typical uses of packages, listed here in increasing order of complexity:

- As collections of related data types and object declarations (for instance, DAYS_MODULE). These packages export objects and types.
- As collections of related subprograms (like CHECK_DATES) and other program units (packages and tasks). These packages export program units.
- As new abstract types together with a set of allowable operations on the type values (like GIANT_INT_ARITHMETIC). These packages export both types and program units.

Finally, as a fourth use, one can design packages that export objects, types, and program units and, in addition, maintain within the package a record of internal states. The next example illustrates this technique.

EXAMPLE   The following package specification deals with stock market indices.

```
Package MARKET is

    type DIRECTION is (DOWN, UNCHANGED, UP ) ;

    type AVERAGE_INDICATORS is private ;

            -- These types might be implemented as an array

            -- of (moving) averages (taken over, say, the

            -- last 5 ,10, or 20 days).

    type OSCILLATORS is private ;

            -- These types might  be   an   array   of   moment

            -- indicators (they would store data on the

            -- speed of market moves).
-- *** MARK ***
```

```
        type LEVEL is digits 8 range 0.00 .. 10000.00 ;
        function CURR_LEVEL return LEVEL ;
            -- The current state of the market is kept
            -- internally within the package (like the
            -- current DOW_JONES value, for instance).
        function NEXT_GUESS ( FORM_LEVEL    : LEVEL ;
                    PREV_FORM_MOVE : DIRECTION ;
                    FORM_OSCILL    : OSCILLATOR ;
                    FORM_AVER      : AVERAGE_INDICATORS);
            -- From  the  value  of  the  formal parameters,
            -- the function returns a certain guess.
                return LEVEL ;
        procedure UPDATE_LEVEL ( FORM_LEVEL : in out LEVEL ;
                        NEW_MOVE   : DIRECTION  ;
                        FORM_MAGN  : LEVEL ) ;
            -- A new level of the market is arrived at by
            -- using the old level and the new changes.
    private
        type AVERAGE_INDICATORS is array ( 1 .. 10 ) of FLOAT ;
        type OSCILLATORS is array ( 1 .. 3 ) of FLOAT ;
        -- ??? MARK ???
    end MARKET      -- A ";" needed for a complete package
                    -- declaration.
```

The package specification MARKET will export declarations (like MOVING_AVERAGES) and subprograms (like UPDATE_LEVEL). The package will, as well, internally maintain the current level of the market.

Of course, Ada packages are encountered in many real-life situations as a mixture of the four types described here.

DEFERRED CONSTANTS

As a final topic in this section, we mention that constants of a private type can be declared as **deferred constants** in the visible part of the package; deferred constants have their value specified in the private part. While the package user does not know the actual value of the constant, he or she may assign it or compare it with other private objects.

The declaration of a deferred constant has the form

```
constant_name : constant type_or_subtype ;
```

For instance, one can insert the following deferred-constant declaration in the package specification MARKET at the *** MARK *** location:

```
STANDARD_OSCILLATOR : constant OSCILLATORS ;
```

The actual values can be supplied by the declaration

```
STANDARD_OSCILLATOR : constant := ( 0.05, 0.55,
   0.95 ) ;
```

to be inserted in the ??? MARK ??? location.

7.2 PACKAGE BODIES

The implementation of a package is carried out in the **package body.** We will introduce two forms for package bodies. The first form contains declarations only:

```
package body package_name is

-- Maybe some declarations are given here.

end package_name ;
```

If a sequence of statements is present, then the package body has the form

```
package body package_name is

-- maybe some declarations

begin

-- sequence_of_statements

end package_name ;
```

Another form for package bodies is used in connection with exceptions. This form will be covered in Chapter 11.

The package_name has to be identical to the corresponding specification name (the package_name following the reserved word "end" is optional). Every declaration of the corresponding package specification is known and can be used within the package body. The opposite is not true: The declarations in a package body are not known and cannot be used by the corresponding package specification (they are not visible outside the package body).

Package specifications and package bodies may be compiled separately. In this case the compilation of the package specification has to precede the compilation of the corresponding package body.

Here is a simple example of a package body:

```
package body DAYS_MODULE is

-- No declarations are given here

-- No sequence of statements is given.

end DAYS_MODULE ;
```

This package body corresponds to the package specification DAYS_MODULE presented at the beginning of the chapter. Because the package DAYS_MODULE contains only type and object declarations, the package body is not required. Whenever the package is a pool of types, constants, and variables, a package body is optional.

A package body is required, however, when the corresponding package specification has subprogram or package declarations. Their bodies have to appear as part of the package body.

EXAMPLE A package body corresponding to the package specification CHECK_ DATES_ALT is as follows:

```
with TEXT_IO ;   use TEXT_IO ;

package body CHECK_DATES_ALT is

       LEAP_YEAR : BOOLEAN;

       INPUT_LEAP : INTEGER;

       package body DAYS_MODULE is

           -- Here the body of DAYS_MODULE is given.

       end DAYS_MODULE ;
```

```
        function IS_VALID_DATE ( FORM_DATE : DATE )

              return BOOLEAN is

          -- The function body is inserted here.

          -- It is identical to the body of the function

          -- with the same name in ACCR_INTEREST.

      end IS_VALID_DATE ;

      procedure FILL_IN_DATE

          ( PROC_F_DATE : in out DATE ;

            GOOD_DATE : out BOOLEAN ) is

          -- The function body is inserted here.

          -- It is identical to the body of the function

          -- with the same name in ACCR_INTEREST.

      end FILL_IN_DATE ;

  end CHECK_DATES_ALT ;
```

The package body CHECK_DATES_ALT in the preceding example has a declarative part but no sequence-of-statements part. A sequence-of-statements part, if it is present, can be used, for instance, to initialize some of the variables of the package. The next example illustrates this process.

EXAMPLE   Here is another version of the package body CHECK_DATES_ALT.

```
package body CHECK_DATES_ALT is

    -- All the declarations of the package body in the preceding

    -- example should be inserted here.

    Package INT_IO is new INTEGER_IO(INTEGER);

    use INT_IO;

begin

    PUT ( " Enter today's date as YYMMDD " ) ; NEW_LINE ;
```

```
            GET ( TODAYS_DATE.YEAR_NO,2 ) ;

            GET ( TODAYS_DATE.MONTH_NO,2 ) ;

            GET ( TODAYS_DATE.DAY_NO,2 ) ;

     end CHECK_DATES_ALT ;
```

The package structure of this CHECK_DATES_ALT is illustrated in Figure 7.1.

We now give some more examples of package specifications and their bodies extracted from some of the programs of previous chapters.

EXAMPLE   We now can collect some of the types in the program YIELD_COMPUTATION of Chapter 6 together with the function "−" in a package useful for yield computations, as follows:

```
with CHECK_DATES_ALT ;

package SECURITIES is

    use CHECK_DATES_ALT ;

    type INTEREST is digits 13 ;

    type DISCOUNT_INTEREST is new INTEREST ;

    type AT_MAT_INTEREST is new INTEREST;

    type INTEREST_KIND is ( COUPON, AT_MATURITY, DISCOUNT ) ;

    type DAY_COUNT_BASIS is ( ACT_ACT, ACT_360, M_30_Y_360 ) ;

    type PRICES is digits 13 ;

    type DISCOUNT_PRICES is new PRICES    ;

    type SECURITY ( INT_PAYM : INTEREST_KIND )   is

        record

            SEC_NAME  : STRING ( 1 .. 10 );

            SETL_DATE : DATE ;

            MAT_DATE  : DATE ;
```

FIGURE 7.1   Package Elements for CHECK_DATES_ALT

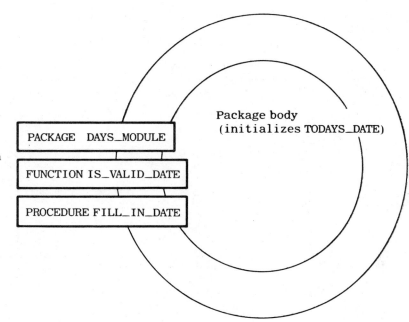

```
            DAY_KIND  : DAY_COUNT_BASIS ;

            YLD       : INTEREST ;

            case INT_PAYM is

                when AT_MATURITY =>

                        ISSUE_DATE : DATE ;

                        S_RATE     : AT_MAT_INTEREST ;

                        QT_PRICE   : PRICES ;

                when DISCOUNT    =>

                        DISC_PRICE : DISCOUNT_PRICES ;

                        DISC_RATE  : DISCOUNT_INTEREST ;

                when others      => null;
```

```
                              end case ;

                     end record;

             function "-" ( X, Y : DATE ) return NATURAL ;

             end SECURITIES ;
```

The corresponding package body is as follows:

```
package body SECURITIES is

function "-" ( X, Y : DATE )

                    -- This procedure computes elapsed days

                    -- assuming M_30_Y_360 day count basis

                    return NATURAL is

begin

            -- A copy of the function body from Chapter

            -- 6 should be inserted here.

end "-";

end SECURITIES ;
```

Another useful package might keep track of legal holidays. Declarations and bodies are taken mostly from ACCR_INTEREST of Chapter 5. The next example presents this package.

EXAMPLE   This package has a sequence-of-statements part initializing the list of holidays. Whenever there is a need to update the list, one can type in the necessary holiday changes. Then the package body can be recompiled.

```
            with CHECK_DATES_ALT ;

            package LEGAL_HOLIDAYS is

                   use CHECK_DATES_ALT ;

                   function IS_LEGAL_HOLIDAY ( FORM_DATE : DATE )

                                       return BOOLEAN ;
```

```
end LEGAL_HOLIDAYS

-- The specification ends here.


package body LEGAL_HOLIDAYS is

     NO_OF_HOLIDAYS : NATURAL := 2 ;

     NO_GOOD_HOLIDAYS : NATURAL;

     GOOD_HOLIDAY : BOOLEAN ;

     type HOLIDAYS  is array ( 1 .. NO_OF_HOLIDAYS) of DATE;

     ACT_HOLIDAYS : HOLIDAYS :=

               -- Initialize the holiday candidates.

               -- Only the MONTH_NO, DAY_NO, and YEAR_NO

               -- components count.

               ( ( MONDAY,JANUARY,7,4,1,1,1985 ) ,

                  ( MONDAY,JANUARY,1,1,1,1,1986 ) ) ;

     function IS_LEGAL_HOLIDAY ( FORM_DATE : DATE )

                         return BOOLEAN is

begin

     for I in 1 .. NO_GOOD_HOLIDAYS

          loop

          if FORM_DATE.TOTAL_DAYS =

               ACT_HOLIDAYS (I).TOTAL_DAYS

               then

               return TRUE ;

          end if ;

     end loop ;

     return FALSE ;

end IS_LEGAL_HOLIDAY ;
```

```
begin

    -- The sequence of statements for the package follows .

    -- The code again taken from ACCR_INTEREST of Chapter 5.

    NO_GOOD_HOLIDAYS := 0;

    for I in 1 .. NO_OF_HOLIDAYS

    loop

        NO_GOOD_HOLIDAYS := NO_GOOD_HOLIDAYS + 1 ;

        FILL_IN_DATE ( ACT_HOLIDAYS(NO_GOOD_HOLIDAYS),

                        GOOD_HOLIDAY );

        if not GOOD_HOLIDAY

            then

            NO_GOOD_HOLIDAYS := NO_GOOD_HOLIDAYS - 1 ;

        end if;

    end loop;

end LEGAL_HOLIDAYS ;
```

Again, remember that the entities declared within the package body (for instance, NO_GOOD_HOLIDAYS and NO_OF_HOLIDAYS) are not known or accessible outside the package body.

The final package to be introduced in this section, presented in the next example, is from the program NAME_PHONE of Chapter 4. It has some usable text-handling features.

EXAMPLE   This package for the NAME_PHONE program is called LINE_HANDLING.

```
package LINE_HANDLING is

    -- The COMMA part is dropped and WRK_LINE becomes a

    -- component of T_REC.

    type LINE_LENTGH is INTEGER range 0 .. 255 ;
```

```
type T_REC ( LINE_LN : LINE_LENGTH ) is

    record

            WRK_LINE : STRING ( 1 .. T_LENGTH );

    end record ;

procedure LOW_TO_UPPER  ( F_REC : in out T_REC ) ;

procedure IGNORE_LEADING_SPACES  ( STRT_POS : out NATURAL ;

                                   F_REC    : in out T_REC ) ;

procedure FIND_NEXT_SP_OR_COMMA  ( STRT_POS : in out NATURAL ;

                                   END_POS  : in out NATURAL ;

                                   F_REC    : in out T_REC );

procedure PLACE_SPACES  ( STRT_POS : in out NATURAL ;

                          END_POS  : in out NATURAL ;

                          F_REC    : in out T_REC ) ;

end LINE_HANDLING ;
```

The corresponding package body (again the code follows closely the code in the NAME_PHONE program) is as follows:

```
package body LINE_HANDLING is

procedure LOW_TO_UPPER  ( F_REC : in out T_REC ) is

begin


    For I in 1 .. F_REC.LINE_LN

        loop

        case F_REC.WRK_LINE (I) is

            when 'a' .. 'z' =>

                    F_REC.WRK_LINE (I) := CHARACTER'VAL (

                    CHARACTER'POS('A') -  CHARACTER'POS('a')  +
```

```
                         CHARACTER'POS( WRK_LINE (I))      ) ;

                when others      => NULL;

                end case ;

        end loop;

end LOW_TO_UPPER;

procedure IGNORE_LEADING_SPACES   ( STRT_POS : out NATURAL ;

                                    F_REC    : in out T_REC ) is

begin

        for I in 1 .. F_REC.LINE_LN

            loop

            STRT_POS := I;

            exit when F_REC.WRK_LINE (I) /= ' ';

        end loop;

end IGNORE_LEADING_SPACES ;

procedure  FIND_NEXT_SP_OR_COMMA ( STRT_POS : in out NATURAL ;

                                   END_POS  : in out NATURAL ;

                                   F_REC    : in out T_REC )   is

        -- This procedure sets END_POS to the position of the last

        -- nonspace or noncomma character after  STRT_POS.

begin

        END_POS := STRT_POS;

        for I in STRT_POS .. F_REC.LINE_LN

            loop

            exit when

                F_REC.WRK_LINE (I) = ' ' or

                F_REC.WRK_LINE (I) = ',' ;
```

```
            END_POS := I;

      end loop;

end   FIND_NEXT_SP_OR_COMMA ;

procedure PLACE_SPACES   ( STRT_POS : in out NATURAL ;

                           END_POS  : in out NATURAL ;

                           F_REC    : in out T_REC )  is


      -- This procedure changes the characters between STRT_POS

      -- and END_POS  into spaces, and turns the first

      -- encountered comma, if any, into a space.

begin

      for I in STRT_POS .. END_POS

          loop

          F_REC.WRK_LINE (I) := ' ' ;

      end loop;

      for I in END_POS + 1 .. LINE_LN

          loop

          if F_REC.WRK_LINE (I) = ','

              then

              F_REC.WRK_LINE (I) := ' ' ;

              exit;

              end if;

          exit when F_REC.WRK_LINE (I) /= ' ';

      end loop;

end PLACE_SPACES;

end LINE_HANDLING;
```

An application of the package LINE_HANDLING is given in the next example, which illustrates an input validation problem.

EXAMPLE Assume that integers are supplied, maybe several per line. The following program will print a message, "Valid integer" or "Invalid integer," for each group of nonspace characters surrounded by at least a space or a comma. (Review the definition of integer literals in Chapter 1.) Only decimal integers are checked. The last line should contain "XX".

```
with LINE_HANDLING ; use LINE_HANDLING ;

with TEXT_IO : use TEXT_IO ;

procedure CHECK_FOR_INTEGERS is

    CURR_REC : T_REC ;

        -- Type T_REC is available and directly

        -- visible from LINE_HANDLING.

    INPUT_LN : NATURAL ;

        -- This declaration gives the line length.

    INP_LINE : STRING ( 1 .. INPUT_LN ) ;

    CURR_ST  : NATURAL ;

    CURR_END : NATURAL ;

    END_A_NO : NATURAL ;

    A_NUMBER : STRING ( 1 .. END_A_NO ) ;

    function CHECK_NUMBER ( F_STRING : STRING ;

                            F_END    : NATURAL )

                            return BOOLEAN is

    begin

    for I in 1 .. F_END

        loop

        case F_STRING ( I ) is
```

```
when '0' .. '9' => null ;

when  '-' ¦ '+' =>

-- Only the first character

-- may be a sign.

                        if I /= 1 then

                                return FALSE ;

                        end if;

when '_'          =>

        -- An underscore is allowed but, but it must

        -- be surrounded by digits or underscores.

        if I = 1 or I = F_END or else

            not ( F_STRING ( I - 1 ) in '0' .. '9' or

                    F_STRING ( I - 1 ) = '_' ) or else

            not ( F_STRING ( I + 1 ) in '0' .. '9' or

                    F_STRING ( I + 1 ) = '_' )

                then

                    return FALSE ;

        end if;

when 'E'          =>

        -- The exponent, if present, has

        -- to be surrounded by digits.

        if I = 1 or I = F_END or else

            F_STRING ( I - 1 ) not in '0' .. '9' or else

            F_STRING ( I + 1 ) not in '0' .. '9'

                then

                    return FALSE ;
```

```
                    end if;

              when others    =>   return FALSE ;

         end case ;

         end loop ;

         return TRUE ;

     end CHECK_NUMBER ;

begin

     GET_LINE ( INP_LINE, INPUT_LN ) ;

     while INP_LINE /= "XX"

     loop

         CURR_REC := ( INPUT_LN, INP_LINE );

             -- An aggregate value is assigned to CURR_REC.

         IGNORE_LEADING_SPACES ( CURR_ST, CURR_REC ) ;

         LOW_TO_UPPER ( CURR_REC ) ;

         while  CURR_ST /= CURR_REC.LINE_LN

             loop

             FIND_NEXT_SP_OR_COMMA ( CURR_ST, CURR_END ,

                                     CURR_REC ) ;

             END_A_NO := CURR_END - CURR_ST ;

             A_NUMBER := CURR_REC.WRK_LINE ( CURR_ST ..

                             CURR_END - 1 ) ;

                 -- A slice assignment is given here.

             PUT ( A_NUMBER, ) ;

             if CHECK_NUMBER ( A_NUMBER, END_A_NO ) = TRUE

                 then

                 PUT ( " Valid number " ) ;
```

```
                    else

                        PUT ( " Invalid number " ) ;

                end if;

                NEW_LINE ;

                PLACE_SPACES    ( CURR_ST, CURR_END, CURR_REC ) ;

                end loop;

            GET_LINE ( INP_LINE, INPUT_LN ) ;

        end loop;

end CHECK_FOR_INTEGERS ;
```

Elaboration of a package declaration involves the elaboration of both the specification and the body part, in that order. The elaboration of the package specification consists of the elaboration of the visible part followed by the elaboration of the private part. The elaboration of the package body consists of the elaboration of its declarative part and then the execution of the sequence of statements. It may not sound right but it is true: The elaboration of the package body includes the execution of its sequence of statements.

7.3 VISIBILITY RULES FOR PACKAGES

Chapter 6 defined the scope and the visibility of an identifier within subprograms and blocks. Now we are going to add to the visibility and scope rules by detailing the way they apply to packages.

We briefly mentioned in Section 7.1 how the visible part of the package specification is exported to other program units. Once the entities in the visible part are exported (for instance, by using package declarations or "use" clauses), these entities have a scope extending to the end of the package, subprogram, or block importing them. The visibility of the exported entities depends on the possible hiding of declarations over parts of the scope, as was illustrated in Chapter 6. Unless the exported entities are directly visible (for instance, by having a "use" clause), the visible entities are referenced with selected-component notation.

Within a package specification and body, declarations can appear in the visible part of the package specification, in the private part of the package specification, and within the package body. The scope of the visible declarations within a package extends to the private part and to the package body itself. The scope of a declaration within the private part extends to the package body, while the declarations appearing in a package body have the package body only as scope. Clearly, an entity cannot be referenced outside its scope.

Some of these visibility and scope rules applying to packages, subprograms, and blocks are illustrated in the next example.

EXAMPLE   The following procedure gives an application of the scope and visibility rules.

```
procedure SCOPE_N_VISIBITY

-- Here a package specification is given.

LL : INTEGER := 8 ;

package AA is

    II : INTEGER ;

            -- The scope of II and JJ covers the

            -- specification and the body of AA. It also

            -- covers SCOPE_N_VISIBILITY from here to

            -- its end.

    type JJ is PRIVATE ;

    function CC ( K_F : INTEGER ) return JJ   ;

  private

    type JJ is new INTEGER ;

            -- The scope and visibility of JJ is from here

            -- to the end of the body of AA.

end AA ;

-- Now we give the package body.

package body AA is

    KK : INTEGER := 5 ;

            -- The scope and visibility of KK starts here

            -- and ends with the end of the body.
```

```
            -- KK is not visible outside this

            -- package body.

      function CC ( K_F : INTEGER ) return JJ  is

      begin

      if K_F > KK

            then

            return JJ ( 2 * K_F ) ;

            -- Here we have a derived type conversion.

            else

            return JJ ( K_F + KK ) ;

            end if ;

            end CC ;

      end AA ;

      use AA ;

MM, NN : JJ ;

-- Variables MM and NN  are variables of private type JJ.

begin

      MM :=  CC ( LL ) ;

      II := LL ;

      -- Variable II is directly visible.

      NN := MM ;

      -- Assignment is allowed for private types.

      PUT ( " now NN and MM are equal " ) ;

            -- A block compound statement follows.

            declare

            II : INTEGER := 13 ;
```

```
            -- The scope of this II

            -- and its visibility is to the block end.

            -- The II declared in AA is now hidden.

            -- It  can  be made visible by  denoting  it

            -- as AA.II.

        begin

            NN := CC ( II ) ;

            if MM = NN then PUT ( " equal " ) ;

                        else PUT ( " unequal " ) ;

            end if ;

        end ;

        -- The block ends here.

        -- The same statements outside the block

        -- would have a different result.

        NN := CC ( II ) ;

        if MM = NN then PUT ( " second equal " ) ;

                        else PUT ( " second unequal " ) ;

end SCOPE_N_VISIBILITY ;
```

7.4 RENAMING DECLARATIONS

So far we have encountered quite a few programs using the selected-component notation. In fact, if we do not have the "use" clause, then we have to use the selected-component notation for the visible identifiers. And things can get cumbersome if packages are nested over several levels. Moreover, at times an advisable procedure is not to have the "use" clause because of possible confusion or conflicts among names. In these situations one can provide a shorthand for deeply nested selected-component notations by using a renaming declaration.

We will introduce three kinds of **renaming declarations:** the first one renames objects; the second one renames subprogram specifications; the third one renames packages. Other kinds of renaming declarations (dealing with exceptions, for instance) will be introduced in Chapter 11.

The first kind of renaming declaration has the following form:

```
identifier : type_or_subtype renames
  object_name ;
```

For instance, in the package CHECK_DATES_ALT (the last version of it) of Section 7.2, we can have the renaming declaration

```
CURRENT_MONTH : MONTH_INT renames
  TODAYS_DATE.MONTH_NO ;
```

The form for renaming subprogram specifications is

```
new_subprog_name renames old_subprog_name ;
```

For instance, if the package LINE_HANDLING is declared in a subprogram, then one can use the declaration

```
L_TO_U renames LINE_HANDLING.LOW_TO_UPPER ;
```

The third kind of renaming declaration has the form

```
package new_pack_name renames old_pack_name ;
```

For example, suppose we have the package declaration

```
package TEXT_MANIP is

package LINE_HANDLING is

end LINE_HANDLING ;

-- More declarations are given here.

end TEXT_MANIP ;
```

Then we can have the package-renaming declaration

```
package NEW_LINE_HAND renames
  TEXT_MANIP.LINE_HANDLING ;
```

A renaming declaration may be ambiguous, and so one should carefully control the use of the "alias" newly introduced.

7.5 INTRODUCTION TO GENERIC PACKAGES

Because of the strong Ada type rules, types should be explicit by the time the programs in which they appear are compiled. Also, the rules regarding the matching of formal and actual parameters are strict. There is little flexibility for writing a subprogram that is general enough to handle a variety of types. The stringency of Ada types is complemented by Ada's **generic facilities,** which allow for the creation of templates or models of packages or subprograms.

The generic facilities cannot be directly executed. Instead, generic packages or subprograms are instantiated. **Instantiation** creates a particular executable package or subprogram by using some actual parameters (actual types) to generate the appropriate version. The matching of actual parameters is done with generic parameters (generic parameters play the role of formal parameters in subprograms).

The general form for a **generic declaration** is

```
generic generic_parameter_declaration ;
```

One can produce a generic package by placing a generic declaration in front of a regular package.

The TEXT_IO package listed in Appendix C gives a number of generic packages. For instance, there is a generic INTEGER_IO package having the following form:

```
generic

    type NUM is range <> ;

        -- This line is the generic declaration.

        -- It is the generic parameter declaration and NUM

        -- is the generic type parameter that matches

        -- any integer type. Any  integer type actual

        -- parameter can be matched  with NUM.

package INTEGER_IO is

    -- Object and subprogram declarations are given here.

end INTEGER_IO ;
```

We instantiated the INTEGER_IO generic package in many of the previous programs, following this pattern:

```
package pack_name is new generic_pack_name
         ( one_or_more_generic_act_param ) ;
```

For instance, if AGE is an integer type, then the instantiation can take the form

```
package INT_IO is new INTEGER_IO ( AGE ) ;
```

In this instantiation the generic actual parameter is the integer type AGE. To instantiate this package with a noninteger type is not valid.

Following the instantiation of the package INTEGER_IO, a package whose name is INT_IO is incarnated by using the actual parameter AGE. That is, in every declaration in the specification of INTEGER_IO, the generic parameter NUM is replaced by AGE. This instantiation process is illustrated in Figure 7.2.

Here are some other generic packages one can find in TEXT_IO. They have also been used in previous programs. The floating-point facilities follow.

```
generic

    type NUM is digits <> ;

            -- This line is the generic declaration.

            -- It is the generic parameter declaration,

            -- where NUM is the generic type parameter

            -- that matches any floating-point type. Any

            -- floating-point type actual parameter

            -- can be matched  with NUM.

package FLOAT_IO is

        -- The content is given in Appendix C.

end FLOAT_IO ;
```

FIGURE 7.2 Instantiation of the Package INTEGER_IO

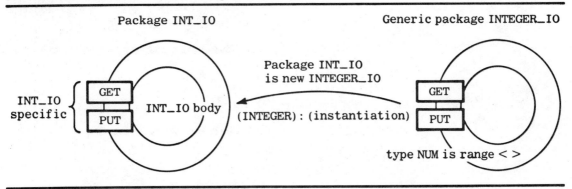

The generic facilities in TEXT_IO corresponding to the fixed-point types are given next.

```
generic

     type NUM is delta <> ;

          -- This line is the generic declaration.

          -- It is the generic parameter declaration,

          -- where NUM is the  generic type parameter

          -- that matches any fixed-point type. Any

          -- fixed-point type actual parameter can be

          -- matched  with NUM.

package FIXED_IO is

     -- The content is given in Appendix C .

end FIXED_IO ;
```

Finally, the enumeration type facilities are as follows:

```
generic

     type ENUM is (<>) ;

          -- This line is the generic declaration.

          -- Is the generic parameter declaration,

          -- where ENUM is the generic type parameter

          -- that matches any enumeration type. Any

          -- enumeration type actual parameter can be

          -- matched  with ENUM.

package ENUMERATION_IO is

     -- The content is given in Appendix C .

end ENUMERATION_IO ;
```

There are some other generic packages in Appendix C, such as DIRECT_IO. We sketch the generic declaration specification of DIRECT_IO next.

```
generic

    type ELEMENT_TYPE is private ;

            -- This line is the generic declaration.

            -- It is the generic parameter declaration, where

            -- ELEMENT_TYPE is the  generic type parameter

            -- that matches  any type that allows for

            -- assignment and tests for equality and

            -- inequality. The actual parameter therefore

            -- can  be  a private type,  a record  type,  an

            -- array type, an integer type, an enumeration

            -- type, a floating-point type, and a few other

            -- types too.

package DIRECT_IO is

            -- The content is given in Appendix C.

end DIRECT_IO ;
```

EXAMPLE We will instantiate the package DIRECT_IO by using a variety of types as actual parameters in order to illustrate the flexibility allowed by private type generic parameters.

```
with SECURITIES, DIRECT_IO ;

use SECURITIES ;

        -- We assume that the  package SECURITIES is compiled.

        -- It was introduced in Section 7.2.

        package INSTANT_DIR_IO is

            --
```

```
package DIR_DATE is new DIRECT_IO ( DATE ) ;

package DIR_SECURITY is new DIRECT_IO ( SECURITY ) ;

package DIR_INTEREST is new DIRECT_IO ( INTEREST ) ;

package DIR_INT_KIND is new DIRECT_IO ( INTEREST_KIND ) ;

--

end INSTANT_DIR_IO ;
```

The package INSTANT_DIR_IO is a collection of four packages, each one able to fully use the facilities of the generic package DIRECT_IO (procedures, functions, and types). The private type generic parameter is replaced by each of the four actual parameters, creating four independent packages, each one with its own set of types, functions, procedures, and so forth.

Note that a private type (or a limited private type) generic declaration is quite general and gives the user remarkable freedom regarding the type of the actual parameter.

Although within a package specification the private and limited private types introduce very tight rules, the opposite is true when they appear as generic type parameters: Any types allowing for operations equally restrictive or with fewer restrictions can be used as actual parameters.

Another generic package in Appendix C is SEQUENTIAL_IO. It has the same generic declaration as the package DIRECT_IO. Each of the generic packages in Appendix C will be studied and used with a number of examples in the next chapter.

Besides containing the generic packages mentioned above, Appendix C contains the specification of the package STANDARD. This package contains predefined objects (such as constants introducing ASCII special characters), types (BOOLEAN, INTEGER, FLOAT, and so on), and functions ("=" for integers, strings, and so forth), together with some representation clauses. This package is directly visible for any Ada program. It plays a special role for Ada programs that will be detailed in Chapter 9.

One may think that generic facilities accomplish a job similar to that of text substitution. But this statement is only partially true, because the replacement of generic formal parameters by the actual parameter is followed by the elaboration of the instantiated package or subprogram at the point of their appearance. Text substitution, in contrast, applies to entities already elaborated.

Writing generic packages is quite a complex job. To explain the design and writing of generic packages is outside the scope of this book. Instead, we have given examples here to make the use of generic packages and instantiation quite straightforward.

EXERCISES FOR CHAPTER 7

1. Rewrite the program DATE_CONVERSION of Chapter 2 by making use of the package CHECK_DATES_ALT (its last version) of Section 7.2.

2. Rewrite the program NAME_PHONE of Chapter 4 by making use of the package LINE_HANDLING of Section 7.2.

3. Extract a relevant package specification and package body for handling student records and grades from the program GR_POINT_AVE of Chapter 4, and rewrite the program by making use of the new package.

4. Enhance the capabilities of the LINE_HANDLING package by providing the specification and the body of new subprograms, such as the following:

Function	Description
EXTRACT	This function returns a portion of the WRK_LINE of specified length and starting at a predefined position
APPEND	This function has two formal parameters of type T_REC, and it returns an object of type T_REC whose WRK_LINE component is the catenation of the WRK_LINE components of the two formal parameters
LOCATE	This function has two formal parameters of type T_REC, denoted F_REC_1 and F_REC_2; it returns the starting position of the first occurrence of the component F_REC_1.WRK_LINE in F_REC_2.WRK_LINE

5. Write a package (both specification and body) that contains two functions, one converting integers to character strings and the other converting character strings to integers.

CHAPTER EIGHT

ADA INPUT/OUTPUT PACKAGES

8.1 INTRODUCTION TO I/O PACKAGES

FILE CONCEPTS

Ada has a number of package-handling files. **Files** (that is, external files) are collections of items placed outside the program, usually on a device such as a disk or a tape. The items are all of the same type. There is always a first item in the external file (unless the file is empty). However, external files are considered to be **unbounded** because, in theory, one can always add another item after the last one. That is, after item 10001 one can add item 10002. In practice, external files are limited in size by the actual storage capacity of a device or the particular details of implementation.

One can liken the concept of external file to the concept of array. There are three key differences, though. First, an array is part of the program, while an external file is part of the external environment. Second, an array has known bounds when the program is running, while the external file (as explained above) does not. Third, array elements are accessed in a uniform manner, while file items can be accessed in a variety of ways.

ADA PACKAGE-HANDLING FILES

Ada has a number of packages that implement essential **input/output** features. These packages facilitate the transfer of information between programs and external files. There is a DIRECT_IO package (dealing with "direct files," which will be explained in this chapter), a SEQUENTIAL_IO package, a TEXT_IO package, and a package named LOW_LEVEL_IO. The LOW_LEVEL_IO package is supposed to support less traditional devices and will not be covered in this book. The specification of the other packages is listed in Appendix C.

A quick inspection of the other three packages reveals that they have some types and subprograms bearing the same name. They all have in common a limited private type called FILE_TYPE, an enumeration type called FILE_MODE, and some procedures having the names OPEN, CLOSE, CREATE, and DELETE. These procedures will be described in the paragraphs that follow.

NAMING A FILE

When files are first created, they are given a NAME. This NAME of type STRING is a formal parameter appearing in a number of subprograms of the input/output packages uniquely identifying the file externally. That is, the file is known to the outside world (including other languages and operating systems) under the actual parameter value matching NAME. This *external name* is given a new name within the scope of the program. The new name is in force as long as the file is in use, and it is akin to an *internal name*. It is the actual parameter value matching the formal parameter FILE_TYPE.

The FILE_TYPE is a type used to identify internally the external file. Whenever we use the term *file* (as opposed to the term *external file*), we mean an object of type FILE_TYPE.

The type FILE_MODE is declared either as

```
type FILE_MODE is ( IN_FILE, INOUT_FILE,
  OUT_FILE ) ;
```

which is version 1, or as

```
type FILE_MODE is ( IN_FILE, OUT_FILE ) ;
```

which is version 2. The first version applies to the DIRECT_IO package, and the second one applies to the SEQUENTIAL_IO and TEXT_IO packages.

The FILE_MODE determines the direction of the information transfer from the (external) file to the program. If the FILE_MODE is IN_FILE, then the file can be read. That is, the only transfer of information is from the file to the program. If the FILE_MODE is OUT_FILE, then items can be written onto the external file. If the FILE_MODE is INOUT_FILE, then one can both read from and write on the external file. This last FILE_MODE is allowed only for the DIRECT_IO packages.

CREATING A FILE

If an external file does not exist, it must be *created* by invoking the procedure CREATE. Its declaration, which is the same for all I/O packages except the default value of the MODE parameter, is

```
procedure CREATE ( FILE : in out FILE_TYPE ;

                   MODE : in    FILE_MODE :=  INOUT_FILE ;

                   NAME : in    STRING    :=  "" ;

                   FORM : in    STRING    :=  "" ; );
```

This procedure is part of the package DIRECT_IO. The MODE formal parameter has the default value OUT_FILE in the SEQUENTIAL_IO and TEXT_IO packages.

The NAME formal parameter has a null string as its default value. If there is no actual parameter supplied for NAME, or if the actual parameter is a null string, then the file created is a temporary one (that is, a file that cannot be accessed after the completion of the main program). If an actual parameter matching NAME is supplied, then it must represent the external file name and has to conform to the external file naming rules of the local computer. Clearly, the NAME parameter is implementation-dependent.

The fourth formal parameter of the procedure CREATE is the FORM. This formal parameter (of type STRING) is implementation-dependent. It may identify details about the external file such as the blocking factor, the retention period, or other file characteristics. If this parameter is omitted, then the default file characteristics of the particular installation will be in force.

EXAMPLE   Here is an example of a procedure call using CREATE:

```
CREATE ( FILE => TRANS_FILE,

         -- This file may be a transaction file, that is, we

         -- intended to record transient information  in it.

         MODE => INOUT_FILE,

         -- This mode applies only to a direct file.

         NAME => "FY8603.DAT",

         -- This line gives the external name (it means
```

```
-- fiscal year 1986 month 03).

FORM => "" ) ;

--   The default assumptions will apply for

--   this parameter. An example for the VAX Ada

--   implementation is :

--   FORM => "ORGANIZATION SEQUENTIAL;"
```

This statement assumes that an instantiation of the package DIRECT_IO is directly visible. An equivalent way to write this statement, this time using positional notation, is

```
CREATE ( TRANS_FILE, INOUT_FILE, "FY8603.DAT", " "
   ) ;
```

OPENING A FILE

Once a file is created and no exception is raised, the file remains opened. Opening a file means that a connection is established between the created external file and the object of type FILE_TYPE. (Remember that the term *file* is understood to mean an object of type FILE_TYPE.)

The external file may already be in existence (that is, it was created before the program started its execution). Then the connection between the object of type FILE_TYPE and the external file is established by a successful invocation of the procedure OPEN (*successful* here means that no exceptions are raised during the execution of the procedure OPEN). The connection between the object of type FILE_TYPE (that is, "the" file) and the external file is broken by the execution of the procedure CLOSE.

The declaration of the procedure OPEN has the same formal parameters as the procedure CREATE:

```
procedure OPEN    ( FILE : in out FILE_TYPE ;

                    MODE : in     FILE_MODE ;

                    NAME : in     STRING    ;

                    FORM : in     STRING    := "" ; );
```

This procedure (as opposed to CREATE) has no default value for MODE and NAME, which means that these parameters are mandatory. Hence one has to spell out the MODE of a file being opened.

EXAMPLE   An example of file opening is as follows:

```
OPEN    ( FILE => TRANS_FILE,

          MODE => INOUT_FILE,

          -- This  mode  implies  the use  of  the  DIRECT_IO

          -- package.

          NAME => "FY8603.DAT",

          -- Here we have the external name of the file.

          FORM => "" ) ;

          -- The default assumptions are given here.
```

The same statement can be written by using the positional notation:

```
OPEN ( TRANS_FILE, INOUT_FILE,
       "FY8603.DAT", " " ) ;
```

Again this statement assumes that an instantiation of the package DIRECT_IO is directly visible.

PERMANENT CHARACTERISTICS OF A FILE

Whenever a file is created, the external file is given some **permanent characteristics.** The exact characteristics are implementation-dependent, but one should expect some characteristics related to the external file organization and maybe some regarding the record size or access rights. These permanent characteristics of the external file are inherited when the external file is opened later. Exceptions are raised whenever the permanent characteristics of an external file are not consistent with characteristics stated by a corresponding OPEN statement (for instance, if the file organization stated by the FORM parameter is not compatible with the file organization of the external file established when the file was created). Exceptions are raised in many other situations, too (for instance, if one tries to open a file already opened). Most of the file-handling exceptions are defined in a package called IO_EXCEPTIONS. These exceptions and their handling will be detailed in Chapter 11.

CLOSING A FILE

The declaration of the procedure CLOSE is

```
procedure CLOSE ( FILE : in out FILE_TYPE ) ;
```

An example for invoking this procedure is

```
CLOSE ( TRANS_FILE );
```

An external file can be opened and closed several times during the execution of a program. A file (internal file) can also be opened and closed several times during the execution of a program, and one can have the same (internal) file name opened at different times in connection with different external files.

ERASING AN EXTERNAL FILE

An external file (assuming that the file is open) can be physically **erased** by invoking the procedure DELETE. Its declaration is

```
procedure DELETE ( FILE : in out FILE_TYPE ) ;
```

An example of its invocation is

```
DELETE ( TRANS_FILE ) ;
```

PROGRAM EXAMPLE

The following program illustrates the features we have discussed so far. It will create 12 external files (using the generic package DIRECT_IO) whose external names are FY8601.DAT through FY8612.DAT.

CREATE_12_TRANS_FILES Program

```
with DIRECT_IO ;

procedure CREATE_12_TRANS_FILES is

-- As it mentioned at the end of Chapter 7, the

-- packages DIRECT_IO and SEQUENTIAL_IO have the generic

-- parameter ELEMENT_TYPE.

type TRANS_RECORD is

    record

        INFO : STRING ( 1 .. 80 ) ;

    end record ;

package DIR_IO is new DIRECT_IO (

        ELEMENT_TYPE => TRANS_RECORD ) ;
```

```
use DIR_IO;

TRANS_FILE : FILE_TYPE ;

        -- We instantiated a DIRECT_IO package having

        -- TRANS_RECORD as element types.

EXT_NAME : STRING (1 .. 10) := "FY8601.DAT" ;

begin

    for I in 1 .. 12

        loop

            CREATE ( FILE => TRANS_FILE,

                     MODE => INOUT_FILE,

                     NAME => EXT_NAME,

                     FORM => "" ) ;

            CLOSE ( TRANS_FILE ) ;

            if EXT_NAME (6) /= '9'

                then

                EXT_NAME := EXT_NAME ( 1 .. 5 ) &

                        CHARACTER'SUCC( EXT_NAME(6) ) &

                        EXT_NAME ( 7 .. 10 ) ;

            else

                EXT_NAME := EXT_NAME ( 1 .. 4 ) &

                        "10" & EXT_NAME ( 7 .. 10 );

            -- The proper name is set up by

            -- incrementing the last digit preceding

            -- the decimal point, unless the digit is 9.

            -- Note that we create 12 external files

            -- but  we use only one (internal)
```

```
                              -- file, which is repeatedly closed and

                              -- reopened (by CREATE).

                    end if;

          end loop;

end CREATE_12_TRANS_FILES ;
```

COMMON FUNCTIONS FOR I/O PACKAGES

Ada has functions common to each of the I/O packages that help in testing various states of a file. Here are their declarations :

```
function NAME ( FILE : FILE_TYPE ) return
   STRING ;
```

This function returns the external name of the file supplied as the actual argument.

```
function END_OF_FILE ( FILE : FILE_TYPE ) return
   BOOLEAN ;
```

This function returns the value TRUE if no more elements can be read from the file supplied as actual argument. This function returns TRUE if it is invoked after the last element of the file is read.

```
function IS_OPEN ( FILE : in FILE_TYPE ) return
   BOOLEAN ;
```

This function returns the value TRUE if the file supplied as the actual argument is open.

```
function MODE ( FILE : FILE_TYPE ) return
   FILE_MODE ;
```

This function returns the current mode of the file supplied as actual argument.

```
function FORM ( FILE : FILE_TYPE ) return
   STRING ;
```

This function returns the current form, as a string, of the file supplied as the actual argument.

8.2 SEQUENTIAL FILE PROCESSING

Sequential files are viewed as a sequence of values of type ELEMENT_TYPE, which is the generic formal parameter of the package SEQUENTIAL_IO. The sequence of values in the file imposes the order for processing the values. When a sequential file is open, then the first element of the file is available for reading. If, say, the third value of the file is needed, though, then one has to read the first two.

The operations needed for sequential file processing are implemented in the generic package SEQUENTIAL_IO, whose specification is listed in Appendix C. Here is the declaration of the sequential READ procedure:

```
procedure READ ( FILE : in FILE_TYPE ;
                 ITEM : out ELEMENT_TYPE ) ;
```

This procedure reads an element from the given file and returns the value in the ITEM parameter. It assumes that the file is opened and that the mode of the file is IN_FILE. The procedure reads the next element of the file. If the next element is the last one of the file, then the END_OF_FILE function, if invoked, returns the value TRUE.

Here is the declaration of the sequential WRITE procedure:

```
procedure WRITE ( FILE : in FILE_TYPE ;
                  ITEM : out ELEMENT_TYPE ) ;
```

This function writes (after the last value of the file) a new value on the file. It assumes that the file is opened and that the mode of the file is OUT_FILE.

At times, one must process a sequential file several times. One may use the RESET procedure, whose declaration is given next, as an alternative to repeatedly closing and reopening the file.

```
procedure RESET ( FILE : in FILE_TYPE ;
                  MODE : in FILE_MODE ) ;
```

This procedure makes the file for reading from or writing on available, starting with the first element of the file. Closing and reopening a file achieves the same result, with the following difference: RESET does not break the connection between the external file and the (internal) file at any time. This procedure is thus less time-consuming. The procedure

```
procedure RESET ( FILE : in FILE_TYPE ) ;
```

is the same as the previous one. However, with this procedure one does not have the option to change the MODE parameter.

BUILDING A SEQUENTIAL FILE

Here we present an Ada program using the generic package SEQUENTIAL_IO requiring the same input and output as the program RECUR_PROC_GRADES of Chapter 5, itself a modification of the program ACCESS_GRADES of Chapter 3. Sample input data were shown in Figures 3.7 and 5.1. However, there is an additional restriction for this program: The test answers are sorted in ascending sequence on subject ID, and the student answer lines are sorted on student ID. Student lines with the same student ID are assumed to be sorted on subject ID.

The program, in addition, builds a sequential file holding the test information and another sequential file containing the student answers.

SEQ_PROC_GRADES Program

```
with TEXT_IO; use TEXT_IO;

with SEQUENTIAL_IO ;

procedure SEQ_PROC_GRADES is

    Package INT_IO is new INTEGER_IO(INTEGER);

    use INT_IO;

    type CHOICES is range 1 .. 5 ;

    type POSSIBLE_QUESTIONS is range 20 .. 50 ;

    Package CHO_IO is new INTEGER_IO(CHOICES);

    use CHO_IO;

    Package POSS_IO is new INTEGER_IO(POSSIBLE_CHOICES);

    use POSS_IO;

    DNO_QUESTIONS : POSSIBLE_QUESTIONS ;

    type ANSWERS is array ( 1 .. DNO_QUESTIONS ) of CHOICES;

    type TEST_KEY is

        record

            SUBJ          : STRING ( 1 .. 5 );

            NO_QUESTIONS : POSSIBLE_QUESTIONS;

            KEY_ANSWERS  : ANSWERS;
```

```
        end record;

CURR_TEST : TEST_KEY ;

GOOD_ANSWERS : INTEGER ;

type IN_REC is

    record

            STUDENT_ID : STRING ( 1 .. 10 );

            SUBJECT_ID : STRING ( 1 .. 5 );

            STUDENT_ANSWERS : ANSWERS ;

    end record;

CURR_REC : IN_REC;

type T_PAIR is

    record

            SUBJ_MAT : STRING ( 1 .. 5 );

            SCORE    : NATURAL ;

    end record;

CURR_PAIR : T_PAIR;

type SEMESTER_TESTS  is array ( 1 .. 25 ) of T_PAIR;

type BIG_REC is

    record

            BIG_ST_ID : STRING ( 1 .. 10 );

            NO_TESTS  : NATURAL ;

            ST_TESTS  : SEMESTER_TESTS ;

    end record ;

                -- The identifiers used so far are identical to those

                -- of RECUR_PROC_GRADES and have the same meaning,

                -- except that we dropped any reference  to access
```

```
                    -- type variables.
        CURR_OUT_REC  : BIG_REC ;
        package TEST_IO is new SEQUENTIAL_IO ( TEST_KEY ) ;
        use TEST_IO;
        package STUD_IO is new SEQUENTIAL_IO  ( BIG_REC ) ;
        use STUD_IO;
        -- Two instantiations of the package SEQUENTIAL_IO are
        -- needed for the two sequential files (a test file  and
        -- a student file).
        TEST_FILE    : TEST_IO.FILE_TYPE ;
        STUDENT_FILE : STUD_IO.FILE_TYPE ;
procedure SAME_STUD_PROC is
        -- This procedure updates a CURR_OUT_REC.
begin
        GET ( CURR_REC.SUBJECT_ID);
        while not END_OF_FILE ( FILE => TEST_FILE ) and
              CURR_TEST.SUBJ  <  CURR_REC.SUBJECT_ID
              loop
              -- Look for the test subject in the TEST_FILE.
              READ ( FILE => TEST_FILE ,
                    ITEM => CURR_TEST ) ;
        end loop;
        if CURR_TEST.SUBJ = CURR_REC.SUBJECT_ID
            then
            -- If the test is TRUE, then subject was found.
            -- Otherwise, there is no such subject in the list.
```

```
        GOOD_ANSWERS := 0;

        for J in 1 .. CURR_TEST.NO_QUESTIONS

            loop

            GET ( CURR_REC.STUDENT_ANSWERS(J), 1);

            if CURR_REC.STUDENT_ANSWERS (J) =

                    CURR_TEST.KEY_ANSWERS (J)

                then

                    GOOD_ANSWERS := GOOD_ANSWERS + 1 ;

            end if;

        end loop;

        NEW_LINE;

        -- The test score is computed now. Next we update

        -- the student record.

        CURR_OUT_REC.NO_TESTS :=

                        CURR_OUT_REC.NO_TESTS + 1 ;

        CURR_PAIR.SUBJ_MAT := CURR_REC.SUBJECT_ID ;

        CURR_PAIR.SCORE     := GOOD_ANSWERS  ;

        CURR_OUT_REC.ST_TESTS(CURR_OUT_REC.NO_TESTS ) :=

                        CURR_PAIR ;

    else

    PUT(" No such subject:");

    PUT(CURR_REC.SUBJECT_ID);

        end if;

end SAME_STUD_PROC ;

--

procedure NEW_STUD_PROC is
```

```
        -- CURR_OUT_REC is now written out (it is a value representing

        -- previous student tests).

begin

        STUD_IO.WRITE ( FILE => STUDENT_FILE ,

                ITEM => CURR_OUT_REC ) ;

        CURR_OUT_REC.BIG_ST_ID := CURR_REC.STUDENT_ID ;

        CURR_OUT_REC.NO_TESTS := 0 ;

        RESET ( FILE => TEST_FILE ) ;

        SAME_STUD_PROC ;

end NEW_STUD_PROC ;

--

begin

        -- Create the test file

        TEST_IO.CREATE ( FILE => TEST_FILE,

                MODE => OUT_FILE,

                -- We need to write test keys  on the file.

                NAME => "TEST_FILE.DAT",

                FORM => "" ) ;

                -- Default file characteristics are requested here.

                -- The file TEST_FILE is opened, ready to write the

                -- first value of type TEST_KEY.

        GET(CURR_TEST.SUBJ);

        while CURR_TEST.SUBJ /= "XXXXX"

            loop

            GET(CURR_TEST.NO_QUESTIONS,2);

            DNO_QUESTIONS := CURR_TEST.NO_QUESTIONS ;
```

```
        SKIP_LINE;

        for I in 1 .. CURR_TEST.NO_QUESTIONS

             loop

             GET ( CURR_TEST.KEY_ANSWERS (I), 1);

        end loop;

        TEST_IO.WRITE ( FILE => TEST_FILE ,

                ITEM => CURR_TEST ) ;

        SKIP_LINE;

        GET(CURR_TEST.SUBJ);

end loop;

-- The test file is now built. We need to sequentially

-- read the file, so we must  close it, and

-- reopen it with mode IN_FILE. Alternatively, we can

-- use RESET.

TEST_IO.CLOSE ( FILE => TEST_FILE ) ;

TEST_IO.OPEN ( FILE => TEST_FILE,

        MODE => IN_FILE,

         -- We need to read test keys  from the file.

        NAME => "TEST_FILE.DAT",

        FORM => "" ) ;

        -- The file above  will be reset for each new

        -- student ID (or it can be closed and reopened)

STUD_IO.CREATE( FILE => STUDENT_FILE,

        MODE => OUT_FILE,

        -- We need to write student records here.

        NAME => "STUDENT_FILE.DAT",
```

```
                    FORM => "" ) ;

                    -- Default file characteristics are requested here.
        SKIP_LINE;

        GET ( CURR_REC.STUDENT_ID ) ;

        CURR_OUT_REC.BIG_ST_ID := CURR_REC.STUDENT_ID ;

        CURR_OUT_REC.NO_TESTS := 0 ;

        while CURR_REC.STUDENT_ID /= "9999999999"

            loop

            if CURR_OUT_REC.BIG_ST_ID /= CURR_REC.STUDENT_ID

                then

                NEW_STUD_PROC ;

            else

                SAME_STUD_PROC ;

            end if ;

            GET ( CURR_REC.STUDENT_ID) ;

        end loop;

        -- All student input lines are processed. However,

        -- the last student record is not written out.

        NEW_STUD_PROC ;

        -- Now the last student record is written.

        STUD_IO.RESET ( FILE => STUDENT_FILE,

        -- We reset the student file at the beginning, and

        -- we change the mode in order to list its values.

                MODE =>  IN_FILE ) ;

        while not STUD_IO.END_OF_FILE ( FILE => STUDENT_FILE )

        -- The test is true if there is no value of STUDENT_FILE
```

```
-- available for a next reading.

    loop

    STUD_IO.READ ( STUDENT_FILE, CURR_OUT_REC ) ;

    -- This statement reads the next value of STUDENT_FILE.

    PUT ( CURR_OUT_REC.BIG_ST_ID ) ;

    for I in 1 .. CURR_OUT_REC.NO_TESTS

        loop

        PUT ( CURR_OUT_REC.ST_TESTS(I).SUBJ_MAT  ) ;

        PUT ( CURR_OUT_REC.ST_TESTS(I).SCORE   ) ;

        NEW_LINE ;

        end loop ;

    end loop;

    TEST_IO.CLOSE ( TEST_FILE ) ;

    STUD_IO.CLOSE ( STUDENT_FILE ) ;

end   SEQ_PROC_GRADES   ;
```

MERGING TWO FILES

Next, we present the merging of two external files, whose external names are STUDENT_FILE_1_IN.DAT and STUDENT_FILE_2_IN.DAT. Merging assumes as input two sorted files; in this case the two external files have values of type BIG_REC and are sorted on BIG_ST_ID. The output of the merging program is a third sorted file (on the same BIG_ST_ID) having the combined information of the two input files.

We make the following simplifying assumption: Whenever two values of the external files have identical BIG_ST_ID components, the test subjects are different, their combined total does not exceed 25, and the test subjects of the value of STUDENT_FILE_1_IN.DAT precede the test subjects of the value of STUDENT_FILE_2_IN.DAT (in the chapter exercises we will drop some of these assumptions).

Figure 8.1 shows some sample input files and the resulting third (merged) file.

FIGURE 8.1 Sample Files for MERGE_PROC_GRADES Program

```
STUD_IN_1
CURR_REC_1_IN
```

BIG_ST_ID	NO_TESTS	ST_TESTS				
		(1)	(2)	(3)	(4) . .	(25)
1234567890	3	AST01 75	CMP05 88	ENG01 89		
2222222222	2	CMP01 89	PHY03 77			
3333333333	2	BSN01 75	CMP01 89			

```
STUD_IN_2
CURR_REC_2_IN
```

BIG_ST_ID	NO_TESTS	ST_TESTS				
BIG_ST_ID	NO_TESTS	ST_TESTS				
		(1)	(2)	(3)	(4) . .	(25)
1234567890	1	PHY01 55				
3333333333	2	ENG01 75	PHY01 95			

```
STUD_OUT_FILE
CURR_REC_OUT
```

BIG_ST_ID	NO_TESTS	ST_TESTS				
		(1)	(2)	(3)	(4) . .	(25)
1234567890	4	AST01 75	CMP05 88	ENG01 89	PHY01 55	
2222222222	2	CMP01 89	PHY03 77			
3333333333	4	BSN01 75	CMP01 89	ENG01 75	PHY01 95	

MERGE_PROC_GRADES Program

```ada
with TEXT_IO; use TEXT_IO;

with SEQUENTIAL_IO ;

procedure MERGE_PROC_GRADES is

    Package INT_IO is new INTEGER_IO(INTEGER);

    use INT_IO;

    type T_PAIR is

        record

            SUBJ_MAT : STRING ( 1 .. 5 );

            SCORE    : NATURAL ;
```

```
            end record;

       CURR_PAIR : T_PAIR;

       type SEMESTER_TESTS  is array ( 1 .. 25 ) of T_PAIR;

       type BIG_REC is

            record

                 BIG_ST_ID : STRING ( 1 .. 10 );

                 NO_TESTS  : NATURAL ;

                 ST_TESTS  : SEMESTER_TESTS ;

            end record ;

                 -- The identifiers used so far are identical to those

                 -- of SEQ_PROC_GRADES and have the same meaning.

       package STUD_IO is new SEQUENTIAL_IO  ( BIG_REC ) ;

       use STUD_IO;

       CURR_REC_1_IN, CURR_REC_2_IN, CURR_REC_OUT : STUD_IO.BIG_REC ;

       STUD_IN_1, STUD_IN_2, STUD_OUT_FILE : STUD_IO.FILE_TYPE ;

--

procedure READ_1 is

begin

    READ ( FILE => STUD_IN_1 ,

           ITEM => CURR_REC_1_IN ) ;

end READ_1 ;

--

procedure READ_2 is

begin

    READ ( FILE => STUD_IN_2 ,

           ITEM => CURR_REC_2_IN ) ;

end READ_2 ;
```

```
        --

        procedure WRITE_OUT is

        begin

                WRITE ( FILE => STUD_OUT_FILE,

                        ITEM => CURR_REC_OUT ) ;

        end WRITE_OUT ;

        --

        procedure COPY_1 is

        begin

                while not STUD_IO.END_OF_FILE ( STUD_IN_1 )

                        loop

                        READ_1 ;

                        CURR_REC_OUT := CURR_REC_1_IN ;

                        WRITE_OUT ;

                end loop ;

                PUT ( " First input file was last processed " ) ;

        end COPY_1 ;

        --

        procedure COPY_2 is

        begin

                while not STUD_IO.END_OF_FILE ( STUD_IN_2 )

                        loop

                        READ_2 ;

                        CURR_REC_OUT := CURR_REC_2_IN ;

                        WRITE_OUT ;

                end loop ;
```

```
        PUT ( " Second input file was last processed " ) ;
end COPY_2 :
--

begin
        STUD_IO.OPEN  ( FILE => STUD_IN_1,
                MODE => IN_FILE ,
                NAME => "STUDENT_FILE_1_IN.DAT",
                FORM => "" ) ;
        STUD_IO.OPEN  ( FILE => STUD_IN_2,
                MODE => IN_FILE ,
                NAME => "STUDENT_FILE_2_IN.DAT",
                FORM => "" ) ;
        STUD_IO.CREATE ( FILE => STUD_OUT_FILE,
                MODE => OUT_FILE ,
                NAME => "STUD-MERGED-FILE.DAT",
                FORM => "" ) ;
        if   not STUD_IO.END_OF_FILE ( STUD_IN_1 ) and
             not END_OF_FILE ( STUD_IN_1)
             then
             READ_1 ;
             READ_2 ;
             loop
               if  CURR_REC_1_IN.BIG_ST_ID <
                   CURR_REC_2_IN.BIG_ST_ID
                   then
                   -- Now we write from the first file.
```

```
                    CURR_REC_OUT := CURR_REC_1_IN ;

                    WRITE_OUT ;

                    if STUD_IO.END_OF_FILE (STUD_IN_1)

                    then

                    -- The last element of the first input file

                    -- was written out .

                    -- Now we write the current element of the second

                    -- input  file; otherwise, COPY_2 will  drop

                    -- it. We end the merge after COPY_2.

                    CURR_REC_OUT := CURR_REC_2_IN ;

                    WRITE_OUT ;

                    COPY_2 ;

                    exit ;

                end if ;

                READ_1 ;

            elsif  CURR_REC_1_IN.BIG_ST_ID >

                   CURR_REC_2_IN.BIG_ST_ID

            then

            -- Now we write from the second file.

            CURR_REC_OUT := CURR_REC_2_IN ;

            WRITE_OUT ;

            if STUD_IO.END_OF_FILE (STUD_IN_2)

                then

                    -- The last element of the second input file

                    -- was written out .

                    -- We write the current element of the first
```

```
            -- input  file; otherwise, COPY_2 will  drop

            -- it. End the merge after COPY_1.

            CURR_REC_OUT := CURR_REC_1_IN ;

            WRITE_OUT ;

            COPY_1 ;

            exit ;

        end if ;

        READ_2 ;

    else

        -- For equality we add  the student tests.

        CURR_REC_OUT := CURR_REC_1_IN ;

        CURR_REC_OUT.NO_TESTS := CURR_REC_OUT.NO_TESTS +

                                CURR_REC_2_IN.NO_TESTS ;

        CURR_REC_OUT.ST_TESTS ( CURR_REC_1_IN.NO_TESTS + 1

            .. CURR_REC_OUT.NO_TESTS ) :=

        CURR_REC_2_IN.ST_TESTS (1..CURR_REC_2_IN.NO_TESTS);

            -- This statement is a slice assignment.

        WRITE_OUT ;

        if STUD_IO.END_OF_FILE (STUD_IN_2)

            then

            COPY_1 ;

            exit ;

        end if ;

        -- We copy the corresponding  file if the other

        -- file is returning an end of file .

        if STUD_IO.END_OF_FILE (STUD_IN_1)
```

```
                                    then

                                    COPY_2 ;

                                    exit ;

                            end if ;

                            READ_1 ;

                            READ_2 ;

                    end if ;

                        -- Two non empty files were merged here.

                        -- At least one file was processed. Now we

                        -- copy the other one.

                    end loop;

            elsif  STUD_IO.END_OF_FILE ( STUD_IN_1 )

                    COPY_2 ;

            else

                        -- STUD_IN_2  must be empty if a value occurs here.

                    COPY_1 ;

            end if ;

            PUT ( " The merge is done " ) ;

            STUD_IO.CLOSE ( STUD_IN_1 ) ;

            STUD_IO.CLOSE ( STUD_IN_2 ) ;

            STUD_IO.CLOSE ( STUD_OUT_FILE ) ;

    end  MERGE_PROC_GRADES  ;
```

8.3 DIRECT FILE PROCESSING

FEATURES OF DIRECT FILES

Direct files are viewed as a sequence of values of type ELEMENT_TYPE, which is the generic formal parameter of the package DIRECT_IO (no difference from the SEQUENTIAL_IO package). Unlike the values of the files in the SEQUENTIAL_IO package, however, the values of the direct files can be processed in any order, regardless of their relative position. In fact, to read or write a value of a direct file, one must supply, among other actual parameters, its relative position—called its **index**—in the file.

Every open direct file has a current index associated with it. The **current index** is the index that will be used to read or write the next element of the file (assuming there is no explicit change of index).

The relative position of the value to be read or written can be controlled with the help of the procedure SET_INDEX (among others). The current position of the file can be found by invoking the procedure INDEX. Their declarations, as indicated in Appendix C, are as follows:

```
procedure SET_INDEX ( FILE : FILE_TYPE ;
                      TO : POSITIVE_COUNT ) ;
```

POSITIVE_COUNT is a subtype of the type COUNT, ranging from 1 to an implementation-defined COUNT'LAST. The index of the file is set to the value of the actual parameter matching TO.

```
function INDEX ( FILE : FILE_TYPE ) return
  POSITIVE_COUNT ;
```

This function returns the current index of a file.

Both SET_INDEX and INDEX operate on a direct file of any mode (IN_FILE, OUT_FILE, or INOUT_FILE). Whenever a file is opened, the current index is set to 1.

The READ and WRITE operations for direct files have the following declarations:

```
procedure READ ( FILE : in FILE_TYPE ;

                 ITEM : out ELEMENT_TYPE ;

                 FROM : in POSITIVE_COUNT ) ;

procedure READ ( FILE : in FILE_TYPE ;

                 ITEM : out ELEMENT_TYPE ) ;
```

In the first form the element of type ELEMENT_TYPE will be read from the file, at the relative position given by the actual parameter matching FROM, and placed in the actual parameter matching ITEM. In the second form the relative position of the value read is given by the current index. The index value is incremented by 1 after the READ statement is executed.

Various exceptions can be raised if abnormal conditions occur. For instance, exceptions will be raised while a READ statement is executed if the file is not open or if its mode is OUT_FILE. Again these exceptions will be discussed in detail in Chapter 11.

The WRITE procedures of the package DIRECT_IO mirror the form of the READ procedures:

```
procedure WRITE ( FILE : in FILE_TYPE ;

                  ITEM : out ELEMENT_TYPE ;

                  TO   : in POSITIVE_COUNT ) ;

procedure WRITE ( FILE : in FILE_TYPE ;

                  ITEM : out ELEMENT_TYPE ) ;
```

In the first form the value of the actual parameter matching ITEM will be written on the file, at the relative position given by the actual parameter matching TO. In the second form the relative position of the value to be written is given by the current index. The index value is incremented by 1 after the WRITE statement is executed. Exceptions may be raised if the file is not open, if the mode is IN_FILE, and so forth.

Direct files have a **size,** which is given by the highest index value used for reading or writing on the file. The current size of a direct file can be obtained by invoking the function SIZE, whose declaration is

```
function SIZE ( FILE : FILE_TYPE ) return COUNT ;
```

Also, whenever the current index exceeds the size of a direct file, a call to the function END_OF_FILE returns the value TRUE; otherwise, the function returns the value FALSE. The function declaration is

```
function END_OF_FILE ( FILE : FILE_TYPE ) return
   BOOLEAN ;
```

The package DIRECT_IO has the kinds of RESET procedures encountered in the SEQUENTIAL_IO package. Their meanings and declarations are the same, except that the MODE parameter can now additionally take the INOUT_FILE value.

PROGRAM USING A DIRECT FILE

We will apply the generic DIRECT_IO package by writing a simple file maintenance program, keeping track of banks for a foreign currency broker. In this program a direct file, whose external name is BANK_MASTER.DAT, holds information about banks. The file is assumed created and holds information for about 150 banks.

The direct file can be updated by adding a new bank or by changing information about a bank, but never by deleting a bank. Also, inquiries can be made about certain banks. The input (from a terminal, for instance) identifies the type of transaction with the first character, which is then followed by the necessary information to perform the transaction. The last transaction line is signaled by a transaction code of 'Z'.

The input lines have the following format:

Column	Data
Column 1	IN_CODE, where 'A' means add, 'C' means change, 'I' means inquiry, and 'Z' means end
Columns 2–21	Bank name
Columns 22–70	Other information like phone, address, and contact persons

The direct file has elements of type BANK_REC, where BANK_REC is a record with a variant part. The variant part covers three kinds of records: One record contains global information such as the number of banks and the maximum number of banks allowed for the file. The second kind of record contains information about a particular bank. And the third kind of record contains posting information (that is, transaction numbers involving the bank). The bank records are sorted in alphabetical order by bank name.

The resources (declarations, subprograms, initializing code) are placed in the package BANK_RESOURCES listed next.

```
with DIRECT_IO ;

package BANK_RESOURCES is

type BANK_INFO is

    record

        BANK_NAME  : STRING ( 1 .. 20 ) ;

        OTHER_INFO : STRING ( 1 .. 49 ) ;

    end record ;

type IN_REC is

    record

        IN_CODE : CHARACTER ;
```

```
                        -- The expected characters are A, C, I, and Z.

                        IN_DATA : BANK_INFO ;

                end record ;

        type REC_KIND is ( GLOB_FILE_DATA, MASTER_DATA, POSTING_DATA) ;

        type TRANS_NUMBER is

                record

                        MO_PART  : INTEGER range 1 .. 12 ;

                        DAY_PART : INTEGER range 1 .. 31 ;

                        NO_PART  : NATURAL ;

                end record ;

        type POST_INFO is array ( 1 .. 12 ) of TRANS_NUMBER ;

        type BANK_REC ( M_TYPE : REC_KIND := MASTER_DATA ) is

                record

                        case M_TYPE is

                                when GLOB_FILE_DATA =>

                                        NO_BANKS   : NATURAL ;

                                        -- This component count how many banks are

                                        -- in the file.

                                        MAX_NO     : NATURAL ;

                                        -- Here we place the limit of the number

                                        -- of banks. Posting data can be written

                                        -- above this limit.

                                when MASTER_DATA   =>

                                        MAST_HEAD  : BANK_INFO ;

                                        FIRST_TRAN : NATURAL ;

                                        -- This variable holds the index of the
```

```
                    -- first POSTING_LINE for a bank (it is  O

                    -- if no transaction is posted for it).

                    LAST_TRAN  : NATURAL ;

                    -- This variable holds the index of the last

                    -- POSTING_LINE for a bank (it is  O if no

                    -- transaction is posted for it ).
                              O
                    LAST_POS   : NATURAL range 1 .. 12 ;

                    -- This variable holds the last position within

                    -- the  last  POSTING_LINE for  a  particular

                    -- bank.

             when POSTING_DATA   =>

                    POSTING_LINE  : POST_INFO  ;

                    NXT_PST_LINE  : NATURAL ;

                    -- There are 12 transactions per POSTING_LINE.

        end case ;

   end record ;
```

Figure 8.2 illustrates the relationships among the different REC_KIND. To continue the package listing:

```
package BANK_IO is new DIRECT_IO ( BANK_REC ) ;

use BANK_IO ;

BANK_FILE : BANK_IO.FILE_TYPE ;

GLOBAL_NO_OF_BANKS : POSITIVE_COUNT ;

procedure RETRIEVE (  FORM_BANK_NAME : in out STRING  ;

                      FORM_POS        : out COUNT ;

                      FORM_FOUND      : out BOOLEAN          ) ;

end BANK_RESOURCES ;
```

FIGURE 8.2   Sample BANK_FILE Records

```
BANK_FILE
First file element of type BANK_REC (GLOB_FILE_DATA):
NO_BANKS    MAX_NO
3           200

Second through fourth file elements of type BANK_REC (MASTER_DATA):
    MAST_HEAD                     FIRST_TRAN   LAST_TRAN   LAST_POS
BANK_NAME           OTHER_INFO
CHASE MANHATTAN     YYYY . . YYY    203          203         2
CHEMICAL BANK       XXXX . . XXX    202          204         3
MARINE MIDLAND      ZZZZ . . ZZZ    201          201         1

File elements 201 through 204 are of type BANK_REC (POSTING_DATA):

        POSTING_LINE
                                      NXT_PST_LINE
(1)        (2)              .. (12)
0723005    0723008                       0
0723001    0723003 . . .     0724002    204
0723002                                  0
0724005    0724006 0724007
```

The body of the package specification BANK_RESOURCES is given next.

```
package body BANK_RESOURCES is

LOCAL_BANK_REC : BANK_REC ;


    -- A direct or sequential file excepts only one type when
    -- its corresponding package is instantiated. By using a
    -- record with a variant part, one can make use of several
    -- kinds of records, however. For the BANK_FILE, one should
    -- keep in mind that  the  size  of  each  kind  of  record
    -- is useful in order to minimize wasted storage. Normally, one
    -- should make sure that the record variant  with the largest
```

```
-- size is the one most often used in the file. For  BANK_FILE
-- the POSTING_DATA kind generates probably most of the file
-- volume, and the number of components of  POST_INFO  should
-- be adjusted so  that  POSTING_LINE has the largest size.
-- A predefined language attribute SIZE (for instance,
-- BANK_REC'SIZE) gives the minimum size (in bits)  needed to
-- hold any possible object of the given type. The size
-- of the file element (which depends on the particular
-- Ada implementation) is somewhere around the value returned
-- by SIZE.
procedure RETRIEVE (  FORM_BANK_NAME : in out STRING  ;
                      FORM_POS       : out COUNT ;
                      FORM_FOUND     : out BOOLEAN        ) is
    -- This procedure looks for an element of BANK_FILE
    -- whose  bank_name is identical  to FORM_BANK_NAME.
    -- If it is found, it returns the  value TRUE in
    -- FORM_FOUND,  and its index in  FORM_POS. Otherwise, it
    -- returns FALSE. The searching technique is called a
    -- binary search .
LEFT_LIM : COUNT := 2 ;
MIDDLE_NDX, RIGHT_LIM : COUNT ;
begin
    RIGHT_LIM  := GLOBAL_NO_OF_BANKS ;
    FORM_FOUND := FALSE ;
    loop
        MIDDLE_NDX := ( LEFT_LIM + RIGHT_LIM ) / 2 ;
```

```
            READ ( FILE => BANK_FILE, ITEM => LOCAL_BANK_REC ,

                    FROM => MIDDLE_NDX ) ;

        if LOCAL_BANK_REC.MAST_HEAD.BANK_NAME = FORM_BANK_NAME

            then

            FORM_FOUND := TRUE ;

            FORM_POS   := MIDDLE_NDX ;

            exit ;

        elsif LOCAL_BANK_REC.MAST_HEAD.BANK_NAME < FORM_BANK_NAME

            then

            LEFT_LIM :=  MIDDLE_NDX ;
            else

            RIGHT_LIM := MIDDLE_NDX ;

        end if;

        if  LEFT_LIM >= RIGHT_LIM

            then

            FORM_POS := RIGHT_LIM ;

            exit ;

        end if ;

    end loop;

end RETRIEVE ;

-- Now here is the initializing code for the package:

begin

    OPEN ( FILE => BANK_FILE ,

          MODE => INOUT_FILE ,-- We need to both read and write

          NAME => "BANK_MASTER.DAT" ,

          FORM  => "" ) ;
```

```
           -- For certain Ada  compilers  one  must supply, as

           -- part of the formal actual parameter, the maximum

           -- record size of the element type when the file is

           -- created (if  the actual parameter is an

           -- unconstrained type, as it here).
    READ ( FILE => BANK_FILE, ITEM => LOCAL_BANK_REC ,

               FROM => 1 ) ;

        -- Read the first element of the BANK_FILE to extract
        -- the number of banks.
    GLOBAL_NO_OF_BANKS := POSITIVE_COUNT(LOCAL_BANK_REC.NO_BANKS);
end BANK_RESOURCES ;
```

The program itself is now listed.

BANK_MAINT Program

```
    with TEXT_IO ; use TEXT_IO ;
    -- The package BANK_RESOURCES, assuming it is  compiled ,
    -- is made directly  visible below
    with BANK_RESOURCES ; use BANK_RESOURCES ;
    --
    procedure BANK_MAINT is
    CURR_IN_REC : IN_REC ;
    ACT_POS : BANK_IO.COUNT ;
    ACT_FOUND : BOOLEAN ;
    CURR_BANK_REC, SAVE_BANK_REC : BANK_REC ;
    begin
            -- The cases 'A' and 'C'  might be better handled
```

```
                    -- with    some    extra  subprograms  in   the    package
                    -- BANK_RESOURCES. Exercise 3 at the end of the chapter
                    -- covers this situation .
                    if not BANK_IO.IS_OPEN ( BANK_FILE )
                         -- Note that both BANK_IO and TEXT_IO packages
                         -- have the function IS_OPEN and the procedure OPEN.
                         then
                         BANK_IO.OPEN (  FILE => BANK_FILE ,
                            MODE => BANK_IO.INOUT_FILE,
                            NAME => "BANK_MASTER.DAT" ,
                            FORM => "" ) ;
                    end if ;
                    GET( CURR_IN_REC.IN_CODE ) ;
                    while CURR_IN_REC.IN_CODE /= 'Z'
                        loop
                        GET(CURR_IN_REC.IN_DATA.BANK_NAME) ;
                        GET(CURR_IN_REC.IN_DATA.OTHER.INFO) ;
                        case CURR_IN_REC.IN_CODE is
                            when 'I'  =>
                                RETRIEVE ( CURR_IN_REC.IN_DATA.BANK_NAME ,
                                    ACT_POS, ACT_FOUND ) ;
                                If ACT_FOUND
                                    then
                                    PUT ( " Bank found " ) ;
                                else
                                    PUT ( " Bank not found " ) ;
```

```
        end if ;
when 'A'  =>
        -- This process is an inefficient way to
        -- update the  bank  file.  It is  done  very
        -- seldom though. However, it exercizes some
        -- DIRECT_IO subprograms.
        for I in 2 .. GLOBAL_NO_OF_BANKS
            loop
            READ ( FILE => BANK_FILE,
                    ITEM => CURR_BANK_REC,
                    FROM => I ) ;
            exit when CURR_IN_REC.IN_DATA.BANK_NAME <
                CURR_BANK_REC.MAST_HEAD.BANK_INFO.BANK_NAME;
        end loop;
        -- The index is incremented by 1 after
        -- data is read.
        ACT_POS := COUNT(INDEX ( BANK_FILE )) -1 ;
        SAVE_BANK_REC := ( MASTER_DATA ,
            CURR_IN_REC.IN_DATA , 0, 0, 1 ) ;
        -- Positional  aggregate  assignment above
        for I in POSITIVE_COUNT(ACT_POS) ..
                GLOBAL_NO_OF_BANKS + 1
            -- This  loop  bumps  records  after
            -- insertion.
            loop
            WRITE ( FILE => BANK_FILE,
```

```
                            ITEM => SAVE_BANK_REC,

                            TO   => I  ) ;

                   SAVE_BANK_REC := CURR_BANK_REC ;

                   READ ( FILE => BANK_FILE ,

                           ITEM => CURR_BANK_REC ) ;

           end loop ;

           -- Update  no of  banks  in  first element

           READ ( BANK_FILE, CURR_BANK_REC ,1   ) ;

           CURR_BANK_REC.NO_BANKS :=

                   POSITIVE(GLOBAL_NO_OF_BANKS) + 1 ;

           WRITE ( BANK_FILE, CURR_BANK_REC ,1  ) ;

   when 'C'  =>   RETRIEVE ( CURR_IN_REC.IN_DATA.BANK_NAME,

           ACT_POS, ACT_FOUND ) ;

           if ACT_FOUND

                then

                READ  ( FILE => BANK_FILE,

                        ITEM => CURR_BANK_REC ,

                        FROM => POSITIVE_COUNT(ACT_POS));

                CURR_BANK_REC.MAST_HEAD :=

                        CURR_IN_REC.IN_DATA ;

                WRITE ( FILE => BANK_FILE,

                        ITEM => CURR_BANK_REC ,

                        TO   => ACT_POS ) ;

                else

                PUT ( " No such bank " ) ;

           end if ;
```

```
              when 'Z' =>    exit ;

              when others => null ;

          end case ;

      SKIP_LINE ;

      GET( CURR_IN_REC.IN_CODE ) ;

      end loop ;

      BANK_IO.CLOSE ( BANK_FILE ) ;

end BANK_MAINT ;
```

ADVANTAGES OF DIRECT FILES

The advantage of using direct files rather than sequential files when accessing and processing file elements in arbitrary order will be illustrated by the two programs presented in this subsection. These programs assume that the BANK_FILE of the previous subsection is available.

The first program records transactions for a foreign currency broker supplied one per line, with the following format:

Column	Data
Columns 1–20	BUYER (must be a bank in the BANK_FILE)
Columns 21–40	SELLER (must be a bank in the BANK_FILE)
Columns 41–43	CURR_BOUGHT (symbol of currency bought, such as US$, DM, or SF)
Columns 44–46	CURR_SOLD (symbol of currency sold)
Columns 47–55	X_RATE (exchange rate)
Columns 56–61	VALUE_DATE (the date when the transaction was agreed upon)
Columns 62–67	TRADE_DATE (the date when money changes hands, usually the next working day)

The last line is signaled by a value of BUYER = "12345678901234567890". There is a commission of $25 per million-dollar equivalent, which is computed but not recorded.

As each line is read, it is examined to see whether it constitutes a valid transaction, that is, has valid dates and proper bank names. If the line represents a good transaction, it is placed in the corresponding transaction file. Otherwise, a warning message is displayed. If the transaction is valid, then a transaction number is generated (the transaction number is generated as a combination of month, day, and daily transaction number). The transaction number is used to locate the file and the index of the file element storing it.

Before we present the program, we place the relevant declarations in the following package specification:

```
with DIRECT_IO ;

package TRANSACTION_RESOURCES is

type   TRANS_HEADER is

    record

            DAY_TRANS_NO : NATURAL ;

            FIRST_TRANS  : NATURAL ;

            LAST_TRANS   : NATURAL ;

    end record ;

type MONTH_HEADER is array ( 1 .. 31 ) of TRANS_HEADER ;

type TRANS_FILE_HEADER is

    record

            YEAR_N_MONTH : STRING ( 1 .. 4 ) ;

            TRANS_STATUS : MONTH_HEADER ;

    end record ;

type SHORT_DATE is

    record

            SHORT_YY : INTEGER range 0 .. 99 ;

            SHORT_MM : INTEGER range 1 .. 12 ;

            SHORT_DD : INTEGER range 1 .. 31 ;

    end record ;

type IN_TRANS is

    record

            BUYER : STRING ( 1 .. 20 ) ;
```

```
            SELLER : STRING ( 1 .. 20 ) ;

            CURR_BOUGHT : STRING ( 1 .. 3 ) ;

            CURR_SOLD   : STRING ( 1 .. 3 )  ;

            X_RATE      : FLOAT ;

            VALUE_DATE  : SHORT_DATE ;

            TRADE_DATE  : SHORT_DATE ;

        end record ;
type TRANS_INFO is

    record

            TRANS_NO    : NATURAL ;

            TRANS_BODY : IN_TRANS ;

            TRANS_NEXT : NATURAL ;

        end record ;

type TRANS_ELEM_KIND is ( TOP_LINE, REC_LINE ) ;

type TRANS_REC ( REC_KIND : TRANS_ELEM_KIND := REC_LINE ) is

    record

        case REC_KIND is

            when TOP_LINE => HEADER_LINE : TRANS_FILE_HEADER ;

                    -- It may turn out that the header line size is

                    -- too big. See exercises at the end of chapter

                    -- for a different record set up

            when REC_LINE    =>  TR_LINE : TRANS_INFO ;

        end case ;

    end record ;
```

An example of a TRANS_FILE and some sample elements of the file are illustrated in Figure 8.3. To continue:

FIGURE 8.3   Sample Records of TRANS_FILE

```
In TRANS_FILE the first file element is of type

TRANS_REC (TOP_LINE):
          TOP_LINE

YEAR_N_MONTH                    TRANS_STATUS
              (1)               (2)        . .  (23)          . .   (31)
8607          01 002 045        02 008 075      23 021 089          0 0 0

All the other file elements are of type

TRANS_REC (REC_LINE). For instance, the 2nd and the 45th elements might
look like this:
TRANS_NO          TRANS_BODY            TRANS_NEXT
001               CHEMICAL BANK . . .       003
034               CHASE . . .               000
```

```
        package TRANS_IO is new DIRECT_IO ( TRANS_REC ) ;

        use TRANS_IO ;

        TRANS_FILE : TRANS_IO.FILE_TYPE ;

        -- We assume that the transaction files are created, maybe by

        -- the program of Section 7.1, even though the transaction

        -- files might have a size of 0 .

        end TRANSACTION_RESOURCES ;
```

The program that follows makes use of a variation of the PUT procedure, appearing in the instantiated package INT_IO. Its declaration is

```
        procedure PUT ( TO : out STRING ; ITEM : NUM ;
                        BASE : in NUMBER_BASE :=
                        DEFAULT_BASE ) ;
```

This procedure places the value of the actual parameter matching ITEM in the string variable matching TO (as opposed to a file whose mode is OUT_FILE).

A symmetric procedure in the package INT_IO has the declaration

```
        GET ( FROM : in STRING ; ITEM : out NUM ;
                        LAST : out NATURAL ) ;
```

As opposed to the corresponding PUT procedure, this GET procedure reads an integer value from the string matching FROM and places it in the actual parameter matching ITEM. The value placed in the variable matching LAST is the index value of the last character read. This kind of GET procedure will be used in the second program of this subsection.

Now assuming that the package TRANSACTION_RESOURCES is already compiled, the first program may be written as follows:

CURR_TRANSACTION_PROC Program

```
with TEXT_IO ; use TEXT_IO ;

with CHECK_DATES_ALT ; use  CHECK_DATES_ALT ;

with BANK_RESOURCES ; use BANK_RESOURCES ;

with TRANSACTION_RESOURCES ; use TRANSACTION_RESOURCES ;

with LEGAL_HOLIDAYS ; use LEGAL_HOLIDAYS ;

      -- The LEGAL_HOLIDAYS package was defined in Chapter 7.

      -- It makes use of the package CHECK_DATES_ALT .

      -- These packages are assumed compiled already

--

procedure CURR_TRANSACTION_PROC is

CURR_IN_TRANS : IN_TRANS ;

CURR_TRANS_REC, SAVE_TRANS_REC : TRANS_REC ;

package INT_IO is new INTEGER_IO (INTEGER) ;

use INT_IO ;

package FLT_IO is new FLOAT_IO ( FLOAT ) ;

use FLT_IO ;

BANK_POS   : POSITIVE_COUNT ;

BANK_FOUND, DATE_VALID : BOOLEAN ;

CURR_DATE  : DATE ;

--

procedure MOVE_SHRT_DATE_TO_REG_DATE
```

```
                  ( FORM_SH_DATE : in SHORT_DATE ;

                    FORM_LG_DATE : out DATE ;        ) is

begin

     FORM_LG_DATE.YEAR_NO := FORM_SH_DATE.SHORT_YY ;

     FORM_LG_DATE.MONTH_NO := FORM_SH_DATE.SHORT_MM ;

      FORM_LG_DATE.DAY_NO   := FORM_SH_DATE.SHORT_DD ;

end MOVE_SHRT_DATE_TO_REG_DATE ;

--

procedure INSERT_REC ( FORM_IN_TRANS : IN_TRANS ) is

EXT_NAME : STRING (1 .. 10) ;

YY_STR , MM_STR  :  STRING ( 1 ..  2 )  ;

LOC_1, LOC_OTHER : TRANS_REC ;

LOCAL_MONTH_HEADER : MONTH_HEADER

                    := ( 1 .. 31 => ( 0, 1, 1 ) );

WRK_LAST_TR  : NATURAL ;

WRK_CURR_TR  : NATURAL ;

begin

     -- First find out the external file name and open it

     PUT ( YY_STR, FORM_IN_TRANS.VALUE_DATE.SHORT_YY ) ;

          -- This statement  converts  integer  values  to

          -- string values.

          -- Next make a 'O' from a leading space.

     If YY_STR ( 1 ) = ' '

          then

          YY_STR ( 1 ) = 'O' ;

     end if ;
```

```
      PUT ( MM_STR, FORM_IN_TRANS.VALUE_DATE.SHORT_MM ) :

      If MM_STR ( 1 ) = ' '

          then

          MM_STR ( 1 ) = 'O' ;

      end if ;

      EXT_NAME := "FY" & YY_STR & MM_STR & ".DAT" ;

      if TRANS_IO.IS_OPEN ( TRANS_FILE )

      then

      TRANS_IO.CLOSE ( TRANS_FILE ) ;

  end if ;

  TRANS_IO.OPEN ( FILE => TRANS_FILE,

      MODE => INOUT_FILE,

      NAME => EXT_NAME,

      FORM => "" ) ;

  if TRANS_IO.SIZE ( TRANS_FILE ) < 1

      -- This condition is true if nothing is written on the

      -- file.

      then

      -- Write the first file element.

      LOC_1 := ( TOP_LINE,

          ( YY_STR & MM_STR, LOCAL_MONTH_HEADER ) ) ;

      TRANS_IO.WRITE ( TRANS_FILE, LOC_1, 1 ) ;

  end if ;

  TRANS_IO.READ ( TRANS_FILE, LOC_1, 1 ) ;

  -- The code below is a prime candidate for using renaming

  -- procedures. It is mentioned in the Exercise 6 at the end
```

```
                -- of the chapter.
                WRK_LAST_TR :=
                     LOC_1.HEADER_LINE.TRANS_STATUS.LAST_TRANS
                           ( FORM_IN_TRANS.VALUE_DATE.SHORT_DD ) ;
                if WRK_LAST_TR /= 1
                     then        -- There are some other transactions
                                 -- for this day of the month, the last
                                 -- transaction becomes next to last.
                TRANS_IO.READ( TRANS_FILE, LOC_OTHER, WRK_LAST_TR );
                -- update next record
                LOC_OTHER.TR_LINE.TRANS_NEXT :=
                     POSITIVE(TRANS_IO.SIZE ( TRANS_FILE )) + 1 ;
                TRANS_IO.WRITE (TRANS_FILE, LOC_OTHER,
                                              WRK_LAST_TR );
                else
                -- Initialize the first transaction of the day
                LOC_1.HEADER_LINE.TRANS_STATUS.FIRST_TRANS
                     ( FORM_IN_TRANS.VALUE_DATE.SHORT_DD ) :=
                           POSITIVE( TRANS_IO.SIZE ( TRANS_FILE )) + 1 ;
            end if;
            WRK_CURR_TR :=
                LOC_1.HEADER_LINE.TRANS_STATUS.DAY_TRANS_NO
                     ( FORM_IN_TRANS.VALUE_DATE.SHORT_DD ) +1 ;
            LOC_1.HEADER_LINE.TRANS_STATUS.DAY_TRANS_NO
                     ( FORM_IN_TRANS.VALUE_DATE.SHORT_DD ):=WRK_CURR_TR ;
            WRK_LAST_TR :=   POSITIVE(TRANS_IO.SIZE ( TRANS_FILE )) + 1      ;
```

```
        LOC_1.HEADER_LINE.TRANS_STATUS.LAST_TRANS

               ( FORM_IN_TRANS.VALUE_DATE.SHORT_DD ) := WRK_LAST_TR;

        -- Next first file element is updated

        TRANS_IO.WRITE ( TRANS_FILE, LOC_1, 1 ) ;

        LOC_OTHER :=

               ( REC_LINE, ( WRK_CURR_TR, FORM_IN_TRANS, 0 ) ) ;

        -- Next write the new transaction

        TRANS_IO.WRITE ( TRANS_FILE, LOC_OTHER, WRK_LAST_TR ) ;

        TRANS_IO.CLOSE ( TRANS_FILE ) ;

end INSERT_REC ;

--

begin

-- Note that as part of the elaboration of BANK_RESOURCES

-- the file BANK_FILE is opened ( elaboration of the package

-- includes the execution of the body ).

GET ( CURR_IN_TRANS.BUYER ) ;

while CURR_IN_TRANS.BUYER /= "12345678901234567890"

   loop

      RETRIEVE ( CURR_IN_TRANS.BUYER, BANK_POS, BANK_FOUND ) ;

      if BANK_FOUND

          then

          GET ( CURR_IN_TRANS.SELLER ) ;

          RETRIEVE ( CURR_IN_TRANS.SELLER, BANK_POS, BANK_FOUND);

      end if ;

      if BANK_FOUND

          then
```

```
                -- If BANK_FOUND is true, we have
                -- a valid buyer and a valid seller.
                GET ( CURR_IN_TRANS.CURR_BOUGHT ) ;
                GET ( CURR_IN_TRANS.CURR_SOLD ) ;
                GET ( CURR_IN_TRANS.X_RATE ) ;
                GET ( CURR_IN_TRANS.VALUE_DATE.SHORT_YY ) ;
                GET ( CURR_IN_TRANS.VALUE_DATE.SHORT_MM ) ;
                GET ( CURR_IN_TRANS.VALUE_DATE.SHORT_DD ) ;
                GET ( CURR_IN_TRANS.TRADE_DATE.SHORT_YY ) ;
                GET ( CURR_IN_TRANS.TRADE_DATE.SHORT_MM ) ;
                GET ( CURR_IN_TRANS.TRADE_DATE.SHORT_DD ) ;
                MOVE_SHRT_DATE_TO_REG_DATE ( CURR_IN_TRANS.VALUE_DATE,
                                CURR_DATE ) ;
                FILL_IN_DATE ( CURR_DATE, DATE_VALID ) ;
                if  DATE_VALID
                    then
                    DATE_VALID:= not IS_LEGAL_HOLIDAYS ( CURR_DATE );
                end if ;
                if DATE_VALID
                    then
                    MOVE_SHRT_DATE_TO_REG_DATE
                        ( CURR_IN_TRANS.TRADE_DATE, CURR_DATE ) ;
                    FILL_IN_DATE ( CURR_DATE, DATE_VALID ) ;
                    if  DATE_VALID
                      then
                      DATE_VALID:= not IS_LEGAL_HOLIDAYS ( CURR_DATE );
```

```
            end if ;

        end if ;

end if ;

SKIP_LINE ;

if DATE_VALID and  BANK_FOUND

    then

        -- The line represents a valid transaction, which will

        -- now be placed in a transaction file.

        INSERT_REC ( CURR_IN_TRANS ) ;

        else

        PUT ( " Invalid transaction " ) ;

end if ;

GET ( CURR_IN_TRANS.BUYER ) ;

  end loop ;

BANK_IO.CLOSE ( BANK_FILE ) ;

end CURR_TRANSACTION_PROC ;
```

The second program, which is presented next, posts transactions from various transaction files on the BANK_FILE so that each bank will have a record of its transactions. We assume that the input consists of one line specifying the year (it must be 1986) and month (entered as two digits), and that the transaction files (from the year 1986) and the BANK_FILE are available.

POSTING_PROC Program

```
with TEXT_IO ; use TEXT_IO ;

with TRANSACTION_RESOURCES ; use TRANSACTION_RESOURCES ;

with BANK_RESOURCES ; use BANK_RESOURCES ;

-- These packages are assumed to be  already compiled.

procedure POSTING_PROC is
```

```
            package INT_IO is new INTEGER_IO (INTEGER) ;

            use INT_IO ;

            CURR_TRANS_REC_1, CURR_TRANS_REC_OTHER : TRANS_REC ;

            YY_AND_MM : STRING ( 1 .. 4 ) ;

            MM_ONLY   : STRING ( 1 .. 2 ) ;

            EXT_NAME  : STRING ( 1 .. 8 )

            WORK_POSITIVE  : NATURAL ;

            CURR_TRANS_HEADER : TRANS_HEADER ;

            CURR_TRANS_INDEX  : POSITIVE_INDEX ;

procedure POST_INDIV_BANK ( ANY_TRANS : TRANS_NUMBER ;

                            ANY_BANK  : STRING  ) is

BK_POS, TR_POS, SAVE_TR_POS : COUNT;

BK_FOUND : BOOLEAN ;

ANY_BANK_REC : BANK_REC ;

ANY_POST_REC : BANK_REC ;

WRK_POST_INFO : POST_INFO ;

begin

     RETRIEVE ( ANY_BANK, BK_POS, BK_FOUND ) ;

     if BK_FOUND

         then

         BANK_IO.READ ( BANK_FILE, ANY_BANK_REC, BK_POS ) ;

         if ANY_BANK_REC.FIRST_TRAN = 0

             -- This condition is true if no transactions were

             -- ever posted for this particular bank.

             then

             if BANK_IO.SIZE ( BANK_FILE ) <= GLOBAL_NO_OF_BANKS
```

```
        -- This condition is true if no transaction were
        -- posted for any bank.
        then
        TR_POS := GLOBAL_NO_OF_BANKS + 1 ;
        else
        TR_POS := BANK_IO.SIZE ( BANK_FILE ) + 1 ;
end if ;
ANY_BANK_REC.FIRST_TRAN := POSITIVE(TR_POS) ;
ANY_BANK_REC.LAST_TRAN  := POSITIVE(TR_POS) ;
ANY_BANK_REC.LAST_POS   := 1 ;
WRK_POST_INFO  :=  ( ANY_TRANS,
                        2 .. 12 => (1,1,1) );
ANY_POST_REC :=
        ( POSTING_DATA, WRK_POST_INFO, 0 ) ;
-- Initialize a posting record with a transaction.
else
if ANY_BANK_REC.LAST_POS = 12
        -- This condition is true if we have full line
        -- of posting data.
        then
        TR_POS := SIZE ( BANK_FILE ) + 1 ;
        BANK_IO.READ ( BANK_FILE, ANY_POST_REC,
                        ANY_BANK_REC.LAST_TRAN ) ;
        ANY_POST_REC.NXT_PST_LINE :=
                        POSITIVE(TR_POS) ;
        BANK_IO.WRITE ( BANK_FILE, ANY_POST_REC,
```

```
                    ANY_BANK_REC.LAST_TRAN ) ;
          ANY_BANK_REC.LAST_TRAN  :=
                     POSITIVE(TR_POS) ;
          ANY_BANK_REC.LAST_POS   := 1 ;
          WRK_POST_INFO  :=  ( ANY_TRANS,
                    2  ..  12 => (1,1,1) );
          ANY_POST_REC :=
             ( POSTING_DATA, WRK_POST_INFO, 0 ) ;
       else
          -- There is room here.
          TR_POS := ANY_BANK_REC.LAST_TRAN ;
          BANK_IO.READ ( BANK_FILE, ANY_POST_REC,
               ANY_BANK_REC.LAST_TRAN ) ;
          ANY_BANK_REC.LAST_POS :=
               ANY_BANK_REC.LAST_POS + 1 ;
          ANY_POST_REC.POSTING_LINE
               (ANY_BANK_REC.LAST_POS)
             :=  ANY_TRANS ;
       end if ;
    end if ;
    BANK_IO.WRITE ( BANK_FILE, ANY_BANK_REC, BK_POS ) ;
    BANK_IO.WRITE ( BANK_FILE, ANY_POST_REC, TR_POS ) ;
    else
    PUT ( " Bank not found : " );
    PUT ( ANY_BANK ) ;
end if ;
```

```
          -- Note that we can post a transaction in the

          -- account of just one bank and not in the account of

          -- its counterpart if the counterpart cannot be found .

          -- Exercise 7 at the end of the chapter asks you to make

          -- necessary changes.

end POST_INDIV_BANK ;

--

procedure POST_BNK ( FORM_TRANS_REC : TRANS_REC ;

                     FORM_DAY : NATURAL ) is

LOCAL_FULL_TRANS_NO : TRANS_NUMBER ;

          -- This procedure is preparing the transaction

          -- for posting in each of the two banks

begin

     LOCAL_FULL_TRANS_NO.DAY_PART   := FORM_DAY ;

     LOCAL_FULL_TRANS_NO.NO_PART    :=

                    FORM_TRANS_REC.TR_LINE.TRANS_NO ;

     GET ( FROM => MM_ONLY, ITEM => LOCAL_FULL_TRANS_NO.MO_PART,

                    LAST => WORK_POSITIVE ) ;

     POST_INDIV_BANK ( LOCAL_FULL_TRANS_NO,

          FORM_TRANS_REC.TR_LINE.TRANS_BODY.BUYER ) ;

     POST_INDIV_BANK ( LOCAL_FULL_TRANS_NO,

          FORM_TRANS_REC.TR_LINE.TRANS_BODY.SELLER ) ;

end POST_BNK ;

--

begin

GET ( YY_AND_MM ) ;
```

```
MM_ONLY := YY_AND_MM ( 3 .. 4 ) ;
if YY_AND_MM < "8601" or YY_AND_MM > "8612"
    then
    PUT ( " Bad date " ) ;
    else
    EXT_NAME := "FY" & YY_AND_MM & ".DAT" ;
    if not TRANS_IO.IS_OPEN ( TRANS_FILE )
        then
        TRANS_IO.OPEN ( FILE => TRANS_FILE,
            MODE => INOUT_FILE,
            NAME => EXT_NAME,
            FORM => "" ) ;
        TRANS_IO.READ ( TRANS_FILE, CURR_TRANS_REC_1, 1 ) ;
    end if ;
    for I in 1 .. 31
    loop
    CURR_TRANS_HEADER :=
        CURR_TRANS_REC_1.HEADER_LINE.TRANS_STATUS ( I ) ;
    CURR_TRANS_INDEX  := CURR_TRANS_HEADER.FIRST_TRANS ;
    if CURR_TRANS_INDEX /= 1
        then
        TRANS_IO.READ ( TRANS_FILE, CURR_TRANS_REC_OTHER ,
                CURR_TRANS_INDEX ) ;
        while CURR_TRANS_REC_OTHER.TR_LINE.TRANS_NEXT  /= 0
            loop
            POST_BNK ( CURR_TRANS_REC_OTHER, I ) ;
```

```
                    CURR_TRANS_INDEX :=

                         CURR_TRANS_REC_OTHER.TR_LINE.TRANS_NEXT ;

                    TRANS_IO.READ ( TRANS_FILE,

                         CURR_TRANS_REC_OTHER, CURR_TRANS_INDEX ) ;

               end loop ;

               POST_BNK ( CURR_TRANS_REC_OTHER, I ) ;

          end if;

     end loop ;

if TRANS_IO.IS_OPEN ( TRANS_FILE )

     then

     TRANS_IO.CLOSE ( TRANS_FILE ) ;

end if ;

if TRANS_IO.IS_OPEN ( BANK_FILE )

     then

     TRANS_IO.CLOSE ( BANK_FILE ) ;

end if ;

end POSTING_PROC ;
```

Other packages, dependent on a particular Ada implementation, should handle files in a variety of shapes. For instance, one may encounter packages that manipulate indexed sequential files or packages that manipulate a mixture of types.

8.4 TEXT_IO PROCESSING

The package TEXT_IO encapsulates the Ada facilities for handling input and output in a convenient way for humans. Many of the TEXT_IO facilities have been used already and described in previous chapters. This section will describe some of the remaining subprograms of TEXT_IO, especially the report-writing facilities.

Once a TEXT_IO file is opened (or created), one can read input files by invoking a GET procedure. One can write on output files by invoking a PUT procedure.

The TEXT_IO package, as shown in Section 7.5, includes several other generic packages. These generic packages must be instantiated if one is to read and write values of type integer, enumeration, or float. Each of the generic packages has its own kind of GET and PUT procedures, and examples of their use are given in many of the programs of previous chapters.

Some of the subprograms of TEXT_IO have several variations. In particular, some of them have options with a FILE formal parameter and options without the FILE parameter. If no FILE parameter is provided when the subprogram is invoked, then it refers to the default input or output file. Every running Ada program has a default input and output file. When a program starts running, the default input and output files are whatever the system considers to be a standard input file and a standard output file. The standard input file is opened as IN_FILE, and the standard output file is opened as OUT_FILE. These assumptions were in force for each of the previous programs.

The package TEXT_IO also contains the procedures SET_INPUT and SET_OUTPUT, which can be used to set the current default files to any other (open) text file. Their declarations are as follows:

```
procedure SET_INPUT ( FILE : in FILE_TYPE ) ;
procedure SET_OUTPUT ( FILE : in FILE_TYPE ) ;
```

One can find the standard input, the standard output, the current input, and the current output file names by invoking one of the following functions:

```
function STANDARD_INPUT return FILE_TYPE ;

function STANDARD_OUTPUT return FILE_TYPE ;

function CURRENT_INPUT return FILE_TYPE ;

function CURRENT_OUTPUT return FILE_TYPE ;
```

The standard input and standard output files may share the same physical device (like a terminal), and they have implementation-defined names (a typical one might be SYS$OUTPUT or SYS$INPUT).

Output TEXT_IO files are seen as sequences of characters making up lines. Positions of characters on a line are given by column numbers; lines make up pages. An end of line is marked by a line terminator, and an end of page is marked by a line terminator and a page terminator. An end of file is marked by a line terminator followed by a page terminator and a file terminator. The user cannot control these terminators, and their actual makeup depends on a particular Ada implementation.

The length of lines and pages is set with the help of the procedures SET_LINE_LENGTH and SET_PAGE_LENGTH. Their declarations are as follows:

```
procedure SET_LINE_LENGTH ( FILE : in FILE_TYPE ;
                              TO : in COUNT ) ;
procedure SET_LINE_LENGTH (   TO : in COUNT ) ;
```

This version applies to the default output file.

```
procedure SET_PAGE_LENGTH ( FILE : in FILE_TYPE ;
                              TO : in COUNT ) ;
procedure SET_PAGE_LENGTH (   TO : in COUNT ) ;
```

Here COUNT is an integer type ranging from 0 to an implementation-defined positive integer.

One can inquire about the maximum line length or page length of a specified output text file with the help of the functions LINE_LENGTH and PAGE_ LENGTH. Their declarations are given in Appendix C.

TEXT_IO has various other subprograms that can be used in the handling of columns, lines, and pages. Besides the procedures NEW_LINE and SKIP_ LINE, which have been used in previous programs, one can make use of several other subprograms. Their declarations are presented next.

```
END_OF_LINE ( FILE : in FILE_TYPE ) return
  BOOLEAN ;
END_OF_LINE return BOOLEAN ;
```

This function returns TRUE if a line terminator or a file terminator is next sensed on an input file.

```
END_OF_PAGE ( FILE : in FILE_TYPE ) return
  BOOLEAN ;
END_OF_PAGE return BOOLEAN ;
```

This function returns TRUE if a line terminator and a page terminator or a file terminator is next sensed on an input file.

```
END_OF_FILE ( FILE : in FILE_TYPE ) return
  BOOLEAN ;
END_OF_FILE return BOOLEAN ;
```

This function returns TRUE if a sequence made up of a line terminator, a page terminator, and a file terminator or a single file terminator is next sensed on an input file.

Current positions of columns, lines, and pages are returned by the following functions:

```
function COL ( FILE : in FILE_TYPE ) return
    POSITIVE_COUNT ;
function COL return POSITIVE_COUNT ;
```

POSITIVE_COUNT is a subtype of COUNT which excludes 0.

```
function LINE ( FILE : in FILE_TYPE ) return
    POSITIVE_COUNT ;
function LINE return POSITIVE_COUNT ;
```

This function returns the current line number within the current page. The system keeps track of the current page, which can be returned by invoking

```
function PAGE ( FILE : in FILE_TYPE ) return
    POSITIVE_COUNT ;
function PAGE return POSITIVE_COUNT ;
```

One can also control the position of columns, lines, and pages with the help of the following procedures:

```
procedure NEW_PAGE (    FILE : in FILE_TYPE ) ;
procedure NEW_PAGE ;
```

These procedures output a line terminator (if the current line is not terminated) and then a page terminator. It assumes a file whose mode is OUT_FILE. The procedures

```
procedure SKIP_PAGE (    FILE : in FILE_TYPE ) ;
procedure SKIP_PAGE ;
```

assume a file whose mode is IN_FILE. It reads and skips all characters until a page terminator is reached. The current page number is incremented by 1, and the current column and line are set to 1. The procedures

```
procedure SET_COL ( FILE : in FILE_TYPE ;
                    TO   : in POSITIVE_COUNT ) ;
procedure SET_COL ( TO   : in POSITIVE_COUNT ) ;
```

can be invoked for files whose mode is IN_FILE or OUT_FILE. The actual parameter value matching TO will be the new column number. The procedures

```
procedure SET_LINE ( FILE : in FILE_TYPE ;
                      TO   : in POSITIVE_COUNT )
                      ;
procedure SET_LINE ( TO   : in POSITIVE_COUNT )
                      ;
```

can be invoked for files whose mode is IN_FILE or OUT_FILE. The actual parameter value matching TO will be the new line number.

The exceptions that may be raised when improper use is made of these subprograms are explained in Chapter 11.

We will apply some of the newly introduced subprograms of the package TEXT_IO in the program that follows. The program will generate monthly statements for certain designated banks by extracting the necessary information from the BANK_FILE and TRANS_FILE of the previous section. The desired report format is given in Figure 8.4.

REPORT_GEN Program

```
with TEXT_IO ; use TEXT_IO ;

with TRANSACTION_RESOURCES ; use TRANSACTION_RESOURCES ;

with BANK_RESOURCES ; use BANK_RESOURCES ;

-- These packages are assumed to be  already compiled.

procedure REPORT_GEN is

package INT_IO is new INTEGER_IO (INTEGER) ;

use INT_IO ;

package FLT_IO is new FLOAT_IO (FLOAT) ;

use FLT_IO ;

DESIRED_BANK : STRING ( 1 .. 20 ) ;
```

FIGURE 8.4   Sample Report Layout

```
Monthly Statement for Bank : XXXXXXXXXXXXXXXXXXXX
                  Month of YYMM
BUYER      SELLER      BOT   SOLD   CROSS_RATE   V_DATE   T_DATE
XXXXXXXX   YYYYYYYYYY   US$   DM     0.30123      MMDD     MMDD
ZZZZZZZZ   YYYYYYYYYY   US$   SF     0.35422      MMDD     MMDD
```

```
REPORT_FILE : TEXT_IO.FILE_TYPE ;

YY_AND_MM : STRING ( 1 .. 4 ) ;

MM_ONLY   : STRING ( 1 .. 2 ) ;

EXT_NAME  : STRING ( 1 .. 8 )

WORK_POSITIVE  : POSITIVE ;

BK_POS, TR_POS, SAVE_TR_POS : POSITIVE_COUNT;

BK_FOUND, TRANS_FILE_FOUND : BOOLEAN ;

ANY_BANK_REC : BANK_REC ;

ANY_POST_REC : BANK_REC ;

procedure WRITE_HEADING is

begin

    -- Start writing on the REPORT_FILE in line 3.

    SET_LINE ( TO => 3 );

    SET_COL  ( TO => 55 );

    PUT      ( PAGE ) ;

    SET_LINE ( TO => 5 ) ;

    SET_COL  ( TO => 5 ) ;

    PUT      ( " Monthly Statement for Bank : " ) ;

    PUT      ( DESIRED_BANK ) ;

    SET_LINE ( TO => 7 ) ;

    SET_COL  ( TO => 20 ) ;

    PUT      ( " Month of " ) ;

    PUT      ( YY_AND_MM ) ;

    SET_LINE ( TO => 10 ) ;

    PUT      ( " BUYER " ); SET_COL ( TO => 21 ) ;

    PUT      ( " SELLER "); SET_COL ( TO => 41 ) ;
```

```
        PUT        ( "  BOT   "  ) ;

        PUT        ( "  SOLD  "  );

        PUT        ( "  CROSS_RATE  "  )  ;

        PUT        ( "  V-DATE  "  )  ;

        PUT        ( "  T-DATE  "  )  ;

        SET_LINE  ( TO => 13 ) ;

end WRITE_HEADING  ;

procedure PRINT_TRAN ( FORM_INFO : TRANS_INFO ) ;

-- This procedure prints a line having the content of a

-- transaction.

begin

        if LINE > 58

                then

                WRITE_HEADING  ;

        end if ;

        PUT ( FORM_INFO.BUYER )  ;

        PUT ( FORM_INFO.SELLER) ; SET_COL ( TO => 43 ) ;

        PUT ( FORM_INFO.CURR_BOUGHT ) ; SET_COL ( TO => 49 ) ;

        PUT ( FORM_INFO.CURR_SOLD )  ;

        PUT ( FORM_INFO.X_RATE,11, 2 );

        SET_COL ( 62 ) ; PUT ( FORM_INFO.VALUE_DATE.SHORT_DD,2) ;

        SET_COL ( 65 ) ; PUT ( FORM_INFO.TRADE_DATE.SHORT_DD,2) ;

end PRINT_TRAN  ;

--

procedure GET_N_WRITE_FULL_TRAN

        ( FORM_TRANS : TRANS_NUMBER  )  is
```

```
        -- This procedure will search sequentially the transactions

        -- on a particular day, and it will display the transaction

        -- body on the file REPORT_FILE. A more efficient way to

        -- search for the desired transaction bodies is requested

        -- in Exercise 9 at the end of the chapter.

    --

LOCAL_TRANS_REC_1, LOCAL_TRANS_REC_OTHER : TRANS_REC ;

WRK_LAST_TR  : POSITIVE_COUNT ;

WRK_CURR_TR  : NATURAL ;

begin

    TRANS_IO.READ ( TRANS_FILE, LOCAL_TRANS_REC_1, 1 ) ;

    WRK_LAST_TR :=

        LOCAL_TRANS_REC_1.HEADER_LINE.TRANS_STATUS.LAST_TRANS

            ( FORM_TRANS.DAY_PART ) ;

    WRK_CURR_TR :=

        LOCAL_TRANS_REC_1.HEADER_LINE.TRANS_STATUS.FIRST_TRANS

            ( FORM_TRANS.DAY_PART ) ;

    TRANS_IO.READ ( TRANS_FILE, LOCAL_TRANS_REC_OTHER, WRK_CURR_TR);

    loop

        if LOCAL_TRANS_REC_OTHER.REG_LINE.TRAN_NO =

                    FORM_TRANS.NO_PART

            then

            PRINT_TRAN ( LOCAL_TRANS_REC_OTHER.REG_LINE ) ;

        end if;

        exit when WRK_CURR_TR = WRK_LAST_TR ;

        WRK_CURR_TR := LOCAL_TRANS_REC_OTHER.REG_LINE.TRAN_NEXT ;

    end loop;
```

```
    end GET_N_WRITE_FULL_TRAN ;

-- Main program starts here

begin

-- Note that, initially, the current input is the standard input.

-- Read the desired bank name.

GET ( DESIRED_BANK );

RETRIEVE ( DESIRED_BANK, BK_POS, BK_FOUND ) ;

if not BK_FOUND

    then

    PUT ( " Bank not in Bank File " ) ;

end if ;

-- Read the desired month in the format YYMM.

GET ( YY_AND_MM ) ;

MM_ONLY := YY_AND_MM ( 3 .. 4 ) ;

if YY_AND_MM < "8601" or YY_AND_MM > "8612"

    then

    PUT ( " Bad date " ) ;

    TRANS_FILE_FOUND := FALSE ;

else

    EXT_NAME := "FY" & YY_AND_MM & ".DAT" ;

    if not IS_OPEN ( TRANS_FILE )

        then

        TRANS_IO.OPEN ( FILE => TRANS_FILE,

                MODE => INOUT_FILE,

                NAME => EXT_NAME,

                FORM => "" ) ;

            TRANS_IO.READ ( TRANS_FILE, CURR_TRANS_REC_1, 1 ) ;
```

```
                    TRANS_FILE_FOUND := TRUE ;

          end if ;

     end if ;

if TRANS_FILE_FOUND and BK_FOUND

     then

     -- Create the file on which the report will be written.

     TEXT_IO.CREATE ( FILE    => REPORT_FILE ,

                      MODE    => OUT_FILE ,

                      NAME    => "BANK_REPORT.DAT" ,

                      FORM    => "" ) ;

     --   Change the default file from the standard file to

     --   the REPORT_FILE

     SET_OUTPUT ( FILE => REPORT_FILE ) ;

     -- Set some desired page and line lengths

     SET_LINE_LENGTH  ( TO => 72 ) ;

     -- The above statement  is equivalent to

     -- SET_LINE_LENGTH ( FILE => REPORT_FILE, TO => 72 ) ;

     -- because the default file is now REPORT_FILE.

     SET_PAGE_LENGTH ( TO => 65 ) ;

     -- If the transactions have been posted according to

     -- POSTING_PROC, then the order of the posted transactions

     -- is consistent with the order of the transactions in

     -- TRANS_FILE. Exercise 8 at the end of this chapter

     -- suggests a more robust approach of posting on BANK_FILE.

     BANK_IO.READ ( BANK_FILE, ANY_BANK_REC, BK_POS ) ;

          if ANY_BANK_REC.FIRST_TRAN = 0
```

```
        -- The condirion is true if no transactions were

        -- ever posted for this particular bank.

        then

        PUT ( " No transaction for this Bank " ) ;

else

        -- Start with the element containing first

        -- posted transactions.

        CURR_POS := 1 ;

        TR_POS := ANY_BANK_REC.FIRST_TRAN ;

        BANK_IO.READ ( BANK_FILE, ANY_POST_REC, TR_POS );

        loop

                -- Does the transaction below have the right

                -- month number?

                if ANY_POST_REC.POSTING_LINE

                        ( CURR_POS ).MO_PART :=

                        CHARACTER'VAL(MM_ONLY) - CHARACTER'VAL('O')

                        then

                        GET_N_WRITE_FULL_TRAN

                           ( ANY_POST_REC.POSTING_LINE ( CURR_POS ));

                end if ;

                -- The expression below is true after the last

                -- transaction for the bank was processed.

                exit when CURR_POS = ANY_BANK_REC.LAST_POS

                        and   TR_POS = ANY_BANK_REC.LAST_TRAN ;

                CURR_POS := CURR_POS + 1 ;

                if CURR_POS > 12
```

```
                                    then

                                    -- Another posting record must be read.

                                    CURR_POS := 1 ;

                                    TR_POS    :=   ANY_POST_REC.NXT_PST_LINE ;

                                    BANK_IO.READ ( BANK_FILE,

                                                      ANY_POST_REC, TR_POS );

                              end if ;

                        end loop ;

                  end if ;

                  TEXT_IO.CLOSE ( REPORT_FILE ) ;

            end if ;

            if TRANS_IO.IS_OPEN (TRANS_FILE)

                  then

                  CLOSE ( TRANS_FILE ) ;

            end if ;

            if BANK_IO.IS_OPEN ( BANK_FILE )

                  then

                  BANK_IO.CLOSE ( BANK_FILE ) ;

            end if ;

      end REPORT_GEN ;
```

EXERCISES FOR CHAPTER 8

1. Modify the program SEQ_PROC_GRADES of Section 8.2 so that it can handle a variable number of tests (changes in the record type BIG_REC are necessary). Also, assume that the test subjects for the same student in each of the two input files do not necessarily precede each other.

2. Modify the program SEQ_PROC_GRADES of Section 8.2 so that the same BIG_ST_ID may appear more than once in each input file. (The two files are still assumed to be sorted.)

3. Rewrite the package BANK_RESOURCES of Section 8.3 by adding subprograms to handle the addition or change of BANK_REC element types. Rewrite the BANK_MAINT program by using the new package.

4. It might be more efficient to have several file elements of type TRANS_FILE_HEADER in the TRANS_FILE used by the program CURR_TRANSACTION_PROC of Section 8.3. Rewrite the program CURR_TRANSACTION_PROC (and the package TRANSACTION_RESOURCES), assuming that the first four file elements are of type TRANS_FILE_RECORD. That is, each of the first four file elements holds information for about eight days (actually, 8, 8, 8, and 7).

5. Write a program using the package TRANSACTION_RESOURCES of Section 8.3 that marks selected transactions of TRANS_FILE as invalid.

6. Rewrite the procedure INSERT_REC of CURR_TRANSACTION_PROC by using renaming declarations so that names are not nested more than two levels deep.

7. Rewrite the procedure POST_INDIV_BANK of the program POSTING_PROC of Section 8.3 so that it will never post a transaction unless both banks are in the BANK_FILE.

8. The program POSTING_PROC of Section 8.3 posts transactions without recording the relative position of the transaction in TRANS_FILE. Make the necessary modifications to both the package BANK_RESOURCES and the program POSTING_PROC so that the posted transactions carry the information about their relative position.

9. Assuming that the modifications of Exercise 8 are in place, rewrite the program REPORT_GEN of Section 8.4 by making use of the relative position of transactions in TRANS_FILE.

10. Write a program reporting on the banks that generate more than 20 transactions for month 07. It should generate a text file with appropriate headings.

CHAPTER NINE

PROGRAM STRUCTURE AND COMPILATION ISSUES

9.1   COMPILATION UNITS AND THE COMPILATION PROCESS

COMPILATION UNITS

Ada programs are made up of one or more **compilation units** kept in a program library. There are two kinds of compilation units, each having the form

```
context Library units
context Secondary units
```

In turn, a **library unit** can be one of the following:

- Subprogram declarations or bodies
- Package declarations
- Generic declarations or instantiation

And **secondary units** can be one of the following:

- Subprogram bodies
- Package bodies
- Subunits

We have already used every compilation unit listed here, except for subunits, which will be described later in this chapter.

The **context** part specifies the library units whose names are necessary within the compilation unit. It has to precede the library or secondary units. An example of a context part is the often-used line

```
with TEXT_IO ; use TEXT_IO ;
```

which makes available subprograms (such as GET and PUT) that are needed to read and write characters, strings, and the like. In a subsequent section we will provide examples and details for the context part of compilation units.

A quick inspection of the list of library units and secondary units shows that subprogram bodies appear in both. For subprogram bodies the following interpretation is in force: If the program library already contains a library unit having the same name, then the subprogram body is considered a secondary unit. Otherwise, the subprogram body is both a library unit and a secondary unit.

MAIN PROGRAMS

Ada does not specify what constitutes a *main program*, that is, a program first invoked by the system environment outside Ada. It is up to the particular implementation to specify the requirements for an Ada main program. However, in any implementation a procedure without formal parameters may be a main program, and every main program must be a subprogram that is a library unit. Clearly, all Ada programs presented so far qualify as main programs because they are procedures lacking formal parameters.

COMPILATION PROCESS

The compilation units making up an Ada program can be compiled in a variety of ways. The obvious way is to submit, for compilation, all the compilation units together in one step. But many other alternative ways are possible for separate compilation of the compilation units. In fact, compilation units can be compiled in any order, subject to certain rules necessary to ensure proper code generation. These rules are mostly derived from a consistent application of visibility rules.

The **compiling process** consists of the submission of some compilation units and of the library file. If the compilation process is successful, then the library file is updated. That is, the new (just compiled) version of the compilation unit replaces old versions (if any) of the compilation unit. This general compilation process is illustrated in Figure 9.1.

CONTEXT PART

We mentioned earlier that the context part of a compilation unit is necessary in order to supply the needed library units for a given compilation unit. The context part takes the form of a "with" clause:

FIGURE 9.1 Compilation Process

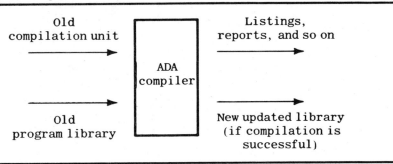

```
with library_unit_simple_name ;
```

If, in addition, a "use" clause is present, its form is

```
with library_unit_simple_name ;
use Package_library_unit_simple_name ;
```

There is no mistake in this "use" form. That is, in a "with" clause any library unit simple name is allowed (one can have subprogram names, package names, or generic instantiations). But in a "use" clause, only package names are allowed. Note as well that every "with" clause creates dependencies among compilation units.

For instance, suppose we have the following compilation unit:

```
with PACK_A ;

procedure PROC_B is

begin

      null;

end  PROC_B ;
```

Then PACK_A must be a library unit, and PROC_B depends on PACK_A. This kind of dependency is important for establishing the allowed order of compilation units, namely, *every library unit on which a compilation unit depends must be compiled prior to the start of the compilation of the compilation unit.* For our example PACK_A must be compiled before the compilation of PROC_B may begin, because the identifiers of PACK_A are visible in PROC_B. This rule is a particular case of a more general visibility rule: If an identifier is visible in a program unit but not declared in it, then the identifier should be part of an already compiled library unit.

Several library unit names may appear in a "with" clause. If they do, the library units must be separated by commas.

Whenever some Ada compilation unit is submitted for compilation, the package STANDARD (listed in Appendix C) is assumed to be part of its context. For this reason the types INTEGER, FLOAT, BOOLEAN, CHARACTER, and STRING, together with the functions operating on these types, are (directly) visible for any Ada program. The package STANDARD contains as well a package ASCII (made up of declarations of constants for control characters and other special characters) and some predefined exception declarations (which will be discussed in Chapter 11).

9.2 SUBUNITS AND BODY STUBS

Subunits were among the possible secondary units listed at the beginning of the chapter. **Subunits** are useful for separate compilation of bodies of program units declared within another compilation unit. The declaration of the program unit within another compilation unit is achieved by a body_stub, which has one of the following three forms:

```
subprogram_specification is separate;
package body package_simple_name is separate ;
task body task_simple_name is separate ;
```

The last form (task body) of a body_stub will be covered in the next chapter.

The body stub keeps the place of the proper body (that is, the actual body code), which is given in the subunit. The subunit has the form

```
separate ( parent_unit_name ) proper_body
```

The parent_unit_name appearing in a subunit is the name of the compilation unit where the body stub appears (this compilation unit is called the **parent unit**).

The advantage of using body stubs is that one may develop a program in its broad outline, compile and design some of its features, and then write some of the proper bodies (that is, some detail code). This approach is sometimes known as a *top-down approach*. In an alternative method, the *bottom-up approach*, a designer uses existing components (perhaps available in certain packages) as building blocks, even though the components may not represent the perfect fit for the intended goal. For instance, we have used the package CHECK_ DATES_ALT (and, in particular, the procedure FILL_IN_DATE) extensively in the preceding chapters for its date conversion capabilities, even though its procedures sometimes perform operations that were unnecessary for the intended application. Clearly, both approaches (and any shades in between) are supported by Ada equally well.

EXAMPLE   In this example we illustrate the use of body stubs by rewriting the declarations of the program NAME_PHONE of Chapter 4.

```
with TEXT_IO ; use TEXT_IO ;

procedure SEP_NAME_PHONE is

-- Use the same declarations from LINE_LN

-- to DIGIT_CT.


-- Now we have some body stubs.


procedure LOW_TO_UPPER_N_CT_COMMAS is separate ;

procedure IGNORE_LEADING_SPACES is separate ;

procedure FIND_NEXT_SP_OR_COMMA is separate ;

procedure PLACE_SPACES is separate ;

procedure IS_CORRECT_NAME is separate ;

-- All the other procedures follow the same "separate" pattern.


begin

-- Use the same body as PHONE_NAME.

end SEP_PHONE_NAME ;


        Now we supply the proper bodies with the following subunits:

separate ( SEP_PHONE_NAME )

procedure LOW_TO_UPPER_N_CT_COMMAS is

-- Use the same code as in the original version.

end  LOW_TO_UPPER_N_CT_COMMAS ;

-- Another subunit follows.

separate ( SEP_PHONE_NAME )

procedure IGNORE_LEADING_SPACES is
```

```
-- Use the same code as in the original version.

end IGNORE_LEADING_SPACES ;
```

Quite similar subunits should be written for the remaining subprograms.

EXAMPLE   In this example we use body stubs and subunits from the program ACCR_
INTEREST of Chapter 5. In the new version the parent unit is given first.

```
procedure SEP_ACCR_INTEREST is

-- Use the same declarations of types and objects.

      function IS_VALID_DATE ( FORM_DATE : DATE )

                              return BOOLEAN is separate ;

      procedure FILL_IN_DATE ( PROC_F_DATE : in out DATE ;

                          GOOD_DATE   : out BOOLEAN )

                      is separate ;

      function FIND_COUP_DATE ( FORM_MAT_DATE ,

          FORM_SETL_DATE : DATE ) return DATE is separate ;

begin

      -- The ACCR_INTEREST body is unchanged.

end SEP_ACCR_INTEREST ;
```

```
      The subunits corresponding to the body stubs are as follows:

separate ( SEP_ACCR_INTEREST )

      function IS_VALID_DATE ( FORM_DATE : DATE )

                              return BOOLEAN is

-- The body of the subprogram goes here.

      end IS_VALID_DATE ;

separate ( SEP_ACCR_INTEREST )
```

```
      procedure FILL_IN_DATE ( PROC_F_DATE : in out DATE ;

                        GOOD_DATE  : out BOOLEAN )  is

-- Body of the subprogram here

      end FILL_IN_DATE ;

separate ( SEP_ACCR_INTEREST )

      function FIND_COUP_DATE ( FORM_MAT_DATE ,

              FORM_SETL_DATE : DATE ) return DATE is

-- The body of the subprogram goes here.

      end FIND_COUP_DATE ;
```

EXAMPLE   Finally, we give an example of a body stub and a corresponding subunit involving packages. The example uses the program BANK_MAINT of Chapter 8.

```
with TEXT_IO ; use TEXT_IO ;

-- The other context information, except for BANK_RESOURCES

-- is left unchanged.


procedure SEP_BANK_MAINT is

-- Here is the change: instead of having

-- with BANK_RESOURCES ; use BANK_RESOURCES ;

-- now we have the following lines:

     package BANK_RESOURCES is

      -- A copy of the package specification

     end BANK_RESOURCES ;

      -- Now comes the body stub.

     package body BANK_RESOURCES is separate ;

      -- Everything else in this  program is left unchanged .

  end SEP_BANK_MAINT ;
```

The corresponding subunit, whose parent unit is SEP_BANK_MAINT, is

```
separate ( SEP_BANK_MAINT )

package body BANK_RESOURCES is

-- A copy of the body from Chapter 8 goes here.

end BANK_RESOURCES ;
```

The basic compilation rule regarding subunits is that the compilation of the parent must precede the compilation of the proper body placed in the corresponding subunit. For instance, before one can compile the subunit containing the proper body of the package BANK_RESOURCES (the previous example), the program SEP_BANK_MAINT must have been compiled already. Clearly, this rule shows another kind of dependency, somewhat complementing the dependency introduced by "with" clauses.

The compilation of the subunit (say, the proper body of BANK_RESOURCES) is done in the context of the parent (in this case SEP_BANK_MAINT). If, in addition, the subunit has its own context part, the assumption at compilation time is that the context part of the subunit is added to the context part of the parent. This rule can be further applied at a higher level if the parent unit is itself a subunit.

9.3 COMPILATION AND RECOMPILATION RULES

To summarize, Ada compilation units can be compiled in any order, provided the following two rules covering the order of compilation are obeyed.

1. A secondary unit must be compiled after the corresponding library unit is compiled. Thus package bodies, subprogram bodies, and subunits must be compiled after the corresponding package specification, subprogram specification, or parent unit. But one should keep in mind that a non-generic subprogram body can be its own specification.
2. A compilation unit must be compiled after all library units mentioned in its context clauses are compiled.

If there is any error during the compilation of a compilation unit, the program library is not modified.

Ada also has two recompilation rules, which are consistent with the two compilation rules.

1. Because secondary units have to be compiled after their corresponding library units, any recompilation of a library unit renders the related

secondary units obsolete, and they have to be recompiled. However, any recompilation of a secondary unit does not render the related library unit obsolete, and there is no need for any library unit recompilation.

2. If any compilation unit of a context part is recompiled, then the compilation unit to which the context applies becomes obsolete and has to be recompiled.

To illustrate the compilation rules, let us consider the program CURR_TRANSACTION_PROC of Section 8.3. The context part lists packages like CHECK_DATES_ALT, BANK_RESOURCES, TRANSACTION_RE-SOURCES, TEXT_IO, and LEGAL_HOLIDAYS. We could simply submit, in one big compilation unit, these packages (their specifications and their bodies) and then the program itself. Or we could supply several separate compilation units, such as CHECK_DATES_ALT, BANK_RESOURCES, and TRANSACTION_RESOURCES, in any order, because they are all packages independent of each other. Then the package LEGAL_HOLIDAYS could be compiled, because it depends on CHECK_DATES_ALT. Finally, the program CURR_TRANSACTION_PROC could be compiled. We can also have many variations of this order. For instance, we could submit two compilation units at a time, perhaps BANK_RESOURCES and TRANSACTION_RESOURCES. Regardless of the order of compilation for a particular program, if the compilation rules are obeyed, the library file will be updated in a consistent manner.

As mentioned above, a compilation consists of one or more compilation units submitted with a program library. A single program library is assumed for each compilation, even though a particular Ada implementation may have several. On a particular installation one should expect some other implementation details dealing with library file manipulation, such as creating a library file, merging library files, and querying the status of library units or secondary units in a library file. Note also that the elaboration of library units at execution time is done in a manner consistent with the compilation rules listed here.

EXERCISES FOR CHAPTER 9

1. Pretend that the program NAME_PHONE of Chapter 4 is written by following a top-down approach. Rewrite the program by using body stubs and subunits for each of the invoked subprograms.

2. Follow the procedure outlined in Exercise 1, but use the program ACCR_INTEREST of Chapter 5.

TASKS

10.1   TASKS AND THE RENDEZVOUS MECHANISM

The Ada programs presented so far were all executed sequentially: That is, no two statements were executed at the same time. Sometimes, though, the real-world problem under consideration can be better expressed by the concurrent execution of two or more actions. For instance, transactions at a bank are often handled by several tellers at the same time; several aircraft are controlled at the same time for landing or takeoff; a telephone company has to handle several conversations conducted concurrently. While each of these examples can be modeled with sequentially executed statements, a more natural approach is to provide the language with features that handle concurrency.

TASKS

In Ada the handling of concurrency is done by entities called tasks whose execution is carried out in parallel. **Tasks** are Ada program units, the last unit to be introduced after subprograms, packages, and generic units. Different tasks can proceed independently, even though tasks have facilities for communicating with each other. Ada does not specify how the parallel tasks are to be implemented, that is, how many computers (at least one) are to be used, or what particular kind of execution is to be used. However, Ada interprets tasks as logical entities behaving as if they were running in parallel on different machines.

Like subprograms and packages, tasks have two parts: a specification and a body. And as with subprograms and packages, a task specification followed by a semicolon constitutes a task declaration. Unlike subprograms and packages, however, tasks cannot be compiled by themselves. Therefore tasks have to be placed in a subprogram or a package in order to be compiled.

RENDEZVOUS

Ada tasks communicate with each other by using entries. Once a task issues an entry call that is accepted by another task, the two tasks lose their independence: The tasks are establishing a **rendezvous,** and as long as the rendezvous is in effect, the tasks are synchronized.

These concepts will be illustrated shortly, but keep in mind that there is no symmetry in the rendezvous mechanism. That is, one task may initiate the possibility of a rendezvous by the issue of an entry call, and another task may or may not accept the call issued by the first task. The rendezvous takes place if and when the second task accepts the call. The rendezvous can be eventually broken off, and each task can proceed independently.

TASK SPECIFICATION

A task specification can define a single task or a task type. A task type is recognized by the appearance of the reserved word "type" in its specification. The simplest form of task specification defining a single task is

```
task task_identifier
```

A semicolon is needed here after the task_identifier for a task declaration. For instance, we might have the following task declaration:

```
task CHECK_BANKS_FOR_OVERFLOW ;
```

ENTRIES

For a task to be called by other tasks, entry points must be provided. The entry points, if they exist, must be declared in the specification part of a task by using an **entry declaration.** The specification then can have the form

```
task task_identifier  is

    entry entry_identifier  (discrete_range) formal_part;

      -- Maybe other entry declarations or

      -- representation clauses (Chapter 7) are given here.

  end task_identifier
```

The discrete_range (used in array types, for instance) and the formal_part (used, for instance, in subprogram specifications) are optional.

EXAMPLE   An example of a task specification is

```
task SOME_TRAN_FILES is

    entry LOOK_FOR_FILES (1 .. 12)

              (FORM_MO : INTEGER ; FORM_DAY : INTEGER) ;

end MAINT_TRAN_FILES ;
```

The entry part of this task declaration has a discrete range (12 elements for 12 possible months) and a formal part with two formal parameters of type INTEGER. Another example is

```
task LOOKING_FOR_BANKS is

    entry INQUIRY

            ( INQ_BANK_NAME : in out STRING   ;

              INQ_POS        : out POSITIVE_COUNT ;

              INQ_FOUND      : out BOOLEAN          ) is

end LOOKING_FOR_BANKS ;
```

The entry INQUIRY has a formal part. It checks to see whether a bank is already in the BANK_FILE. Then it returns the answer TRUE in INQ_FOUND if the bank is found. It is similar to RETRIEVE of the package BANK_RESOURCES of Chapter 8, except that it can handle several parallel requests at a time.

Note that entry declarations have a form similar to that of subprogram specification. The similarity goes one step further: A task entry may be invoked whenever it is allowed to invoke a subprogram, and the rules for matching actual parameters with formal parameters are the same for tasks and subprograms.

There is no concept of recursive call for tasks, however. And to have a task invoking itself, either directly or indirectly, is a mistake, as shown in the final subsection of this section.

The formal parameters appearing in the formal part of an entry declaration, as the preceding example shows, can have a mode of "in," "in out," or "out."

Entry calls issued by a calling task also have the form of procedure calls:

The entry name is followed by the list of actual parameters, if any, within parentheses and a semicolon. The prefix consisting of the task name is mandatory when one is calling a task because the "use" clause is not allowed for tasks (remember that tasks are not compilation units).

Possibly, several tasks will call the same entry, in which case only one task at a time will be permitted to rendezvous. The other tasks must wait in a queue, which has to be provided by any Ada implementation. The tasks waiting in a queue will be accepted by the called task on a first-come, first-served basis. As long as the tasks are in the queue, they are said to be **suspended.** If two or more tasks issue calls for the same task at the same time, there is no predefined order assigned to the calling tasks.

Here is an example of an entry call:

```
LOOKING_FOR_BANKS.INQUIRY (THIS_BANK,
    THIS_POS ,IS_THERE) ;
```

This entry call (assuming the named task is visible) will attempt a rendezvous with LOOKING_FOR_BANKS. If the rendezvous is not immediately possible, the call will be placed in the queue provided for the entry INQUIRY.

TASK BODY

As mentioned earlier, task types are specified in the same way as single tasks, except that the reserved word "type" follows the reserved word "task." Of course, once a task type is declared, one can declare objects of the declared task. The use of objects of a task type is quite restrictive, because task types are of a limited private type: They cannot be compared for equality or inequality, and they cannot be assigned.

The body of a task has the form

```
task body task_identifier is

        -- The declarative part goes here.

begin

        -- The sequence_of_statements part goes here.

end task_identifier ;
```

After the sequence_of_ statements part there is an optional exception-handling part, which will be covered in Chapter 11.

ACCEPT STATEMENTS

If the corresponding task specification has an entry declaration, then the task body should contain at least one **accept statement.** The rough meaning of this term is as follows: A task discloses, in its specification, whether it can be called by another task (by the presence of the entry declarations) and the form of the proper call. The actual conditions under which the rendezvous takes place are spelled out in the corresponding accept statements (an entry declaration can have more than one corresponding accept statement).

The simplest form of the accept statement is

```
accept entry_identifier ;
```

This form is used if the corresponding entry declaration has no discrete range or formal part (these parts are optional for an entry declaration, as mentioned above). If some of these optional features are present in the entry declaration, then the corresponding accept statement should have them, too. For instance, an accept statement can have the form

```
accept entry_identifier (expression) formal_part;
```

The complete form of an accept statement may have a sequence_of_statements part enclosed within the reserved words "do . . . end" preceding the semicolon, which is executed during the rendezvous. This form is

```
accept entry_identifier (expression) formal_part
      do sequence_of_statements end ;
```

As we mentioned before, the rendezvous of a calling and a called task starts with the matching of actual parameters with formal parameters. It then continues with the execution of the sequence of statements (if any) of the accept statement, and the rendezvous ends when the semicolon is reached. During the rendezvous the tasks can exchange information (through their parameter matching), and the tasks are synchronized as well: The sequence-of-statements part of the accept statement is executed on behalf of both tasks.

MASTERS

We stated earlier that tasks are not compilation units, and they cannot be compiled by themselves. They are generally placed in the declarative part of a package or a subprogram. Thus a task must be dependent on a **master,** which can be a subprogram, a block, a package, or another task. If a task appears in the declarative part of a block, for instance, then the block is a master for the task. A task can have several masters. For instance, if the block containing the task is activated by another task, the activating task is a master too for the task whose master is the block. Clearly, then, a task may depend on several program units or blocks. The concept of master is important in establishing the circumstances of task completion, as we will show shortly.

EXAMPLES AND A PROGRAM

EXAMPLE   This example illustrates how one may write a task body for the specification of the task LOOKING_FOR_BANKS given earlier.

```
task body LOOKING_FOR_BANKS is

NO_FILES_PROCESSED : NATURAL :=0 ;

-- The declarations  of the   package BANK_RESOURCES

-- are assumed to be visible  and the package is

-- assumed to be elaborated.

begin

loop

    accept INQUIRY

            ( INQ_BANK_NAME : in out STRING  ;

              INQ_POS        : out POSITIVE_COUNT ;

              INQ_FOUND      : out BOOLEAN        )

        do

            -- The statements below will be executed

            -- during the rendezvous.

            RETRIEVE ( FORM_BANK_NAME => INQ_BANK_NAME ,

                       FORM_POS        => INQ_POS ,

                       FORM_FOUND      => INQ_FOUND);

        if INQ_BANK_NAME = "12345678901234567890"

            then

            NO_FILES_PROCESSED :=

                    NO_FILES_PROCESSED + 1 ;
```

```
                    end if ;

                    -- The rendezvous ceases when the statement

                    -- below is reached.

                end INQUIRY ;

            exit when NO_FILES_PROCESSED = 2  ;

            -- When the number of closed files equals 2

            -- no more input is expected.

        end loop;

        CLOSE (BANK_FILE) ;

    end LOOKING_FOR_BANKS ;
```

This task specification and the body of LOOKING_FOR_BANKS can be placed in a new package called PARALLEL_BANK_RESOURCES, with the following specification:

```
with BANK_RESOURCES ; use BANK_RESOURCES ;

package PARALLEL_BANK_RESOURCES is

    -- The task specification for  LOOKING_FOR_BANKS goes here.

end PARALLEL_BANK_RESOURCES ;

--

package body PARALLEL_BANK_RESOURCES is

    -- The task body for  LOOKING_FOR_BANKS goes here.

begin

end PARALLEL_BANK_RESOURCES ;
```

The program that follows makes use of two tasks in addition to the one in the package PARALLEL_BANK_RESOURCES. The program reads bank names from two sequential files and checks to see whether the names are found in the BANK_FILE. When both sequential files reach the END_OF_FILE, the program displays the ratio of banks in the BANK_FILE to the total number of banks in each file, and the program ends.

GATHER_BANK_STATISTICS Program

```
with TEXT_IO; use TEXT_IO ;

with SEQUENTIAL_IO, DIRECT_IO, PARALLEL_BANK_RESOURCES ;

use  DIRECT_IO, PARALLEL_BANK_RESOURCES ;

procedure GATHER_BANK_STATISTICS is

package SEQ_1 is new  SEQUENTIAL_IO (STRING (1 .. 20)) ;

package SEQ_2 is new  SEQUENTIAL_IO (STRING (1 .. 20)) ;

use SEQ_1, SEQ_2 ;

package INT_IO is new INTEGER_IO (INTEGER) ;

use INT_IO ;

FILE_1 : SEQ_1.FILE_TYPE ;

FILE_2 : SEQ_2.FILE_TYPE ;

-- Two task specifications, CHECK_FILE_1 and CHECK_FILE_2,

-- without entries, are given next.

--

task CHECK_FILE_1 ;

task CHECK_FILE_2 ;

--

task body CHECK_FILE_1 is

NO_HITS_FILE_1, TOT_FILE_1 : NATURAL := 0 ;

BNK_1 : STRING (1 .. 20) ;

BNK_1_POS : NATURAL ;

IS_1_THERE : BOOLEAN ;

FILE_1 : FILE_TYPE ;

    begin

        OPEN ( FILE => FILE_1 ,
```

```
            MODE => IN_FILE,

            NAME => "FILE1.DAT" ,

            FORM => "") ;

while  not END_OF_FILE (FILE_1)

       loop

       READ (FILE => FILE_1, ITEM => BNK_1 ) ;

       TOT_FILE_1 := TOT_FILE_1 + 1 ;

       LOOKING_FOR_BANKS.INQUIRY

                 (BNK_1 ,BNK_1_POS, IS_1_THERE) ;

       -- This statement is an entry call to the

       -- LOOKING_FOR_BANKS task .

       -- As long as the rendezvous is not completed,

       -- this task will be suspended. When the

       -- rendezvous is initiated, then this task

       -- and the called task will be synchronized,

       -- and information will be exchanged. IS_1_THERE

       -- will hold, for instance, the information about

       -- whether the bank supplied as an actual parameter

       -- is in the BANK_FILE .

       -- Starting with the statement below, the two tasks

       -- will  be  again  independent  until  the  next

       -- rendezvous.

       if IS_1_THERE

           then

           NO_HITS_FILE_1 := NO_HITS_FILE_1 + 1 ;

           end if ;
```

```
end loop ;
LOOKING_FOR_BANKS.INQUIRY ("12345678901234567890",

                  BNK_1_POS, IS_1_THERE) ;
-- This  entry call is used to make sure
-- that the called task will end eventually .
PUT (" The number of banks in FILE1.DAT  is ");
PUT ( TOT_FILE_1) ;
PUT   ( "  The  number  of  banks  in  FILE1.DAT " &

                  "  and BANK_FILE  is ");
      PUT (NO_HITS_FILE_1) ;
      CLOSE (FILE_1) ;

end CHECK_FILE_1 ;
--

--  This task is a copy of CHECK_FILE_2 using the second
--  sequential file. Exercise 1 at the end of the chapter
--  asks for a different approach .
--

task body CHECK_FILE_2 is
NO_HITS_FILE_2, TOT_FILE_2 : NATURAL := 0 ;
BNK_2 : STRING (1 .. 20) ;
BNK_2_POS : NATURAL ;
IS_2_THERE : BOOLEAN ;
FILE_2 : FILE_TYPE ;

   begin
        OPEN ( FILE => FILE_2 ,

                MODE => IN_FILE,
```

```
                    NAME => "FILE2.DAT" ,

                    FORM => "") ;

          while   not END_OF_FILE (FILE_2)

                loop

                READ (FILE => FILE_2, ITEM => BNK_2 ) ;

                TOT_FILE_2 := TOT_FILE_2 + 1 ;

                LOOKING_FOR_BANKS.INQUIRY

                          (BNK_2 ,BNK_2_POS, IS_2_THERE) ;

                if IS_2_THERE

                    then

                        NO_HITS_FILE_2 := NO_HITS_FILE_2 + 1 ;

                    end if ;

          end loop ;

          LOOKING_FOR_BANKS.INQUIRY ("12345678901234567890",

                        BNK_2_POS, IS_2_THERE) ;

          PUT (" The number of banks in FILE2.DAT  is ");

          PUT ( TOT_FILE_2) ;

          PUT   ( "  The  number  of  banks  in  FILE2.DAT " &

                  "  and BANK_FILE  is ");

          PUT (NO_HITS_FILE_2) ;

          CLOSE (FILE_2) ;

end CHECK_FILE_2 ;

--

begin
      -- The main program starts here. It needs at least

      -- one null statement.

      null;

end GATHER_BANK_STATISTICS ;
```

TASK STATES

Tasks become **active**—that is, they start their logically independent execution acting as if they were running on logically different machines—when the "begin" reserved word is reached (signaling the start of the sequence-of-statements part) in the package or subprogram containing the tasks. Activation of a task means the sequential execution of the statements part of its body.

A task is **completed** (and this completion holds, as each of the previous programs demonstrates, for subprograms or blocks, too) when the end of the body is reached. A task, a subprogram, or a block can be completed in a variety of other ways—for instance, when exceptions are raised, a situation that will be covered in the next chapter.

There are three tasks in the previous program (in addition to the main program, which is considered a task, too). The master of the tasks CHECK_ FILE_1 and CHECK_FILE_2 is the procedure GATHER_BANK_STATISTICS. The master of the third task, LOOKING_FOR_BANKS, is the package PARALLEL_BANK_RESOURCES. These tasks may be in one of these three states: running (executing statements), suspended (waiting for a rendezvous, for instance), or terminated (for instance, the task is completed and all its dependent tasks are completed). Task termination, which will be discussed in detail in the next section, is more general than task completion. Completion means merely that the task, in its sequential execution of statements, has reached the reserved word "end." Completion of a task has nothing to do with the activity of dependent tasks that might very well be active. In contrast, the concept of termination of a task covers its completion and, possibly, the termination of dependent or master tasks.

Refer again to the previous program. If the task LOOKING_FOR_BANKS reaches the accept statement, it may be that none of the other tasks have issued a call yet, in which case LOOKING_FOR_BANKS will become suspended; it will stay suspended until a rendezvous is possible. Actually, if no call is ever forthcoming, the task will never leave this state (to prevent this event, we introduced a counter of the number of closed input files, and we exited the loop when all input files were processed).

Possibly, all three tasks may be running (when they are first activated, each task is independently opening a file), but we can have one or two tasks suspended at a time. For example, two tasks are suspended if the accept statement is executed and the other task is suspended, waiting for a rendezvous. In this case one task is waiting in the queue associated with the accept statement. For the previous program we can never have more than one task waiting, because each task reading an input sequential file is suspended after each reading until its rendezvous with LOOKING_FOR_BANKS is completed. This situation arises because there is no buffering task and the calling task waits until the rendezvous is completed. It probably takes longer to check several records in the BANK_FILE until a decision is reached than to read a record of the sequential file.

Now we summarize some asymmetric features of the rendezvous mechanism:

- The called task does not know which task is the calling task (the calling task does). That is, the task LOOKING_FOR_BANKS does not know whether it is having a rendezvous with CHECK_FILE_1 or CHECK_FILE_2.
- The called task suspends the calling task for the duration of the rendezvous.

Note that during a rendezvous the called task may initiate another rendezvous with a different task. In this situation the new rendezvous has to be completed before the old one is.

Figure 10.1 illustrates the three tasks of the program GATHER_BANK_STATISTICS and their various states under a number of assumptions.

DEADLOCK

One should be quite careful to avoid the possibility of every task in a program being suspended, waiting for another task of the program to execute. This situation is called **deadlock,** and we provide a simple deadlock example next.

EXAMPLE Consider the following procedure:

```
procedure DEADLOCK_EXAMPLE is

    task CALLS_ITSELF is

        entry ENTRY_POINT ;

    end CALLS_ITSELF ;

    procedure INTERM is

        CALLS_ITSELF.ENTRY_POINT ;

    end INTERM ;

    task body CALLS_ITSELF is

        INTERM ;

        accept ENTRY_POINT ;

    end CALLS_ITSELF ;

    begin
```

FIGURE 10.1 Rendezvous Mechanism

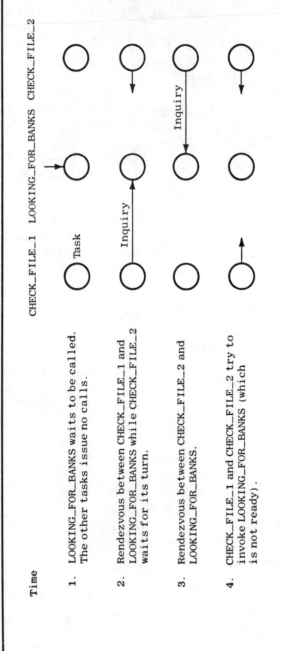

Time

CHECK_FILE_1   LOOKING_FOR_BANKS   CHECK_FILE_2

1. LOOKING_FOR_BANKS waits to be called. The other tasks issue no calls.

2. Rendezvous between CHECK_FILE_1 and LOOKING_FOR_BANKS while CHECK_FILE_2 waits for its turn.

3. Rendezvous between CHECK_FILE_2 and LOOKING_FOR_BANKS.

4. CHECK_FILE_1 and CHECK_FILE_2 try to invoke LOOKING_FOR_BANKS (which is not ready).

```
    null;

end DEADLOCK_EXAMPLE ;
```

In this program the task CALLS_ITSELF is activated; then it invokes the procedure INTERM, which in turn issues an entry call for ENTRY_POINT. Because the access statement is not reached, the call becomes suspended. But the access statement will not be reached because the previous statement must be completed first. This simple example of a deadlock situation is illustrated in Figure 10.2.

Avoiding and recognizing the possibility of deadlock is quite complex. In contrast to the situation here, in other situations the reasons for deadlock, when it occurs, might not be obvious at all.

10.2 STATEMENTS AND ATTRIBUTES FOR TASKS

DELAY STATEMENT

The execution of a task can be suspended temporarily with the help of a **delay statement.** Its form is

```
delay duration_expression ;
```

The duration_expression is an expression of the predefined fixed-point type DURATION, part of the package STANDARD listed in Appendix C. The delay

FIGURE 10.2 Deadlock

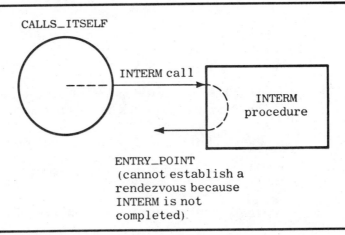

CALLS_ITSELF

INTERM call

INTERM procedure

ENTRY_POINT
(cannot establish a
rendezvous because
INTERM is not
completed)

statement will suspend the activity of the task for at least the number of seconds given by duration_expression.

A predefined package CALENDAR, listed in Appendix C, defines the operations possible on values of the private type TIME. Some of the overloaded operators defined in this package are $+$, $-$, $<$, $<=$, $>$, and $>=$. These functions return values of type TIME or DURATION and have formal parameters of type TYPE or DURATION.

The package CALENDAR has some other useful subprograms like SPLIT (given time, it returns the YEAR, MONTH, DAY, and SECONDS) and TIME_OF (which is the complement of SPLIT; given YEAR, MONTH, DAY, and SEC-ONDS, it returns a value of type TIME), as well as functions that independently manipulate some of the listed types. The CALENDAR package will be used in the program PLANT_SCHED that is presented later.

SELECT STATEMENT: SELECTIVE WAIT

There are three kinds of **select statements,** called selective wait, conditional entry call, and timed entry call. We will discuss each kind in turn.

The form of a **selective wait** is

```
select

      select_alternative

      -- One or more select alternatives are given here.

   or

   select_alternative

   else

         sequence_of_statements

   end select ;
```

It is valid to have zero or several "or" alternatives, and the "else" part is optional. The select alternative can have three flavors, which are listed below:

```
when condition => accept_statement

                              sequence_of_statements


when condition => delay_statement
```

```
                                    sequence_of_statements


when condition => terminate ;
```

The sequence_of_statements and the "when condition = >" parts of the select alternatives are optional.

If there is no "when" reserved word for an alternative, or if the condition following "when" is always true, the corresponding select alternative is said to be **open.** Otherwise, it is said to be **closed.** These concepts are useful for an understanding of how selective wait statements work.

There must be at least one accept alternative in a selective wait. The execution of a selective wait is carried out as follows: The conditions after the reserved word "when" are evaluated in some arbitrary order. In the next step one of the select alternatives or the "else" part, if present, will compete for execution. Preference is given to any open alternatives with an accept statement, which can establish a rendezvous. If several alternatives satisfy this condition, then one of these alternatives is selected at random. The selection of an accept alternative means that both the sequence of statements within the accept statement (if any) and the sequence of statements following the accept statement (if any) are executed.

If no rendezvous is possible for any accept alternative, and if there is no "else" part, then the task starts waiting. If there is an "else" part, however, it is now selected and executed.

While the task is waiting, an open delay alternative will be selected if the specified delay has elapsed and no accept alternative can be selected. If there are several delay alternatives of equal duration, one of them will be selected at random.

Finally, a terminate alternative will be selected if all dependent tasks of the master have terminated or are waiting at a terminate alternative and no calls are queued at any entry of the task.

The exception PROGRAM_ERROR is raised if all alternatives are closed and the "else" part is missing (this exception will be explained in Chapter 11).

Note that the selection of a terminate alternative in a selective wait statement does not mean that the task containing this alternative terminates. In this situation a task terminates if the task master is completed and all tasks dependent on the master have terminated or are waiting at a terminate alternative.

EXAMPLE   In this example we illustrate the use of a selective wait statement in a package. The package includes a modification of the task specification and the task body LOOKING_FOR_BANKS in order to allow for both reading and updating of bank records.

```
task LOOKING_FOR_BANKS is

    entry INQUIRY

                ( INQ_BANK_NAME : STRING (1 .. 20) ;

                    INQ_POS           : out POSITIVE_COUNT ;

                    INQ_FOUND         : out BOOLEAN          ) ;

    entry BK_CHANGE

                ( CHANGE_BANK_NAME : STRING (1 .. 20) ;

                    CHANGE_POS          : out POSITIVE_COUNT ;

                    CHANGE_INFO         : STRING (1 .. 49) ;

                    CHANGE_FOUND        : out BOOLEAN          ) ;

end LOOKING_FOR_BANKS ;

--

    task body LOOKING_FOR_BANKS is

    NO_FILES_PROCESSED : NATURAL :=0 ;

    CHANGE_HEAD : BANK_INFO ;

    CHANGE_BANK_REC : BANK_REC ;

    begin

    loop

        -- An example of a select statement follows.

        select

            -- There is no "when" part for this

            -- alternative, but there is a

            -- sequence-of-statements part.

            accept INQUIRY

                ( INQ_BANK_NAME : STRING (1 .. 20) ;

                    INQ_POS          : out POSITIVE_COUNT ;
```

```
        INQ_FOUND         : out BOOLEAN              )

   do

   RETRIEVE ( FORM_BANK_NAME => INQ_BANK_NAME ,

                 FORM_POS        => INQ_POS ,

                 FORM_FOUND      => INQ_FOUND);

   if INQ_BANK_NAME = "12345678901234567890"

         then

         NO_FILES_PROCESSED :=

                     NO_FILES_PROCESSED + 1 ;

      end if ;

   end INQUIRY ;

or

accept BK_CHANGE

      ( CHANGE_BANK_NAME : STRING (1 .. 20) ;

        CHANGE_POS         : out POSITIVE_COUNT ;

        CHANGE_INFO        : STRING (1 .. 49) ;

        CHANGE_FOUND       : out BOOLEAN           )

      do

      RETRIEVE(FORM_BANK_NAME => CHANGE_BANK_NAME ,

                  FORM_POS        => CHANGE_POS ,

                  FORM_FOUND      => CHANGE_FOUND);

      if CHANGE_BANK_NAME = "12345678901234567890"

            then

            NO_FILES_PROCESSED :=

                        NO_FILES_PROCESSED + 1 ;

      else
```

```
                        --   If the bank is found, then the

                        --   record is updated .

                    if CHANGE_FOUND

                        then

                        CHANGE_BANK_REC.MAST_HEAD.BANK_NAME :=

                            FORM_BANK_NAME ;

                        CHANGE_BANK_REC.MAST_HEAD.OTHER_INFO :=

                            CHANGE_INFO ;

                        WRITE (FILE => BANK_FILE ,

                                ITEM => CHANGE_BANK_REC ,

                                FROM => CHANGE_POS) ;

                    end if ;

                end if ;

            end BK_CHANGE ;

        or    terminate ;

        end select ;

        exit when NO_FILES_PROCESSED = 3  ;

        -- When the number of closed files equals 3

        -- No more input is expected.

    end loop;

    CLOSE (BANK_FILE) ;

    -- Note that the loop is executed  as long as the

    -- three  files  processed  by three independent tasks are open.

    -- No task will access BANK_FILE after these three files

    -- are closed.

    end LOOKING_FOR_BANKS ;
```

The task body of this example also implements a mechanism to ensure mutual exclusion of certain events. **Mutual exclusion** refers to operations that cannot be performed at the same time for consistency reasons. For instance, we cannot have data being updated and read concurrently, because one task may read data that just became obsolete by new data written or modified by a different task. The select statement in the task body achieves the desired mutual exclusion, because just one alternative can be selected at any given time, and data can be read or modified only through the select statement.

EXAMPLE The task CHANGE_FILE_1 described here updates the content of the BANK_FILE with information extracted from the file CHNG_FILE. It represents a straightforward modification of the tasks CHECK_FILE_1 and CHECK_FILE_2. This new task is placed in the same program.

```
task CHANGE_FILE_1 ;

task body CHANGE_FILE_1 is

CHNG_BNK_1 : STRING (1 .. 20) ;

CHNG_INFO_1 : STRING (1 .. 49) ;

NO_HITS_FILE_CHNG, TOT_FILE_CHNG : NATURAL := 0 ;

BNK_CHNG_POS : NATURAL ;

IS_CHNG_THERE : BOOLEAN ;

CHNG_FILE : FILE_TYPE ;
    begin
        OPEN ( FILE => CHNG_FILE ,
              MODE => IN_FILE,
              NAME => "CHANG1.DAT" ,
              FORM => "") ;
        while  not END_OF_FILE (CHNG_FILE)
            loop
            READ (FILE => CHNG_FILE,
                  ITEM => CHNG_BNK_1 ) ;
```

```
                    TOT_FILE_CHNG  := TOT_FILE_CHNG + 1 ;

                    LOOKING_FOR_BANKS.BK_CHANGE

                        ( CHANGE_BANK_NAME => CHNG_BNK_1 ,

                            CHANGE_POS          => BNK_CHNG_POS ,

                            CHANGE_INFO         => CHNG_INFO_1 ,

                            CHANGE_FOUND        => IS_CHNG_THERE ) ;

                    if IS_CHNG_THERE

                        then

                            NO_HITS_FILE_CHNG := NO_HITS_FILE_CHNG + 1 ;

                        end if ;

                end loop ;

                LOOKING_FOR_BANKS.BK_CHANGE

                        ( CHANGE_BANK_NAME => "12345678901234567890" ,

                            CHANGE_POS          => BNK_CHNG_POS ,

                            CHANGE_INFO         => CHNG_INFO_1 ,

                            CHANGE_FOUND        => IS_CHNG_THERE ) ;

                PUT (" The number of banks in CHNG_FILE  is ");

                PUT ( TOT_FILE_CHNG);

                PUT    ( " The  number  of  banks  in  CHNG_FILE " &

                        "  and BANK_FILE  is ");

                PUT (NO_HITS_FILE_CHNG  ;

                CLOSE (CHNG_FILE) ;

        end CHANGE_FILE_1 ;
```

SELECT STATEMENT: CONDITIONAL ENTRY AND TIMED ENTRY CALLS

While selective wait statements establish conditions under which a rendezvous is possible with a called task, the conditional entry call and the timed entry call statements can be used by calling tasks to attempt a rendezvous that may be canceled under certain conditions. With a **conditional entry** call the attempted rendezvous is canceled immediately if it is not possible. The entry call is canceled after a given delay with a **timed entry** call.

The complete form of a conditional entry call is

```
select

      entry_call_statement

      sequence_of_statements

else

      sequence_of_statements

end select ;
```

The sequence_of_statements following the entry_call_statement is optional.

The conditional entry call statement is executed as follows: The actual parameters of the entry_call_statement, if present, are evaluated; then an attempt is made to rendezvous with the called task. If the rendezvous is not immediately possible for any reason, the "else" part of the statement is executed. If the rendezvous is successful, upon its completion the sequence of statements following the entry_call_statement (if present) is executed.

A conditional entry call is useful for gaining some time and performing some useful work if a rendezvous is not immediately possible. The call is not placed in a queue; instead, the sequence_of_statements part following the "else" reserved word is executed, and the call may be tried again later. Exercise 2 at the end of the chapter modifies the program GATHER_BANK_STATISTICS in order to use conditional entry calls.

The complete form of a timed entry call statement is

```
select

      entry_call_statement

      sequence_of_statements

or

      delay_alternative

      sequence_of_statements

end select ;
```

As for conditional entry calls, the sequence of statements following the entry_ call_statement and the delay_alternative is optional.

The execution of the timed entry call statement is carried out as follows: The actual parameters of the entry_call_statement, if any, are evaluated; then the expression following the "delay" reserved word is evaluated. An attempt is made to rendezvous with the called task within the evaluated duration. If the rendezvous is possible, then it is initiated. Upon its completion the sequence-of-statements part (if any) following the call is executed. If no rendezvous is possible within the allowed duration, the sequence-of-statements part (if any) following the delay statement is executed.

For both the conditional entry call and timed entry call, the exception TASKING_ERROR is raised if the called task has completed its execution. (An example in Chapter 11 will show how this situation can be handled.)

ENTRY AND TASK ATTRIBUTES

An example of the use of timed entry calls is given in the program that follows. It deals with a simplified manufacturing problem, whereby a product needs two operations, OPER1 and OPER2, in order to be finished. The program also makes use of the entry attribute

E'COUNT

which returns the number of entry calls queued at a particular moment on the entry E of a task T.

Some other useful attributes apply to any task objects or task types. They are as follows (T denotes the task object):

T'CALLABLE	Returns the Boolean value FALSE when the task is completed, terminated, or abnormal; returns TRUE otherwise
T'TERMINATED	Returns the Boolean value TRUE if the task denoted by T is terminated; returns the value FALSE otherwise

A manufacturer's floor has three machines, MACH1, MACH2, and MACH3, to perform needed operations. MACH1 is able to perform OPER1 in about 3 minutes, MACH2 can perform OPER2 in about 7 minutes, and MACH3 can perform both OPER1 and OPER2 (always in succession) in about 11 minutes. Once the product is finished, it is inspected. The inspection takes about 2 minutes, and 5% of the products are rejected. Every 2 hours the inspector takes a coffee break of 15 minutes (but not in the middle of inspecting a product). Rejected products must go through OPER1 and OPER2 again.

The times mentioned here for operations and inspections represent averages of some assumed probability distributions. The package DISTRIBUTIONS is used to obtain the actual times.

Assuming that the day starts with a batch of 200 unfinished products, the program determines approximately how long it will take the machines to complete the batch.

PLANT_SCHED Program

```
with CALENDAR; use CALENDAR;

package DISTRIBUTIONS is

type DIST_KINDS is (TIME_MACH1, TIME_MACH2, TIME_MACH3 ,

                    INSPECTION ) ;

    -- The probabilities returned are in seconds rather than

    -- minutes in order to shorten the simulation time.

function PROBABILITY (FORM_DIST : in out DIST_KINDS) return

                    DURATION;

function INSP_RESULT return BOOLEAN ;

    -- The function returns the value TRUE if the inspection

    -- is passed.

end DISTRIBUTIONS ;

--

with DISTRIBUTIONS ; use DISTRIBUTIONS ;

with CALENDAR ; use CALENDAR ;

-- This package is needed for CLOCK and "-" functions.

with TEXT_IO; use TEXT_IO;

procedure PLANT_SCHED is

        -- Exercise 4 at the end of the chapter takes a different

        -- approach  by  interpreting the 200  products  as

        -- a family of tasks.

N_OF_FINISHED_PROD : NATURAL := 0 ;

N_OF_REJECTS  : NATURAL := 0 ;
```

```
    MACH1_AVAIL ,MACH2_AVAIL ,MACH3_AVAIL : NATURAL := 0 ;
        -- These variables count how many of the products
        -- were processed by each machine but were not
        -- accepted  immediately by the next processing step.
        -- They are "shared" variables, and their exact
        -- behavior will be explained in the next section.
    task COORDINATOR is
        entry SCHED ;
    end COORDINATOR ;
        task MACH1 is
            entry OPER1 ;
        end MACH1 ;
        cask MACH2 is
            entry OPER2 ;
        end MACH2 ;
        task MACH3 is
            entry OPER1_N_2 ;
        end MACH3 ;
        task STOP_INSPECTION ;
        task INSPECT is
            entry PRODUCT ;
            entry TAKE_A_BREAK ;
        end INSPECT ;
    --

        task body MACH1 is
        MACH1_JOB_DURATION : DURATION ;
```

```
begin

     MACH1_JOB_DURATION := PROBABILITY (TIME_MACH1) ;

     loop

          accept OPER1 ;

          delay MACH1_JOB_DURATION ;

          -- The select statement below makes sure

          -- that the task does not become suspended

          -- (and the machine does not become idle) if

          -- the second machine is unavailable. The same

          -- process is applied to all three machines.

          select

               MACH2.OPER2 ;

          else

               MACH1_AVAIL := MACH1_AVAIL + 1 ;

          end select ;

          MACH1_JOB_DURATION := PROBABILITY (TIME_MACH1) ;

     end loop ;

end MACH1 ;

--

task body MACH2 is

MACH2_JOB_DURATION : DURATION ;

begin

     MACH2_JOB_DURATION := PROBABILITY (TIME_MACH2) ;

     loop

          loop

               -- This select statement   insures
```

```
                    -- that the machine does not sit idle if

                    -- there is no immediate call from MACH1.

                    -- Exercise 3 at the end of the chapter

                    -- suggests another approach by using

                    -- a buffer task.

                    select

                         accept OPER2 ;

                         exit ;

                    else

                         if MACH1_AVAIL > 0

                              then

                              MACH1_AVAIL := MACH1_AVAIL - 1 ;

                              exit;

                         end if ;

                    end select ;

               end loop ;

               delay MACH2_JOB_DURATION ;

               select

                    INSPECT.PRODUCT ;

               else

                    MACH2.AVAIL := MACH2.AVAIL + 1 ;

               end select ;

               MACH2_JOB_DURATION := PROBABILITY (TIME_MACH2) ;

          end loop;

     end MACH2 ;
```

```
task body MACH3 is

MACH3_JOB_DURATION : DURATION ;

begin

     MACH3_JOB_DURATION := PROBABILITY (TIME_MACH3) ;

     loop

          accept OPER1_N_2  ;

          delay MACH3_JOB_DURATION ;

          select

               INSPECT.PRODUCT ;

          else

               MACH3_AVAIL := MACH3_AVAIL + 1 ;

          end select ;

          MACH3_JOB_DURATION := PROBABILITY (TIME_MACH3) ;

     end loop;

  end MACH3 ;

--

task body COORDINATOR is

begin

     -- As long as there are calls to this task, or as long as

     -- the number of rejected products is positive, a timed

     -- entry call will attempt to rendezvous with MACH1 or

     -- MACH3 by switching from one task to the other if

     -- the rendezvous is not possible every 0.01 second.

     -- The simulation here introduces some extra overhead

     -- because of the possible delay of 0.01.

     accept SCHED ;
```

```
        -- This accept statement makes sure that we start
        -- by processing calls from the main program.
        loop

            loop

                select

                    MACH1.OPER1 ;

                    exit ;

                or

                    delay 0.01 ;

                end select ;

                select

                    MACH3.OPER1_N_2 ;

                    exit ;

                or

                    delay 0.01 ;

                end select ;

                -- An alternative way to model this situation

                -- (without the extra 0.01 delay) is to

                -- use  a conditional entry call, as follows:

                -- loop

                --    select

                --      MACH1.OPER1 ;

                --      exit ;

                --    else

                --      null ;

                --    end select ;
```

```
--    select
--        MACH3.OPER1_N_2 ;
--        exit ;
--    else
--        null ;
--    end select ;
        end loop ;
        select
            accept SCHED ;
            else
            -- This alternative is taken if all 200 products
            -- are processed and  there are some rejects to
            -- be reprocessed.
            -- Note that one can look at the number of
            -- rejects here in order to decide whether to
            -- schedule a product. Further discussion of
            -- this  possibility is given  in  the
            -- next section.
                null ;
        end select;
    end loop ;
end COORDINATOR ;
--
    task body STOP_INSPECTION is
    begin
    loop
```

```
            delay  120.00 ;

            INSPECT.TAKE_A_BREAK ;

    end loop;

    end STOP_INSPECTION ;

    --

    task body INSPECT is

    INSP_PASSED    : BOOLEAN ;

    EXAM_TIME : DURATION ;

    START_MANUFACT, STOP_MANUFACT : TIME ;

    DURATION_MANUFACT : DURATION ;

    package DURATION_IO is new FIXED_IO (DURATION) ;

    use DURATION_IO ;

    begin

    -- As mentioned earlier DURATION is a predefined

    -- part of the predefined Ada environment. CLOCK is the

    -- function part of the package CALENDAR and returns

    -- the current TIME.

    START_MANUFACT := CLOCK ;

        INSP_PASSED :=   INSP_RESULT ;

        EXAM_TIME := PROBABILITY (INSPECTION) ;

        loop

                -- The loop below makes sure that the

                -- inspection is started only if there

                -- are items to be inspected.

                -- A buffer task might be used instead (see

                -- the same Exercise 3 at the end of the
```

```
-- chapter).
loop
    select
        accept PRODUCT ;
        exit;
    else
        if MACH2_AVAIL > 0
            then
            MACH2_AVAIL := MACH2_AVAIL - 1 ;
            exit ;
        end if ;
        if MACH3_AVAIL > 0
            then
            MACH3_AVAIL := MACH3_AVAIL - 1 ;
            exit ;
        end if ;
    end select ;
end loop;
delay EXAM_TIME    ;
if INSP_PASSED
    then
    N_OF_FINISHED_PROD := N_OF_FINISHED_PROD + 1;
    else
    N_OF_REJECTS  := N_OF_REJECTS + 1 ;
    -- These two variables can be accessed
    -- by some other tasks, two. For instance,
```

```
                    -- the task COORDINATOR might use them

                    -- to test when to stop scheduling products.

      end if ;

      EXAM_TIME := PROBABILITY (INSPECTION) ;

      INSP_PASSED :=   INSP_RESULT ;

      exit when  N_OF_FINISHED_PROD = 200 ;

      -- Should the inspector take a break ?

      if TAKE_A_BREAK'COUNT > 0

            -- This condition is TRUE when there is a call

            -- waiting.  It  means  it is time to take  a

            -- break.

            then

            accept TAKE_A_BREAK ;

            delay 15 ;

      end if ;

      -- This "if" statement might be replaced

      -- with a select statement, such as the following:

      -- select

      --          accept TAKE_A_BREAK ;

      --               delay 15 ;

      --        else

      --               null;

      -- end select ;

end loop ;

-- Here one might have some abort statements  (to be

-- discussed in the next section)  to terminate some of
```

```
          -- the tasks suspended and waiting to be called.
      STOP_MANUFACT := CLOCK ;

      DURATION_MANUFACT := START_MANUFACT - STOP_MANUFACT ;

      -- Note that the operator "-" is an overloaded

      -- operator, and the context indicates that it is a

      -- function defined in the package CALENDAR.

      PUT (DURATION_MANUFACT, 10, 2) ;

      end INSPECT ;

      begin

      for I in 1 .. 200

          loop


          COORDINATOR.SCHED ;

      end loop ;

      -- Make the attempt to schedule 200 products .

      -- Some more products may be actually scheduled because

      -- a few will be rejected.

  end  PLANT_SCHED ;
```

Figure 10.3 illustrates the working of various tasks of the program PLANT_SCHED. In step 1 the coordinator just found MACH1 available, while MACH2 waits for a product and MACH3 attempts a rendezvous with the IN-SPECTOR. In step 3 each task is running independently.

ABORT STATEMENTS

Ada provides the **abort statement** for the explicit termination of tasks. The statement consists of the reserved word "abort" followed by the names of tasks to be aborted (separated by commas) and a semicolon. For example,

```
    abort TASK1, TASK2 ;
```

Here tasks TASK1 and TASK2 are terminated. But first, any aborted task becomes **abnormal,** which is a kind of pretermination state. A task in an abnormal

FIGURE 10.3   Possible Rendezvous in PLANT_SCHED Program

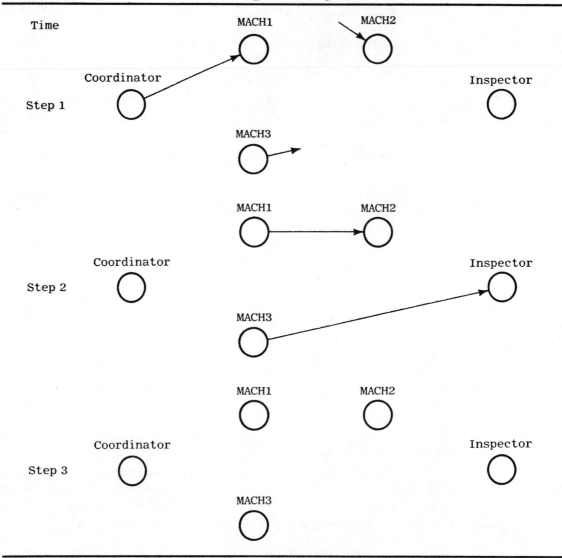

state cannot further participate in a new rendezvous. Any task depending on an abnormal task becomes itself abnormal unless it is already terminated. However, an abnormal task is allowed to complete a rendezvous it started before becoming abnormal.

If a task becomes abnormal while it is suspended or is in the middle of a delay statement, then the abnormal task is completed immediately. Otherwise, the abnormal task is completed as soon as it reaches a **synchronizing point** like an "end" reserved word, another abort statement, the start or the end of an accept statement, a select statement, or an exception handler (to be covered in Chapter 11).

A task is allowed to abort any other task (whose name it knows via visibility rules), including itself. This feature is a powerful one, and the programmer should carefully justify its use.

10.3 SHARED VARIABLES AND THE PRIORITY PRAGMA

SHARED VARIABLES

Generally, one should not have two or more tasks reading and updating the same variable. A variable that is accessible and can be modified by several tasks is called a **shared variable.** It can take new values while some of the tasks are operating on some other (older) values. This situation may happen because tasks are independent and assumed to run in parallel; the only time two tasks can access the same copy is when they are synchronized.

However, every Ada implementation should enforce some additional rules applying to shared variables of scalar or access types only. These rules make the use of scalar or access type shared variables somewhat less unpredictable, because they force on the particular Ada implementation the following discipline: If a task, denoted by T, reads a shared variable between two consecutive synchronization points, say A and B, then no other task is allowed to update the shared variable while T has passed A and has not reached B. In a similar way, if task T changes the value of a shared variable between A and B, then no other task is allowed to either change or read the shared variable while T has passed A and has not reached B.

For instance, in the program PLANT_SCHED the variables N_OF_FINISHED_PROD and N_OF_REJECTS are two shared variables of scalar type. One of these two variables is updated by the task INSPECT. According to the rules for shared variables, no other task can either update or read the variable N_OF_FINISHED_PROD or N_OF_REJECTS while the task INSPECT executes statements between the synchronization point "accept PRODUCT" and the next synchronization point, which may be the same "accept PRODUCT," a new point, such as "accept TAKE_A_BREAK," or the completion of the task. The shared-variables rules ensure, in this case, that the program properly tests for zero rejected products in the task COORDINATOR. Only the updated copy of the variable N_OF_REJECTS will be made available in COORDINATOR, preventing the scheduling of more products than are required.

Note that in the last version of the task LOOKING_FOR_BANKS, presented in Section 10.2, the variables CHANGE_HEAD and CHANGE_BANK_REC are not shared variables, because only task LOOKING_FOR_BANKS can access them. Therefore the updating of the elements of

BANK_FILE cannot be disturbed by other tasks. If these record type variables, however, are made accessible to other tasks (for instance, by declaring them before all task specification parts of GATHER_BANK_STATISTICS), then the rules for scalar and access variables do not apply. In this situation the updating of these variables is even more unpredictable.

Sometimes, though, the use of shared variables is justified. For instance, consider the program POSTING_PROC of Chapter 8. In this program one can make use of several tasks, maybe one task for each day having transactions. Therefore one can proceed to post transactions in parallel. While the posting starts by reading several days in parallel from the TRANS_FILE, the posting ends by writing corresponding transaction numbers in file elements associated with the bank part of the transaction.

Again one can imagine a number of tasks involved in posting transaction numbers for several banks at a time. One may use a variable, however, that may be necessary for every task posting on the BANK_FILE. This variable should contain the up-to-date allocation of the elements of BANK_FILE in order to properly write transactions belonging to certain banks. The use of the SIZE function only would be a mistake, though, because by the time a task is ready to write a new element of the BANK_FILE, the size of the file might be different from the size initially used. An alternative way to treat this problem is to use another task solely responsible for allocating new elements for the BANK_FILE, as shown in the example that follows.

EXAMPLE   For this example we extract the procedure POST_INDIV_BANK of the program POSTING_PROC of Chapter 8, and we rewrite it as a task type. But first, we will present the task OBTAIN.

```
task OBTAIN is

     -- This task returns the position of a newly

     -- allocated file element .

     entry FILE_ELEM (FORM_TR_POS :  out  POSITIVE_COUNT) ;

end OBTAIN ;

--

task body OBTAIN is

DUMMY_BANK_REC : BANK_REC (POSTING_DATA) :=

          ( POSTING_DATA, (1 .. 12 => (0,0,1), 0 ) ;

-- This record is needed for writing a dummy element.
```

```
begin

    accept FILE_ELEM (FORM_TR_POS : out POSITIVE_COUNT)

        do

            if SIZE (BANK_FILE) <= GLOBAL_NO_OF_BANKS

                then

                FORM_TR_POS := GLOBAL_NO_OF_BANKS + 1 ;

                else

                FORM_TR_POS := SIZE (BANK_FILE) + 1 ;

            end if ;

        WRITE (BANK_FILE, DUMMY_BANK_REC, FORM_TR_POS) ;

        -- Write a dummy element  here.

        end ;

end OBTAIN ;
```

Now the POST_INDIV_BANK part of the program POSTING_PROC is rewritten as the task type PARALLEL_POST_INDIV_BANK, making use of the task OBTAIN.

```
task type PARALLEL_POST_INDIV_BANK is

    entry  TRANSACT (FORM_TRANS : TRANS_NUMBER ;

                     FORM_BANK  : STRING (1 .. 20) ;

end PARALLEL_POST_INDIV_BANK ;

--

task body PARALLEL_POST_INDIV_BANK is

BK_POS, TR_POS, SAVE_TR_POS : POSITIVE_COUNT;

BK_FOUND : BOOLEAN ;

ANY_BANK  : STRING (1 .. 20) ;

ANY_TRANS : TRANS_NUMBER ;

ANY_BANK_REC : BANK_REC ;
```

```
ANY_POST_REC : BANK_REC ;

WRK_POST_INFO : POST_INFO ;

begin

        accept TRANSACT (FORM_TRANS : TRANS_NUMBER ;

                         FORM_BANK  : STRING )

            do

            -- Just copy the formal parameters to be used

            -- by the task

            ANY_BANK  := FORM_BANK ;

            ANY_TRANS := FORM_TRANS ;

            end ;

        RETRIEVE (ANY_BANK, BK_POS, BK_FOUND) ;

        if BK_FOUND

then

READ (BANK_FILE, ANY_BANK_REC, BK_POS) ;

if ANY_BANK_REC.FIRST_TRAN = 0

        then

        -- This codition is TRUE when no transactions

        -- are posted for this bank.

        OBTAIN.FILE_ELEM (TR_POS) ;

        -- This statement replaces an "if" statement

        -- setting  the last element of the file.

        ANY_BANK_REC.FIRST_TRAN := TR_POS ;

        ANY_BANK_REC.LAST_TRAN  := TR_POS ;

        ANY_BANK_REC.LAST_POS   := 1 ;

        WRK_POST_INFO  :=  ( ANY_TRANS,
```

```
                                2  ..  12  => (1,1,1));

     ANY_POST_REC :=

          (POSTING_DATA, WRK_POST_INFO, O) ;

else

     if ANY_BANK_REC.LAST_POS = 12

          then

          -- A full line of posting data is given here.

          -- The statement

          -- TR_POS := SIZE (BANK_FILE) + 1 ;

          -- is replaced by the following statements.

          OBTAIN.FILE_ELEM (TR_POS) ;

          READ (BANK_FILE, ANY_POST_REC,

                    ANY_BANK_REC.LAST_TRAN) ;

          ANY_POST_REC.NXT_PST_LINE := TR_POS ;

          WRITE (BANK_FILE, ANY_POST_REC,

                    ANY_BANK_REC.LAST_TRAN) ;

          ANY_BANK_REC.LAST_TRAN  := TR_POS ;

          ANY_BANK_REC.LAST_POS   := 1 ;

          WRK_POST_INFO  :=  ( ANY_TRANS,

                         2  ..  12  => (1,1,1));

          ANY_POST_REC :=

               (POSTING_DATA, WRK_POST_INFO, O) ;

     else

          -- There is room here.

          TR_POS := ANY_BANK_REC.LAST_TRAN ;

          READ (BANK_FILE, ANY_POST_REC,
```

```
                               ANY_BANK_REC.LAST_TRAN) ;

                  ANY_BANK_REC.LAST_POS :=

                          ANY_BANK_REC.LAST_POS + 1 ;

                  ANY_POST_REC.POSTING_LINE (ANY_BANK_REC.LAST_POS)

                          :=   ANY_TRANS ;

           end if ;

       end if ;

       WRITE (BANK_FILE, ANY_BANK_REC, BK_POS) ;

       WRITE (BANK_FILE, ANY_POST_REC, TR_POS) ;

       else

       PUT (" Bank not found : ");

       PUT (ANY_BANK) ;

   end if ;
end PARALLEL_POST_INDIV_BANK ;
```

PROGRAM USING SHARED VARIABLES

In the program that follows we show how you can actually use task types and access types pointing at task objects. This program presents a modification of the POSTING_PROC that allows the user to generate as many posting tasks as there are days carrying transactions.

SEVERAL_POSTING_PROC Program

```
with TEXT_IO ; use TEXT_IO ;

with TRANSACTION_RESOURCES ; use TRANSACTION_RESOURCES ;

with BANK_RESOURCES ; use BANK_RESOURCES ;

-- These packages, defined in Chapter 8, are

-- assumed to be compiled and available.

procedure SEVERAL_POSTING_PROC is

package INT_IO is new INTEGER_IO (INTEGER) ;
```

```
        use INT_IO ;

        CURR_TRANS_REC_1, CURR_TRANS_REC_OTHER : TRANS_REC ;

        YY_AND_MM : STRING (1 .. 4) ;

        MM_ONLY   : STRING (1 .. 2) ;

        EXT_NAME  : STRING (1 .. 8)

        WORK_POSITIVE  : NATURAL ;

        CURR_TRANS_HEADER : TRANS_HEADER ;

        CURR_TRANS_INDEX  : POSITIVE_INDEX ;

        NO_OF_DAILY_JOBS : NATURAL ;


        -- There are no changes in declarations  up to this point.
        procedure POST_BNK_PAR (FORM_TRANS_REC : TRANS_REC ;

                         FORM_DAY : NATURAL) is

        LOCAL_FULL_TRANS_NO : TRANS_NUMBER ;

        begin
-- The sequence of statements of the procedure POST_BNK part
-- of POSTING_PROC should be inserted here
end POST_BNK ;
--

task type DAY_POSTING is
        -- This task type will be used to generate task objects ,
        -- one per day, and will be activated in order to
        -- read the daily transactions.
        entry GET_THIS_DAY (I : INTEGER range 1 .. 31) ;
end DAY_POSTING ;
--

type DAY_POST_PTR is access DAY_POSTING ;
```

```
-- This is an access type pointing at a task of
-- type DAY_POSTING.
type MONTHLY_COLLECTION_OF_JOBS is array (1 .. 31) of
          DAY_POST_PTR ;
-- This type is an array type whose elements are pointers
-- to tasks.
ACT_MONTHLY_JOBS : MONTHLY_COOLECTION_OF_JOBS ;
--

task body DAY_POSTING is
--

-- This task body is a liberal modification of the inner-most
-- loop of the sequence of  statements of the POSTING_PROC.
-- First, a day ID is saved in THIS_DAY. Next, all transactions
-- corresponding to THIS_DAY are read, and the relevant
-- information is passed  for processing by the procedure
-- POST_BNK_PAR. Actually, a better way (perhaps avoiding a
-- a large queue of  suspended tasks) to  write the program
-- is to provide a buffer task.
THIS_DAY_TRANS_HEADER : TRANS_HEADER ;
THIS_DAY_TRANS-INDEX  : POSITIVE_INDEX ;
THIS_DAY : INTEGER range 1 .. 31 ;
DAILY_TRANS_REC : TRANS_REC ;
begin
      accept GET_THIS_DAY (I : INTEGER range 1 .. 31)
           do
              -- Make a record of this  day.
```

```
        THIS_DAY := I ;

end GET_THIS_DAY ;

        THIS_DAY_TRANS_HEADER :=

            CURR_TRANS_REC_1.HEADER_LINE.TRANS_STATUS

                (THIS_DAY) ;

        THIS_DAY_TRANS_INDEX  :=

                THIS_DAY_TRANS_HEADER.FIRST_TRANS ;

        if THIS_DAY_TRANS_INDEX /= 1

            then

            READ (TRANS_FILE, DAILY_TRANS_REC ,

                    THIS_DAY_TRANS_INDEX) ;

            -- The first transaction of the day was

            -- just read.

            while DAILY_TRANS_REC.REG_LINE.TRAN_NEXT  /= 0

                loop

                -- The procedure POST_BNK_PAR is

                -- invoked here.

                POST_BNK_PAR (DAILY_TRANS_REC, THIS_DAY) ;

                THIS_DAY_TRANS_INDEX :=

                    DAILY_TRANS_REC.REG_LINE.TRAN_NEXT ;

                READ (TRANS_FILE, DAILY_TRANS_REC ,

                    THIS_DAY_TRANS_INDEX) ;

            end loop ;

            -- The next  call applies to the last transaction

            -- only.

            POST_BNK_PAR (DAILY_TRANS_REC, THIS_DAY) ;
```

```
                    end if;

             -- The task is completed here.

     end DAY_POSTING ;

     -- The specification and body of the task

     -- PARALLEL_POST_INDIV_BANK should be placed here as well

     -- as some additional task specifications and bodies

     -- necessary for buffer management (see Exercise 5

     -- at the end of the chapter).

     begin

     GET (YY_AND_MM) ;

     MM_ONLY := YY_AND_MM (3 .. 4) ;

     if YY_AND_MM < "8601" or YY_AND_MM > "8612"

          then

            PUT (" Bad date ") ;

          else

          EXT_NAME := "FY" & YY_AND_MM & ".DAT" ;

          if not TRANS_IO.IS_OPEN (TRANS_FILE)

               then

               TRANS_IO.OPEN (FILE => TRANS_FILE,

                       MODE => INOUT_FILE,

                       NAME => EXT_NAME,

                       FORM => "") ;

               READ (TRANS_FILE, CURR_TRANS_REC_1, 1) ;

          end if ;

          NO_OF_DAILY_JOBS := 0 ;

          for I in 1 .. 31
```

```
loop

CURR_TRANS_HEADER :=

        CURR_TRANS_REC_1.HEADER_LINE.TRANS_STATUS (I) ;

CURR_TRANS_INDEX   := CURR_TRANS_HEADER.FIRST_TRANS ;

if CURR_TRANS_INDEX /= 1

        then

            -- The test is true if there are transactions

            -- for this day. If there are, a corresponding task

            -- is activated next.

            ACT_MONTHLY_JOBS (I) := new DAY_POSTING ;

            NO_OF_DAILY_JOBS := NO_OF_DAILY_JOBS + 1 ;

            -- While the whole program is not written here ,

            -- one may use the count of the number of active

            -- tasks in order to sense when all transactions

            -- have been posted.

        end if;

    end loop ;

-- The close statements below should be executed only after all

-- transactions have been posted.

-- TRANS_IO.CLOSE (TRANS_FILE) ;

-- BANK_IO.CLOSE (BANK_FILE) ;

end SEVERAL_POSTING_PROC ;
```

PRIORITY PRAGMA

To indicate the degree of urgency of an Ada task, one may use the pragma
PRIORITY. Its form is

```
pragma PRIORITY (static_expression) ;
```

A PRIORITY pragma may appear only once in a task specification. The evaluation of the static_expression should return an integer value, which should be compatible with the range of the subtype PRIORITY of the predefined package SYSTEM listed in Appendix C. The higher the value, the more urgent the corresponding task is.

The degree of urgency implied by the PRIORITY of a task is supposed to help a particular implementation to decide which tasks should execute if the resources available cannot support all the active tasks. That is, no implementation can allow the execution of a task of lower priority and deny at the same time the execution of a task of higher priority (assuming that the two tasks require the same resources).

EXERCISES FOR CHAPTER 10

1. Modify the program GATHER_BANK_STATISTICS so that it will accept calls only after checking that at least one of the files FILE_1 or FILE_2 is open. (The parts dealing with an end-of-file value like "12345678901234567890" should be dropped.)

2. Rewrite the program GATHER_BANK_STATISTICS by using task attributes and the package CALENDAR in order to derive information about the average waiting time for calls issued by CHECK_FILE_1 and CHECK_FILE_2.

3. The program PLANT_SCHED of Section 10.2 uses some loops at the beginning of the sequence-of-statements part for tasks MACH1, MACH2, MACH3, and INSPECT. Their role is to make sure that each task continues its independent useful work even if no immediate rendezvous is possible. An alternative (and probably better) way to handle this situation is to have a buffer task between

FIGURE 10.4   Illustration for Exercise 3

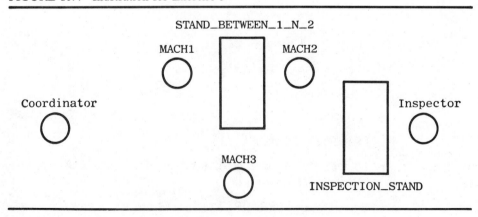

MACH1 and MACH2 (call it STAND_BETWEEN_1_N_2) and another one between (MACH2 or MACH3) and INSPECT (call it INSPECTION_STAND). That is, whenever MACH1 finishes its operation, it should call an entry of STAND_BETWEEN_1_N_2 and make a record of the additional product available for processing by MACH2 (perhaps just a counter should be incremented). In turn, MACH2 should be able to independently establish a rendezvous with STAND_BETWEEN_1_N_2 and decide whether to start processing another product (if it is available). Similar considerations apply to INSPECTION_ STAND. The relationships of the new tasks with the other ones is illustrated in Figure 10.4.

4. Suppose that the 200 products for the manufacturing problem presented in Section 10.2 are animated, and they represent independent tasks that are interested in being processed. That is, these tasks should call either MACH1 and MACH2 and INSPECT or MACH3 and INSPECT. Of course, the calls must be repeated if the product fails inspection. Rewrite the program PLANT_SCHED by incorporating this new approach and implementing a new constraint: No product should issue a call if more than three other waiting calls precede it. (Perhaps product task types and access types pointing to objects of type product should be used.)

5. Incorporate the task OBTAIN and the task DAY_POSTING of Section 10.3 in a new version of the program SEVERAL_POSTING_PROC. Make any other necessary modifications.

CHAPTER ELEVEN

EXCEPTIONS

11.1 DECLARING AND RAISING EXCEPTIONS

Ada provides facilities for dealing with either errors or selected special events during program execution through the use of **exceptions.** When an error or a selected special event occurs, the normal sequential execution of the statements is abandoned, and the error or the event is signaled. This process is called **raising an exception.** The action taken when an exception is raised is called **handling the exception,** and it can be controlled by the programmer through the declaration of exceptions and exception handler sections of Ada code. Exceptions can be raised unexpectedly when an unforeseen error or situation occurs. Exceptions can be raised in a less unpredictable manner, too, during the execution of raise statements, as will be shown later in this section.

PREDEFINED AND USER-DEFINED EXCEPTIONS

Certain exceptions are **predefined** in Ada, and they are associated with situations defining many of the common errors occurring in programs. The predefined exceptions are as follows:

Error	Description
CONSTRAINT_ERROR	This exception is raised if range, index, or discriminant constraints are violated (including the attempt to use a record com-

	ponent unavailable for the current discriminant value). It is also raised if an attempt is made to use a selected component, an indexed component, a slice, or an attribute of an object that can be pointed at by an access value, when in fact the access value is null.
NUMERIC_ERROR	This exception is raised when the execution of a predefined numeric operation cannot provide a correct result. The actual meaning of this exception is dependent on the particular Ada implementation and may include integer overflow, division by zero, or floating-point overflow. It is also raised if a conversion results in an out-of-range value.
PROGRAM_ERROR	This exception is raised when a subprogram is called, a task is activated, or a generic instantiation is elaborated, and these actions are attempted before the corresponding bodies are elaborated. This exception may also be raised if a function reaches the "end" reserved word (instead of a "return") or if all alternatives are found closed during the execution of a selective wait statement and there is no "else" alternative. This exception may cover as well some situations whose detection is optional by a particular Ada implementation. For instance, this exception may be raised if a program assumes a certain order of some actions, when in fact Ada warns against relying on any particular order (the matching of formal with actual parameters is an example).
STORAGE_ERROR	This exception is raised whenever run-time storage is not sufficient. Storage may be allocated while the program is running when declarative items are elaborated, when a task is activated, or when an object is created by an allocator.
TASKING_ERROR	This exception is raised when certain events occur during intertask communications. Details and examples are given in Section 11.3.

These predefined exceptions are all listed in the package STANDARD given in Appendix C.

A package of predefined IO_EXCEPTIONS is also associated with the Ada I/O packages of Appendix C, and its use will be discussed in Section 11.2.

Besides predefined exceptions, there are **user-defined exceptions,** which must be declared. The exception declarations have the form

```
list_of_exception_names : exception ;
```

For instance, we might have

```
ALARM_1 : exception ;
EMPTY_FILE, UNEXPECTED_END_OF_FILE : exception ;
```

Once declared, user-defined exceptions (and predefined exceptions, too) can be raised when certain chosen conditions occur.

EXCEPTION HANDLERS

As mentioned earlier, the raising of an exception results in the transfer of control to an **exception handler.** The provision of an exception handler is optional, however; and if it is present, it is placed at the end of a block statement or at the end of the body of a subprogram, package, or task unit.

The programs written in the previous chapters had no exception handlers. As a consequence, the raising of any of the predefined exceptions means that program execution is abandoned and the exceptions are propagated to the calling environment. That is, if the exception is raised within, say, a procedure or a function, then if there is no exception handler within the respective subprogram, the exception will be raised next in the calling subprogram, and so on, until the main program is reached or a corresponding exception handler is encountered. If the main program is reached and no corresponding exception handler is found, the main program is terminated and an explanatory message is listed. This process was the way the programs of previous chapters handled exceptions whenever any of the predefined exceptions occurred.

The specification of exception handlers is quite similar to case statements and has the form

```
when

    exception_names => sequence_of_statements

    -- One or more choices like the one above are

    -- given here.

    -- An others optional choice may be given.
```

The exception handlers are preceded by the reserved word "exception." After exception handlers and the associated sequence of statements, one encounters the reserved word "end," which signals the end of the block statement, subprogram, task, or package containing the exception handler.

For instance, we can have (assuming we have the previously given exception declarations) the following exception handler:

```
exception

    when   NUMERIC_ERROR => PUT (" Bad computation ") ;

    when   ALARM_1        => PUT (" Call police ") ;

    when   others         => PUT (" Unexpected error ") ;

end ;
```

As with the case statement, the choice "others" is allowed only as the last exception handler, and it covers any other exception (predefined or otherwise) not mentioned in previous exception handlers.

RAISE STATEMENT

The **raise statement,** which can be used to transfer control to the exception handler, has the form

```
raise exception_name ;
```

If the raise statement happens to be within an exception handler it may have the following form, under certain conditions:

```
raise;
```

For instance, we can have, assuming the same exception declarations,

```
raise ALARM_1 ;
```

A raise statement followed by an exception_name will raise the named exception. If there is a corresponding exception handler, then it will be given control. Otherwise, the exception will be propagated.

The second option of the raise statement raises again the exception that made the execution of the raise statement possible in the first place.

PROGRAM USING EXCEPTION HANDLERS

Here we present an example of exception handling in a modification of the program DAY_CONVERSION of Section 1.4. The program will read several lines, each line containing a Julian day and the weekday (MON through SUN)

on which the first of January falls. For each line it will display the weekday corresponding to the Julian day. The last line is signaled by a Julian day of 0.

EXC_DAY_CONVERSION Program

```
with TEXT_IO; use TEXT_IO;

procedure EXC_DAY_CONVERSION is

     type DAY is (MON,TUE,WED,THU,FRI,SAT,SUN) ;

     package INT_IO is new INTEGER_IO(INTEGER);

     use INT_IO;

     package DAY_IO is new ENUMERATION_IO(DAY);

     use DAY_IO;

     type JULIAN is range 1..366;

     JULIAN_DAY : JULIAN ;

     CURRENT_DAY,FIRST_JAN_DAY: DAY;

     CURRENT_DAY_POS : INTEGER;

     -- Next two declarations are new.

     IN_DAY     : NATURAL ;

     BAD_IN_DAY      : EXCEPTION ;

     -- This exception will be raised if the IN_DAY exceeds

     -- the value 366.

begin

     GET(IN_DAY,3);

     -- An exception will be raised if  the

     -- IN_DAY is negative.

     while IN_DAY /= 0

          loop

          if IN_DAY > 366
```

```
                    then

                    -- This statement is an example of a

                    -- "raise" statement.

                    raise BAD_IN_DAY ;

          else

                    -- ** Statements identical to DAY_CONVERSION start

                    -- here.

                    JULIAN_DAY := IN_DAY ;

                    -- An exception CONSTRAINT_ERROR would be raised

                    -- if IN_DAY is outside the range 0 .. 366.

                    GET(FIRST_JAN_DAY);

                    CURRENT_DAY_POS :=   JULIAN_DAY mod 7   +

                             DAY'POS(FIRST_JAN_DAY) ;

                    if CURRENT_DAY_POS > 7

                        then

                        CURRENT_DAY_POS := CURRENT_DAY_POS - 7;

                    end if;

                    CURRENT_DAY := DAY'VAL(CURRENT_DAY_POS);

                    -- An exception will be raised (namely a

                    -- CONSTRAINT_ERROR) if CURRENT_DAY_POS

                    -- is outside the range 1 .. 7 (this error is

                    -- not possible though for this statement).

                    NEW_LINE;

                    PUT(" This julian day falls on a ");

                    PUT(CURRENT_DAY);

                    if CURRENT_DAY not in Mon .. Fri
```

```
                    then

                    PUT("  is a weekend");

                    else

                    PUT(" is a working day ");

              end if;

                    -- **  Statements identical to DAY_CONVERSION

                    -- end here.


              end if ;

              SKIP_LINE;

              GET(IN_DAY,3);

        end loop;

        exception

              when  NUMERIC_ERROR  :  CONSTRAINT_ERROR

                                        => PUT (" Numeric error  or" );

                                        => PUT (" Constraint error ") ;

              when BAD_IN_DAY         => PUT (" Bad julian day") ;

              when others             =>

                        -- Maybe  some  of  the input  data  was  not

                        -- valid.

                        PUT (" Other error " );

end EXC_DAY_CONVERSION;
```

RAISING EXCEPTIONS

Note that the same exception can be raised in different places of the unit. For instance, in the previous program we noted at least two places where the exception CONSTRAINT_ERROR might be raised. So for this program one may run the risk of guessing exactly where the exception was raised. This situation may be repaired by enclosing sensitive statements in subprograms or block statements, as shown in the program of the next section.

Exceptions may be raised either during the execution of statements (as in the previous program) or during the elaboration of declarations. If an exception is raised during the elaboration of the declarative part of a package body, block, or subprogram or during the elaboration of a package declaration, then the elaboration is abandoned and the same exception is immediately raised again (propagated), as follows:

- The exception is raised at the point of call for a subprogram (unless the subprogram is a main program, in which case the main program is abandoned).
- The exception is raised after the block statement when a block statement is involved.
- If the package body or package declaration is a declarative item, then the exception is raised in the outer declarative part.
- If the package body is that of a subunit, then the exception is raised at the place of the corresponding body stub.
- If the package body or package declaration is a library unit, then the execution of the main program is abandoned.

If an exception is raised during the elaboration of a task body, the elaboration is abandoned and the task becomes completed. At the point of activation of the task, the exception TASKING_ERROR is raised. If the exception is raised during the elaboration of a task declaration, then the exception is propagated to the outer declarative part. Further details about the handling of exceptions by tasks during the execution of statements will be presented in Section 11.3.

SUPPRESSING CHECKS

As discussed at the beginning of the section, Ada has predefined exceptions (like CONSTRAINT_ERROR) that cover a variety of possible events. Sometimes, one may wish to inhibit the raising of a particular exception for some particular events or some particular types within a unit. The omission of certain run-time checks is allowed in Ada with the help of the pragma SUPPRESS. Its form is

```
pragma SUPPRESS (check_name );
```

If, in addition, one desires to apply the pragma only to a particular object, type, subprogram, and so on, the form is

```
pragma SUPPRESS (check_name, ON => name );
```

Some of the check_names corresponding to the exception CONSTRAINT_ERROR are as follows:

Name	Description
ACCESS_CHECK	Applies to selected components, indexed components, slices, or attributes of an object pointed at by an access value
DISCRIMINANT_CHECK	Applies to discriminant values; determines whether the value supplied is consistent with the constraint type or whether it exists for the current given record object
INDEX_CHECK	Applies to bounds of array values and to index values of particular components
LENGTH_CHECK	Applies to components that need matching (for instance, during array assignments)
RANGE_CHECK	Applies to values that need checking of range constraints, to subtypes that are elaborated, to index or discriminant values that need checking of appartenence to a given subtype, and so forth

Some of the name_checks corresponding to the predefined exception NUMERIC_ERROR are as follows:

Name	Description
DIVISION_CHECK	Applies when the second operand in /, rem, or mod is zero
OVERFLOW_CHECK	Applies when the result of a numeric operation overflows

The pragma SUPPRESS, if used, should be one of the first lines of a declarative part or a package specification. One should also be aware that this pragma only gives the compiler the permission to omit a given check. This permission may or may not be taken up by the compiler. In fact, the compiler may choose not to implement this pragma for certain checks deemed too expensive.

One example of this pragma is

```
pragma SUPPRESS (RANGE_CHECK) ;
```

Here the compiler is given the permission to omit the RANGE_CHECK for every object. Another example is

```
pragma SUPPRESS (ACCESS_CHECK, ON => DATE) ;
```

Here the compiler is given the permission to omit the ACCESS_CHECK for all objects of type DATE.

11.2 IO_EXCEPTIONS

The exceptions defined for the packages SEQUENTIAL_IO, DIRECT_IO, and TEXT_IO are placed in the package IO_EXCEPTIONS. The exceptions defined in IO_EXCEPTIONS, together with a brief description of these exceptions, follows.

Exception	Description
`STATUS_ERROR: exception;`	This exception is raised if the file is not open and an attempt is made to use functions like MODE, FORM, and NAME or procedures like READ, WRITE, RESET, and DELETE. It is also raised if the file is open and an attempt is made to reopen it.
`MODE_ERROR: exception ;`	This exception is raised when the program is reading from a file whose current mode is OUT_FILE; when the program is trying to detect the end-of-file condition for an OUT_FILE; or when the program is trying to write to a file whose current mode is IN_FILE. In addition, if the package TEXT_IO is in use, then this exception is raised for an OUT_FILE whenever the following subprograms are invoked: SET_INPUT, SKIP_LINE, END_OF_LINE, SKIP_PAGE, and END_OF_PAGE. This exception is also raised if the mode is IN_FILE and any of the following subprograms are called: SET_OUTPUT, SET_LINE_LENGTH, SET_PAGE_LENGTH, LINE_LENGTH, PAGE_LENGTH, NEW_LINE, and NEW_PAGE.

`NAME_ERROR: exception ;`

This exception is raised if the string given as the actual parameter to a CREATE or an OPEN procedure fails to establish a connection with an external file. For instance, the string may not be acceptable because of special characters, or the string in an OPEN statement may not correspond to any existing external file.

`USE_ERROR: exception ;`

This exception is raised when certain events occur that are incompatible with some characteristics of an external file. For instance, it may be raised when the program is trying to CREATE a file and at the same time is choosing a mode of IN_FILE, and the file resides on a device (like printers) that can only support the mode OUT_FILE. Or it may be raised when the program uses a FORM actual parameter incompatible with the one used when the file was created.

`DEVICE_ERROR: exception;`

This exception is raised when certain hardware errors are detected during an input/output operation. *Note:* Certain Ada implementations may not use this exception; instead, hardware errors are handled by some other exceptions, like USE_ERROR.

`END_ERROR: exception ;`

This exception is raised when an attempt is made to read past the end of a file.

`DATA_ERROR: exception ;`

This exception is raised when the procedure READ is invoked and the element that is read is not of the proper type. It is also raised when the procedure GET of the package TEXT_IO is invoked and the input element does not have the expected format or is outside the prescribed range.

`LAYOUT_ERROR: exception;`

This exception is raised by subprograms of TEXT_IO if COL, LINE, or PAGE return values exceeding COUNT-LAST; if too many characters are placed in a string used as the actual argument for a PUT; or if an attempt is made to set the column or the lines per page to values exceeding some preset limits.

The IO_EXCEPTIONS package is visible for each of the input/output packages. All its exceptions appear in renaming declarations of the following kind (see also Appendix C):

```
For SEQUENTIAL_IO package :
STATUS_ERROR : exception renames
   IO_EXCEPTIONS.STATUS_ERROR ;
```

This format allows one to distinguish exceptions in different input/output packages, because one can refer to SEQUENTIAL_IO.NAME_ERROR or DIRECT_IO.NAME_ERROR without the use of an extra qualifier.

Now we will rewrite the program MERGE_PROC_GRADES of Chapter 8 in order to illustrate the use of IO_EXCEPTIONS and their propagation. There is some redundancy in the use of exceptions in the procedures READ_1 and READ_2, for instance, but this situation is addressed in Exercise 1 at the end of the chapter. Also, the redundancy helps to preserve some of the original program design, which facilitates understanding of the new version.

EXCEP_MERGE_PROC_GRADES Program

```
with TEXT_IO; use TEXT_IO;

with SEQUENTIAL_IO ;

procedure EXCEP_MERGE_PROC_GRADES is
```

```
Package INT_IO is new INTEGER_IO(INTEGER);

use INT_IO;

type T_PAIR is

    record

        SUBJ_MAT : STRING (1 .. 5 );

        SCORE    : NATURAL ;

    end record;

CURR_PAIR : T_PAIR;

type SEMESTER_TESTS  is array (1 .. 25) of T_PAIR;

type BIG_REC is

    record

        BIG_ST_ID : STRING (1 .. 10 );

        NO_TESTS  : NATURAL ;

        ST_TESTS  : SEMESTER_TESTS ;

    end record ;

        -- The identifiers used so far are identical to those

        -- of SEQ_PROC_GRADES and have the same meaning.

package STUD_IO is new SEQUENTIAL_IO  (BIG_REC) ;

use STUD_IO;

CURR_REC_1_IN, CURR_REC_2_IN, CURR_REC_OUT: STUD_IO.BIG_REC ;

STUD_IN_1, STUD_IN_2, STUD_OUT_FILE : STUD_IO.FILE_TYPE ;

--

procedure READ_1 is

begin

    READ (FILE => STUD_IN_1 ,

          ITEM => CURR_REC_1_IN) ;
```

```
exception

    when STUD_IO.STATUS_ERROR =>

                    -- Maybe the file was not open.

                    PUT (" Status error reading file " &

                        "STUDENT-FILE-1-IN.DAT" );

                raise ;

                        -- The same STATUS_ERROR is

                        -- raised again. It will be propagated

                        -- up to the calling subprogram. Note that

                        -- if    an exception   is   declared   locally

                        -- (within this procedure, for instance)

                        -- it is not visible, and therefore it

                        -- cannot   be   referred   to   outside   the

                        -- procedure.

    when STUD_IO.MODE_ERROR   =>

                    -- Maybe the mode is wrong

                    -- if the file was open as OUT_FILE.

                    PUT (" Mode error reading file " &

                        "STUDENT_FILE_1_IN.DAT" );

                raise ;

                        -- The same MODE_ERROR is

                        -- raised again. It will be propagated

                        -- up to the calling subprogram.

    when STUD_IO.DEVICE_ERROR   =>

                    -- This error is a hardware malfunction.

                    PUT (" Device error reading file " &
```

```
                    "STUDENT-FILE-1-IN.DAT" );

           raise ;

-- NAME_ERROR is not a possible exception here because

-- there is no NAME parameter for the READ procedure.

-- USE_ERROR  is also an unlikely exception here, however

-- certain implementation might raise this exception

-- when a hardware failure of some kind occurs.

when STUD_IO.END_ERROR     =>

                    -- Maybe an attempt is made to

                    -- read past the end of file .

              PUT (" End error reading file " &

                    "STUDENT-FILE-1-IN.DAT" );

              raise ;

when STUD_IO.DATA_ERROR    =>

                    -- Maybe the element read

                    -- is not (or cannot be interpreted to be )

                    -- of type BIG_REC .

              PUT (" Data error reading file " &

                    "STUDENT-FILE-1-IN.DAT" );

              raise ;

when others        =>

                    -- Anything else goes here

              PUT (" Unusual  kind of error reading file "

                    & "STUDENT-FILE-1-IN.DAT" );

              raise;

end READ_1 ;
```

```
        --

procedure READ_2 is

begin

        READ (FILE => STUD_IN_2 ,

            ITEM => CURR_REC_2_IN) ;

        exception

            -- The exceptions for this procedure mirror the

            -- ones for READ_1 .

            when STUD_IO.STATUS_ERROR =>

                    PUT (" Status error reading file " &

                        "STUDENT-FILE-2-IN.DAT" );

                    raise ;

            when STUD_IO.MODE_ERROR   =>

                        PUT (" Mode error reading file " &

                        "STUDENT-FILE-2-IN.DAT" );

                    raise ;

            when STUD_IO.END_ERROR     =>

                    PUT (" End error reading file " &

                        "STUDENT-FILE-2-IN.DAT" );

                    raise ;

            when STUD_IO.DATA_ERROR    =>

                    PUT (" Data error reading file " &

                        "STUDENT-FILE-1-IN.DAT" );

                    raise ;

            when others        =>

                    PUT (" Unusual  kind of error reading file "
```

```
                            & "STUDENT-FILE-2-IN.DAT" );

                    raise;

end READ_2 ;

--

procedure WRITE_OUT is
 begin
        WRITE (FILE => STUD_OUT_FILE,

                ITEM => CURR_REC_OUT) ;

        exception

            when STUD_IO.STATUS_ERROR =>

                        -- Maybe the file was not open.

                    PUT (" Status error writing file " &

                        "STUD-MERGED-FILE.DAT" ) ;

                    raise ;

                        -- The same STATUS_ERROR is

                        -- raised again. It will be propagated

                        -- up to the calling subprogram.

            when STUD_IO.MODE_ERROR   =>

                        -- Maybe the mode is wrong

                        -- if the file was opened as IN_FILE

                    PUT (" Mode error writing file " &

                        "STUD-MERGED-FILE.DAT" ) ;

                    raise ;

                        -- The same MODE_ERROR is

                        -- raised again. It will be propagated

                        -- up to the calling subprogram.
```

```
            -- NAME_ERROR is not a possible exception here because
            -- there is no NAME parameter for the WRITE procedure.
            -- USE_ERROR  is  also  an  unlikely  exception  here.
            -- However, certain implementation might raise this
            -- exception when a hardware failure of some kind occurs.
            -- END_ERROR is not a possible error here.
        when STUD_IO.DATA_ERROR   =>
                    -- Maybe the element written
                    -- is not (or cannot be interpreted to be )
                    -- of type BIG_REC.
                PUT (" Data error writing file " &
                    "STUD-MERGED-FILE.DAT" ) ;
            raise ;
        when others        =>
                    -- Anything else goes here.
                PUT (" Unusual  kind of error writing file "
                    "STUD-MERGED-FILE.DAT" ) ;
            raise;
    end WRITE_OUT ;
    --
    procedure COPY_1 is
    begin
        while not STUD_IO.END_OF_FILE (STUD_IN_1)
            loop
            READ_1 ;
            CURR_REC_OUT := CURR_REC_1_IN ;
```

```
        WRITE_OUT ;

    end loop ;

    PUT (" First input file was last processed ") ;

    -- One may place an exception handler here for those

    -- exceptions that are propagated (or raised again)

    -- from READ_1 or WRITE_OUT.

end COPY_1 ;
--

  procedure COPY_2 is

  begin

      while not STUD_IO.END_OF_FILE (STUD_IN_2)

          loop

          READ_2 ;

          CURR_REC_OUT := CURR_REC_2_IN ;

          WRITE_OUT ;

      end loop ;

      PUT (" Second input file was last processed ") ;

      -- An exception handler might be placed here (as in COPY_1 )

  end COPY_2 ;
--

  procedure CLOSE_IT is

  begin

      if STUD_IO.IS_OPEN (STUD_IN_1 )

          then

          STUD_IO.CLOSE (STUD_IN_1) ;

      end if ;
```

```
        if STUD_IO.IS_OPEN (STUD_IN_2

            then

            STUD_IO.CLOSE (STUD_IN_2) ;

        end if ;

        if STUD_IO.IS_OPEN (STUD_OUT_FILE )

            then

            STUD_IO.CLOSE (STUD_OUT_FILE) ;

        end if ;

    end CLOSE_IT;

    --

    begin

        -- The block statement is useful because it allows one to

        -- identify the statement causing the exception  (otherwise,

        -- one does not know which of the OPEN or CREATE

        -- statements was at fault).

        begin

        STUD_IO.OPEN  (FILE => STUD_IN_1,

                MODE => IN_FILE ,

                NAME => "STUDENT_FILE_1_IN.DAT" ,

                FORM => "") ;

                            -- Default   file  characteristics   are

                            -- used.

        exception

            when STUD_IO.STATUS_ERROR =>

                            -- Maybe the file is already open.

                        PUT (" Status error opening file " &
```

```
                    "STUDENT-FILE-1-IN.DAT" );

          raise ;

                    -- The same STATUS_ERROR is

                    -- raised again. It will be propagated

                    -- further (actually the program will

                    -- stop its execution and the control

                    -- will be passed to the environment.

                    -- MODE_ERROR is an unlikely error here.
     when STUD_IO.NAME_ERROR =>

                    -- Maybe the external  file does not

                    -- exist, or the string is unacceptable

          PUT (" Name error opening file " &

                    "STUDENT-FILE-1-IN.DAT" );

          raise ;

     when STUD_IO.USE_ERROR  =>

                    -- Maybe the form actual parameter

                    -- is not proper, or some other kind of

                    -- incompatibility occurs.

          PUT (" Use error opening file " &

                    "STUDENT-FILE-1-IN.DAT" );

          raise ;

          -- END_ERROR is an unlikely error when

          -- opening a file. DATA_ERROR is not a possible

          -- error.

     when others      =>

          -- Anything else goes here.
```

```
                          PUT (" Unusual  kind of error opening file "
                               & "STUDENT-FILE-1-IN.DAT" );
                      raise;

     end;
     begin
     STUD_IO.OPEN  (FILE => STUD_IN_2,
            MODE => IN_FILE ,
            NAME => "STUDENT_FILE_2_IN.DAT" ,
            FORM => "") ;
     exception
         -- These exceptions are similar to the ones for
         -- STUD_IN_1 file.
         when STUD_IO.STATUS_ERROR =>
                 PUT (" Status error opening file " &
                      "STUDENT-FILE-2-IN.DAT" );
                 raise ;
         when STUD_IO.NAME_ERROR =>
                 PUT (" Name error opening file " &
                      "STUDENT-FILE-2-IN.DAT" );
                 raise ;
         when STUD_IO.USE_ERROR  =>
                 PUT (" Use error opening file " &
                      "STUDENT-FILE-2-IN.DAT" );
                 raise ;
         when others        =>
                 PUT (" Unusual  kind of error opening file "
```

```
                    & "STUDENT-FILE-2-IN.DAT" );

              raise;

end;

begin

STUD_IO.CREATE (FILE => STUD_OUT_FILE,

          MODE => OUT_FILE ,

          NAME => "STUD-MERGED-FILE.DAT" ,

          FORM => "") ;

                    -- Create the merged file.

exception

      when STUD_IO.STATUS_ERROR =>

                    -- Maybe the file is already open.

                  PUT (" Status error creating the file " &

                      "STUD-MERGED-FILE.DAT" );

              raise ;

      when STUD_IO.MODE_ERROR   =>

                    -- An error occurs if the file is created

                    -- and the  mode is IN_FILE.

                  PUT (" Mode error creating the file " &

                      "STUD-MERGED-FILE.DAT" );

              raise ;

      when STUD_IO.NAME_ERROR =>

                    -- Maybe the external  file name

                    -- has unacceptable characters.

                  PUT (" Name error creating the file " &

                      "STUD-MERGED-FILE.DAT" );
```

```
                    raise ;
            when STUD_IO.USE_ERROR  =>  --

                        -- Maybe the FORM actual parameter

                        -- is not proper, or some other kind of

                        -- incompatibility occurs.

                PUT (" Use error creating the file " &

                    "STUD-MERGED-FILE.DAT" );

                raise ;

            -- END_ERROR is an unlikely error in the creation of a

            -- file. DATA_ERROR is not a possible error.

            when others         =>

                        -- Anything else goes here.

                PUT (" Unusual  kind of error creating file "

                    "STUD-MERGED-FILE.DAT" );

                raise;

    end ;

--  Another block containing the main processing

begin

    if   not STUD_IO.END_OF_FILE (STUD_IN_1) and

        not STUD_IO.END_OF_FILE (STUD_IN_1)

        then

        READ_1 ;

        READ_2 ;

        loop

          if  CURR_REC_1_IN.BIG_ST_ID <

                CURR_REC_2_IN.BIG_ST_ID
```

```
then

-- Write from the first file.

CURR_REC_OUT := CURR_REC_1_IN ;

WRITE_OUT ;

if STUD_IO.END_OF_FILE (STUD_IN_1)

    then

    -- The last element of the first input file

    -- was written out .

    -- Write the current element of the second

    -- input  file. Otherwise, COPY_2 will  drop

    -- it. End the merge after COPY_2.

    CURR_REC_OUT := CURR_REC_2_IN ;

    WRITE_OUT ;

    COPY_2 ;

    exit ;

end if ;

READ_1 ;

elsif  CURR_REC_1_IN.BIG_ST_ID >

    CURR_REC_2_IN.BIG_ST_ID

then

-- Write from the second file

CURR_REC_OUT := CURR_REC_2_IN ;

WRITE_OUT ;

if STUD_IO.END_OF_FILE (STUD_IN_2)

    then

    -- The last element of the second input file
```

```
                    -- was written out .

                    -- Write the current element of the first

                    -- input  file,  otherwise COPY_2 will  drop

                    -- it. End the merge after COPY_1

                    CURR_REC_OUT := CURR_REC_1_IN ;        .

                    WRITE_OUT ;

                    COPY_1 ;

                    exit ;

                end if ;

                READ_2 ;

            else

                -- For equality, add  the student tests.

                CURR_REC_OUT := CURR_REC_1_IN ;

                CURR_REC_OUT.NO_TESTS :=

                    CURR_REC_OUT.NO_TESTS + CURR_REC_2_IN ;

                CURR_REC_OUT.ST_TESTS (CURR_REC_1_IN.NO_TESTS + 1

                    .. CURR_REC_OUT.NO_TESTS) :=

                CURR_REC_2_IN.ST_TESTS (1..CURR_REC_2_IN.NO_TESTS);

                    -- This statement is a slice assignment.

                WRITE_OUT ;

                if STUD_IO.END_OF_FILE (STUD_IN_2)

                    then

                    COPY_1 ;

                    exit ;

                end if ;

                -- Copy the corresponding  file if the other
```

```
                -- file is returning an end-of-file.

                if STUD_IO.END_OF_FILE (STUD_IN_1)

                        then

                        COPY_2 ;

                        exit ;

                    end if ;

                    READ_1 ;

                    READ_2 ;

            end if ;

                    -- Two nonempty files were merged.

                    -- At least one file was processed.

                    -- Copy the other one .

            end loop;

    elsif   STUD_IO.END_OF_FILE (STUD_IN_1 ).pn509

            COPY_2 ;

            else

            -- STUD_IN_2  must be empty if the condition is true.

            COPY_1 ;

        end if ;

        PUT (" The merge is done ") ;

    exception

            -- This exception is used whenever some of the errors

            -- are propagated  from the procedures READ, WRITE, COPY,

            -- and so on.

            when others    => CLOSE_IT ;

end;
```

```
-- The end of the main processing block ossurs here.

CLOSE_IT;

-- This call is executed if the processing was successful.

end  EXCEP_MERGE_PROC_GRADES  ;
```

11.3 EXCEPTION HANDLING IN A CONCURRENT ENVIRONMENT

As mentioned in Section 11.1, TASKING_ERROR is the predefined exception raised when certain events occur during intertask communication. These events include the following:

- The failure of a task to be activated.
- An attempt to communicate with a task that is abnormal or completed.
- An explicit raising of TASKING_ERROR during a rendezvous.

The exception TASKING_ERROR is raised either in the calling task, at the place of the call (when the called task is completed, for instance), or within the called task if the exception is raised within a rendezvous.

If an exception is raised within a called task, then its propagation to the calling task depends on whether the exception is handled locally. If the exception is raised within an accept statement and it has a local exception handler, then the exception does not have to be propagated, even though one still has the option to raise the exception again and propagate it. If there is no corresponding local exception handler, then the exception is propagated, and the exception is raised in the calling task. Note that whenever a calling task becomes abnormal, the called task is unaffected. That is, no exception is raised within it.

We illustrate the use of tasking exceptions in the program that follows, which is a modification of the program PLANT_SCHED of Chapter 10. This program will be modified to allow for a possible breakdown in any of the three machines involved in processing. If a machine breaks down, it is not repaired in time to be reused for the processing of the batch. Also, to simplify the program, we left out the first loop statement of the tasks MACH1, MACH2, MACH3, and INSPECT.

EXCEP_PLANT_SCHED Program

```
with DISTRIBUTIONS ; use DISTRIBUTIONS ;

with CALENDAR ; use CALENDAR ;

procedure EXCEP_PLANT_SCHED is
```

```
N_OF_FINISHED_PROD : NATURAL := 0 ;

N_OF_REJECTS  : NATURAL := 0 ;

task COORDINATOR is

     entry SCHED ;

end COORDINATOR ;

     task MACH1 is

          entry OPER1 ;

          entry DISABLE ;

     end MACH1 ;

     task MACH2 is

          entry OPER2 ;

          entry DISABLE ;

     end MACH2 ;

     task MACH3 is

          entry OPER1_N_2 ;

          entry DISABLE ;

     end MACH3 ;

     task STOP_INSPECTIONS ;

     task INSPECT is

          entry PRODUCT ;

          entry TAKE_A_BREAK ;

     end INSPECT ;

--   The following task is an extra task that can disable MACH1,
--   MACH2 or  MACH3   whenever   the   function   BREAK_DOWN
--   returns, respectively, the value 1,  2,  or 3.  If the
--   returned value is 4,  the process cannot continue (for
```

```
--   instance, MACH2 and MACH3 are disabled). Any other returned
--   value   means   that   the  current  states   of   the   machines
--   remain unchanged.

     task DISABLE_MACHINES ;
--

     task body MACH1 is
     MACH1_JOB_DURATION : DURATION ;
     begin
         MACH1_JOB_DURATION := PROBABILITY (TIME_MACH1) ;
         loop

             -- This part is added to handle the possible
             -- DISABLE call. Identical code is provided
             -- for MACH2 and MACH3. An alternative
             -- way of coding this part is as follows:
             -- if DISABLE'COUNT > 0
             --    then
             --    accept DISABLE do
             --        loop null ; end loop ;
             --    end ;
             -- end if ;
             select

                 accept DISABLE do

                     loop

                         null;

                     end loop;
```

```
            end ;

            else

                null;

        end select;

        --  Additional code  ends here.

        accept OPER1 ;

        delay MACH1_JOB_DURATION ;

        -- Place  the  task call  in  a  block.

        begin

            MACH2.OPER2 ;

            exception

                when TASKING_ERROR =>

                        PUT( " Possibly terminated MACH2 ");

                        raise;

            end;

            MACH1_JOB_DURATION := PROBABILITY (TIME_MACH1) ;

        end loop ;

    end MACH1 ;

--

task body MACH2 is

MACH2_JOB_DURATION : DURATION ;

begin

    MACH2_JOB_DURATION := PROBABILITY (TIME_MACH2) ;

    loop

        -- The compressed extra code starts here.

        select
```

```
                    accept DISABLE do

                         loop    null; end loop; end ;

                    else   null;

               end select;

               -- The compressed extra code ends  here.


               accept OPER2 ;

               delay MACH2_JOB_DURATION ;

               -- Place  the  task call  in  a  block.

               begin

                    INSPECT.PRODUCT ;

                    exception

                         when TASKING_ERROR =>

                              PUT( " Possibly terminated INSPECT ");

                              raise;

                    end;

                    MACH2_JOB_DURATION := PROBABILITY (TIME_MACH2) ;

               end loop;

          end MACH2 ;

     --

     task body MACH3 is

     MACH3_JOB_DURATION : DURATION ;

     begin

          MACH3_JOB_DURATION := PROBABILITY (TIME_MACH3) ;

          loop

               -- The compressed extra code starts here.
```

```
select

        accept DISABLE do

            loop   null; end loop; end ;

        else  null;

    end select;

    -- The compressed extra code ends  here

    accept OPER1_N_2  ;

    delay MACH3_JOB_DURATION ;

    -- Place  the  task call  in  a  block.

    begin

        INSPECT.PRODUCT ;

        exception

            when TASKING_ERROR =>

                PUT( " Possibly terminated INSPECT ");

                raise;

        end;

        MACH3_JOB_DURATION := PROBABILITY (TIME_MACH3) ;

    end loop;

end MACH3 ;

--

task body COORDINATOR is

begin

    accept SCHED ;

    loop

        loop

            select
```

```
                        MACH1.OPER1 ;

                        exit ;

                or

                        delay 0.01 ;

                end select ;

                select

                        MACH3.OPER1_N_2 ;

                        exit ;

                or

                        delay 0.01 ;

                end select ;

        end loop ;

        select

                accept SCHED ;

                else

                        null ;

        end select;

    end loop ;

    exception

        when TASKING_ERROR =>

                PUT( " Problem in one of the calls ") ;

                raise;

end COORDINATOR ;

--

    task body STOP_INSPECTION is

    begin
```

```
loop

     delay  120.00 ;

     INSPECT.TAKE_A_BREAK ;

end loop;

end STOP_INSPECTION ;

--

task body INSPECT is

INSP_PASSED     : BOOLEAN ;

EXAM_TIME : DURATION ;

START_MANUFACT, STOP_MANUFACT : TIME ;

DURATION_MANUFACT : DURATION ;

package DURATION_IO is new FIXED_IO (DURATION) ;

use DURATION_IO ;

begin

START_MANUFACT := CLOCK ;

    INSP_PASSED :=    INSP_RESULT ;

    EXAM_TIME := PROBABILITY (INSPECTION) ;

    loop

        accept PRODUCT ;

        delay EXAM_TIME    ;

        if INSP_PASSED

            then

            N_OF_FINISHED_PROD := N_OF_FINISHED_PROD + 1;

            else

            N_OF_REJECTS   := N_OF_REJECTS + 1 ;

        end if ;
```

```
                    EXAM_TIME := PROBABILITY (INSPECTION) ;

                    INSP_PASSED :=    INSP_RESULT ;

                    exit when  N_OF_FINISHED_PROD = 200 ;

                    if TAKE_A_BREAK'COUNT > 0

                        then

                        accept TAKE_A_BREAK ;

                        delay 15 ;

                    end if ;

                end loop ;

            STOP_MANUFACT := CLOCK ;

            DURATION_MANUFACT := START_MANUFACT - STOP_MANUFACT ;

            PUT (DURATION_MANUFACT, 10, 2) ;

            abort STOP_INSPECTION ;

--    Note that when this task is  completed, then any call to

--    this task will raise the exception   TASKING_ERROR in the

--    calling task at the calling point. So MACH2, and later on,

--    MACH1, MACH3, and in turn COORDINATOR will raise this same

--    exception.

            end INSPECT ;

--    The body of the task DISABLE_MACHINES follows. Every

--    second (corresponding to 1 minute on the manufacturing

--    floor) the function BREAK_DOWN is invoked. BREAK_DOWN

--    is a function whose specification should be added to the

--    package DISTRIBUTIONS, as follows:

--    function BREAK_DOWN return NATURAL ;

--    The package should also keep track, in its body, of which

--    machines are malfunctioning so that the same machine
```

```
--      does   not break down twice.

        task body DISABLE_MACHINES ;

        MAYBE_IS_BROKE : NATURAL ;

        begin

            loop

                delay 1.0 ;

                MAYBE_IS_BROKE := BRAKE_DOWN ;

                case MAYBE_IS_BROKE is

                    when 1         =>    MACH1.DISABLE;

                    when 2         =>    MACH2.DISABLE;

                    when 3         =>    MACH3.DISABLE;

                    when 4         =>    abort MACH2;

                                        abort MACH3;

                                        -- INSPECT may still

                                        -- be active.

                                        abort INSPECT ;

                    when others    =>   null;

                end case ;

            end loop;

        end DISABLE_MACHINES ;

--

        begin

        for I in 1  .. 200

            loop

            COORDINATOR.SCHED ;

        end loop ;

end  EXCEP_PLANT_SCHED ;
```

EXERCISES FOR CHAPTER 11

1. Rewrite the program EXCEP_MERGE_PROC_GRADES, replacing the procedures READ_1 and READ_2 by a new procedure with a formal parameter that can identify the file that is to be read. Make any other needed modifications in order to properly identify the exceptions, should they occur.

2. Rewrite every program of Chapter 5 in order to incorporate appropriate exception-handling facilities.

3. Rewrite the package BANK_RESOURCES and the program BANK_MAINT of Chapter 8 in order to incorporate adequate exception-handling facilities.

APPENDIX

Appendix material is reprinted from ANSI/MIL-STD-1815A.

A. Predefined Language Attributes
B. Predefined Language Pragmas
C. Predefined Language Environment
D. Glossary
E. Syntax Summary

A. PREDEFINED LANGUAGE ATTRIBUTES

This annex summarizes the definitions given elsewhere of the predefined attributes.

P'ADDRESS

For a prefix P that denotes an object, a program unit, a label, or an entry:

Yields the address of the first of the storage units allocated to P. For a subprogram, package, task unit, or label, this value refers to the machine code associated with the corresponding body or statement. For an entry for which an address clause has been given, the value refers to the corresponding hardware interrupt. The value of this attribute is of the type ADDRESS defined in the package SYSTEM. (See 13.7.2.*)

---

* Section references are to the *Reference Manual for the Ada Programming Language.*

P'AFT

For a prefix P that denotes a fixed point subtype:

Yields the number of decimal digits needed after the point to accommodate the precision of the subtype P, unless the delta of the subtype P is greater than 0.1, in which case the attribute yields the value one. (P'AFT is the smallest positive integer N for which (10∗∗N) ∗P'DELTA is greater than or equal to one.) The value of this attribute is of the type *universal_integer*. (See 3.5.10.)

P'BASE

For a prefix P that denotes a type or subtype:

This attribute denotes the base type of P. It is only allowed as the prefix of the name of another attribute: for example, P'BASE' FIRST. (See 3.3.3.)

P'CALLABLE

For a prefix P that is appropriate for a task type:

Yields the value FALSE when the execution of the task P is either completed or terminated, or when the task is abnormal; yields the value TRUE otherwise. The value of this attribute is of the predefined type BOOLEAN. (See 9.9.)

P'CONSTRAINED

For a prefix P that denotes an object of a type with discriminants:

Yields the value TRUE if a discriminant constraint applies to the object P, or if the object is a constant (including a formal parameter or generic formal parameter of mode **in**); yields the value FALSE otherwise. If P is a generic formal parameter of mode **in out,** or if P is a formal parameter of mode **in out** or **out** and the type mark given in the corresponding parameter specification denotes an unconstrained type with discriminants, then the value of this attribute is obtained from that of the corresponding actual parameter. The value of this attribute is of the predefined type BOOLEAN. (See 3.7.4.)

P'CONSTRAINED

For a prefix P that denotes a private type or subtype:

Yields the value FALSE if P denotes an unconstrained nonformal private type with discriminants; also yields the value FALSE if P denotes a generic formal private type and the associated actual subtype is either an unconstrained type with discriminants or an unconstrained array type; yields the value TRUE otherwise. The value of this attribute is of the predefined type BOOLEAN. (See 7.4.2.)

P'COUNT

For a prefix P that denotes an entry of a task unit:

Yields the number of entry calls presently queued on the entry (if the attribute is evaluated within an accept statement for the entry P, the count does not include the calling task). The value of this attribute is of the type *universal_integer*. (See 9.9.)

P'DELTA

For a prefix P that denotes a fixed point subtype:

Yields the value of the delta specified in the fixed accuracy definition for the subtype P. The value of this attribute is of the type *universal_real*. (See 3.5.10.)

P'DIGITS

For a prefix P that denotes a floating point subtype:

Yields the number of decimal digits in the decimal mantissa of model numbers of the subtype P. (This attribute yields the number D of section 3.5.7.) The value of this attribute is of the type *universal_integer*. (See 3.5.8.)

P'EMAX

For a prefix P that denotes a floating point subtype:

Yields the largest exponent value in the binary canonical form of model numbers of the subtype P. (This attribute yields the product $4*B$ of section 3.5.7.) The value of this attribute is of the type *universal_integer*. (See 3.5.8.)

P'EPSILON

For a prefix P that denotes a floating point subtype:

Yields the absolute value of the difference between the model number 1.0 and the next model number above, for the subtype P. The value of this attribute is of the type *universal_real*. (See 3.5.8.)

P'FIRST

For a prefix P that denotes a scalar type, or a subtype of a scalar type:

Yields the lower bound of P. The value of this attribute has the same type as P. (See 3.5.)

P'FIRST

For a prefix P that is appropriate for an array type, or that denotes a constrained array subtype:

Yields the lower bound of the first index range. The value of this attribute has the same type as this lower bound. (See 3.6.2 and 3.8.2.)

P'FIRST(N)

For a prefix P that is appropriate for an array type, or that denotes a constrained array subtype:

Yields the lower bound of the N-th index range. The value of this attribute has the same type as this lower bound. The argument N must be a static expression of type *universal_integer*. The value of N must be positive (nonzero) and no greater than the dimensionality of the array. (See 3.6.2 and 3.8.2.)

P'FIRST_BIT

For a prefix P that denotes a component of a record object:

Yields the offset, from the start of the first of the storage units occupied by the component, of the first bit occupied by the component. This offset is measured in bits. The value of this attribute is of the type *universal_integer*. (See 13.7.2.)

P'FORE

For a prefix P that denotes a fixed point subtype:

Yields the minimum number of characters needed for the integer part of the decimal representation of any value of the subtype P, assuming that the representation does not include an exponent, but includes a one-character prefix that is either a minus sign or a space. (This minimum number does not include superfluous zeros or underlines, and is at least two.) The value of this attribute is of the type *universal_integer*. (See 3.5.10.)

P'IMAGE

For a prefix P that denotes a discrete type or subtype:

This attribute is a function with a single parameter. The actual parameter X must be a value of the base type of P. The result type is the predefined type STRING. The result is the *image* of the value of X, that is, a sequence of characters representing the value in display form. The image of an integer value is the corresponding decimal literal; without underlines, leading zeros, exponent, or trailing spaces; but with a one character prefix that is either a minus sign or a space.

The image of an enumeration value is either the corresponding identifier in upper case or the corresponding character literal (including the two apostrophes); neither leading nor trailing spaces are included. The image of a character other than a graphic character is implementation-defined. (See 3.5.5.)

P'LARGE

For a prefix P that denotes a real subtype:

The attribute yields the largest positive model number of the subtype P. The value of this attribute is of the type *universal_real*. (See 3.5.8 and 3.5.10.)

P'LAST

For a prefix P that denotes a scalar type, or a subtype of a scalar type:

Yields the upper bound of P. The value of this attribute has the same type as P. (See 3.5.)

P'LAST	For a prefix P that is appropriate for an array type, or that denotes a constrained array subtype:
	Yields the upper bound of the first index range. The value of this attribute has the same type as this upper bound. (See 3.6.2 and 3.8.2.)
P'LAST(N)	For a prefix P that is appropriate for an array type, or that denotes a constrained array subtype:
	Yields the upper bound of the N-th index range. The value of this attribute has the same type as this upper bound. The argument N must be a static expression of type *universal_integer*. The value of N must be positive (nonzero) and no greater than the dimensionality of the array. (See 3.6.2 and 3.8.2.)
P'LAST_BIT	For a prefix P that denotes a component of a record object:
	Yields the offset, from the start of the first of the storage units occupied by the component, of the last bit occupied by the component. This offset is measured in bits. The value of this attribute is of the type *universal_integer*. (See 13.7.2.)
P'LENGTH	For a prefix P that is appropriate for an array type, or that denotes a constrained array subtype:
	Yields the number of values of the first index range (zero for a null range). The value of this attribute is of the type *universal_integer*. (See 3.6.2.)
P'LENGTH(N)	For a prefix P that is appropriate for an array type, or that denotes a constrained array subtype:
	Yields the number of values of the N-th index range (zero for a null range). The value of this attribute is of the type *universal_integer*. The argument N must be a static expression of type *universal_integer*. The value of N must

be positive (nonzero) and no greater than the dimensionality of the array. (See 3.6.2 and 3.8.2.)

P'MACHINE_EMAX

For a prefix P that denotes a floating point type or subtype:

Yields the largest value of *exponent* for the machine representation of the base type of P. The value of this attribute is of the type *universal_integer*. (See 13.7.3.)

P'MACHINE_EMIN

For a prefix P that denotes a floating point type or subtype:

Yields the smallest (most negative) value of *exponent* for the machine representation of the base type of P. The value of this attribute is of the type *universal_integer*. (See 13.7.3.)

P'MACHINE_MANTISSA

For a prefix P that denotes a floating point type or subtype:

Yields the number of digits in the *mantissa* for the machine representation of the base type of P (the digits are extended digits in the range 0 to P'MACHINE_RADIX − 1). The value of this attribute is of the type *universal_integer*. (See 13.7.3.)

P'MACHINE_OVERFLOWS

For a prefix P that denotes a real type or subtype:

Yields the value TRUE if every predefined operation on values of the base type of P either provides a correct result, or raises the exception NUMERIC_ERROR in overflow situations; yields the value FALSE otherwise. The value of this attribute is of the predefined type BOOLEAN. (See 13.7.3.)

P'MACHINE_RADIX

For a prefix P that denotes a floating point type or subtype:

Yields the value of the *radix* used by the machine representation of the base type of P. The value of this attribute is of the type *universal_integer*. (See 13.7.3.)

P'MACHINE_ROUNDS	For a prefix P that denotes a real type or subtype:
	Yields the value TRUE if every predefined arithmetic operation on values of the base type of P either returns an exact result or performs rounding; yields the value FALSE otherwise. The value of this attribute is of the predefined type BOOLEAN. (See 13.7.3.)
P'MANTISSA	For a prefix P that denotes a real subtype:
	Yields the number of binary digits in the binary mantissa of model numbers of the subtype P. (This attribute yields the number B of section 3.5.7 for a floating point type, or of section 3.5.9 for a fixed point type.) The value of this attribute is of the type *universal_integer*. (See 3.5.8 and 3.5.10.)
P'POS	For a prefix P that denotes a discrete type or subtype:
	This attribute is a function with a single parameter. The actual parameter X must be a value of the base type of P. The result type is the type *universal_integer*. The result is the position number of the value of the actual parameter. (See 3.5.5.)
P'POSITION	For a prefix P that denotes a component of a record object:
	Yields the offset, from the start of the first storage unit occupied by the record, of the first of the storage units occupied by the component. This offset is measured in storage units. The value of this attribute is of the type *universal_integer*. (See 13.7.2.)
P'PRED	For a prefix P that denotes a discrete type or subtype:
	This attribute is a function with a single parameter. The actual parameter X must be a value of the base type of P. The result type is the base type of P. The result is the value whose position number is one less than that

of X. The exception CONSTRAINT_
ERROR is raised if X equals P'BASE'FIRST.
(See 3.5.5.)

P'RANGE

For a prefix P that is appropriate for an array
type, or that denotes a constrained array subtype:

Yields the first index range of P, that is, the
range P'FIRST . . P'LAST. (See 3.6.2.)

P'RANGE(N)

For a prefix P that is appropriate for an array
type, or that denotes a constrained array subtype:

Yields the N-th index range of P, that is, the
range P'FIRST(N) . . P'LAST(N). (See
3.6.2.)

P'SAFE_EMAX

For a prefix P that denotes a floating point
type or subtype:

Yields the largest exponent value in the binary canonical form of safe numbers of the
base type of P. (This attribute yields the number E of section 3.5.7.) The value of this
attribute is of the type *universal_integer*. (See
3.5.8.)

P'SAFE_LARGE

For a prefix P that denotes a real type or
subtype:

Yields the largest positive safe number of the
base type of P. The value of this attribute is
of the type *universal_real*. (See 3.5.8 and
3.5.10.)

P'SAFE_SMALL

For a prefix P that denotes a real type or
subtype:

Yields the smallest positive (nonzero) safe
number of the base type of P. The value of
this attribute is of the type *universal_real*.
(See 3.5.8 and 3.5.10.)

P'SIZE

For a prefix P that denotes an object:

Yields the number of bits allocated to hold
the object. The value of this attribute is of
the type *universal_integer*. (See 13.7.2.)

P'SIZE	For a prefix P that denotes any type or subtype:
	Yields the minimum number of bits that is needed by the implementation to hold any possible object of the type or subtype P. The value of this attribute is of the type *universal_integer*. (See 13.7.2.)
P'SMALL	For a prefix P that denotes a real subtype:
	Yields the smallest positive (nonzero) model number of the subtype P. The value of this attribute is of the type *universal_real*. (See 3.5.8 and 3.5.10.)
P'STORAGE_SIZE	For a prefix P that denotes an access type or subtype:
	Yields the total number of storage units reserved for the collection associated with the base type of P. The value of this attribute is of the type *universal_integer*. (See 13.7.2.)
P'STORAGE_SIZE	For a prefix P that denotes a task type or a task object:
	Yields the number of storage units reserved for each activation of a task of the type P or for the activation of the task object P. The value of this attribute is of the type *universal_integer*. (See 13.7.2.)
P'SUCC	For a prefix P that denotes a discrete type or subtype:
	This attribute is a function with a single parameter. The actual parameter X must be a value of the base type of P. The result type is the base type of P. The result is the value whose position number is one greater than that of X. The exception CONSTRAINT_ERROR is raised if X equals P'BASE'LAST. (See 3.5.5.)
P'TERMINATED	For a prefix P that is appropriate for a task type:
	Yields the value TRUE if the task P is terminated; yields the value FALSE otherwise.

The value of this attribute is of the predefined type BOOLEAN. (See 9.9.)

P'VAL

For a prefix P that denotes a discrete type or subtype:

This attribute is a special function with a single parameter X which can be of any integer type. The result type is the base type of P. The result is the value whose position number is the *universal_integer* value corresponding to X. The exception CONSTRAINT_ ERROR is raised if the *universal_integer* value corresponding to X is not in the range P'POS(P'BASE'FIRST) . . P'POS(P'BASE' LAST). (See 3.5.5.)

P'VALUE

For a prefix P that denotes a discrete type or subtype:

This attribute is a function with a single parameter. The actual parameter X must be a value of the predefined type STRING. The result type is the base type of P. Any leading and any trailing spaces of the sequence of characters that corresponds to X are ignored.

For an enumeration type, if the sequence of characters has the syntax of an enumeration literal and if this literal exists for the base type of P, the result is the corresponding enumeration value. For an integer type, if the sequence of characters has the syntax of an integer literal, with an optional single leading character that is a plus or minus sign, and if there is a corresponding value in the base type of P, the result is this value. In any other case, the exception CONSTRAINT_ERROR is raised. (See 3.5.5.)

P'WIDTH

For a prefix P that denotes a discrete subtype:

Yields the maximum image length over all values of the subtype P (the *image* is the sequence of characters returned by the attribute IMAGE). The value of this attribute is of the type *universal_integer*. (See 3.5.5.)

B. PREDEFINED LANGUAGE PRAGMAS

This annex defines the pragmas LIST, PAGE, and OPTIMIZE, and summarizes the definitions given elsewhere of the remaining language-defined pragmas.

Pragma	Meaning
CONTROLLED	Takes the simple name of an access type as the single argument. This pragma is only allowed immediately within the declarative part or package specification that contains the declaration of the access type; the declaration must occur before the pragma. This pragma is not allowed for a derived type. This pragma specifies that automatic storage reclamation must not be performed for objects designated by values of the access type, except upon leaving the innermost block statement, subprogram body, or task body that encloses the access type declaration, or after leaving the main program (see 4.8).
ELABORATE	Takes one or more simple names denoting library units as arguments. This pragma is only allowed immediately after the context clause of a compilation unit (before the subsequent library unit or secondary unit). Each argument must be the simple name of a library unit mentioned by the context clause. This pragma specifies that the corresponding library unit body must be elaborated before the given compilation unit. If the given compilation unit is a subunit, the library unit body must be elaborated before the body of the ancestor library unit of the subunit (see 10.5).
INLINE	Takes one or more names as arguments; each name is either the name of a subprogram or the name of a generic subprogram. This pragma is only allowed at the place of a declarative item in a declarative part or package specification, or after a library unit in a compilation, but before any subsequent compilation unit. This pragma specifies that the subprogram bodies should be expanded inline at each call whenever possible; in the case of a generic subprogram, the pragma applies to calls of its instantiations (see 6.3.2).
INTERFACE	Takes a language name and a subprogram name as arguments. This pragma is allowed at the place of a declarative item, and must apply in this case to a subprogram declared by an earlier declarative item of the same dec-

larative part or package specification. This pragma is also allowed for a library unit; in this case the pragma must appear after the subprogram declaration, and before any subsequent compilation unit. This pragma specifies the other language (and thereby the calling conventions) and informs the compiler that an object module will be supplied for the corresponding subprogram (see 13.9).

LIST — Takes one of the identifiers ON or OFF as the single argument. This pragma is allowed anywhere a pragma is allowed. It specifies that listing of the compilation is to be continued or suspended until a LIST pragma with the opposite argument is given within the same compilation. The pragma itself is always listed if the compiler is producing a listing.

MEMORY_SIZE — Takes a numeric literal as the single argument. This pragma is only allowed at the start of a compilation, before the first compilation unit (if any) of the compilation. The effect of this pragma is to use the value of the specified numeric literal for the definition of the named number MEMORY_SIZE (see 13.7).

OPTIMIZE — Takes one of the identifiers TIME or SPACE as the single argument. The pragma is only allowed within a declarative part and it applies to the block or body enclosing the declarative part. It specifies whether time or space is the primary optimization criterion.

PACK — Takes the simple name of a record or array type as the single argument. The allowed positions for this pragma, and the restrictions on the named type, are governed by the same rules as for a representation clause. The pragma specifies that storage minimization should be the main criterion when selecting the representation of the given type (see 13.1).

PAGE — This pragma has no argument, and is allowed anywhere a pragma is allowed. It specifies that the program text which follows the pragma should start on a new page (if the compiler is currently producing a listing).

PRIORITY — Takes a static expression of the predefined integer subtype PRIORITY as the single argument. This pragma is only allowed within the specification of a task unit or immediately within the outermost declarative part of a main program. It specifies the priority of the task (or tasks of the task type) or the priority of the main program (see 9.8).

SHARED

Takes the simple name of a variable as the single argument. This pragma is allowed only for a variable declared by an object declaration and whose type is a scalar or access type; the variable declaration and the pragma must both occur (in this order) immediately within the same declarative part or package specification. This pragma specifies that every read or update of the variable is a synchronization point for that variable. An implementation must restrict the objects for which this pragma is allowed to objects for which each of direct reading and direct updating is implemented as an indivisible operation (see 9.11).

STORAGE_UNIT

Takes a numeric literal as the single argument. This pragma is only allowed at the start of a compilation, before the first compilation unit (if any) of the compilation. The effect of this pragma is to use the value of the specified numeric literal for the definition of the named number STORAGE_UNIT (see 13.7).

SUPPRESS

Takes as arguments the identifier of a check and optionally also the name of either an object, a type or subtype, a subprogram, a task unit, or a generic unit. This pragma is only allowed either immediately within a declarative part or immediately within a package specification. In the latter case, the only allowed form is with a name that denotes an entity (or several overloaded subprograms) declared immediately within the package specification. The permission to omit the given check extends from the place of the pragma to the end of the declarative region associated with the innermost enclosing block statement or program unit. For a pragma given in a package specification, the permission extends to the end of the scope of the named entity.

If the pragma includes a name, the permission to omit the given check is further restricted: it is given only for operations on the named object or on all objects of the base type of a named type or subtype; for calls of a named subprogram; for activations of tasks of the named task type; or for instantiations of the given generic unit (see 11.7).

SYSTEM_NAME

Takes an enumeration literal as the single argument. This pragma is only allowed at the start of a compilation, before the first compilation unit (if any) of the compilation. The effect of this pragma is to use the enumeration literal with the specified identifier for the definition of the constant SYSTEM_NAME. This pragma is only allowed if the specified identifier corresponds to one of the literals of the type NAME declared in the package SYSTEM (see 13.7).

C. PREDEFINED LANGUAGE ENVIRONMENT

This annex outlines the specification of the package STANDARD containing all predefined identifiers in the language. The corresponding package body is implementation-defined and is not shown.

The operators that are predefined for the types declared in the package STANDARD are given in comments since they are implicitly declared. Italics are used for pseudo-names of anonymous types (such as *universal_real*) and for undefined information (such as *implementation_defined* and *any_fixed_point_type*).

package STANDARD **is**

type BOOLEAN **is** (FALSE, TRUE);

— The predefined relational operators for this type are as follows:

— **function** *"="*   (LEFT, RIGHT : BOOLEAN) **return** BOOLEAN;
— **function** *"/="*   (LEFT, RIGHT : BOOLEAN) **return** BOOLEAN;
— **function** *"<"*   (LEFT, RIGHT : BOOLEAN) **return** BOOLEAN;
— **function** *"<="*   (LEFT, RIGHT : BOOLEAN) **return** BOOLEAN;
— **function** *">"*   (LEFT, RIGHT : BOOLEAN) **return** BOOLEAN;
— **function** *">="*   (LEFT, RIGHT : BOOLEAN) **return** BOOLEAN;

— The predefined logical operators and the predefined logical negation operator are as follows:

— **function** *"and"*   (LEFT, RIGHT : BOOLEAN) **return** BOOLEAN;
— **function** *"or"*   (LEFT, RIGHT : BOOLEAN) **return** BOOLEAN;
— **function** *"xor"*   (LEFT, RIGHT : BOOLEAN) **return** BOOLEAN;

— **function** *"not"*   (RIGHT : BOOLEAN) **return** BOOLEAN;

— The universal type *universal_integer* is predefined.

type INTEGER **is** *implementation_defined;*

— The predefined operators for this type are as follows:

— **function** *"="*   (LEFT, RIGHT : INTEGER) **return** BOOLEAN;
— **function** *"/="*   (LEFT, RIGHT : INTEGER) **return** BOOLEAN;
— **function** *"<"*   (LEFT, RIGHT : INTEGER) **return** BOOLEAN;
— **function** *"<="*   (LEFT, RIGHT : INTEGER) **return** BOOLEAN;
— **function** *">"*   (LEFT, RIGHT : INTEGER) **return** BOOLEAN;
— **function** *">="*   (LEFT, RIGHT : INTEGER) **return** BOOLEAN;

— **function** *"+"*   (RIGHT : INTEGER) **return** INTEGER;

— **function** *"~"*   (RIGHT : INTEGER) **return** INTEGER;
— **function** *"abs"*   (RIGHT : INTEGER) **return** INTEGER;

— **function** *"+"*   (LEFT, RIGHT : INTEGER) **return** INTEGER;
— **function** *"-"*   (LEFT, RIGHT : INTEGER) **return** INTEGER;
— **function** *"*"*   (LEFT, RIGHT : INTEGER) **return** INTEGER;
— **function** *"/"*   (LEFT, RIGHT : INTEGER) **return** INTEGER;
— **function** *"rem"*   (LEFT, RIGHT : INTEGER) **return** INTEGER;
— **function** *"mod"*   (LEFT, RIGHT : INTEGER) **return** INTEGER;

— **function** *"**"*   (LEFT : INTEGER; RIGHT : INTEGER) **return** INTEGER;

— An implementation may provide additional predefined integer types. It
— is recommended that the names of such additional types end with INTE-
— GER as in SHORT_INTEGER or LONG_INTEGER. The specification
— of each operator for the type *universal_integer,* or for any additional
— predefined integer type, is obtained by replacing INTEGER by the name
— of the type in the specification of the corresponding operator of the type
— INTEGER, except for the right operand of the exponentiating operator.
— The universal type *universal_real* is predefined.

type FLOAT **is** *implementation_defined;*

— The predefined operators for this type are as follows:

— **function** "="   (LEFT, RIGHT : FLOAT) **return** BOOLEAN;
— **function** "/="   (LEFT, RIGHT : FLOAT) **return** BOOLEAN;
— **function** "<"   (LEFT, RIGHT : FLOAT) **return** BOOLEAN;
— **function** "<="   (LEFT, RIGHT : FLOAT) **return** BOOLEAN;
— **function** ">"   (LEFT, RIGHT : FLOAT) **return** BOOLEAN;
— **function** ">="   (LEFT, RIGHT : FLOAT) **return** BOOLEAN;

— **function** "+"   (RIGHT : FLOAT) **return** FLOAT;
— **function** "-"   (RIGHT : FLOAT) **return** FLOAT;
— **function** "abs"   (RIGHT : FLOAT) **return** FLOAT;

— **function** "+"   (LEFT, RIGHT : FLOAT) **return** FLOAT;
— **function** "-"   (LEFT, RIGHT : FLOAT) **return** FLOAT;
— **function** "*"   (LEFT, RIGHT : FLOAT) **return** FLOAT;
— **function** "/"   (LEFT, RIGHT : FLOAT) **return** FLOAT;

— **function** "**"   (LEFT : FLOAT; RIGHT : INTEGER) **return** FLOAT;

— An implementation may provide additional predefined floating point
— types. It is recommended that the names of such additional types end
— with FLOAT as in SHORT_FLOAT or LONG_FLOAT. The specifi-
— cation of each operator for the type *universal_real,* or for any additional

— predefined floating point type, is obtained by replacing FLOAT by the
— name of the type in the specification of the corresponding operator of
— the type FLOAT.

— In addition, the following operators are predefined for universal types:

— **function** "*" (LEFT : *universal_integer;*   RIGHT : *universal_real*)   **return** *universal_real;*
— **function** "*" (LEFT : *universal_real;*   RIGHT : *universal_integer*)   **return** *universal_real;*
— **function** "/" (LEFT : *universal_real;*   RIGHT : *universal_integer*)   **return** *universal_real;*

— The type *universal_fixed* is predefined. The only operators declared for
this type are

— **function** "*" (LEFT : *any_fixed_point_type;* RIGHT : *any_fixed_point_type*) **return** *universal_fixed;*
— **function** "/" (LEFT : *any_fixed_point_type;* RIGHT : *any_fixed_point_type*) **return** *universal_fixed;*

— The following characters form the standard ASCII character set. Character literals corresponding to control characters are not identifiers; they are indicated in italics in this definition.

type CHARACTER **is**

(*nul,*	*soh,*	*stx,*	*etx,*	*eot,*	*enq,*	*ack,*	*bel,*
bs,	*ht,*	*lf,*	*vt,*	*ff,*	*cr,*	*so,*	*si,*
dle,	*dc1,*	*dc2,*	*dc3,*	*dc4,*	*nak,*	*syn,*	*etb,*
can,	*em,*	*sub,*	*esc,*	*fs,*	*gs,*	*rs,*	*us,*
' ',	'!',	'"',	'#',	'$',	'%',	'&',	''',
'(',	')',	'*',	'+',	',',	'−',	'.',	'/',
'0',	'1',	'2',	'3',	'4',	'5',	'6',	'7',
'8',	'9',	':',	';',	'<',	'=',	'>',	'?',
'@',	'A',	'B',	'C',	'D',	'E',	'F',	'G',
'H',	'I',	'J',	'K',	'L',	'M',	'N',	'O',
'P',	'Q',	'R',	'S',	'T',	'U',	'V',	'W',
'X',	'Y',	'Z',	'[',	'/',	']',	'^',	'_',
'`',	'a',	'b',	'c',	'd',	'e',	'f',	'g',
'h',	'i',	'j',	'k',	'l',	'm',	'n',	'o',
'p',	'q',	'r',	's',	't',	'u',	'v',	'w',
'x',	'y',	'z',	'{',	'|',	'}',	'~',	*del*);

for CHARACTER **use** — 128 ASCII character set without holes
(0, 1, 2, 3, 4, 5, . . . , 125, 126, 127);

— The predefined operators for the type CHARACTER are the same as
— for any enumeration type.

package ASCII **is**

— Control characters:

NUL	: **constant** CHARACTER : = *nul;*
STX	: **constant** CHARACTER : = *stx;*
EOT	: **constant** CHARACTER : = *eot;*
ACK	: **constant** CHARACTER : = *ack;*
BS	: **constant** CHARACTER : = *bs;*
LF	: **constant** CHARACTER : = *lf;*
FF	: **constant** CHARACTER : = *ff;*
SO	: **constant** CHARACTER : = *so;*
DLE	: **constant** CHARACTER : = *dle;*
DC2	: **constant** CHARACTER : = *dc2;*
DC4	: **constant** CHARACTER : = *dc4;*
SYN	: **constant** CHARACTER : = *syn;*
CAN	: **constant** CHARACTER : = *can;*
SUB	: **constant** CHARACTER : = *sub;*
FS	: **constant** CHARACTER : = *fs;*
RS	: **constant** CHARACTER : = *rs;*
DEL	: **constant** CHARACTER : = *del;*
SOH	: **constant** CHARACTER : = *soh;*
ETX	: **constant** CHARACTER : = *etx;*
ENQ	: **constant** CHARACTER : = *enq;*
BEL	: **constant** CHARACTER : = *bel;*
HT	: **constant** CHARACTER : = *ht;*
VT	: **constant** CHARACTER : = *vt;*
CR	: **constant** CHARACTER : = *cr;*
SI	. **constant** CHARACTER : = *si;*
DC1	: **constant** CHARACTER : = *dc1;*
DC3	: **constant** CHARACTER : = *dc3;*
NAK	: **constant** CHARACTER : = *nak;*
ETB	: **constant** CHARACTER : = *etb;*
EM	: **constant** CHARACTER : = *em;*
ESC	: **constant** CHARACTER : = *esc;*
GS	: **constant** CHARACTER : = *gs;*
US	: **constant** CHARACTER : = *us;*

— Other characters:

```
EXCLAM         : constant CHARACTER := '!';
SHARP          : constant CHARACTER := '#';
PERCENT        : constant CHARACTER := '%';
COLON          : constant CHARACTER := ':';
QUERY          : constant CHARACTER := '?';
L_BRACKET      : constant CHARACTER := '[';
R_BRACKET      : constant CHARACTER := ']';
UNDERLINE      : constant CHARACTER := '_';
L_BRACE        : constant CHARACTER := '{';
R_BRACE        : constant CHARACTER := '}';
QUOTATION      : constant CHARACTER := '"';
DOLLAR         : constant CHARACTER := '$';
AMPERSAND      : constant CHARACTER := '&';
SEMICOLON      : constant CHARACTER := ';';
AT_SIGN        : constant CHARACTER := '@';
BACK_SLASH     : constant CHARACTER := '\';
CIRCUMFLEX     : constant CHARACTER := '^';
GRAVE          : constant CHARACTER := '`';
BAR            : constant CHARACTER := '|';
TILDE          : constant CHARACTER := '~';
```

— Lower case letters:

```
LC_A : constant CHARACTER := 'a';

...

LC_Z : constant CHARACTER := 'z';

end ASCII;
```

— Predefined subtypes:

```
subtype NATURAL is INTEGER range 0 . . INTEGER'LAST;
subtype POSITIVE is INTEGER range 1 . . INTEGER'LAST;
```

— Predefined string type:

type STRING **is array**(POSITIVE **range** <>) **of** CHARACTER;

pragma PACK(STRING);

— The predefined operators for this type are as follows:

— **function** *"="*   (LEFT, RIGHT : STRING) **return** BOOLEAN;
— **function** *"/="*   (LEFT, RIGHT : STRING) **return** BOOLEAN;
— **function** *"<"*   (LEFT, RIGHT : STRING) **return** BOOLEAN;
— **function** *"<="* (LEFT, RIGHT : STRING) **return** BOOLEAN;
— **function** *">"*   (LEFT, RIGHT : STRING) **return** BOOLEAN;
— **function** *">="* (LEFT, RIGHT : STRING) **return** BOOLEAN;

— **function** *"&"* (LEFT : STRING;   RIGHT : STRING)   **return** STRING;
— **function** *"&"* (LEFT : CHARACTER; RIGHT : STRING)   **return** STRING;
— **function** *"&"* (LEFT : STRING;   RIGHT : CHARACTER) **return** STRING;
— **function** *"&"* (LEFT : CHARACTER; RIGHT : CHARACTER) **return** STRING;

type DURATION **is delta** *implementation_defined* **range** *implementation_defined;*

— The predefined operators for the type DURATION are the same as for any fixed point type.

— The predefined exceptions:

CONSTRAINT_ERROR   : **exception;**
NUMERIC_ERROR   : **exception;**
PROGRAM_ERROR   : **exception;**
STORAGE_ERROR   : **exception;**
TASKING_ERROR   : **exception;**

end STANDARD;

— The package MACHINE_CODE (if provided)   (see 13.8)
— The generic procedure UNCHECKED_DEALLOCATION   (see 13.10.1)
— The generic function UNCHECKED_CONVERSION   (see 13.10.2)

```
package CALENDAR is
  type TIME is private;

  subtype YEAR_NUMBER   is INTEGER   range 1901 . . 2099;
  subtype MONTH_NUMBER is INTEGER   range 1 . . 12;
  subtype DAY_NUMBER    is INTEGER   range 1 . . 31;
  subtype DAY_DURATION  is DURATION range 0.0 . . 86_400.0;

  function CLOCK return TIME;

  function YEAR    (DATE : TIME) return YEAR_NUMBER;
  function MONTH   (DATE : TIME) return MONTH_NUMBER;
  function DAY     (DATE : TIME) return DAY_NUMBER;
  function SECONDS (DATE : TIME) return DAY_DURATION;

  procedure SPLIT  ( DATE    : in  TIME;
                     YEAR    : out YEAR_NUMBER;
                     MONTH   : out MONTH_NUMBER;
                     DAY     : out DAY_NUMBER;
                     SECONDS : out DAY_DURATION);

  function TIME_OF ( YEAR    : YEAR_NUMBER
                     MONTH   : MONTH_NUMBER;
                     DAY     : DAY_NUMBER;
                     SECONDS : DAY_DURATION := 0.0) return
                               TIME;

function "+"  (LEFT : TIME;      RIGHT : DURATION) return TIME;
function "+"  (LEFT : DURATION; RIGHT : TIME)      return TIME;
function "-"  (LEFT : TIME;      RIGHT : DURATION) return TIME;
function "-"  (LEFT : TIME;      RIGHT : TIME)      return DURATION;

function "<"  (LEFT, RIGHT : TIME) return BOOLEAN;
function "<=" (LEFT, RIGHT : TIME) return BOOLEAN;
function ">"  (LEFT, RIGHT : TIME) return BOOLEAN;
function ">=" (LEFT, RIGHT : TIME) return BOOLEAN;

  TIME_ERROR : exception; — can be raised by TIME_OF, "+",
  and "-"

private
  — implementation-dependent
end;
```

```
package SYSTEM is
    type ADDRESS is implementation_defined;
    type NAME      is implementation_defined_enumeration_type;

    SYSTEM_NAME      : constant NAME : = implementation_defined;

    STORAGE_UNIT     : constant : = implementation_defined;
    MEMORY_SIZE      : constant : = implementation_defined;

    — System-Dependent Named Numbers:

    MIN_INT          : constant : = implementation_defined;
    MAX_INT          : constant : = implementation_defined;
    MAX_DIGITS       : constant : = implementation_defined;
    MAX_MANTISSA     : constant : = implementation_defined;
    FINE_DELTA       : constant : = implementation_defined;
    TICK             : constant : = implementation_defined;

    — Other System-Dependent Declarations

    subtype PRIORITY is INTEGER range implementation_defined;

    . . .
end SYSTEM;


with IO_EXCEPTIONS;
generic
    type ELEMENT_TYPE is private;
package SEQUENTIAL_IO is

    type FILE_TYPE   is limited private;

    type FILE_MODE is (IN_FILE, OUT_FILE);

    — File management

    procedure CREATE (FILE    : in out FILE_TYPE;
                      MODE : in FILE_MODE : = OUT_FILE;
                      NAME : in STRING : = " ";
                      FORM : in STRING : = " ");

    procedure OPEN    (FILE    : in out FILE_TYPE;
                      MODE : in FILE_MODE;
                      NAME : in STRING;
                      FORM : in STRING : = " ");

    procedure CLOSE   (FILE : in out FILE_TYPE);
    procedure DELETE  (FILE : in out FILE_TYPE);
    procedure RESET   (FILE : in out FILE_TYPE; MODE : in
                       FILE_MODE);
```

```
          procedure RESET    (FILE : in out FILE_TYPE);

          function MODE       (FILE : in FILE_TYPE) return FILE_MODE;
          function NAME       (FILE : in FILE_TYPE) return STRING;
          function FORM       (FILE : in FILE_TYPE) return STRING;

          function IS_OPEN    (FILE : in FILE_TYPE) return BOOLEAN;

          — Input and output operations

          procedure READ     (FILE : in FILE_TYPE; ITEM : out
                               ELEMENT_TYPE);
          procedure WRITE    (FILE : in FILE_TYPE; ITEM : in
                               ELEMENT_TYPE);

          function END_OF_FILE(FILE : in FILE_TYPE) return BOOLEAN;

          — Exceptions

          STATUS_ERROR    : exception renames
                            IO_EXCEPTIONS.STATUS_ERROR;
          MODE_ERROR      : exception renames
                            IO_EXCEPTIONS.MODE_ERROR;
          NAME_ERROR      : exception renames
                            IO_EXCEPTIONS.NAME_ERROR;
          USE_ERROR       : exception renames
                            IO_EXCEPTIONS.USE_ERROR;
          DEVICE_ERROR    : exception renames
                            IO_EXCEPTIONS.DEVICE_ERROR;
          END_ERROR       : exception renames
                            IO_EXCEPTIONS.END_ERROR;
          DATA_ERROR      : exception renames
                            IO_EXCEPTIONS.DATA_ERROR;

private
   — implementation-dependent
end SEQUENTIAL_IO;


with IO_EXCEPTIONS;
generic
   type ELEMENT_TYPE is private;
package DIRECT_IO is

   type FILE_TYPE is limited private;

   type     FILE_MODE is (IN_FILE, INOUT_FILE, OUT_FILE);
   type     COUNT        is range 0 . . implementation_defined;
   subtype  POSITIVE_COUNT is COUNT range 1 . . COUNT'LAST;
```

— File management

procedure CREATE (FILE   : **in out** FILE_TYPE;
                    MODE : **in** FILE_MODE := INOUT_FILE;
                    NAME : **in** STRING := " ";
                    FORM : **in** STRING := " ");

procedure OPEN   (FILE   : **in out** FILE_TYPE;
                    MODE : **in** FILE_MODE;
                    NAME : **in** STRING;
                    FORM : **in** STRING := " ");

procedure CLOSE   (FILE : **in out** FILE_TYPE);
procedure DELETE (FILE : **in out** FILE_TYPE);
procedure RESET   (FILE : **in out** FILE_TYPE; MODE :
                    in FILE_MODE);
procedure RESET   (FILE : **in out** FILE_TYPE);

function MODE   (FILE : **in** FILE_TYPE) **return** FILE_MODE;
function NAME   (FILE : **in** FILE_TYPE) **return** STRING;
function FORM   (FILE : **in** FILE_TYPE) **return** STRING;

function IS_OPEN   (FILE : **in** FILE_TYPE) **return** BOOLEAN;

— Input and output operations

procedure READ   (FILE : **in** FILE_TYPE; ITEM : **out**
                   ELEMENT_TYPE; FROM : POSITIVE_
                   COUNT);
procedure READ   (FILE : **in** FILE_TYPE; ITEM : **out**
                   ELEMENT_TYPE);

procedure WRITE   (FILE : **in** FILE_TYPE; ITEM : **in**
                    ELEMENT_TYPE; TO : POSITIVE_COUNT);
procedure WRITE   (FILE : **in** FILE_TYPE; ITEM : **in**
                    ELEMENT_TYPE);

procedure SET_INDEX(FILE : **in** FILE_TYPE; TO : **in**
                    POSITIVE_COUNT);

function INDEX(FILE : **in** FILE_TYPE) **return** POSITIVE_COUNT;
function SIZE   (FILE : **in** FILE_TYPE) **return** COUNT;

function END_OF_FILE (FILE : **in** FILE_TYPE) **return** BOOLEAN;

— Exceptions

STATUS_ERROR   : **exception renames**
                    IO_EXCEPTIONS.STATUS_ERROR;
MODE_ERROR   : **exception renames**
                    IO_EXCEPTIONS.MODE_ERROR;

```
        NAME_ERROR      : exception renames
                          IO_EXCEPTIONS.NAME_ERROR;
        USE_ERROR       : exception renames
                          IO_EXCEPTIONS.USE_ERROR;
        DEVICE_ERROR    : exception renames
                          IO_EXCEPTIONS.DEVICE_ERROR;
        END_ERROR       : exception renames
                          IO_EXCEPTIONS.END_ERROR;
        DATA_ERROR      : exception renames
                          IO_EXCEPTIONS.DATA_ERROR;

private
  — implementation-dependent
end DIRECT_IO;


with IO_EXCEPTIONS;
package TEXT_IO is

    type FILE_TYPE is limited private;

    type FILE_MODE is (IN_FILE, OUT_FILE);

    type COUNT is range 0 . . implementation_defined;
    subtype POSITIVE_COUNT is COUNT range 1 . . COUNT'LAST;
    UNBOUNDED : constant COUNT := 0; — line and page length

    subtype FIELD is INTEGER range 0 . . implementation_defined;
    subtype NUMBER_BASE is INTEGER range 2 . . 16;

    type TYPE_SET is (LOWER_CASE, UPPER_CASE);

    — File Management

    procedure CREATE  ( FILE  : in out FILE_TYPE;
                        MODE : in FILE_MODE := OUT_FILE;
                        NAME : in STRING     := " ";
                        FORM : in STRING     := " ");

    procedure OPEN    ( FILE  : in out FILE_TYPE;
                        MODE : in FILE_MODE;
                        NAME : in STRING;
                        FORM : in STRING := " ");
```

```
procedure CLOSE      (FILE : in out FILE_TYPE);
procedure DELETE     (FILE : in out FILE_TYPE);
procedure RESET      (FILE : in out FILE_TYPE; MODE : in
                        FILE_MODE);
procedure RESET      (FILE : in out FILE_TYPE);

function  MODE       (FILE : in FILE_TYPE) return FILE_MODE;
function  NAME       (FILE : in FILE_TYPE) return STRING;
function  FORM       (FILE : in FILE_TYPE) return STRING;

function  IS_OPEN    (FILE : in FILE_TYPE) return BOOLEAN;
```

— Control of default input and output files

```
procedure SET_INPUT    (FILE : in FILE_TYPE);
procedure SET_OUTPUT   (FILE : in FILE_TYPE);

function  STANDARD_INPUT    return FILE_TYPE;
function  STANDARD_OUTPUT   return FILE_TYPE;

function  CURRENT_INPUT     return FILE_TYPE;
function  CURRENT_OUTPUT    return FILE_TYPE;
```

— Specification of line and page lengths

```
procedure SET_LINE_LENGTH  (FILE : in FILE_TYPE; TO : in
                              COUNT);
procedure SET_LINE_LENGTH  (TO : in COUNT);

procedure SET_PAGE_LENGTH  (FILE : in FILE_TYPE; TO : in
                              COUNT);
procedure SET_PAGE_LENGTH  (TO : in COUNT);

function  LINE_LENGTH    (FILE : in FILE_TYPE) return COUNT;
function  LINE_LENGTH    return COUNT;

function  PAGE_LENGTH    (FILE : in FILE_TYPE) return COUNT;
function  PAGE_LENGTH    return COUNT;
```

— Column, Line, and Page Control

```
procedure NEW_LINE       (FILE : in FILE_TYPE; SPACING : in
                            POSITIVE_COUNT := 1);
procedure NEW_LINE       (SPACING : in POSITIVE_COUNT :=
                            1);

procedure SKIP_LINE      (FILE : in FILE_TYPE; SPACING : in
                            POSITIVE_COUNT := 1);
procedure SKIP_LINE      (SPACING : in POSITIVE_COUNT :=
                            1);
```

```
function    END_OF_LINE      (FILE : in FILE_TYPE) return
                                 BOOLEAN;
function    END_OF_LINE       return BOOLEAN;

procedure NEW_PAGE           (FILE : in FILE_TYPE);
procedure NEW_PAGE;

procedure SKIP_PAGE          (FILE : in FILE_TYPE);
procedure SKIP_PAGE;

function    END_OF_PAGE      (FILE : in FILE_TYPE) return
                                 BOOLEAN;
function    END_OF_PAGE       return BOOLEAN;

function    END_OF_FILE      (FILE : in FILE_TYPE) return
                                 BOOLEAN;
function    END_OF_FILE       return BOOLEAN;

procedure SET_COL            (FILE : in FILE_TYPE; TO : in
                                 POSITIVE_COUNT);
procedure SET_COL            (TO   : in POSITIVE_COUNT);

procedure SET_LINE           (FILE : in FILE_TYPE; TO : in
                                 POSITIVE_COUNT);
procedure SET_LINE           (TO   : in POSITIVE_COUNT);

function COL     (FILE : in FILE_TYPE) return POSITIVE_COUNT;
function COL      return POSITIVE_COUNT;

function LINE    (FILE : in FILE_TYPE) return POSITIVE_COUNT;
function LINE     return POSITIVE_COUNT;

function PAGE    (FILE : in FILE_TYPE) return POSITIVE_COUNT;
function PAGE     return POSITIVE_COUNT;
```

— Character Input-Output

```
procedure GET(FILE  : in  FILE_TYPE; ITEM : out CHARACTER);
procedure GET(ITEM : out CHARACTER);
procedure PUT(FILE  : in  FILE_TYPE; ITEM : in CHARACTER);
procedure PUT(ITEM : in  CHARACTER);
```

— String Input-Output

```
procedure GET(FILE  : in  FILE_TYPE; ITEM : out STRING);
procedure GET(ITEM : out STRING);
procedure PUT(FILE  : in  FILE_TYPE; ITEM : in STRING);
procedure PUT(ITEM : in  STRING);


procedure GET_LINE(FILE : in   FILE_TYPE; ITEM : out STRING;
                                 LAST : out NATURAL);
```

```
procedure GET_LINE(ITEM : out STRING; LAST : out NATURAL);
procedure PUT_LINE(FILE : in   FILE_TYPE; ITEM : in STRING);
procedure PUT_LINE(ITEM : in   STRING);
```

— Generic package for Input-Output of Integer Types

```
generic
   type NUM is range <>;
package INTEGER_IO is

   DEFAULT_WIDTH  : FIELD := NUM'WIDTH;
   DEFAULT_BASE   : NUMBER_BASE := 10;

   procedure GET(FILE   : in  FILE_TYPE; ITEM : out NUM; WIDTH
                        : in FIELD := 0);
   procedure GET(ITEM   : out NUM; WIDTH : in FIELD := 0);

   procedure PUT(FILE     : in FILE_TYPE;
                 ITEM     : in NUM;
                 WIDTH    : in FIELD := DEFAULT_WIDTH;
                 BASE     : in NUMBER_BASE := DEFAULT_
                            BASE);
   procedure PUT(ITEM     : in NUM;
                 WIDTH    : in FIELD := DEFAULT_WIDTH;
                 BASE     : in NUMBER_BASE := DEFAULT_
                            BASE);

   procedure GET(FROM   : in  STRING; ITEM : out NUM; LAST :
                        out POSITIVE);
   procedure PUT(TO       : out STRING;
                 ITEM     : in  NUM;
                 BASE     : in  NUMBER_BASE := DEFAULT_
                            BASE);

end INTEGER_IO;
```

— Generic packages for Input-Output of Real Types

```
generic
   type NUM is digits <>;
package FLOAT_IO is

   DEFAULT_FORE  : FIELD := 2;
   DEFAULT_AFT   : FIELD := NUM'DIGITS-1;
   DEFAULT_EXP   : FIELD := 3;

   procedure GET(FILE   : in FILE_TYPE; ITEM : out NUM; WIDTH :
                        in FIELD := 0);
   procedure GET(ITEM : out NUM; WIDTH : in FIELD := 0);
```

```
            procedure PUT(FILE    : in FILE_TYPE;
                          ITEM    : in NUM;
                          FORE    : in FIELD := DEFAULT_FORE;
                          AFT     : in FIELD := DEFAULT_AFT;
                          EXP     : in FIELD := DEFAULT_EXP);
            procedure PUT(ITEM    : in NUM;
                          FORE    : in FIELD := DEFAULT_FORE;
                          AFT     : in FIELD := DEFAULT_AFT;
                          EXP     : in FIELD := DEFAULT_EXP);

        procedure GET(FROM    : in STRING; ITEM : out NUM; LAST : out
                                 POSITIVE);
        procedure PUT(TO      : out STRING;
                      ITEM    : in NUM;
                      AFT     : in FIELD := DEFAULT_AFT;
                      EXP     : in FIELD := DEFAULT_EXP);
    end FLOAT_IO;

    generic
      type NUM is delta <>;
    package FIXED_IO is

      DEFAULT_FORE  : FIELD := NUM'FORE;
      DEFAULT_AFT   : FIELD := NUM'AFT;
      DEFAULT_EXP   : FIELD := 0;

      procedure GET(FILE    : in FILE_TYPE; ITEM : out NUM; WIDTH
                            : in FIELD := 0);
      procedure GET(ITEM    : out NUM; WIDTH : in FIELD := 0);

      procedure PUT(FILE    : in FILE_TYPE;
                    ITEM    : in NUM;
                    FORE    : in FIELD := DEFAULT_FORE;
                    AFT     : in FIELD := DEFAULT_AFT;
                    EXP     : in FIELD := DEFAULT_EXP);
      procedure PUT(ITEM    : in NUM;
                    FORE    : in FIELD := DEFAULT_FORE;
                    AFT     : in FIELD := DEFAULT_AFT;
                    EXP     : in FIELD := DEFAULT_EXP);

      procedure GET(FROM    : in STRING; ITEM : out NUM; LAST : out
                            POSITIVE);
      procedure PUT(TO      : out STRING;
                    ITEM    : in NUM;
                    AFT     : in FIELD := DEFAULT_AFT;
                    EXP     : in FIELD := DEFAULT_EXP);
```

end FIXED_IO;

— Generic package for Input-Output of Enumeration Types

generic
  type ENUM **is** (<>);
  package ENUMERATION_IO **is**

  DEFAULT_WIDTH   : FIELD := 0;
  DEFAULT_SETTING : TYPE_SET := UPPER_CASE;

  procedure GET(FILE   : **in** FILE_TYPE; ITEM : **out** ENUM);
  procedure GET(ITEM   : **out** ENUM);

  procedure PUT(FILE   : **in** FILE_TYPE;
             ITEM   : **in** ENUM;
             WIDTH : **in** FIELD   := DEFAULT_WIDTH;
             SET   : **in** TYPE_SET := DEFAULT_SETTING);
  procedure PUT(ITEM   : **in** ENUM;
             WIDTH : **in** FIELD   := DEFAULT_WIDTH;
             SET   : **in** TYPE_SET := DEFAULT_SETTING);

  procedure GET(FROM : **in** STRING; ITEM : **out** ENUM; LAST : **out**
                    POSITIVE);
  procedure PUT(TO   : **out** STRING;
             ITEM   : **in** ENUM;
             SET   : **in** TYPE_SET := DEFAULT_SETTING);
end ENUMERATION_IO;

— Exceptions

  STATUS_ERROR   : **exception renames**
                 IO_EXCEPTIONS.STATUS_ERROR;
  MODE_ERROR   : **exception renames**
                 IO_EXCEPTIONS.MODE_ERROR;
  NAME_ERROR   : **exception renames**
                 IO_EXCEPTIONS.NAME_ERROR;
  USE_ERROR   : **exception renames**
                 IO_EXCEPTIONS.USE_ERROR;
  DEVICE_ERROR   : **exception renames**
                 IO_EXCEPTIONS.DEVICE_ERROR;
  END_ERROR   : **exception renames**
                 IO_EXCEPTIONS.END_ERROR;
  DATA_ERROR   : **exception renames**
                 IO_EXCEPTIONS.DATA_ERROR;
  LAYOUT_ERROR   : **exception renames**
                 IO_EXCEPTIONS.LAYOUT_ERROR;

```
private
— implementation-dependent
end TEXT_IO;

package IO_EXCEPTIONS is

    STATUS_ERROR      : exception;
    MODE_ERROR        : exception;
    NAME_ERROR        : exception;
    USE_ERROR         : exception;
    DEVICE_ERROR      : exception;
    END_ERROR         : exception;
    DATA_ERROR        : exception;
    LAYOUT_ERROR      : exception;

end IO_EXCEPTIONS;


package LOW_LEVEL_IO is
    — declarations of the possible types for DEVICE and DATA;
    — declarations of overloaded procedures for these types:
    procedure SEND_CONTROL        (DEVICE : device_type; DATA : in
                                        out data_type);
    procedure RECEIVE_CONTROL     (DEVICE : device_type; DATA : in
                                        out data_type);

end;
```

D. GLOSSARY

This appendix is informative and is not part of the standard definition of the Ada programming language. Italicized terms in the abbreviated descriptions below either have glossary entries themselves or are described in entries for related terms.

Accept statement. See *entry.*

Access type. A value of an access type (an *access value*) is either a null value, or a value that *designates* an *object* created by an *allocator.* The designated object can be read and updated via the access value. The definition of an access type specifies the type of the objects designated by values of the access type. See also *collection.*

Actual parameter. See *parameter.*

Aggregate. The evaluation of an aggregate yields a value of a *composite type.* The value is specified by giving the value of each of the *components.* Either *positional association* or *named association* may be used to indicate which value is associated with which component.

Allocator. The evaluation of an allocator creates an *object* and returns a new *access value* which *designates* the object.

Array type. A value of an array type consists of *components* which are all of the same *subtype* (and hence, of the same type). Each component is uniquely distinguished by an *index* (for a one-dimensional array) or by a sequence of indices (for a multidimensional array). Each index must be a value of a *discrete type* and must lie in the correct index *range.*

Assignment. Assignment is the *operation* that replaces the current value of a *variable* by a new value. An *assignment statement* specifies a variable on the left, and on the right, an *expression* whose value is to be the new value of the variable.

Attribute. The evaluation of an attribute yields a predefined characteristic of a named entity; some attributes are *functions.*

Block statement. A block statement is a single statement that may contain a sequence of statements. It may also include a *declarative part,* and *exception handlers;* their effects are local to the block statement.

Body. A body defines the execution of a *subprogram, package,* or *task.* A *body stub* is a form of body that indicates that this execution is defined in a separately compiled *subunit.*

Collection. A collection is the entire set of *objects* created by evaluation of *allocators* for an *access type.*

Compilation unit. A compilation unit is the *declaration* or the *body* of a *program unit,* presented for compilation as an independent text. It is optionally preceded by a *context clause,* naming other compilation units upon which it depends by means of one more *with* clauses.

Component. A component is a value that is a part of a larger value, or an *object* that is part of a larger object.

Composite type. A composite type is one whose values have *components.* There are two kinds of composite type: *array types* and *record types.*

Constant. See *object.*

Constraint. A constraint determines a subset of the values of a *type.* A value in that subset *satisfies* the constraint.

Context clause. See *compilation unit*.

Declaration. A declaration associates an identifier (or some other notation) with an entity. This association is in effect within a region of text called the *scope* of the declaration. Within the scope of a declaration, there are places where it is possible to use the identifier to refer to the associated declared entity. At such places the identifier is said to be a *simple name* of the entity; the *name* is said to *denote* the associated entity.

Declarative Part. A declarative part is a sequence of *declarations*. It may also contain related information such as *subprogram bodies* and *representation clauses*.

Denote. See *declaration*.

Derived Type. A derived type is a *type* whose operations and values are replicas of those of an existing type. The existing type is called the *parent type* of the derived type.

Designate. See *access type, task*.

Direct visibility. See *visibility*.

Discrete Type. A discrete type is a *type* which has an ordered set of distinct values. The discrete types are the *enumeration* and *integer types*. Discrete types are used for indexing and iteration, and for choices in case statements and record *variants*.

Discriminant. A discriminant is a distinguished *component* of an *object* or value of a *record type*. The *subtypes* of other components, or even their presence or absence, may depend on the value of the discriminant.

Discriminant constraint. A discriminant constraint on a *record type* or *private type* specifies a value for each *discriminant* of the *type*.

Elaboration. The elaboration of a *declaration* is the process by which the declaration achieves its effect (such as creating an *object*); this process occurs during program execution.

Entry. An entry is used for communication between *tasks*. Externally, an entry is called just as a *subprogram* is called; its internal behavior is specified by one or more *accept statements* specifying the actions to be performed when the entry is called.

Enumeration type. An enumeration type is a *discrete type* whose values are represented by enumeration literals which are given explicitly in the *type declaration*. These enumeration literals are either *identifiers* or *character literals*.

Evaluation. The evaluation of an *expression* is the process by which the value of the expression is computed. This process occurs during program execution.

Exception. An exception is an error situation which may arise during program execution. To *raise* an exception is to abandon normal program execution so as to signal that the error has taken place. An *exception handler* is a portion of program text specifying a response to the exception. Execution of such a program text is called *handling* the exception.

Expanded name. An expanded name *denotes* an entity which is *declared* immediately within some construct. An expanded name has the form of a *selected component*: the *prefix* denotes the construct (a *program unit;* or a *block*, loop, or *accept statement*); the *selector* is the *simple name* of the entity.

Expression. An expression defines the computation of a value.

Fixed point type. See *real type*.

Floating point type. See *real type*.

Formal parameter. See *parameter*.

Function. See *subprogram*.

Generic unit. A generic unit is a template either for a set of *subprograms* or for a set of *packages*. A subprogram or package created using the template is called an *instance* of the generic unit. A *generic instantiation* is the kind of *declaration* that creates an instance. A generic unit is written as a subprogram or package but with the specification prefixed by a *generic formal part* which may declare *generic formal parameters.* A generic formal parameter is either a *type,* a *subprogram,* or an *object.* A generic unit is one of the kinds of *program unit.*

Handler. See *exception.*

Index. See *array type.*

Index constraint. An index constraint for an *array type* specifies the lower and upper bounds for each index *range* of the array type.

Indexed component. An indexed component *denotes* a *component* in an *array.* It is a form of *name* containing *expressions* which specify the values of the *indices* of the array component. An indexed component may also denote an *entry* in a family of entries.

Instance. See *generic unit.*

Integer type. An integer type is a *discrete type* whose values represent all integer numbers within a specific *range.*

Lexical element. A lexical element is an identifier, a *literal,* a delimiter, or a comment.

Limited type. A limited type is a *type* for which neither assignment nor the predefined comparison for equality is implicitly declared. All *task* types are limited. A *private type* can be defined to be limited. An equality operator can be explicitly declared for a limited type.

Literal. A literal represents a value literally, that is, by means of letters and other characters. A literal is either a numeric literal, an enumeration literal, a character literal, or a string literal.

Mode. See *parameter.*

Model number. A model number is an exactly

representable value of a *real type. Operations* of a real type are defined in terms of operations on the model numbers of the type. The properties of the model numbers and of their operations are the minimal properties preserved by all implementations of the real type.

Name. A name is a construct that stands for an entity: it is said that the name *denotes* the entity, and that the entity is the meaning of the name. See also *declaration, prefix.*

Named association. A named association specifies the association of an item with one or more positions in a list, by naming the positions.

Object. An object contains a value. A program creates an object either by *elaborating* an *object declaration* or by *evaluating* an *allocator.* The declaration or allocator specifies a *type* for the object: the object can only contain values of that type.

Operation. An operation is an elementary action associated with one or more *types.* It is either implicitly declared by the *declaration* of the type, or it is a *subprogram* that has a *parameter* or *result* of the type.

Operator. An operator is an operation which has one or two operands. A unary operator is written before an operand; a binary operator is written between two operands. This notation is a special kind of *function call.* An operator can be declared as a function. Many operators are implicitly declared by the *declaration* of a *type* (for example, most type declarations imply the declaration of the equality operator for values of the type).

Overloading. An identifier can have several alternative meanings at a given point in the program text: this property is called *overloading.* For example, an overloaded enumeration literal can be an identifier that appears in the definitions of two or more *enumeration types.*

The effective meaning of an overloaded identifier is determined by the context. *Subprograms, aggregates, allocators,* and string *literals* can also be overloaded.

Package. A package specifies a group of logically related entities, such as *types, objects* of those types, and *subprograms* with *parameters* of those types. It is written as a *package declaration* and a *package body.* The package declaration has a *visible part,* containing the *declarations* of all entities that can be explicitly used outside the package. It may also have a *private part* containing structural details that complete the specification of the visible entities, but which are irrelevant to the user of the package. The *package body* contains implementations of *subprograms* (and possibly *tasks* as other *packages*) that have been specified in the package declaration. A package is one of the kinds of *program unit.*

Parameter. A parameter is one of the named entities associated with a *subprogram, entry,* or *generic unit,* and used to communicate with the corresponding subprogram body, *accept statement* or generic body. A *formal parameter* is an identifier used to denote the named entity within the body. An *actual parameter* is the particular entity associated with the corresponding formal parameter by a *subprogram call, entry call,* or *generic instantiation.* The *mode* of a formal parameter specifies whether the associated actual parameter supplies a value for the formal parameter, or the formal supplies a value for the actual parameter, or both. The association of actual parameters with formal parameters can be specified by *named associations,* by *positional associations,* or by a combination of these.

Parent type. See *derived type.*

Positional association. A positional association specifies the association of an item with a position in a list, by using the same position in the text to specify the item.

Pragma. A pragma conveys information to the compiler.

Prefix. A prefix is used as the first part of certain kinds of name. A prefix is either a *function call* or a *name.*

Private part. See *package.*

Private type. A private type is a *type* whose structure and set of values are clearly defined, but not directly available to the user of the type. A private type is known only by its *discriminants* (if any) and by the set of *operations* defined for it. A private type and its applicable operations are defined in the *visible part* of a *package,* or in a *generic formal part.* Assignment, equality, and inequality are also defined for private types, unless the private type is *limited.*

Procedure. See *subprogram.*

Program. A program is composed of a number of *compilation units,* one of which is a *subprogram* called the *main program.* Execution of the program consists of execution of the main program, which may invoke subprograms declared in the other compilation units of the program.

Program unit. A program unit is any one of a *generic unit, package, subprogram,* or *task unit.*

Qualified expression. A qualified expression is an *expression* preceded by an indication of its *type* or *subtype.* Such qualification is used when, in its absence, the expression might be ambiguous (for example as a consequence of *overloading*).

Raising an exception. See *exception.*

Range. A range is a contiguous set of values of a *scalar type.* A range is specified by giving the lower and upper bounds for the values. A value in the range is said to *belong* to the range.

Range constraint. A range constraint of a *type* specifies a *range*, and thereby determines the subset of the values of the type that *belong* to the range.

Real type. A real type is a *type* whose values represent approximations to the real numbers. There are two kinds of real type: *fixed point types* are specified by absolute error bound; *floating point types* are specified by a relative error bound expressed as a number of significant decimal digits.

Record type. A value of a record type consists of *components* which are usually of different *types* or *subtypes*. For each component of a record value or record *object,* the definition of the record type specifies an identifier that uniquely determines the component within the record.

Renaming declaration. A renaming declaration declares another *name* for an entity.

Rendezvous. A rendezvous is the interaction that occurs between two parallel *tasks* when one task has called an *entry* of the other task, and a corresponding *accept statement* is being executed by the other task on behalf of the calling task.

Representation clause. A representation clause directs the compiler in the selection of the mapping of a *type,* an *object*, or a *task* onto features of the underlying machine that executes a program. In some cases, representation clauses completely specify the mapping; in other cases, they provide criteria for choosing a mapping.

Satisfy. See *constraint, subtype.*

Scalar type. An *object* or value of a scalar *type* does not have *components.* A scalar type is either a *discrete type* or a *real type.* The values of a scalar type are ordered.

Scope. See *declaration.*

Selected component. A selected component is a *name* consisting of a *prefix* and of an identifier called the *selector.* Selected components are used to denote record components, *entries,* and *objects* designated by access values; they are also used as *expanded names.*

Selector. See *selected component.*

Simple name. See *declaration, name.*

Statement. A statement specifies one or more actions to be performed during the execution of a *program.*

Subcomponent. A subcomponent is either a *component,* or a component of another subcomponent.

Subprogram. A subprogram is either a *procedure* or a *function.* A procedure specifies a sequence of actions and is invoked by a *procedure call* statement. A function specifies a sequence of actions and also returns a value called the *result,* and so a *function call* is an *expression.* A subprogram is written as a *subprogram declaration,* which specifies its *name, formal parameters,* and (for a function) its result; and a *subprogram body* which specifies the sequence of actions. The subprogram call specifies the *actual parameters* that are to be associated with the formal parameters. A subprogram is one of the kinds of *program unit.*

Subtype. A subtype of a *type* characterizes a subset of the values of the type. The subset is determined by a *constraint* on the type. Each value in the set of values of a subtype *belongs* to the subtype and *satisfies* the constraint determining the subtype.

Subunit. See *body.*

Task. A task operates in parallel with other parts of the program. It is written as a *task specification* (which specifies the *name* of the task and the names and *formal parameters* of its entries), and a *task body* which defines its execution. A *task unit* is one of the kinds of *program unit.* A *task type* is a *type* that permits the subsequent *declaration* of any number of similar tasks of the type. A value of a task type is said to *designate* a task.

Type. A type characterizes both a set of values, and a set of *operations* applicable to those values. A *type definition* is a language construct that defines a type. A particular type is either an *access type*, an *array type*, a *private type*, a *record type*, a *scalar type*, or a *task type*.

Use clause. A use clause achieves *direct visibility* of *declarations* that appear in the *visible parts* of named *packages*.

Variable. See *object*.

Variant part. A variant part of a *record* spec-

ifies alternative record *components*, depending on a *discriminant* of the record. Each value of the discriminant establishes a particular alternative of the variant part.

Visibility. At a given point in a program text, the *declaration* of an entity with a certain identifier is said to be *visible* if the entity is an acceptable meaning for an occurrence at that point of the identifier. The declaration is *visible* by *selection* at the place of the *selector* in a *selected component* or at the place of the name in a *named association*. Otherwise, the declaration is *directly visible*, that is, if the identifier alone has that meaning.

Visible part. See *package*.

With clause. See *compilation unit*.

E. SYNTAX SUMMARY

This syntax summary is not part of the standard definition of the Ada programming language.

2.1*
graphic_character :: = basic_graphic_character
| lower_case_letter | other_special_character

basic_graphic_character :: =
upper_case_letter | digit
| special_character | space_character

basic_character :: =
basic_graphic_character | format_effector

2.3
identifier :: =
letter {[underline] letter_or_digit}

letter_or_digit :: = letter | digit

letter :: = upper_case_letter | lower_case_letter

2.4
numeric_literal :: = decimal_literal | based_literal

2.4.1
decimal_literal :: = integer [.integer] [exponent]

integer :: = digit {[underline] digit}

exponent :: = E [+] integer | E − integer

2.4.2
based_literal :: =
base # based_integer [.based_integer] # [exponent]

base :: = integer

based_integer :: =
extended_digit {[underline] extended_digit}

extended_digit :: = digit | letter

2.5
character_literal :: = 'graphic_character'

2.6
string_literal :: = "{graphic_character}"

2.8
pragma :: =
pragma identifier [(argument_association {, argument_association})];

argument_association :: =
[*argument*_identifier =>] name
| [*argument*_identifier =>] expression

3.1
basic_declaration :: =
object_declaration | number_declaration
| type_declaration | subtype_declaration
| subprogam_declara- | package_declaration
tion
| task_declaration | generic_declaration
| exception_declara- | generic_instantiation
tion
| renaming_declaration | deferred_constant_
declaration

3.2
object_declaration :: =
identifier_list : [**constant**] subtype_indication [: = expression];
| identifier_list : [**constant**] constrained_array_ definition [: = expression];

number_declaration :: =
identifier_list : **constant** : = *universal_static_* expression;

identifier_list :: = identifier {, identifier}

3.3.1
type_declaration :: = full_type_declaration
| incomplete_type_declaration | private_type_ declaration

full_type_declaration .. =
type identifier [discriminant_part] **is** type_defi- nition;

type_definition :: =
enumeration_type_ | integer_type_
definition definition
| real_type_definition | array_type_definition
| record_type_defini- | access_type_defini-
tion tion
| derived_type_definition

*Section numbers refer to the *Reference Manual for the Ada Programming Language.*

3.3.2
subtype_declaration :: =
  subtype identifier **is** subtype_indication;

subtype_indication :: = type_mark [constraint]

type_mark :: = *type*_name | *subtype*_name

constraint :: =
| range_constraint | floating_point_con-
| straint
| | fixed_point_con- | index_constraint
| straint
| | discriminant_constraint

3.4
derived_type_definition :: = **new** subtype_indica-
tion

3.5
range_constraint :: = **range** range

range :: = *range*_attribute
  | simple_expression . . simple_expression

3.5.1
enumeration_type_definition :: =
  (enumeration_literal_specification
  {, enumeration_literal_specification})

enumeration_literal_specification :: = enumera-
tion_literal

enumeration_literal :: = identifier | character_
literal

3.5.4
integer_type_definition :: = range_constraint
3.5.6
real_type_definition :: =
  floating_point_constraint | fixed_point_con-
straint

3.5.7
floating_point_constraint :: =
  floating_accuracy_definition [**range**_constraint]

floating_accuracy_definition :: =
  digits *static*_simple_expression

3.5.9
fixed_point_constraint :: =
  fixed_accuracy_definition [range_constraint]

fixed_accuracy_definition :: =
  delta *static*_simple_expression

3.6
array_type_definition :: =
  unconstrained_array_definition | constrained_ar-
ray_definition

unconstrained_array_definition :: =
  array(index_subtype_definition {, index_sub-
type_definition}) **of** *component*_subtype_indi-
cation

constrained_array_definition :: =
  array index_constraint **of** *component*_subtype_
indication

index_subtype_definition :: = type_mark **range** <>

index_constraint :: = (discrete_range {, discrete_
range})

discrete_range :: = *discrete*_subtype_indication |
range

3.7
record_type_definition :: =
  record
    component_list
  end record

component_list :: =
    component_declaration {component_declara-
tion}
  | {component_declaration} variant_part
  | **null;**

component_declaration :: =
    identifier_list : component_subtype_definition
[: = expression];

component_subtype_definition :: = subtype_in-
dication

3.7.1
discriminant_part :: =
  (discriminant_specification {; discriminant_spe-
cification})

discriminant_specification :: =
  identifier_list : type_mark [: = expression]

3.7.2
discriminant_constraint :: =
  (discriminant_association {, discriminant_associa-
tion})

discriminant_association :: =
  [*discriminant*_simple_name {| *discriminant*_sim-
ple_name} = >] expression

3.7.3

variant_part :: =
   case *discriminant*_simple_name **is**
      variant
      { variant}
   end case;

variant :: =
   when choice {| choice} = >
      component_list

choice :: = simple_expression
   | discrete_range | **others** | *component*_simple_
      name

3.8

access_type_definition :: = **access** subtype_indica-
tion

3.8.1

incomplete_type_declaration :: =
   type identifier [discriminant_part];

3.9

declarative_part :: =
   {basic_declarative_item} {later_declarative_item}

basic_declarative_item :: = basic_declaration
   | representation_clause | use_clause

later_declarative_item :: = body
   | subprogram_declara- | package_declaration
      tion
   | task_declaration | generic_declaration
   | use_clause | generic_instantiation

body :: = proper_body | body_stub

proper_body :: =
   subprogram_body | package_body | task_body

4.1

name :: = simple_name
   | character_literal | operator_symbol
   | indexed_component | slice
   | selected_component | attribute

simple_name :: = identifier

prefix :: = name | function_call

4.1.1

indexed_component :: = prefix(expression {, ex-
pression})

4.1.2

slice :: = prefix(discrete_range)

4.1.3

selected_component :: = prefix.selector

selector :: = simple_name
   | character_literal | operator_symbol | **all**

4.1.4

attribute :: = prefix'attribute_designator

attribute_designator :: =
   simple_name [(*universal_static*_expression)]

4.3

aggregate :: =
   (component_association {, component_associa-
tion})

component_association :: =
   [choice {| choice} =>] expression

4.4

expression :: =
   relation {**and** relation} | relation {**and then** re-
                                     lation}
   | relation {**or** relation} | relation {**or else** rela-
   | relation {**xor** relation]   tion}

relation :: =
   simple_expression [relational_operator simple_
   expression]
   | simple_expression [**not**] **in** range
   | simple_expression [**not**] **in** type_mark

simple_expression :: =
   [unary_adding_operator] term {binary_adding_
   operator term]

term :: = factor {multiplying_operator factor}

factor :: = primary [** primary] | **abs** primary | **not**
   primary

primary :: =
   numeric_literal | **null** | aggregate | string_literal
   | name | allocator | function_call | type_conver-
   sion
   | qualified_expression | (expression)

4.5

logical_operator :: = **and** | **or** | **xor**

relational_operator :: = = | /= | < | <= | > | >=

binary_adding_operator :: = + | − | &

unary_adding_operator :: = + | −

multiplying_operator :: = * | / | **mod** | **rem**

highest_precedence_operator :: = ** | **abs** | **not**

4.6

type_conversion :: = type_mark(expression)

4.7

qualified_expression :: =
   type_mark'(expression) | type_mark'aggregate

4.8

allocator :: =
   new subtype_indication | **new** qualified_expression

5.1

sequence_of_statements :: = statement {statement}

statement :: =
   { label} simple_statement | {label} compound_
      statement

   simple_statement :: = null_statement
      | assignment_state- | procedure_call_
         ment   statement
      | exit_statement | return_statement
      | goto_statement | entry_call_state-
      | delay_statement   ment
      | raise_statement | abort_statement
                                 | code_statement

compound_statement :: =
      if_statement | case_statement
   | loop_statement | block_statement
   | accept_statement | select_statement

label :: = <<*label*_simple_name>>

null_statement :: = **null**;

5.2

assignment_statement :: =
   *variable*_name := expression;

5.3

if_statement :: =
   if condition **then**
      sequence_of_statements
   { **elsif** condition **then**
      sequence_of_statements}
   [**else**
      sequence_of_statements]
   end if;

condition :: = *boolean*_expression

5.4

case_statement :: =
   case expression **is**

      case_statement_alternative
      { case_statement_alternative}
   end case;

case_statement_alternative :: =
   when choice {| choice } =>
      sequence_of_statements

5.5

loop_statement :: =
   [*loop*_simple_name:]
      [iteration_scheme] **loop**
         sequence_of_statements
      end loop [*loop*_simple_name];

iteration_scheme :: = **while** condition
   | **for** loop_parameter_specification

loop_parameter_specification :: =
   identifier **in** [**reverse**] discrete_range

5.6

block_statement :: =
   [*block*_simple_name:]
      [**declare**
         declarative_part]
      begin
         sequence_of_statements
      [**exception**
         exception_handler
         {exception_handler}]
      end [*block*_simple_name];

5.7

exit_statement :: =
   exit [*loop*_name] [**when** condition];

5.8

return_statement :: = **return** [expression];

5.9

goto_statement :: = **goto** *label*_name;

6.1

subprogram_declaration :: = subprogram_specifi-
   cation;

subprogram_specification :: =
      procedure identifier [formal_part]
   | **function** designator [formal_part] **return** type_
      mark

designator :: = identifier | operator_symbol

operator_symbol :: = string_literal

formal_part :: =
  (parameter_specification {; parameter_specification})

parameter_specification :: =
  identifier_list : mode type_mark [: = expression]

mode :: = **[in]** | **in out** | **out**

6.3

subprogram_body :: =
  subprogram_specification **is**
    [declarative_part]
  begin
    sequence_of_statements
  [**exception**
    exception_handler
    {exception_handler}]
  end [designator];

6.4

procedure_call_statement :: =
  *procedure*_name [actual_parameter_part];

function_call :: =
  *function*_name [actual_parameter_part]

actual_parameter_part :: =
  (parameter_association {, parameter_association})

parameter_association :: =
  [formal_parameter = >] actual_parameter

formal_parameter :: = *parameter*_simple_name

actual_parameter :: =
  expression | *variable*_name | type_
    mark(*variable*_name)

7.1

package_declaration :: = package_specification;

package_specification :: =
  package identifier **is**
    {basic_declarative_item}
  [**private**
    {basic_declarative_item}]
    end [*package*_simple_name]

package_body :: =
  package body *package*_simple_name **is**
    [declarative_part]
  [**begin**
    sequence_of_statements
  [**exception**

    exception_handler
    { exception_handler}]]
  end [*package*_simple_name];

7.4

private_type_declaration :: =
  type identifier [discriminant_part] **is [limited] private;**

deferred_constant_declaration :: =
  identifier_list : **constant** type_mark;

8.4

use_clause :: = **use** *package*_name {, *package*_name};

8.5

renaming_declaration :: =
  identifier : type_mark **renames** *object*_name;
  | identifier : **exception** **renames** *exception*_name;
  | **package** identifier **renames** *package*_name;
  | subprogram_specification **renames** *subprogram_or_entry*_name;

9.1

task_declaration :: = task_specification;

task_specification :: =
  task [type] identifier **[is**
    {entry_declaration}
    {representation_clause}
  end [*task*_simple_name]]

task_body :: =
  task body *task*_simple_name **is**
    [declarative_part]
  begin
    sequence_of_statements
  [**exception**
    exception_handler
    { exception_handler}]
  end [*task*_simple_name];

9.5

entry_declaration :: =
  entry identifier [(discrete_range)] [formal_part];

entry_call_statement :: =
  *entry*_name [actual_parameter_part];

accept_statement :: =

accept *entry*_simple_name [(entry_index)] [formal_part] [**do** sequence_of_statements
end [*entry*_simple_name]];

entry_index :: = expression

9.6
delay_statement :: = **delay** simple_expression;

9.7
select_statement :: = selective_wait
| conditional_entry_call | timed_entry_call

9.7.1
selective_wait :: =
   select
     select_alternative
  { **or**
     select_alternative}
  [**else**
     sequence_of_statements]
   end select;

select_alternative :: =
  [**when** condition =>]
     selective_wait_alternative

selective_wait_alternative :: = accept_alternative
| delay_alternative | terminate_alternative

accept_alternative :: =
  accept_statement [sequence_of_statements]

delay_alternative :: =
  delay_statement [sequence_of_statements]

terminate_alternative :: = **terminate;**

9.7.2
conditional_entry_call :: =
  select
   entry_call_statement
  [sequence_of_statements]
  else
   sequence_of_statements
  end select;

9.7.3
timed_entry_call :: =
  select
    entry_call_statement
   [sequence_of_statements]
  or
    delay_alternative
  end select;

9.10
abort_statement :: = **abort** *task*_name
  {, *task*_name};

10.1
compilation :: = {compilation_unit}

compilation_unit :: =
  context_clause library_unit
  | context_clause secondary_unit

library_unit :: =
  subprogram_declaration | package_declaration
  | generic_declaration | generic_instantiation
  | subprogram_body

secondary_unit :: = library_unit_body | subunit

library_unit_body :: = subprogram_body | package_body

10.1.1
context_clause :: = {with_clause {use_clause}}

with_clause :: =
  with *unit*_simple_name {, *unit*_simple_name};

10.2
body_stub :: =
  subprogram_specification **is separate;**
  | **package body** *package*_simple_name **is
    separate;**
  | **task body** *task*_simple_name **is separate;**

subunit :: = **separate** (*parent_unit*_name) proper_body

11.1
exception_declaration :: = identifier_list : **exception;**

11.2
exception_handler :: =
  when exception_choice {| exception_choice} =>
    sequence_of_statements

exception_choice :: = *exception*_name | **others**

11.3
raise_statement :: = **raise** [*exception*_name];

12.1
generic_declaration :: = generic_specification;

generic_specification :: =
  generic_formal_part subprogram_specification
  | generic_formal_part package_specification

generic_formal_part :: = **generic** {generic_parameter_declaration}

generic_parameter_declaration :: =
    identifier_list : [**in** [**out**]] type_mark [: = expression];
    | **type** identifier **is** generic_type_definition;
    | private_type_declaration
    | **with** subprogram_specification [**is** name];
    | **with** subprogram_specification [**is** <>];

generic_type_definition :: =
    (<>) | **range** <> | **digits** <> | **delta** <>
    | array_type_definition | access_type_definition

12.3

generic_instantiation :: =
    package identifier **is**
      new *generic_package*_name [generic_actual_part];
    | **procedure** identifier **is**
      new *generic_procedure*_name [generic_actual_part];
    | **function** designator **is**
      new *generic_function*_name [generic_actual_part];

generic_actual_part :: =
    (generic_association {, generic_association})

generic_association :: =
    [generic_formal_parameter =>] generic_actual_parameter

generic_formal_parameter :: =
*parameter*_simple_name | operator_symbol

generic_actual_parameter :: = expression | *variable*_name
    | *subprogram*_name | *entry*_name | type_mark

13.1

representation_clause :: =
    type_representation_clause | address_clause

type_representation_clause :: = length_clause
    | enumeration_representation_clause
    | record_representation_clause

13.2

length_clause :: = **for** attribute **use** simple_expression;

13.3

enumeration_representation_clause :: =
    for *type*_simple_name **use** aggregate;

13.4

record_representation_clause :: =
    for *type*_simple_name **use**
      record [alignment_clause]
      {component_clause}
      end record;

alignment_clause :: = **at mod** *static*_simple_expression;

component_clause :: =
    *component*_name **at** *static*_simple_expression
                range *static*_range;

13.5

address_clause :: =
    for simple_name **use at** simple_expression;

13.8

code_statement :: = type_mark'*record*_aggregate;

SYNTAX CROSS REFERENCE

In the list given below each syntactic category is followed by the section number where it is defined.* For example:

adding_operator   4.5

In addition, each syntactic category is followed by the names of other categories in whose definition it appears. For example, adding_operator appears in the definition of simple_expression:

adding_operator   4.5
   simple_expression   **4.4**

An ellipsis (. . .) is used when the syntactic category is not defined by a syntax rule. For example:

lower_case_letter   . . .

All uses of parentheses are combined in the term "()". The italicized prefixes used with some terms have been deleted here.

abort	. . .	**actual_parameter_part**	6.4
abort_statement	9.10	entry_call_statement	9.5
		function_call	6.4
abort_statement	9.10	procedure_call_statement	6.4
simple_statement	5.1		
		address_clause	13.5
abs	. . .	representation_clause	13.1
factor	4.4		
highest_precedence_operator	4.5	**aggregate**	4.3
		code_statement	13.8
accept	. . .	enumeration_representation_clause	13.3
accept_statement	9.5	primary	4.4
		qualified_expression	4.7
accept_alternative	9.7.1		
selective_wait_alternative	9.7.1	**alignment_clause**	13.4
		record_representation_clause	13.4
accept_statement	9.5		
accept_alternative	9.7.1	**all**	. . .
compound_statement	5.1	selector	4.1.3
access	. . .	**allocator**	4.8
access_type_definition	3.8	primary	4.4
access_type_definition	3.8	**and**	. . .
generic_type_definition	12.1	expression	4.4
type_definition	3.3.1	logical_operator	4.5
actual_parameter	6.4		
parameter_association	6.4		

*Section numbers refer to the *Reference Manual for the Ada Programming Language.*

INDEX

533

Date Due

AUG 01 1988			